REFERENCE REBORN

REFERENCE REBORN

Breathing New Life into Public Services Librarianship

DIANE ZABEL, EDITOR

Preface by Linda C. Smith

AN IMPRINT OF ABC-CLIO, LLC
Santa Barbara, California • Denver, Colorado • Oxford, England

Library of Congress Cataloging-in-Publication Data

Reference reborn : breathing new life into public services librarianship / Diane Zabel, editor ; preface by Linda C. Smith.
p. cm.
Includes bibliographical references and index.
ISBN 978-1-59158-828-3 (acid-free paper) — ISBN 978-1-59158-829-0 (ebook) 1. Reference services (Libraries)—United States. 2. Public services (Libraries)—United States. 3. Electronic reference services (Libraries) 4. Internet in library reference services. I. Zabel, Diane.
Z711.R4454 2011
025.5'2—dc22 2010041105

ISBN: 978-1-59158-828-3
EISBN: 978-1-59158-829-0

15 14 13 12 11 1 2 3 4 5

This book is also available on the World Wide Web as an eBook.
Visit www.abc-clio.com for details.

Libraries Unlimited
An Imprint of ABC-CLIO, LLC

ABC-CLIO, LLC
130 Cremona Drive, P.O. Box 1911
Santa Barbara, California 93116-1911

This book is printed on acid-free paper ∞

Manufactured in the United States of America

CONTENTS

PREFACE

In 2008, Robert H. Kieft, one of the contributors to this volume, observed, "The service edifice built by reference librarians beginning in the late nineteenth century does not so much threaten to collapse as to be reborn in ways that we are still groping to discern" (Kieft, 2008, 6). As a teacher of reference related courses since 1977 and the coeditor of a reference textbook since the first edition was published in 1991 (Bopp and Smith, 1991), I have continually sought to discern new trends in reference services and the roles new librarians can play in shaping them and to share those with my own students and readers of the textbook. Editor Diane Zabel and the more than 30 other contributors to *Reference Reborn: Breathing New Life into Public Services Librarianship* have given readers a timely examination of developments in public services librarianship and an affirmation that this remains a vital and creative part of the profession. This book will be of value not only to beginning librarians looking ahead to the opportunities and challenges that will shape their careers but also to librarians who began their careers at any time since the 1970s. At that time reference services transitioned from a period of certainty regarding roles, resources, and methods to a period of change and challenge, driven in large part by developments in computer and communications technology (Rettig, 2006).

The organization of this volume highlights major themes that should be of interest to anyone concerned with the future of public services librarianship: the current and potential users of our services, new and improved service models, new and revised roles for reference librarians, the role of technology in reference services, reference collection development, staffing in 21st-century libraries, and the education and training of reference librarians.

Contributors, include several who are well known for their contributions to reference research and practice and some who are newer to the profession. This new generation will lead the way in ensuring that reference services—in forms that we are just beginning to discern—will continue to be a vital part of libraries. Concluding on a personal note, it is rewarding to count among the contributors a number of graduates of our master's program at Illinois: Diane Zabel herself, as well as Jim Hahn, M. Kathleen Kern, James LaRue, Meris A. Mandernach, Amber A. Prentiss, and David A. Tyckoson.

Linda C. Smith

WORKS CITED

Bopp, R. E., and L. C. Smith, eds. 1991. *Reference and information services: An introduction*. Englewood, CO: Libraries Unlimited.

Kieft, R. H. 2008. The return of the *Guide to Reference* (Books). *Reference & User Services Quarterly* 48 (1): 4–10.

Rettig, J. 2006. Reference service: From certainty to uncertainty. *Advances in Librarianship* 30: 105–143.

ACKNOWLEDGMENTS

This happy collaboration with more than 30 creative contributors happened by accident. I had no intention of working on a book project at this stage in my career and was taken completely by surprise when Barbara Ittner, a senior acquisitions editor at Libraries Unlimited, invited me to develop a proposal for a book on trends in reference and public services librarianship. Anyone who has ever met Barbara knows that she is both charming and persuasive. Before I knew it, I was recruiting wonderful authors whom I had worked with on other projects, and enlisting other authors whose work I had long admired. I also had the good sense to invite some rising stars to contribute. I have worked with many editors over the years, and Barbara is simply the best. We just clicked and I will never forget her warmth, generosity, patience, and understanding.

Much of my thinking about reference and public services librarianship has been shaped by my participation in the Reference and User Services Association (RUSA), a division of the American Library Association. I have been active in RUSA for almost a quarter century, and my RUSA colleagues (too numerous to list by name) have enriched my life. Many of the contributors to this volume are part of my RUSA network. RUSA was also my forum for finding a mentor early on in my career. I would be remiss if I did not acknowledge the important role that David Kohl, a past RUSA president, played in my professional development.

Completion of this project would not have been possible without the support provided by my institution, the Pennsylvania State University Libraries. In particular, I want to thank associate dean Sally Kalin, who is the embodiment of service excellence in our profession. I also want to acknowledge the assistance provided by Emily Robins Sharpe, the gifted doctoral student who served as an editorial assistant, thanks to financial support provided through the Louis and Virginia Benzak Business Librarian Endowment. My colleagues in the Schreyer Business Library also need to be recognized for their enthusiastic support of this project. Finally, I want to thank my family, especially my husband (Craig) and son (Zachary), for their continued encouragement.

INTRODUCTION

The time is right for a balanced look at trends in reference and public services librarianship (in both academic and public libraries in the United States) and a consideration of future scenarios. Rather than worrying about reference's demise, many librarians have been energized by their newly expanded roles, many of which allow for creative ways of delivering enhanced services, thanks in part to Web 2.0 and other user-centric technologies.

THE REBIRTH OF REFERENCE

In the past few years there has been a renewed interest in studying best practices for reference delivery. All of a sudden, reference is the rage. Reference-related programs at conferences pack rooms. A participant at a reference retreat that I attended in 2007 commented, "I'm glad reference is back" (Zabel, 2007, 109). While reference never went away, more librarians are recognizing that providing excellent public service is critical to the future of libraries. Perhaps evidence of this is the tremendous positive response to the guest editorial that Lorraine J. Pellack contributed to the Fall 2009 issue of *Reference & User Services Quarterly.* The message of this article, titled "First Impressions and Rethinking Restroom Questions," is very simple: Patrons' first impressions matter, and polite responses to the most routine questions create a welcoming environment. I have been editor of this journal since 2006; no other article has generated so much discussion. Many readers posted comments on the Web site of the journal's online companion (www.rusq.org). Others wrote to me directly to let me know how much they appreciated the reminder that courteous service never goes out of style. Some readers also indicated that they intended to assign this article to students enrolled in master of library science (MLS) courses or library staff during training programs.

I was humbled to learn that "A Reference Renaissance," an editorial I wrote for the Winter 2007 issue of *Reference & User Services Quarterly,* has been background reading for reference retreats and assigned reading for continuing education courses. I was also informed that this editorial was the inspiration in part for the theme of Reference Renaissance: Current and Future Trends, a 2008 conference sponsored by the Bibliographical Center for Research and the Reference and User Services Association (a division of the American Library Association). Marie Radford, the program chair for this Denver conference, has been instrumental in bringing reference to the forefront in our profession. The conference drew more than 500 attendees; based on its success, a second Reference Renaissance conference took place in August 2010.

I invited Marie Radford to write a guest editorial on reference service excellence for the Winter 2008 issue of *Reference & User Services Quarterly.* She used this forum to "celebrate the rise and revitalization of reference service excellence" (Radford, 2008, 109). She wrote, "I have been involved in reference for twenty years on the front line in school and academic libraries, and as a researcher for an over-lapping time of twenty-three years. I have never seen a more exciting time for reference. In fact, I've never seen any time that has even come remotely close" (109). That's quite an assessment from someone who has given numerous conference presentations and workshops on reference and has published extensively on various aspects of reference services, including groundbreaking research on interpersonal communication in face-to-face and virtual reference encounters.

There have been other manifestations of increasing interest in reference and public services librarianship. Columbia University Libraries has been hosting an annual library symposium on 21st-century reference service since 2001. This conference "invites representatives of large private academic research libraries in the Northeast to share ideas, plans, and concerns about reference services," (Free, 250). The theme of the 2008 symposium was "Beyond the Desk." Nor is interest in new reference models limited to elite institutions or academic libraries. The January–February 2007 issue of *Public Libraries* (the official publication of the Public Library Association, a division of the American Library Association) focused on reference—bringing together articles on reference transaction statistics and trends, collaborative virtual reference service, roving reference, digital formats of reference materials, and librarians' evolving role.

Significantly, broader publications have also featured articles on the future of reference. The cover of the April 20, 2007, issue of the *Chronicle of Higher Education* posed the question, "Reference Desks: Endangered Species?" This provocative question was the lead-in to Scott Carlson's thoughtful article, "Are Reference Desks Dying Out?" which examines how academic libraries continue to grapple with how best to redefine roles and services. Carlson notes that arguments for eliminating the desk began to surface in the mid-1980s, culminating with the publication of Jerry Campbell's controversial article in the Spring 2000 issue of *Reference & User Services Quarterly* arguing that librarians should enhance technology and move away from the traditional reference desk model.[1] Campbell's call to adopt technology almost seems quaint in 2010, and librarians of a certain generation (myself included) can recall with some fondness early experimentation with tiered reference and other models of service. Librarians have been rethinking reference since the 1993 publication of Virginia Massey-Burzio's seminal article ("Rethinking the Reference Desk") on the topic. *Reference Reborn* is a vehicle to share interesting perspectives on how we can best serve library users. This volume brings together essays on new public service configurations, the impact of e-resources on reference and collection development, innovative outreach, and other timely topics.

THE IMPACT OF THE RECESSION

I developed the proposal for this book in May 2008, before the recession had profoundly impacted many libraries. This severe economic downturn has precipitated major changes in public services for many libraries across the country. In her retelling of this crisis, *portal* editor Sarah M. Pritchard recalled that "the effects began to hit many libraries in early 2009, with mid-year budget take-backs, hiring freezes, and large endowment drops; and, over the course of the spring, the forecasts for FY 2010 got increasingly grim. As librarians gathered at professional association meetings this last summer, it was clear that the financial trends look bad or worse for FY 2011" (2009, 437). In terms of the impact on academic libraries, Pritchard noted that "we are seeing a flurry of news bulletins and electronic list messages about branch closings, service point consolidations, layoffs, serials cancellations, shorter hours, delayed building projects, outsourcing, consortial contracting and the like" (437). The forecast is unfortunately gloomy for many academic libraries.

The recession has had dire consequences for America's public libraries as well. While public library use has soared during the recession (especially since public libraries provide resources to assist job seekers), funding has been slashed. A recent news release from the American Library Association (2010) reported that "half of states have reduced funding to public libraries and to state library agencies, and close to one-quarter of urban libraries have reduced open hours. Adequate staffing is the leading challenge to aiding job seekers." In response, the American Library Association has mounted an aggressive campaign to promote the value of American libraries.

ARE THERE OPPORTUNITIES IN A RECESSION?

My home institution, the Pennsylvania State University, has been closely monitoring how other academic libraries have responded to cutbacks. The

University Park Libraries at Penn State, my specific library, used this crisis as an opportunity to create a more coordinated and cohesive approach to the delivery of reference services at University Park, a campus serving more than 42,000 students.

At the beginning of 2008, associate dean Sally Kalin (a contributor to *Reference Reborn*) created the Reference and Consultation Services Council, a cross-departmental leadership team charged with providing direction for the improvement of reference-related services at University Park. I had the good fortune to be a member of the initial council (serving as cochair along with *Reference Reborn* contributor Anne Behler). Within the first few months, with considerable input from other librarians and staff working on the front lines in our libraries, our team developed a tactical plan for delivery and improvement of reference services at University Park, one that aligned with the goals of our library's strategic plan. This concise plan consists of 10 tactics and includes more than 40 action items that have been identified as immediate (achievable within 6 months), short-term (achievable between 6 and 18 months), or long-term (actions that require more than 18 months for completion or are ongoing).[2] Several teams have been appointed to address specific issues and to complete these action items. This tactical plan is serving as our blueprint for reference service excellence at University Park. While the plan's goal is to improve services for our users, some tactics and actions address the need for more effective sharing of staff across service points, and the need for more strategic and cost-effective reference service delivery, using a variety of delivery modes and mechanisms.

The Reference and Consultation Services Council was also charged with the task of tracking national trends, identifying best practices, and fostering discussions about reference and user services. One of our mechanisms for promoting dialogue about user services has been sponsorship of an ongoing forum (usually held monthly) that we have named "UP Public Services Unplugged." Some of these forums have been designed as "report backs" from relevant meetings and conferences where public service trends, new reference service models, and successful technological applications have been discussed. So what are some of the predominant trends in reference and public services librarianship? In forums held throughout 2009 and early 2010, my colleagues and I identified the following trends based on attendance and participation in various regional and national venues:

- Elimination of service points
- Consolidation of reference/service points (e.g., merged reference and circulation or merged reference and information technology help)
- Closure or merger of branch or discipline-based libraries
- Use of technology to assist patrons (e.g., icons on library computers that enable patrons to ask for help)
- Increased usage of two specific models of reference service: the triage-tiered model and the shared staffing model

- Expansion of self-service options (e.g., self-checkout, online group study room reservations, self-service reserves, and touch-screen FAQs [frequently asked questions])
- Reduction of staff due to hiring freezes and greater use of nine-month contracts
- Increased liaison roles for subject librarians (with an emphasis on getting out of the building)
- Greater emphasis on virtual reference
- Acceptance of instant messaging and text messaging as mainstream reference mediums
- Growing usage of telephone reference (a trend fueled by the ubiquitous cell phone)
- Reconfiguration of reference services and reference resources for smartphones and other mobile devices
- Increased use of software programs to track and manage reference transactions and to manage referrals
- Development of core competencies for reference service providers and development of formal ongoing training programs
- Greater focus on candidates' "soft skills" in the hiring process
- Reduction of print collections due to aggressive weeding and policies that discourage duplication
- Accelerated growth of e-book collections
- Greater marketing and promotion of e-book readers

SOME THEMES IN *REFERENCE REBORN*

Many of the trends identified in the preceding are discussed in this collection of essays. In addition, chapter contributors have identified and expanded on the following themes:

- While there are varying opinions about how to best prepare the next generation of reference librarians, our profession's core values (e.g., sensitivity to the needs of our users, commitment to connect our users to the information and materials they need, recognition of the educational role of librarians) will continue to underpin library education.
- A good public services librarian is always tracking economic, social, cultural, and technological trends that may drive change in libraries. Librarians can use data from external environmental scans (such as those conducted by the Online Computer Library Center [OCLC] and the Pew Internet & American Life Project) and local surveys to plan new services or reconfigure existing services.
- Libraries must offer multiple modes of reference delivery as users want a range of services.

- Librarians are rethinking the traditional liaison role. It extends beyond collection development to encompass a variety of library services. Susan Sharpless Smith and Lynn Sutton write about embedding librarians in academic departments so librarians can become active partners in the educational mission. In the public library environment, James LaRue refers to this trend as "community reference work." Linda Friend describes the powerful role reference librarians can play in fostering dialogue on open access and other issues in scholarly communication.
- Readers' advisory service is experiencing a renaissance in public libraries, according to Barry Trott and Neil Hollands. Anne Behler observes that a growing number of academic libraries are creating leisure reading collections and introducing readers' advisory services as strategies to encourage reading and promote use of book collections.
- Reference librarians need to go where users are. This might mean leaving the library for residence halls or having a presence on Facebook, Second Life, or other online communities.
- Since a library's Web site is the first service point for many users, it is imperative that libraries focus on improving the interface. Users want easy-to-use and customizable Web sites. With the large-scale migration from print to e-reference collections, it is critical that libraries create usable interfaces so users can find resources.
- We can't forget that the physical library plays an important role as a learning space. Juliet Rumble describes how information commons support learning communities.
- While we need to deliver reference service using multiple modes, this delivery of service should be seamless to the user. Organizationally, reference should be viewed as a single centralized service.
- Since libraries are under greater scrutiny to account for return on dollars spent, systematic data collection is critical to document outcomes and assess services. Evaluation of reference service must be ongoing. It is important that libraries follow through and act in response to the data that can be collected using the various methods and tools described by Julie A. Gedeon and Joseph A. Salem, Jr.
- Marketing is key, as many of our users (and nonusers) are not aware of the services that libraries offer. In addition to marketing reference services, libraries should market how they are strategically different from Google and other competitors.
- Ongoing training for reference providers is essential. Training needs to emphasize the importance of empathy in face-to-face and virtual interactions. Greater focus needs to be placed on the behavioral aspects of reference service, for example, incorporation of those model behaviors outlined in national guidelines for professional practice.

And finally, while librarians tend to focus on new tools and emerging technologies, there are two important threads throughout *Reference Reborn*. First, there is an overwhelming belief in the sustainability of reference service.

Reference will remain an important service since users value the human touch. Sally Kalin writes eloquently about the enduring qualities of reference librarians: "Even though the progression of my career has seen a dramatic change in what reference librarians do, what has not changed is the formula of how they do it: with skill, courtesy, and kindness." Second, there is tremendous optimism about the ability of librarians to adapt to change. Charlotte Ford and Lili Luo sum this up best: "Reference librarians are known for their resourcefulness, wide-ranging curiosity, and capacity for learning. . . . Reference librarianship is an adaptable profession, and in this adaptability lies its salvation."

Diane Zabel

NOTES

1. This was not Campbell's first controversial article on reference service. His 1992 article, "Shaking the Conceptual Foundations of Reference," published in *Reference Services Review*, is a classic. To understand Campbell's immense influence on changing models of reference, see Marcy Simons's excellent 2008 profile of him: "ChangeMasters All: A Series on Librarians Who Steered a Clear Course toward the Twenty-first Century: An Interview with Dr. Jerry Campbell" (*Library Administration and Management* 22 [4]: 168–171).

2. The 2009 tactical plan for reference and consultation services for the University Park Libraries at Penn State consists of the following 10 tactics:

> 1. "Develop a set of standards and policies that govern reference and consultation services in all areas of the University Park libraries."
> 2. "Develop a model of reference as a single centralized service with multiple delivery modes."
> 3. "Identify and implement models of effectively sharing staff across service points."
> 4. "Focus on proactive reference strategies and practices that anticipate library user needs."
> 5. "Identify fail points in the navigation of the physical library and of the Web interface, and implement safety nets to help users better navigate those spaces."
> 6. "Explore delivery options for 24/7 Virtual Reference Service."
> 7. "Establish a formal referral/availability system and develop both immediate and delayed (synchronous/asynchronous) internal communication mechanisms which are interoperable and flexible (agile) for all service points. Core functionality should be similar across systems for sharing ideas."
> 8. "Establish a curriculum and standard level of training for all new faculty and staff hires (including part-time)."
> 9. "Market reference services."
> 10. "Engage in ongoing assessment of reference services."

Several actions identified in the plan were accomplished in the first year, including the following: creation of a public statement stating our commitment to excellence in delivery of patron services, a pilot involving shared staffing of a general service point, implementation of a commercially developed software product to record reference transactions, and use of instant messaging software at all service desks for communication among service points.

WORKS CITED

American Library Association. 2010. *A new survey shows U.S. public libraries in financial jeopardy.* Retrieved January 21, 2010, from http://www.ala.org/ala/newspresscenter/news/pressreleases2010/january2010/trendstudy_ors.cfm.

Campbell, J. D. 2000. Clinging to traditional reference services: An open invitation to Libref.com. *Reference & User Services Quarterly* 39 (3): 223–227.

Carlson, S. 2007. Are reference desks dying out? *Chronicle of Higher Education* (April 20): A37–A39.

Free, D. 2008. News from the field. *College & Research Libraries News* 69 (5): 250–253.

Massey-Burzio, V. 1993. Rethinking the reference desk. In *Rethinking reference in academic libraries,* ed. A. G. Lipow, 43–48. Berkeley, CA: Library Solutions Press.

Pellack, L. J. 2009. First impressions and rethinking restroom questions. *Reference & User Services Quarterly* 49 (1): 4, 6.

Pritchard, S. M. 2009. Crises and opportunities. *portal: Libraries and the Academy* 9 (4): 437–440.

Radford, M. 2008. A personal choice: Reference service excellence. *Reference & User Services Quarterly* 48 (2): 109–115.

Zabel, D. 2007. A reference renaissance. *Reference & User Services Quarterly* 47 (2): 108–110.

I

OUR CHANGING USERS

1

WHO ARE OUR USERS? SCANNING THE ENVIRONMENT TO DETECT TRENDS

Ellysa Stern Cahoy

Knowing your users involves more than placing a prominent suggestion box on the reference desk, considering e-mailed kudos or criticisms, or conducting patron focus groups. To truly understand and encapsulate the current and future needs of the library's users, librarians must systematically and regularly collect, analyze, and disseminate both internal and external information on trends that impact user behaviors and needs. *Environmental scanning* is an organizational practice of screening external demographic, social, cultural, political, legal, and technological trends in an effort to better anticipate and meet future user needs. This chapter provides an overview of environmental scanning in libraries, shares scanning strategies, gives examples of existing library-related environmental scans, and explains the importance of comparing local data with national trends. Albright states, "Success requires a keen understanding of external influences in order to respond in ways that will ensure the organization's survival and success. Environmental scanning is one tool in an organization's arsenal that can be used to gain this understanding" (2004, 39).

Francis Aguilar, a Harvard Business School professor, coined the term *environmental scanning* in 1967 to describe the action of "scanning for information about events and relationships in a company's outside environment, the knowledge of which would assist top management in charting the company's future course of action" (Aguilar, 1967, 1). Used heavily in the corporate world, environmental scanning helps organizations "assess and respond to external environmental change that may have a decisive impact on strategic business decisions, organizational performance, and viability" (Castiglione, 2008, 528). Originating in the social sciences, environmental scanning emerged as a method for qualitative research. Environmental scanning is an example of a "naturalistic" study that seeks to understand an event or a series of events without altering the occurrence. The practice of scanning was more widely adopted in higher education (and in libraries in general) in the 1980s and 1990s, most frequently as part of a visioning or strategic planning process (Hatch and Pearson, 1998). Environmental scanning can help libraries understand external threats and opportunities, leading to change that will maximize user satisfaction and support (Crist, Daub, and MacAdam, 1994). The environmental scan, "a product of the collection of relevant data on social, economic, technological, and other developments over an extended period of time, connects the organization with the larger world and is used to identify trends and forecast their possible impact on the organization" (Prentice, 1989, 713). The knowledge uncovered by a scan is most integral when the library has undergone significant changes and must newly assess the impact on users' views of the library and its services. Libraries entering a period of strategic planning or contemplating significant change are also ripe candidates for scanning.

A comprehensive environmental scan helps librarians gain an understanding of the library's relationship with the external environment, whether it is positive, negative, or neutral. If the findings of a scan are utilized properly, they can help librarians improve the library's symbiotic relationship with the external environment.

For libraries, the materials used to assess the external environment can include a host of different audiences and organizations. External resources include conference papers and presentations; print and Web-based reports on user trends and attitudes; blog posts; media articles on political, social, or legal developments; and white papers on current issues. Internal information sources include the feedback of other employees in the organization, interviews with personal contacts, focus groups or meetings with user groups, and internal surveys or reports conducted with the organization's primary user base or other relevant constituencies (Castiglione, 2008).

Khandwalla (1977) identifies three types of existing relationships between organizations and their external environment. A comprehensive environmental scan will help identify the library's current relationship with the external environment and will provide the organization with direction in better balancing the library's current and future environment.

—*Dominant organization/dominated environment*

The organization maximizes the opportunities and challenges presented by the external environment, effectively meeting the needs of its users and adequately anticipating and preparing for future needs. A current example of a dominant organization is Google. Google's many products and services, including Google Books and the Google search engine, have dominated the market and, in many respects, have shaped the development of search and retrieval on the Internet, including local search tools maintained by individual libraries.

—Dominant environment/dominated organization

In this setting, developments in the external environment impact the organization and its ability to reach users and provide needed services. The external environment dominates many libraries. Slow to change because of bureaucracy, a lack of funding for new initiatives, or other barriers to innovation and change, libraries find themselves impacted by (and, in many cases, later emulating) commercially provided online resources and services.

—Symbiotic relationship: Neither the organization nor the company dominates

A symbiotic relationship provides perhaps the best of both worlds—an organization that understands and responds to external threats and opportunities, and an environment that is in sync with the organization's priorities and developments (Abels, 2002). Symbiosis should be the goal for libraries as information providers.

THE BASICS OF ENVIRONMENTAL SCANNING AS A PROCESS

The practice of environmental scanning is of use to all types of libraries—public, school, academic, and special libraries. How the scan is conducted, and the sources that are used to compile the scan, will differ by type of library. Specific types of libraries will have sources inherent to the audiences they are studying that will be of greater importance than others.

Environmental scanning focuses on strategic thinking and strategic planning, keeping the organization more abreast of current trends and future challenges. A well-conducted scan should result in a new management and marketing style that is more anticipatory and forward-thinking. It is not meant to be a stagnant process or a one-shot endeavor. Good environmental scanning is conducted as a continuous process, helping the organization to "maintain a preparative stance" as environmental circumstances change (Albright, 2004, 40).

In *Future-Driven Library Marketing*, Weingand (1998) identifies questions for librarians to ask of their organization when considering undertaking an environmental scan. Does the organization have an intense internal focus, with little understanding of external factors that may influence future user needs? Are there valuable opportunities that are not being seized because the library lacks an understanding of the external environment? Is the library's staff adequately skilled and ready to deal with users' changing needs, ensuring future success? Is the library in peril of hitting an "iceberg"—an unanticipated danger? Weingand states that a "yes" to any of these questions is evidence that environmental scanning will be of use in a library. An environmental scan places greatest emphasis on what the library may face as challenges in the next three to five years. It also gives librarians a needed perspective on where librarianship is headed in general, as a profession.

—*What resources are needed for an environmental scan?*

The most significant resource needed to effectively complete an environmental scan is staff time and dedication. Because the results of an environmental scan are subjective and culled from a variety of sources, the staff conducting the scan must be librarians or administrative staff, perhaps those working in a marketing or public relations capacity or at a managerial level in the organization. The library staff conducting the scan is also responsible for collecting sources, coordinating analysis, and widely disseminating the scan's results. Staff may also oversee a comparison of local user studies with environmental scan results.

Before undertaking an environmental scan, librarians should reflect on the following organizational considerations:

—*Does the library currently capture environmental information?*

Some libraries may have a structure already in place for scanning print and electronic media and other sources for information relevant to future challenges. Many do not. If your library is not currently involved in environmental scanning, it is important to think about where, organizationally speaking, the responsibility for environmental scanning will reside. Does the library have a marketing office, a marketing committee, or an administrative team that oversees marketing? Groups formally tied to strategic planning and marketing provide a natural home for the sort of visioning activity and analysis that environmental scanning provides.

—*Is the sort of information that environmental scanning provides internally considered important to the strategic planning process?*

Environmental scanning provides an opportunity to reflect on the library's existing flow and process for strategic planning. Does the library's strategic planning process provide for and support preliminary exploration of new trends, current challenges, and other information provided by internal and external sources? A related question—is the library administrative structure flexible and open to new ideas (and responding to external threats)?—has a similar focus, asking whether the library is ready to undertake and implement recommendations provided by environmental scanning information.

If conducted at the right time in the strategic planning process, environmental scanning can help administrators identify and evaluate leading-edge trends and organizational strengths and weaknesses early enough to address these challenges head-on within the strategic plan. Castiglione warns that "high impact ES (environmental scanning) is not a 'one shot' process. Effective ES is conducted continuously in an effort to identify emerging changes and trends that may have a significant impact on library operations and stakeholder satisfaction" (2008, 530). Conducted properly, environmental scans merge marketing and strategic planning into a symbiotic, responsive process.

—*How is an environmental scan conducted?*

The following outlines the essential steps in conducting an effective environmental scan in a library:

1. *Identify the library's environmental scanning needs.* How often does the library need to conduct an environmental scan? Which external and internal documents are of greatest importance with regard to a scan? Who are the staff members that will direct or be involved in the scanning process? What is the library's current strategic planning process timeline, and how will the scan inform that process?
2. *Conduct an analysis of the library's external environment.* The external environment can include any factors that are influencing or are currently adopted by users. This analysis could refer to a wide variety of external documents in order to present a portrait of current user needs and trends. A current document useful for determining the external environment is the 2009 *ECAR Study of Undergraduate Students and Information Technology* (Educause, 2009). This regularly updated study provides a comprehensive portrait of students' technology use, forecasting future trends that are likely to impact libraries and other technology-focused organizations. Aaker (1983) recommends scanning on two different levels. At the first level, librarians and staff assigned to project teams can look comprehensively at the current economy (local and national), current and emerging patron demographics, and service requirements. At the second level of scanning, there is a singular focus on technological changes that will have a significant future impact on user services and library instruction (Castiglione, 2008).
3. *Assess the library's existing strengths and limitations.* This is an audit of the library's internal environment. As much as it is important to look at external factors and our users' future plans, it is also critical to understand the current climate, direction, opportunities, and limitations that exist in the library. This internal assessment of current conditions will temper the overall scan's recommendations and will ground future planning in a realm (that is) appropriate to the library's needs. According to Albright, "Internal information includes organization-specific information that can be compared to the findings of external scanning in order to maximize organizational responsiveness" (2004, 44).
4. *Evaluate the identified trends, opportunities, and issues, ranking each in importance according to its relevance to user needs and potential positive impact on user services.* Ranking trends can be accomplished as a group activity within the library. Publicizing the scan findings in a forum for library staff, and asking librarians and other staff to rank issues identified as relevant to the library, can increase internal investment in the scan's relevance to the organization's needs.
5. *Communicate the results of the scan widely to the local library community and to the library's user base.* Avenues for publicizing scan results include the library's Web site, library newsletters, and public forums for library users. Sharing results widely will help users better understand the library's current challenges, while increasing their confidence in the library's ability to address and develop (better) future user services.

6. *Employ a decision-making process to apply the information collected and analyzed within the environmental scan to the library's current marketing plan and strategy-making process.* This activity may fall to the library's strategic planning group, in consultation with the librarians and staff involved in conducting and analyzing the scan.
7. *Continue to conduct environmental scans on a regular basis, reassessing trends, opportunities, and issues for their relevance to emerging user needs.* According to Karim, "Assessment should lead to the strategic integration of the environmental scanning process with organizational strategic planning" (2004, 362).

Organizational adoption of continued environmental scanning is a critical first step in changing a library's organizational structure to focus on adaptive decision making (Hambrick, 1981). Castiglione reiterates the importance of organizational adoption of scanning: "The use of environmental scanning by library administrators may reduce complacency; inform the progressive adaptation of our profession; enhance the importance of our professional activities; and facilitate the development of appropriate stakeholder services" (2008, 531).

EXAMPLES OF EXISTING LIBRARY-RELATED USER STUDIES AND ENVIRONMENTAL SCANS

Conducting environmental scans on a regular basis is a staff-intensive process. Libraries with many marketing demands or small staff may not have the resources to conduct scans locally. A wide variety of more globally produced environmental scans exist to fill this need and assist libraries in envisioning future goals.

Since 2003, the Online Computer Library Center (OCLC) has periodically published "landscape reports" (OCLC, 2007). The reports are primarily technology focused and seek to help librarians understand "the emerging library services environment" (Castiglione, 2008, 533). OCLC's first report in this area, the 2003 *Environmental Scan: Pattern Recognition,* identified current issues and trends likely to impact library services in the near future, targeted to OCLC decision makers and librarians engaged in strategic planning. In 2005, OCLC published *Perceptions of Libraries and Information Resources.* This report looked almost exclusively at the library "brand" and how users perceived the value of libraries as information providers. The publication's introduction nicely sums up its focus as an environmental scan:

> There are no major recent empirical studies that look specifically and broadly at the role that libraries and librarians play in the infosphere, from the point of view of the information consumer. How are libraries perceived by today's information consumer? Do libraries still matter? On what level? Will library use likely increase or decrease in the future? (OCLC, 2005, vii)

OCLC published *College Students' Perceptions of Libraries and Information Resources* in 2006. This report was a subset of the data compiled for the 2005 report and was of specific use to the academic library audience. The 2007 report, *Sharing, Privacy, and Trust in Our Networked World,* cast a wider net, looking closely at how Internet users share information and social data on the Web, with specific analysis and recommendations for how libraries can maximize services incorporating social media. Its most recent report, *Online Catalogs: What Users and Librarians Want* (2009), targets current and emerging issues in enhancing and developing new online public access catalog (OPAC) interfaces.

The Pew Internet & American Life Project issues numerous reports of interest to libraries. A "non-partisan, non-profit 'fact tank,'" the project shares information about trends and current issues impacting America and the world (Pew Internet & American Life Project, 2009). Recurring Pew report topics relevant to librarians include the use of the social Web (including Facebook and Twitter), data on generations of users online, use of the mobile Web by various age groups, and information-seeking patterns online. Recent Pew reports include *Information Searches That Solve Problems: How People Use the Internet, Libraries and Government Agencies When They Need Help* (Rainie, Estabrook, and Witt, 2007) and *Teens and Social Media* (Lenhart, Madden, Smith, and Macgill, 2007). Each Pew report surveys a large number of U.S. residents on a specific emerging topic. While not all Pew reports are related to libraries or the Web, they provide compelling data that highlight changing and growing trends online and elsewhere.

Annually, the New Media Consortium (NMC) publishes "The Horizon Report" (2006). Focused on technology, the report details emerging technologies predicted to have an impact on teaching and learning over the coming year. Critical challenges, technologies to watch, and key trends are highlighted. Primarily focused on higher education, the NMC now also publishes (as of 2009) a "Horizon Report" for the K–12 environment. Libraries interested in understanding new user technologies impacting the learning environment (including the time to adoption for specific technologies) will find much to use in the "Horizon Report" in order to forecast and plan for addressing new technology initiatives in the library.

The Association of College and Research Libraries (ACRL) has issued several environmental scans (in 2003 and 2007) to "identify the trends that will define the future of academic librarianship, to support research aimed at improving the practice of librarianship in academic and research environments, and to develop resources and programming that support the continuing professional education needs of its membership" (ACRL Research Committee, 2007). Previous to that, ACRL issued a report, *Top Issues Facing Academic Libraries,* that was summarized by Hisle (2002). The environmental scans are linked to related research agendas produced by ACRL sections, including the "Research Agenda for Library Instruction and Information

Literacy" (last revision in 2006) and the "Scholarly Communications Research Agenda" (2004). Each ACRL environmental scan looks at "major assumptions" currently shaping academic librarianship, as well as emerging issues likely to significantly impact libraries and librarians (ACRL Research Committee, 2007). The assumptions, which include forecasted challenges and predicted issues impacting libraries, are culled from a survey of academic librarians. In this respect, the ACRL scans give academic librarians a summary of new trends while providing a barometer for the opportunities and challenges at the forefront of librarianship. The parent organization of the ACRL, the American Library Association (ALA), is currently collecting resources for an association-wide environmental scan in 2015. This new scan is an interesting exercise in harnessing the combined knowledge of the library community to build a collection of scan resources. ALA members are invited to contribute recommended documents for use in the scan, available on the association's community software platform, ALA Connect (ALA, 2009). This collaborative process provides a new social model that may ease individual libraries' burden of collecting a wide range of resources for a comprehensive scan.

Two academic organizations, JISC and Ithaka, have also released reports useful for libraries undertaking environmental scans. JISC, a U.K.-based organization, is focused on the integration of emerging technologies in higher education. In 2008, JISC released "Information Behaviour of the Researcher of the Future." The report contains the results of a study commissioned by the JISC and the British Library regarding how children and young adults will interact with information resources over the next 5 to 10 years. The report contains the results of a massive literature review focused on several areas of information literacy and information access over the past 50 years, combined with a "deep log analysis" of the use of BL Learning, a British Library database. While the report does not contain significant original research, it provides compelling projections and conclusions for libraries, primarily based on their wide-ranging review of the existing literature (JISC, 2008).

The Ithaka project "helps the academic community use digital technologies to preserve the scholarly record and to advance research and teaching in sustainable ways" (Ithaka, 2009). The 2006 Ithaka report, "Studies of Key Stakeholders in the Digital Transformation in Higher Education," surveyed faculty and asked them to rate the importance of the library as a gateway to information, as an archive and as a buyer of information (Housewright and Schonfeld, 2008). The Ithaka reports contain essential information regarding stakeholder groups—in addition to faculty, the Ithaka Project has also surveyed and analyzed academic librarians in the past. For libraries seeking to understand the current mindset and future needs of faculty, the Ithaka reports are invaluable tools.

STRATEGIES FOR COMPLEMENTING NATIONAL DATA WITH STUDIES OF LOCAL USERS

Using national or international findings for environmental scanning can suggest future needs and challenges that may face a library. To extrapolate the data effectively to a specific library's needs, additional data from local surveys should be used to provide a more complete picture of the user population. One option is to join with local libraries or library consortiums for collaborative, cooperative scanning. Cooperative scanning programs may help develop wider and more frequent environmental scanning among libraries. Castiglione notes that

> individual library professionals, library schools, and our professional associations must become part of an interconnected system of learning, adaptation and renewal; based on collective environmental scanning and the sharing of intelligence. This process will be facilitated—not hindered—by the evolution of our library associations into a more global, interconnected and coordinated group of concerned library professionals operating on behalf of our stakeholders. (2008, 534–536)

Castiglione identifies external factors that librarians should monitor on a regular basis. These include the impact of new technologies on library services and collections; changes in copyright and intellectual property law; state and local changes in budgetary finances for library operations; new information services competitors (whether online or physically based); workforce trends and the availability of qualified, trained staff; regulatory changes impacting employment and human resources procedures, and the current and future economic outlook in general. All of these factors influence how a library plans, designs, and delivers its services and collections. It is important to remember that environmental scanning done in isolation will not be entirely useful to an organization. To be most useful, environmental scanning must be conducted in tandem with other assessment efforts to discern user needs and learning gaps (Hatch and Pearson, 1998).

Resources useful for local scanning efforts can take the form of user surveys, usability analyses of library Web pages or of locally based online library tools (such as the library catalog), user population surveys done at the community or campus level, articles in the local media, and socioeconomic data and trends relevant to the local area. Cyert and March (1963) warned against "bounded rationality," which can occur when individuals scan their own local environment so extensively that they may be unaware of the impact of important, externally occurring factors (Castiglione, 2008). It is important to retain a balance between scanning of local resources and a more wide-ranging scan of external national and international sources.

Libraries that are considering undertaking a local assessment of users or other populations should consider the following questions:

1. *Are there already-existing local studies that can be utilized?* Within colleges and universities, local communities, and school districts, an office for assessment or other assessment-related unit may have existing survey data that could prove helpful. Conducting a local environmental scan of existing data may prove useful in identifying any relevant data, as well as refining the need and focus for a new study.
2. *Who will conduct the study?* Are there support systems in place on campus or in your local community that could assist you in conducting a local user study? At colleges and universities, other units of campus (such as student affairs offices or educational technology units) may have experience, expertise, and resources for conducting local surveys.
3. *What is the focus of the study?* Are there specific areas that you would like to study with regard to current and future users (for example, library spaces, instructional technologies, or the library Web site)? Narrowing the focus of the study will assist in providing reasonable goals and a defined scope for your survey.
4. *What are the timeline and staffing for the study?* When undertaking a local study, planning ahead is essential. Consider how much time and staff effort are needed in planning and refining the survey instrument, conducting the survey, and analyzing the results. Finalizing and implementing the timeline up front will assist staff in understanding the flow and measurable goals of the study, as well as maximizing the time and staff resources available.
5. *Are there national studies that can be used for benchmarking purposes?* Identifying one or more complementary studies relevant to your research will assist in providing a more seamless connection between local and national data. Look for national studies that cover the same user population and/or topic area that you are interested in. Most studies make their survey questions available to the public. Consider using similar wording in the questions on your survey instrument in order to make correlations and analysis much easier and more powerful.
6. *How will results be analyzed and implemented?* Will the results of your study be used to inform a current strategic planning process or other current planning initiative in your library? Knowing beforehand how results will be deployed to inform future decisions will help add power and a time-sensitive focus to your survey. It may also assist in bringing more administrative resources to your study.

Local studies can provide valuable information to libraries. In "Library Service Perceptions: A Study of Two Universities," Sutton, Bazirjian, and Zerwas (2009) replicated the 2005 OCLC study, *Perceptions of Libraries and Information Resources,* on two North Carolina university campuses. The study found that local factors in place at a specific university can affect student responses. The authors stressed the importance of using local data to drive decision making, rather than relying on more globally focused data. The importance of conducting local surveys to discern the needs of a library's specific user pool is stressed throughout the article. According to Albright,

"Internal information includes organization-specific information that can be compared to the findings of external scanning in order to maximize organizational responsiveness" (2004, 44).

CONCLUSION

Abels (2002) notes,

> Competitive intelligence, knowing what competitors are doing, requires one to define the competition. In an environmental scan, the competition has to be defined in the broadest sense, going beyond obvious competitors to potential competitors in other industries. Libraries have often considered information brokers to be competitors; now libraries have to compete with bookstores, the Internet, and search engines.

Conducted properly, an environmental scan can help libraries look at new and emerging user needs and trends locally, nationally, and internally. A scan can serve as an "early warning system," helping libraries maintain preparedness for potential organizational threats (Albright, 2004, 45). Think about your library community, your library's needs, and your user population. Are there opportunities for collaboration on local user studies? Are there existing scans that could be utilized to help direct efforts to serve your local population? Is there a group in your library that would serve as a natural guide for designing and implementing scanning in tandem with a strategic planning process? Using the guidelines shared in this chapter, your library can develop a plan for environmental scanning that can help move the library forward in a future-thinking, purposeful manner, while giving librarians and staff the opportunity to engage in creative problem solving and forecasting regarding the library's future services and activities.

WORKS CITED

Aaker, D. 1983. Organizing a strategic information scanning system. *California Management Review* 25 (2): 76–83.

Abels, E. 2002. Hot topics: Environmental scanning. *Bulletin of the American Society for Information Science and Technology* 28 (3). Retrieved December 19, 2009, from http://www.asis.org/Bulletin/Mar-02/abels.html.

Aguilar, F. 1967. *Scanning the business environment.* New York: Macmillan.

Albright, K. 2004. Environmental scanning: Radar for success. *Information Management Journal* 38 (3): 38–45.

American Library Association. 2009. ALA 2015 environmental scan. *ALA Connect.* Retrieved December 19, 2009, from http://connect.ala.org/2015scan.

Association of College and Research Libraries. 2003. *Environmental scan 2003.* Retrieved December 19, 2009, from http://www.ala.org/ala/mgrps/divs/acrl/publications/whitepapers/03environmentalscanfinal.pdf.

Association of College and Research Libraries Instruction Section. 2006. *Research agenda for library instruction.* American Library Association. Retrieved

September 14, 2010 from http://www.ala.org/ala/mgrps/divs/acrl/about/sections/is/projpubs/researchagendalibrary.cfm.

Association of College and Research Libraries Research Committee. 2007. *Environmental scan 2007.* Retrieved December 19, 2009, from http://www.ala.org/ala/mgrps/divs/acrl/publications/whitepapers/Environmental_Scan_2007%20FINAL.pdf.

Association of College and Research Libraries Scholarly Communications Committee. 2007. *Establishing a Research Agenda for Scholarly Communication: A Call for Community Engagement.* Retrieved September 14, 2010 from http://www.ala.org/ala/mgrps/divs/acrl/issues/scholcomm/SCResearchAgenda.pdf.

Castiglione, J. 2008. Environmental scanning: An essential tool for twenty-first century librarianship. *Library Review* 57 (7): 528–536.

Crist, M., P. Daub, and B. MacAdam. 1994. User studies: Reality check and future perfect. *Wilson Library Bulletin* 68 (6): 38–41.

Cyert, R. M., and J. G. March 1963. *A behavioral theory of the firm.* Englewood Cliffs, NJ: Prentice-Hall.

Educause. 2009. *The ECAR study of undergraduate students and information technology.* Retrieved December 19, 2009, from http://www.educause.edu/ers0906.

Hambrick, D. 1981. Specialization of environmental scanning activities among upper level executives. *Journal of Management Studies* 18: 299–320.

Hatch, T., and T. Pearson. 1998. Using environmental scans in educational needs assessment. *Journal of Continuing Education in the Health Professions* 18: 179–184.

Hisle, W. L. 2002. Top issues facing academic librarians: A report of the Focus on the Future Task Force. *College & Research Libraries News* 63 (10). Retrieved December 19, 2009, from http://www.ala.org/ala/mgrps/divs/acrl/publications/crlnews/2002/nov/topissuesfacing.cfm.

Housewright, R., and T. Schonfeld. 2008. *Ithaka's 2006 studies of key stakeholders in the digital transformation in higher education.* Retrieved December 19, 2009, from http://www.ithaka.org/research/Ithakas%202006%20Studies%20of%20Key%20Stakeholders%20in%20the%20Digital%20Transformation%20in%20Higher%20Education.pdf.

Ithaka. 2009. *Ithaka Project.* Retrieved December 19, 2009, from http://www.ithaka.org.

JISC. 2008. *Information behaviour of the researcher of the future: A ciber briefing paper.* Retrieved December 19, 2009, from http://www.jisc.ac.uk/media/documents/programmes/reppres/gg_final_keynote_11012008.pdf.

Karim, N. S. A. 2004. The link between environmental scanning (ES) and organizational information behavior: Implications for research and the role of information professionals. *Library Review* 53 (7): 356–362.

Khandwalla, P. 1977. *The design of organizations.* New York: Harcourt Brace Jovanovich.

Lenhart, A., M. Madden, A. Smith, and A. Macgill. 2007. *Teens and social media.* Pew Internet & American Life Project. Retrieved December 19, 2009, from http://www.pewinternet.org/~/media//Files/Reports/2007/PIP_Teens_Social_Media_Final.pdf.pdf.

New Media Consortium. 2006. *Horizon Project.* Retrieved on December 19, 2009, from http://www.nmc.org/horizon.

Online Computer Library Center. 2003. *Environmental scan: Pattern recognition.* Retrieved December 19, 2009, from http://www.oclc.org/reports/escan/default.htm.

Online Computer Library Center. 2005. *Perceptions of libraries and information resources.* Retrieved December 19, 2009, from http://www.oclc.org/reports/2005perceptions.htm.

Online Computer Library Center. 2006. *College students' perception of libraries and information resources.* Retrieved December 19, 2009, from http://www.oclc.org/reports/perceptionscollege.htm.

Online Computer Library Center. 2007. *Sharing, privacy, and trust in our networked world.* Retrieved December 19, 2009, from http://www.oclc.org/reports/sharing/default.htm.

Online Computer Library Center. 2009. *Online catalogs: What users and librarians want.* Retrieved December 19, 2009, from http://www.oclc.org/reports/onlinecatalogs/default.htm.

Pew Internet & American Life Project. 2009. *About us.* Pew Research Center's Internet & American Life Project. Retrieved December 19, 2009, from http://www.pewinternet.org/About-Us.aspx.

Prentice, A. E. 1989. The environmental scan. *College & Research Libraries News* 50 (8): 713–715.

Rainie, L., E. Estabrook, and W. Witt. 2007. *Information searches that solve problems: How people use the Internet, libraries and government agencies when they need help.* Pew Internet & American Life Project. Retrieved December 19, 2009, from http://www.pewinternet.org/ /media/Files/Reports/2007/Pew_UI_LibrariesReport.pdf.pdf.

Sutton, L., R. Bazirjian, and S. Zerwas. 2009. Library service perceptions: A study of two universities. *College & Research Libraries* 70 (5): 474–485.

Weingand, D. E. 1998. *Future-driven library marketing.* Chicago: ALA Editions.

ADDITIONAL READINGS

Dempsey, K. 2009. *The accidental library marketer.* Medford, NJ: Information Today.

II

NEW AND IMPROVED SERVICE MODELS

2

DEMYSTIFYING VIRTUAL REFERENCE

Daniel Hickey

BY FOOT OR BY FINGERTIP?

When one thinks about a library, it's not unlikely that the mind will conjure up an image of collections housed within a physical building. However, another front door to the library demands increased attention from librarians and patrons alike: the library's Web site. Within the space of a human lifetime the medium and method for disseminating and retrieving information have shifted drastically, from tangible to digital media. This shift's repercussions have transformed the information landscape. Although the challenges that the changes in information retrieval and dissemination have posed now seem mundane, libraries are still struggling with the long-term, far-reaching consequences.

Before the advent of the networked computer, libraries served as a primary hub for information dissemination. Today, libraries must compete with a multitude of formal and informal information providers in the digital sphere. One aspect of information retrieval that libraries still have a corner on, however, is reference. The profession places a high priority on reference as a traditional and increasingly valued role of librarians. With the exponential proliferation of available information, users—regardless of their level of information literacy—often require research assistance beyond that which a search algorithm or frequently asked questions (FAQs) page can provide.

Virtual reference services have become ubiquitous for libraries with an online presence. However, these services rarely occupy a space of prominence on a library's main Web site. At the time of this writing, only 6 of the 124 member libraries of the Association of Research Libraries have chat widgets on the main page that allow patrons to immediately contact a library employee for assistance. (In contrast, almost all the member libraries contain prominent search boxes that let users directly interact with collections.) In almost all cases, virtual reference services are at least one click deeper into the Web site. These links often occupy very little screen real estate, making it difficult for them to compete with other Web content.

Why Aren't Virtual Reference Services at the Fore at More or All Libraries?

Increasingly, researchers are calling into question the cost-effectiveness of staffing a physical reference desk with librarians. The outcome of one study, conducted by Susan Ryan (2008), suggested that 74 percent of questions received at a traditional reference desk did not require the expertise of a trained professional to answer. With evidence-based decision making decreasing the need for librarians at a desk, the logical place for reference librarians to assist patrons is "out and about meeting users when and where the help is needed" (Watstein and Bell, 2008, 6). In the current research milieu, meeting patrons at their point of need is almost synonymous with providing virtual reference services. Libraries have a unique, and largely unexploited, opportunity to highlight their strength in reference by pushing these services to the forefront in online environments. Doing so is only one method that librarians can employ to make virtual reference services a priority at their library.

ASTOUNDING SAMUEL GREEN

In 1876, in the first issue of *Library Journal,* Samuel Green of the Worcester Public Library published an article entitled "Personal Relations between Librarians and Readers" in which he chronicled the many situations in which a librarian might be of assistance in fulfilling a patron's information need. Notably absent from these interactions was the use of letter writing to communicate with people at a distance. In the vision of reference services that Green presents to readers, the patron invariably "calls for the work, and takes it home to study" (Green, 1876, 77). Now, the patron, the materials she's looking for, and even the librarian answering her question need not reside in a library for a reference transaction to occur.

Joan Reitz's *Online Dictionary for Library and Information Science* (2007) defines *digital reference* as "services requested and provided over the Internet, usually via e-mail, instant messaging ('chat'), or Web-based submission forms, usually answered by librarians in the reference department of a library, sometimes by the participants in a collaborative reference system serving more than one institution." The core of this slightly antiquated definition rings surprisingly true, despite methods (such as virtual worlds and text messaging) that don't strictly rely on the use of a Web browser to access the Internet.

Although technology evolves rapidly, it is useful to frame current virtual reference services in terms of the history of remote reference. Whether a librarian chooses to send a letter, write an e-mail, or video chat with a user, his intended goal is the same. The only difference is the medium he selects and the constraints that medium places on communication. As mainstream methods of communication change, librarians must ensure that their approach to virtual reference is flexible enough to accommodate necessary revisions to services.

As of December 2009, the Pew Internet & American Life Project reported that 93 percent of Americans aged 18 to 29 use the Internet (Rainie, 2010). Although older Americans are less likely to use the Internet, it is important to note that as educational attainment increases so does the statistical likelihood that one is an Internet user. While 63 percent of people with a high school education use the Internet, the percentage jumps to 87 percent for those with a college degree and 94 percent for those with tertiary education (Rainie, 2010).

Between 2005 and 2008 all age groups polled (from age 12 to 76 and over) experienced growth in Internet use (Jones and Fox, 2010). In the foreseeable future, it seems likely that Internet use will increase and eventually level off to a constant across age groups and levels of educational attainment. To remain relevant, libraries must be ready for patron bases that increasingly expect reference interactions to take place in a technologically mediated, virtual environment. In addition, librarians must be receptive to unanticipated changes in how their users initiate contact in virtual environments:

> Despite the power that email holds among adults as a major mode of personal and professional communication, it is not a particularly important part of the communication arsenal of today's teens. Only 14% of all teens report sending emails to their friends every day, making it the least popular form of daily social communication on the list we queried [landline, mobile phone, in person, IM, text message, messaging over social networking sites, email]. (Lenhart, Madden, Smith, and Macgill, 2009, iv)

While e-mail is a primary mode of professional communication for librarians, there may come a time when maintaining a presence in a prevailing social networking Web site becomes just as important to conversing with patrons.

In the same year that Green's landmark article was published, Alexander Graham Bell was awarded a patent for the telephone, a technology still used today by librarians to provide reference services at a distance. Although we don't know whether Green found the advent of telecommunication particularly striking or relevant to his interactions with patrons, hindsight allows today's librarians to imagine the unique set of challenges new technologies can pose to interpersonal communication.

THE HARDEST BUTTON TO BUTTON

The *Virtual Reference Bibliography* (http://vrbib.rutgers.edu/index.php), first established by Bernie Sloan and now maintained at Rutgers by Marie Radford, is an index of over 900 works about virtual reference. Searching a library science database such as Library and Information Science Abstracts (LISA) will yield approximately the same number of citations. Clearly, a very large corpus of literature already surrounds virtual reference. Why are librarians still talking about it? The answer to this question is multipronged and illustrates the challenges that face virtual reference providers.

Many of the problems that virtual reference practitioners deal with are technological in nature. First and foremost, much of the software that librarians employ to connect with remote users was never designed with the reference interview in mind. Instead, these young technologies were created to facilitate casual communication and thus lacked the functionality required to coordinate online reference at a library. Examples of technologies that have achieved widespread use due to their popularity with users are programs such as AOL Instant Messenger or services such as text messaging. As these technologies developed over time, their creators' goals were focused on a set of needs distinct from those in reference work.

At the same time, software specifically designed for librarians and virtual reference has proven less than competitive. Vendor products became notorious for lagging behind technologically, imposing unreasonable constraints on users (such as having to install software on their computers), and generally not meeting needs as easily as free products. Only recently have freely available and vendor products begun to meet the needs of both the librarian and the user.

Libraries also have philosophical tendencies that serve as hurdles to excellence in virtual reference. Although this is a stereotype and not true of all institutions or individuals, libraries have a reputation for being slow to change, taking conservative or wait-and-see approaches. Instead of taking risks and seizing opportunities, libraries hesitate and are subsequently forced to change to avoid obsolescence. For visionary virtual reference providers, institutional resistance to change may be the largest challenge to overcome for virtual reference implementation. Libraries of the 21st century that are stuck with late 20th-century technological infrastructures need to remain cognizant of advances in virtual reference. Lina Coelho (2009) summed up this sentiment perfectly when she stated that "it is essential to know what is happening beyond 'the limits of the possible' set by your institution's IT department."

If libraries want software tailored to both librarians' and users' needs, one option is to build and maintain the tool in-house. Although not focused on virtual reference, an excellent example of open-source software is Oregon State University's *Library à la Carte*. Ideally, instead of one library designing and disseminating virtual reference software, several libraries could band together in a consortium to design and support virtual reference software across several institutions. Gaining traction, buy-in, and funding for such a project may be difficult, but it is a challenge that virtual reference providers should rise to rather than shy away from.

A bevy of challenges face online reference providers, be they technological, philosophical, or monetary in origin. However, the literature contained within the previously mentioned *Virtual Reference Bibliography* and library databases provides an excellent starting point for addressing the hurdles that must be overcome to provide virtual reference services.

THE LONG AND WINDING ROAD TO ASSESSMENT

Selection, implementation, and assessment of library-wide virtual reference services are topics each worthy of their own book, and as such a multitude of monographs is dedicated to each of them. The important first step is to perform a needs assessment for the service. The results of a successful needs assessment can provide valuable insights for informed decision making throughout all subsequent steps of virtual reference service implementation.

Users' needs should shape an institution's technical and operational approach to reference. Before librarians begin vetting different software, hardware, or service plans, they should identify how patrons want to connect to the library. Outlining, and later articulating, clear service-level expectations (such as hours staffed and types of questions answered) will help with measuring the success of the implemented service. Based on the patron base being served and resources available to meet the said need, service levels will vary widely between different types of libraries.

The needs of virtual reference service operators should be taken into consideration as well. In many cases a virtual reference service should centralize the flow of queries yet still allow for flexibility, especially in multilibrary systems. A virtual reference service should supply librarians with the tools to effectively fill patrons' information needs, the functionality to make seamless referrals, and a framework from which to draw meaningful metrics.

Benchmarking with peer institutions can provide valuable insight into what similar libraries do to meet user and librarian needs. Reviewing other libraries' decisions may also alert librarians to considerations that they had not yet anticipated. Libraries will have to consider several salient points. Will the library select a vendor product or develop one in-house? Will the library staff the service with librarians or paraprofessionals (or even outsource the service in whole or part)? Will the library place the responsibility for virtual reference on one or several librarians, departments, and so on? There are no foolproof courses of action for any of these decisions; rather, having a firm understanding of an institution's resources and patron base will guide librarians to realistic and manageable choices.

Anyone who has spent some time in the Zs knows that there's a plethora of sources about assessing virtual reference services. In the past, at the most basic level, reference services have been evaluated based on the number of patrons served. A remnant of this system can be seen in Association of Research Libraries statistics, which still record reference transactions as a lump sum associated with a library. However, collecting quantitative data without context has been outmoded for some time. Increasingly, reference assessment has been blended with qualitative data garnered through surveys such as LibQUAL+ to provide a more holistic picture of services at an institution. A patron's "willingness to return" and use a service again is increasingly a measure that has become shorthand for quality (Nielson and Ross, 2006, 63). A baseline for quality can be easily achieved by following the Reference and User Services Association's behavioral and the International Federation of Library Associations and Institutions' digital reference guidelines, suggested courses of action that current virtual reference providers follow to greater and lesser extents (Shachaf and Horowitz, 2008).

The next logical step in assessing virtual reference services is to move beyond user perceptions of quality to a system that places an internal emphasis on excellence in customer service. Although many librarians will recoil at such corporate verbiage, internalizing the need for distinction in patron relations should be a clearly articulated job responsibility for reference providers. The days of splitting hairs over which desk (reference, lending, or tech help) a question should be asked at are over. (In the virtual environment, services are rarely divided in this way.) In the patron's mind, she is consulting the correct person to help her: a library employee.

Of course, not all assessment will focus on users. Virtual reference services will invariably come under financial scrutiny, not only for the cost of technology, but also for employee time expended. The important thing to remember is that, should a particular approach to virtual reference prove ineffectual, librarians should be willing to revisit and revise past decisions to reinvigorate the service. Although the process seems commonplace, establishing professional virtual reference services includes a certain amount of risk that library administrators must be willing to take on. Assessment, as a result, shouldn't be a one-time process. Continual evaluation with incremental changes will result in a dynamic virtual reference service that changes to meet the needs of the institution, professional, and patron.

BACK TO THE FUTURE: OLD PROBLEMS OR NEW OPPORTUNITIES?

Several hot topics in reference relate directly or indirectly to virtual reference services. While some are unique opportunities for librarians to innovate and provide superior service, others are known problems that must be addressed for professionals to move forward in their work.

As Lenhart and colleagues (2009) mentioned in their Pew Internet & American Life report on *Teens and Social Media,* the social aspects of Web 2.0 are increasingly a primary method for young people to communicate. These channels, often considered informal, are a logical place for librarians to extend reference services should they prove overwhelmingly popular among a patron base. The key is to prioritize, but not write off, new modes of virtual reference. An academic librarian may find that it is imperative to offer reference services in a university's course management system, where all students must log on to find course readings, grades, and so on. Meanwhile, that same librarian might abandon an interesting platform such as a virtual world due to the small percentage of the patron base that actually uses this service point. Alternative and novel venues for virtual reference allow librarians to reach highly specific groups of patrons. Such activities should be appropriately balanced with methods of communication that allow librarians to reach the widest possible audience.

As mobile computing technologies become increasingly affordable and functional, more and more patrons are using mobile platforms to access library resources and services. According to the Pew Internet & American Life Project, "more than half of Americans—56%—have accessed the internet wirelessly on some device, such as a laptop, cell phone, MP3 player, or game console" (Horrigan, 2009, 1). The challenge of helping a patron navigate a physical space will put increased emphasis on wayfinding aids in both physical and virtual environments. In addition to allowing patrons to move during a reference interaction, technology will increasingly empower virtual reference providers to get out from behind the computer and meet "virtual" patrons who are actually within the library to provide face-to-face service. Librarians will also be able to multitask more effectively when using mobile devices, roving when not engaged in a virtual reference interaction.

Unfortunately, the future of virtual reference service isn't all about possibilities. Privacy, as it relates to digital communications, should be a persistent concern for librarians. The American Library Association's *Code of Ethics* states that library professionals must "protect each library user's right to privacy and confidentiality with respect to information sought or received and resources consulted, borrowed, acquired or transmitted" (American Library Association Council, 2008). Librarians must be canny when it comes to privacy, vetting virtual reference software to ensure that patrons' privacy is respected. Currently, many popular, free, Web-based e-mail services employ data mining to display targeted advertisements. While data mining is usually automated, it still violates the profession's ethical conviction of confidentiality and should thus be avoided. In addition, building an institutional knowledge base or data warehouse of reference interactions must be done with care, removing identifiable patron information to safeguard privacy.

There are many future challenges that face virtual reference service providers. Some, such as providing reference services despite reductions in staffing, are complex, institution-specific problems beyond the scope of this chapter. However, many of the issues facing virtual reference today require librarians to revisit the profession's core values, affirm their importance, and work to ensure that they will be upheld in the digital sphere.

BUSTING MYTHS, TAKING NAMES

A librarian's receptivity to virtual reference should, of course, not be taken for granted. There are persistent myths about virtual reference that need to be dispelled. The first is that virtual reference is for the next generation of professionals, that crowd of 20- or 30-somethings for whom implementing technology in libraries seems like a breeze. Fluency in a virtual environment doesn't correspond with age but rather with familiarity and practice. People of any age can become adept at virtual reference.

Another myth is that virtual reference is, quite simply, a lot of extra work. This idea most likely sprang from one individual being asked to spearhead virtual reference services at a library. When added to preestablished job responsibilities, serving as the axis on which virtual reference services turn could be overwhelming. In such cases, journal articles with titles like "Doing Virtual Reference along with Everything Else" begin to take on a darker, ominous tone. Ideally, even at the smallest libraries, virtual reference responsibilities should be shared. With proper management of the service, no practitioner should feel overwhelmed by his workload.

Finally, although virtual reference used to be viewed as a service that could be offered inexpensively, needing only free tools and a skeleton crew to be implemented, it is increasingly viewed as a service with a price tag, especially at large libraries. However, purchasing software, hardware, labor, or data plans is still not necessary to implement virtual reference successfully. Even at large libraries, reasonably priced and free options are still being employed to provide service.

Offering virtual reference services involves implicitly or explicitly answering a series of questions. For the practitioner, it's important to keep in mind that reference skills are transferable and can be adapted to new technologies. Actively participating in the process by which these technologies are implemented and evaluated affords the opportunity to shape the resultant system. Librarian input facilitates a virtual reference service that grows increasingly efficient behind the scenes and is user centered—custom tailored to librarian and patron alike.

What's the next step for a professional who wants to get involved with virtual reference or is already in the thick of it? The answer is simple: Talk to those who excel at remote reference. Seek out the people who are passionate about excellent service and the most effective ways to provide it. Staying hip to developments at one's library and within the profession is easier when one's in good company. No virtual reference librarian need work in a vacuum.

WORKS CITED

American Library Association Council. 2008. *Code of ethics of the American Library Association*. Retrieved January 15, 2010, from http://www.ala.org/ala/aboutala/offices/oif/statementspols/codeofethics/codeethics.cfm.

Coelho, L. 2009. Information tomorrow: Reflections on technology and the future of public and academic libraries. *Ariadne* 61 (October 30). Retrieved January 2, 2010, from http://www.ariadne.ac.uk/issue61/coelho-rvw/.

Green, S. S. 1876. Personal relations between librarians and readers. *Library Journal* 1 (October): 74–81.

Horrigan, J. 2009. *Wireless internet use*. Pew Internet & American Life Project. Retrieved January 13, 2010, from http://www.pewinternet.org/~/media//Files/Reports/2009/Wireless Internet Use.pdf.

Jones, S., and S. Fox. 2010. *Generations online in 2009*. Pew Internet & American Life Project. Retrieved January 28, 2010, from http://www.pewinternet.org/~/media//Files/Reports/2009/PIP_Generations_2009.pdf.

Lenhart, A., M. Madden, A. Smith, and A. Macgill. 2009. *Teens and social media*. Pew Internet & American Life Project. Retrieved December 27, 2009, from http://pewinternet.org/~/media//Files/Reports/2007/PIP_Teens_Social_Media_Final.pdf.pdf.

Nielson, K., and C. S. Ross. 2006. Evaluating virtual reference from the user's perspective. In *Assessing reference and user services in a digital age*, ed. E. Novotny, 53–79. Binghamton, NY: Haworth Information Press.

Rainie, L. 2010. *Internet, broadband, and cell phone statistics*. Pew Internet & American Life Project. Retrieved January 10, 2010, from http://www.pewinternet.org/~/media//Files/Reports/2010/PIP_December09_update.pdf.

Reitz, J. M. 2007. *ODLIS—Online dictionary for library and information science*. Libraries Unlimited. Retrieved December 25, 2009, from http://lu.com/odlis/odlis_d.cfm.

Ryan, S. M. 2008. Reference transactions analysis: The cost effectiveness of staffing a traditional academic reference desk. *Journal of Academic Librarianship* 34 (5): 389–399.

Shachaf, P., and S. M. Horowitz. 2008. Virtual reference service evaluation: Adherence to RUSA behavioral guidelines and IFLA digital reference guidelines. *Library & Information Science Research* 30 (2): 122–137.

Watstein, S. B., and S. J. Bell. 2008. Is there a future for the reference desk? A point-counterpoint discussion. *Reference Librarian* 49 (1): 1–20.

3

GOING BEYOND THE DESK: 21ST-CENTURY REFERENCE, OUTREACH, AND TEACHING SERVICES

Elizabeth McKeigue and Laura Farwell Blake

Changing scholarly practices and economic constraints require that the library profession revisit many of the assumptions that have long been the basis for academic library programs and services. Much of the academic library world has been affected by a global economic crisis that has strained our capacity to sustain programs, services, and collections. Some argue that reference desks are no longer sustainable. However, we argue that, not in all, but in many environments, they are still essential and that, to sustain the business of reference services, librarians must balance the need to guide users in a library setting and the need to serve them wherever they are.

Long before there was an economic crisis, discussion in the library literature indicated that academic libraries and their services would look very different in the 21st century than they had during the 20th. In the last years of the 20th and the first years of the 21st century, a hybrid environment prevailed. In this environment, there was a constantly and locally (institutionally based) shifting balance between in-person and virtual services, print and digital collections, local and distance education, on-campus and online resources. One cause of the new library's evolution was the growing influence of technology on research: "The information landscape of early 21st century higher education is characterized by ubiquitous, digitized, indexed, online access to content" (Council on Library and Information Resources, 2008, 1). Another was a change in patterns of scholarship, specifically, the rise of cross-disciplinary research. These two causes combined to require institutions of higher learning to rethink their internal organization (Council on Library and Information Resources, 2008). While these factors are distinctly present in the ongoing mix, libraries now have to confront these challenges in an era of sharply limited financial resources. Faced with crisis, it can be tempting to look for solutions that seem to yield immediate rewards. Closing reference desks may seem like a straightforward savings, but it is not so. Reference and research services enhance the overall value of academic libraries' collections. Reducing costs is a necessity; sustaining value is a greater good. At the same time that we seek innovative solutions to these challenges, we can also seek guidance in a longer view. Where reference and research services are concerned, library voices from earlier centuries can still speak to us.

SOME TRUTHS PERSIST

We may speak of outreach and support for teaching by reference librarians as new, as having developed in response to changing patterns of library use, and yet, in some strong sense, outreach and teaching support are a natural extension of an old tradition of reference work. In 1876, in the first volume of *Library Journal,* edited by Melvil Dewey, with Charles Cutter as bibliographer, the article "Personal Relations between Librarians and Readers" appeared. Its author, Samuel Swett Green, was writing in the tradition of the great public librarians of the 19th century. While his voice and views are clearly from another time, he articulates certain truths that persist and still inform successful reference work. He says,

> *First.* If you gain the respect and confidence of readers, and they find you easy to get along with and pleasant to talk with, great opportunities are afforded of stimulating the love of study and of directing investigators to the best sources of information.
>
> *Second.* You find out what book the actual users of the library need, and your judgment improves in regard to the kind of books it is best to add to it.
>
> *Third.* One of the best means of making a library popular is to mingle freely with its users, and help them in every way. (Green, 1876, 78)

Though Green speaks from the public library tradition, he further asserts, "Personal intercourse and relations between librarian and readers are useful in all libraries." (1876, 79). This holds true for academic libraries now more than ever. The article concludes with this affirmation of the pleasures of reference work: "There are few pleasures comparable to that of associating continually with curious and vigorous minds, and of aiding them in realizing their ideals" (Green, 1876, 81). Any reference or research librarian who has been present at the moment when a student or faculty member discovers a new intellectual connection or a new research or teaching pathway knows this pleasure.

FROM THE 19TH TO THE 21ST CENTURY

What was true for Green in 1876 continues to be true for effective reference librarianship. It is, in an important sense, personal. What allows the reference librarian's work to remain personal in an era of remote research is that the work is increasingly mobile, as well as virtual. A 2004 Association of Research Libraries (ARL) study conducted by Aamot and Hiller concluded that three major benefits of offering library services in nonlibrary spaces are increasing the visibility of "librarians and the library by providing services on users' turf"; providing services on users' own terms; and creating opportunities to "connect with faculty and students in a way that can't be done in a traditional library setting" (12). Reference librarians leave the desk and the library to involve themselves in the academic life of the college or university, both as a way to reach students and faculty outside of the library and as a way of connecting the library to campus curriculum and student life. These choices are strategic: *We leave the library to help sustain its place at the heart of the university.*

Researchers' need for personal mediation by librarians prevails despite the increasing availability of effective search engines like Google or Bing. The proliferation of search engines may lead people to believe that all information is equal and that they can find any information they need for free, instantly and easily, online. However, ubiquitous digital information allows researchers to work more independently but not necessarily more effectively. A Pew Internet & American Life Project report in 2007 notes that an increasing number of questions at library services desks come from researchers who have not been able to find what they need using a Web search engine (Rainie, Estabrook, and Witt, 2007). A 2009 article on the future of reference services in academic and public libraries comments that while "sometimes it is because the information is not there," it is also often because "their search skills are not . . . focused" (O'Gorman and Trott, 2009, 328). Though in the 21st century, many students and faculty have access to a rich digital landscape on the Internet and through their libraries' considerable investment in licensed electronic resources (which consume an ever-increasing amount of library funds), the personal relationships to which Green refers are still necessary for the effective use of those resources.

OUR ENVIRONMENT AND OUR ROLES

As mentioned earlier, reference and research librarians serve the essential role of intermediary between library collections and scholarly communities. The intermediary role is one traditional and significant aspect of reference work, but the depth and scope of the current activities of most reference and research librarians reveal that their fundamental role is that of educator.

In the first years of the 21st century, the Faculty of Arts and Sciences at Harvard University completed a multiyear review of the college's curriculum. A new plan for general education was developed. The *Report of the Committee on General Education* stated,

> We recognize that the boundaries between disciplines today are porous and shifting. It is less clear than it was thirty years ago where chemistry stops and biology begins, where literary theory stops and art history begins, where computer science stops and linguistics begins, where economics stops and government begins, where neuroscience stops and psychology begins, where mathematics stops and philosophical logic begins. Research today is not only *multi*disciplinary, but *trans*disciplinary. (*Report of the Committee,* 2005, 23)

The report stated, "Additionally, there is the question of institutional DNA. . . . Harvard has not been a place of required foundational courses. It is a university dedicated to the pursuit of excellence in specialized areas of expertise, and its curriculum reflects this" (*Report of the Committee,* 2005, 31).

To design effective reference programs and services, it is essential to understand and respect the "institutional DNA" of the institution whose mission the library supports. Each institution offers opportunities and constraints. For example, there are deep traditions of decentralization at Harvard University that have informed much of the organizational structures of the libraries there. An old Harvard maxim, "Every tub rests on its own bottom," or ETOB, has been a guiding principle in the organization. This operating principle must now shift to accommodate the demands of transdisciplinary research and to achieve necessary efficiencies, including centralized functions, services, and resources. There is always a dynamic tension between centralization and specialization. On the one hand, as Dave Tyckoson stated in his essay, "That Thing You Do," "all librarianship is local" (2007, 112). So programs and services must be designed to support the teaching and research needs of a library's primary community: They must be local. On the other hand, because of transdisciplinarity, students and researchers need to move easily across multiple libraries on a single campus, which may not share structures or processes; they can be frustrated by a scheme that takes "local" too far. Therein lie the challenges to the model of ETOB.

Transdisciplinary research and new modes of teaching in the curriculum drive organizations to revisit decentralized organizational structures, coordinate their services, and think creatively. In the case of reference and research services, this means thinking about developing a strong network of librarians who leave the reference desk to support faculty teaching. The human network must be sustained alongside the fiber: For reference and research services to thrive, a strong network of reference and research librarians who get out from behind the desk and out of the library is vital to the ongoing success of libraries.

BEYOND THE LIBRARY: REAL PERSONAL LIBRARIANSHIP

While libraries provide a wide range of virtual resources and services to meet new user demands, surveys and other research reveal that users find the library information environment increasingly complex and difficult to navigate. Library users want assistance at time of need and in their space. They also value personal contact with library staff as a way to ask questions and resolve problems.

Research libraries and librarians continue to seek new strategies for providing services to library users, including expanding services beyond library facilities and offering in-person library services in non-library spaces. (Aamot and Hiller, 2004)

The Association of Research Libraries has affirmed the wisdom of Green's 1876 assertions. This begs the question of which strategies are effective in achieving "personal contact" and building "personal relations."

Formal outreach programs, such as liaison programs, offer reference librarians the opportunity to get out from behind their desks in a meaningful way. The concept of roving reference was an early attempt to develop these kinds of services, but liaison programs are not about establishing remote general reference service points in nonlibrary settings. In fact, they are about developing relationships with curricular programs, with student organizations, with residential units, and with other key members of the academic community. Effective programs for providing reference services outside of the library are based on ongoing relationships with academic programs and on getting reference librarians engaged with student life. This level of outreach allows library services to be truly mobile and creates reference services that are the basis for what is known in some circles as the "embedded librarian."[1]

Despite a national downward trend in the actual number of questions received at reference desks, we assert that reference work continues to occur at the same rate. It is occurring, and increasingly so, in places and modes where we do not have traditional ways of quantifying services and gathering data at an institutional level. As important as library spaces are, the library is only one place to encounter researchers. "Teachable moments" are happening all over campus, and librarians need to identify where and when they are.

How do librarians identify where and when these teachable moments occur? They have to gather data and analyze it, and they have to get out there and network. They have to create and build relationships with key constituencies on campus. For example, there are nearly 6,700 undergraduates enrolled at Harvard College and over 3,700 graduates in the programs of the Graduate School of Arts and Sciences (Office of Institutional Research, Harvard University, 2008, 6). Looking at the data to identify where critical masses of users exist outside the library exposes several significant opportunities.

At Harvard, 97 percent of all undergraduates live on campus in one of the 12 residential houses. Each house accommodates 350 to 500 students and has its own dining hall, study spaces, common rooms, and facilities for academic, recreational, and cultural activities. The Harvard College Web site explains, "Houses are places where learning occurs all the time, whether in the dining hall as students share a meal with instructors and visiting scholars, or in house tutorials or seminars taken for degree credit."[2] The houses differ from traditional dormitories in that each house offers instructional opportunities (tutorials and small classes) and promotes activities related to music, drama, theater, sports, public services, and other special interests. The house system encourages interaction among students, faculty, and other house affiliates. These houses are a key constituency for librarians serving undergraduates. Librarians who connect with the college faculty and administrative staff of these houses can create opportunities to participate in the life of the house and connect with students in a way that does not happen in a classroom or across a reference desk. As a nonresident adviser in a house, a librarian might find him- or herself in the dining hall a few times a week. An informal setting can open a whole new range of questions.

Because the librarian has gone to where the students are, students who didn't think they needed the library or a librarian suddenly see the opportunity to ask what's on their minds, without special effort. They see an opportunity, and, in the moment, they take it. In turn, this gives the librarian an opportunity to demystify the library system, to ask what students are thinking, and to directly assist them outside of the library. When these moments are successful for both sides, students tell their friends, and librarians gain valuable insights into students' needs. Whatever other outreach programs we may build, positive word of mouth is the most valuable publicity the reference and research library service can have. It seems deceptively simple, but it requires an investment of time on the part of individual librarians. This is not work that occurs between 9 A.M. and 5 P.M., Monday through Friday. Institutions that wish to invest must consider both the cost of extra time and the need for flexible work schedules for staff to pursue these opportunities.

For institutions with graduate programs, librarians have a special role. Graduate work often begins in a collective experience and develops in a continuous arc toward the solitude of dissertation work. There are economies of scale to be realized: The library can participate in orientations, create online resources that welcome graduate students to their new environment, and offer various institution-wide messages. But, most effectively, librarians who are liaisons or who have an official responsibility to academic programs can make an early effort to affect graduate students' experience. These students are future members of the faculty, whose experience can teach them to value reference librarians in their future scholarship and teaching. Librarians can partner with graduate students to effect change in the perceptions of academic libraries nationally. It is possible to raise the collective expectations of future faculty through library outreach programs to graduate students. As graduate students progress from courses to teaching, librarians who have established relationships can support the nascent teaching efforts of these students and thereby gain valuable insight into the future of scholarship and pedagogy.

This is not to say, by any means, that librarians can have an impact only in graduate programs. Most undergraduates do not go on to graduate education. This is all the more reason for librarians to engage with undergraduates at every opportunity. Research literacy and the ethical use of sources must be taught within the undergraduate curriculum, and librarians must take on that responsibility. In the age of ubiquitous digital information, this is a profound responsibility.

Liaison work has been an activity common to a great enough number of academic libraries—and for a long enough time—that there has been time to reflect on it, study it, and publish about it. In the 2003 article "New Roles and Opportunities for Academic Library Liaisons: A Survey and Recommendations," research librarians at Rutgers University found that their top recommendation for effective liaisonship was to make "direct and personal contact with faculty and students whenever possible" (Glynn and Wu, 2003, 122). The Rutgers article also analyzed the data from a survey of librarian liaisons about their liaison work. Another survey was done at Harvard in 2008, using the same questions Rutgers asked in their survey so that the results could be compared. The Rutgers survey (see figure 3.1) revealed that the top three most useful ways to connect with faculty were via e-mail, in person, and by telephone. The 2008 Harvard survey (see figures 3.1 and 3.2) confirmed that e-mail and face-to-face contact were still the most useful methods of making connections with faculty, yet at Harvard, the value of giving a formal presentation not only outranked e-mail and face-to-face as a method but was ranked most useful by all of the poll respondents. Getting out and being seen "on stage," as it were, seemed to be getting the attention of Harvard faculty more than any other way.

Rutgers (2003)	*Harvard (2008)*
1. E-mail	1. Presentations
2. Face to face	2. E-mail
3. Telephone	3. Face to face

Figure 3.1. Top Three (*Most* Useful) Ways to Connect with Faculty

Rutgers (2003)	*Harvard (2008)*
1. Newsletters	1. Newsletters
2. Campus mail	2. Campus mail
3. Office hours	3. Office hours

Figure 3.2. Bottom Three (*Least* Useful) Ways to Connect with Faculty

Unsurprisingly, the 2008 results at Harvard for the most (figure 3.3) and least (figure 3.4) useful ways to connect with students were entirely in agreement with the 2003 results at Rutgers. However, while it is true that what worked well then still works well today, we also must acknowledge that new ways of connecting have emerged since then.

Rutgers (2003)	*Harvard (2008)*
1. Face to face	1. Face to face
2. Instruction	2. E-mail
3. E-mail	3. Instruction

Figure 3.3. Top Three (*Most* Useful) Ways to Connect with Students

Rutgers (2003)	*Harvard (2008)*
1. Consultation forms	1. Office hours
2. Telephone	2. Telephone
3. Office hours	3. Consultation forms

Figure 3.4. Bottom Three (*Least* Useful) Ways to Connect with Students

HOW LIAISON WORK IS CHANGING

A crucial question in the Rutgers survey asks, "Do you see the need for liaison work as increasing?" In the Rutgers results, 66 percent said yes to this question in 2003. In the Harvard survey, 80 percent said yes. One of our colleagues expounded on this opinion in his comments: "I think that the scope of library liaison activities is expanding. In addition to research guides, consultations, special tours, and research classes, I have also been engaged to discuss course assignments, advise on department and course webpages, consult on humanities computing projects, meet with prospective grad students, visit scholarly institutes, and more. The trend, I think, is towards a more scholarly engagement with departments in the form of co-teaching, introducing students to special collections, adding 'library' components to course sites, etc."[3]

A vivid example of this type of engagement is the experience of librarians who connect with faculty as a new course is being developed. Though there are many examples across many disciplines, one that is instructive as a model of transdisciplinary teaching arose from the Silk Road Project, a nonprofit cultural and educational organization founded in 1998 by cellist Yo-Yo Ma. This creative intellectual association led Harvard's Cogan University Professor Stephen Greenblatt to design a new course called

Imaginary Journeys: Travel and Transformation in the Early 17th Century, wherein three imaginary ships leave England and travel, ultimately, to Virginia and Massachusetts. Students assume the role of travelers, reading *The Merchant of Venice, Othello,* and *The Tempest* in tandem with accounts of first encounters from the period. Librarians were integrated into the course, attending lectures and contributing to the course's rich virtual environment. When they considered which digital resources might be useful to the course, it was immediately apparent that the range included those for anthropology, astronomy, history, economics, the history of science, literature in several languages, the arts, music, geography, and a host of other disciplines. Librarians saw that this course defied their normal approaches. It was offered as a general education course, a nondepartmental course, representing well the concept of transdisciplinarity. The Program in General Education at Harvard arose from a historic review of the undergraduate curriculum. It led to a new course planning structure: Librarians began to work collaboratively with instructional technologists and consultants from writing programs, with educators from museums of the arts and sciences, with experts from the university's teaching and learning center, and, most significantly, with deans and faculty in support of these courses, rather than responding with offers of support after the courses had been published in the course catalog.

We initially wanted to avoid using the phrase *embedded librarian,* but in fact, it's not a bad analogy. Reference and research librarians are doing more than tagging along for the ride. Increasingly, librarians are working with faculty and their teaching fellows as a member of the team, integrating their services into the development, preparation, and execution of the course. In addition, librarians are not only involving themselves in the design of new courses but becoming students themselves. At Harvard, some of our colleagues audit courses each semester in one of the areas to which they serve as liaison. This is understood as a valuable activity. One liaison reports that faculty usually introduce her at the beginning of the semester and sometimes call on her to provide information; as a result, students tend to recognize her and feel more comfortable e-mailing her with questions, while she in turn has opportunities to gain subject knowledge and to understand the student experience better.[4]

As important as it is to get out there and engage with people in person, new technologies, particularly those that fall into the broad category of Web 2.0 tools, are providing librarians with many new ways to interact with faculty and students. The research guides of today are more than lists of useful links. Customized research portals deliver library content in a more holistic way. We have recently developed research portals with multiple librarians across disciplines, with faculty across departments, and with graduate students. The products of this collaboration include guides that rely on the course management software and can easily be integrated into interdisciplinary course sites: guides that are topical and are based on local special collections, include submissions from contributors to the field, and offer graduate students opportunities to showcase their work, such as *poetry@harvard*;[5] interdisciplinary guides based on historical periods that cross disciplinary boundaries, like *Rinascimento: Research Guide for Renaissance Studies*[6] and *Interlibros: Research Guide for Classics & Medieval Studies*;[7] and guides that recognize fields of study whose methods require multiple approaches to knowledge, such as *Traditions: Research Guide for Folklore and Folkloristics*.[8]

These portals include deep links to library catalog records and search results; links to e-books, recommended articles, and electronic reference book entries; library-produced videos on everything from how to use the catalog to the library's special collections, featuring librarians, students, and faculty; auto-rotating content like resource spotlights or slideshows featuring digital collection images; RSS feeds from online newspapers and other media; and instant messaging chat widgets.

The Internet, with all of its evolving uses, is ultimately only the means to an end. The goal is academic discovery. Librarians must create Web resources that bring students to the library collections. In research libraries with significant historical collections, there is much that promises to remain available in print form only for some time to come.

The nature of reference work today is that we must step outside of our traditional comfort zones in the library or behind the computer workstation and position ourselves physically in the communities we serve. We must communicate in multiple ways by making equal use of technology for creating a virtual presence and of our social skills for creating trust with students and faculty. Chatting with a student about his or her dissertation research at a department gathering is more likely to serve as a catalyst for forging a lasting connection than a Web page posting about library services. The Rutgers survey found that the most effective method of communication with students was not e-mail but face-to-face interaction. We continue to find that this is still true.

Facebook is good, but face time is better.

GETTING OUT THERE: PRACTICAL ADVICE

Getting out from behind the desk and into the life of the campus can take many forms. Formalizing the embedded librarian relationship with a class represents a deep commitment. A librarian might target a few key courses with large enrollments in his or her area. Supporting the course with guides, consultations, and in-class research instruction are goals: A first step might be to ask the faculty member to introduce you as librarian for the course during a lecture or during section discussions.

Another way to connect outside the library is to serve the student community; for example, if your institution offers such a program, serve as an academic adviser to students. Many institutions have programs that invite librarians to participate in student advising, as requested by academic departments or programs. If your college or university doesn't have such a program, you might work with college administration to find out what it would take to start one.

A crucial way to connect with student life is to become an affiliate of a dorm, house, or other student social organization in order to get to know students beyond the classroom. Once in these spaces and places, and once you've established your role, you might ask students how they approach research, if they know their library liaisons or personal librarians, or if they have suggestions for how library liaisons can be more effective. Connecting is not just about going where the students are. Meet faculty and administrative staff by seeking out opportunities to serve on university-wide committees. Connect with your academic department by getting to know the staff. Another tactic to draw attention to services is to vary your method of communication: Don't only send e-mail—make flyers and hand deliver them to your departments' faculty and graduate students mailboxes. You might also run into some of them when you drop by. Social networking tools can be useful, with appropriate boundaries. Facebook, Twitter, and so on are spaces where your students can encounter you if you maintain a consistent and professional presence.

SHOWING UP IS HALF THE BATTLE: A SHORT LIST

- Once you're known in your community, schedule regular office hours in academic departments, houses, or a student cafeteria.
- Audit an advanced class in the program you serve.
- Join in and support nonprofit organizations on campus.
- Support your faculty by attending departmental parties, colloquia, or lecture series.
- Every encounter is an opportunity to help faculty, students, and the library: Go out of your way to greet students and faculty when you see them on campus, in restaurants, or in the grocery store. (A very important connection was once forged between a librarian who introduced herself to a well-known faculty member as they stood together in line at the grocery store on a holiday, commiserating over waiting until the last minute to do their grocery shopping.)
- Plan and execute receptions, or, if you have the opportunity, host symposia or other events in the library for specific user groups.
- Welcome graduate students to the library in social gatherings, colloquia, or with talks by library experts.

STATING THE OBVIOUS: MUST DO'S

- Read the campus newspaper or other campus publications daily.
- Subscribe to departmental or student discussion lists.
- Understand the structure of the university and know who the key players are.
- Draw on the expertise of colleagues, especially those who are not directly involved in liaison or reference work. Respect their insights.
- Participate in the scholarship of academic programs; be an observer and an active listener.
- Recognize the obligation: This work does not align well with an expectation that a workweek is Monday to Friday, from 9 A.M. to 5 P.M. Institutions that support this work will support flexible schedules based on strategic priorities.
- Find out what library services the program or department to which you liaise values the most. Find opportunities for integration and seek administrative support for your focus on that.

NOT EITHER/OR BUT BOTH/AND: IT'S ABOUT BALANCE

Though we assert that reference desk service continues to be important, particularly in large research library settings, we advocate balance in levels of staffing and funding for those services, and a strategic understanding that administrators must be able to move funds across activities on an annual basis, in an organizational framework that allows flexibility.

Traditionally, large research library reference services have relied on teams of generalists, many of whom have subject specializations as well. It is not at all surprising that these services, which span centuries and are based on a model of apprenticeship, value deep knowledge of local library collections and resources. For institutions of this kind, it is crucial that this model be respected and that senior librarians be charged to pass on their institutional knowledge to newer colleagues. The unique collections of these institutions in turn create unique service obligations, which must be met in-person, as visiting scholars and the needs of global scholarship dictate. These costs are part of the obligation large research libraries have to the development of new knowledge. For institutions that do not depend on deep legacy print collections, other additional kinds of expertise are necessary. Librarianship is, in these cases, not only about the collections and spaces in which librarians work but also about their special skills in navigating a global information network and in creating context for the information they identify with their researchers. In teaching those methods and in creating a climate of research literacy, major contributions are made. Neither model is truly dependent solely on buildings or spaces. In both cases, the ability to see local resources and to see beyond them, to see the disciplinary literatures as part of a seamless whole, and to meet the students and faculty where they are in their search for meaning defines a successful research servicсs program.

NOTES

1. A useful description of what it means to be "embedded" can be found in the article "Creating Opportunities: Embedded Librarians." The authors state that among the key factors of embedded librarianship are integration and collaboration:

> Embedded librarians are, first and foremost, integrated into their settings, be they traditional or non-traditional. In academic settings, embedded librarians are in collaborative learning environments. They are on research teams. They are in academic departments. They are co-instructors in the classroom and in the online classroom. They play a major leadership role in pushing an academic co-creator model for scholarship and scholarly communication. . . . Embedded librarians are . . . integral to these environs as key players on research and instructional teams. (Kesselman and Watstein, 2009, 387)

2. From the Web site of the Office of Student Life, Harvard University. Retrieved November 15, 2009, from http://www.orl.fas.harvard.edu/icb/icb.do?keyword=k11447&tabgroupid=icb.tabgroup17718.
3. Experience of the library liaison to the Program on the Study of Religion and the Program in Folklore and Mythology in 2008.
4. Comments of the library liaison to the Department of Classics and to the Program on Medieval Studies at Harvard in 2008.
5. See *poetry@harvard*, http://poetry.harvard.edu.
6. See *Rinascimento*, http://isites.harvard.edu/icb/icb.do?keyword=k6246.
7. See *Interlibros*, http://isites.harvard.edu/icb/icb.do?keyword=k3286.
8. See *Traditions*, http://isites.harvard.edu/icb/icb.do?keyword=k25081.

WORKS CITED

Aamot, G., and S. Hiller. 2004. *Library services in non-library spaces.* ARL Spec Kit 285. Retrieved November 12, 2009, from http://www.arl.org/bm~doc/spec285web.pdf.

Council on Library and Information Resources. 2008. *No brief candle: Reconceiving research libraries for the 21st century.* Retrieved November 10, 2009, from http://www.clir.org/pubs/reports/pub142/pub142.pdf.

Glynn, T., and C. Wu. 2003. New roles and opportunities for academic library liaisons: A survey and recommendations. *Reference Services Review* 31(2): 122–128.

Green, S. S. 1876. Personal relations between librarians and readers. *Library Journal* 1(1): 74–81.

Kesselman, M., and S. B. Watstein. 2009. Creating opportunities: Embedded librarians. *Journal of Library Administration* 49(4): 383–400.

Office of Institutional Research, Harvard University. 2008. *Harvard University fact book 2008–2009.* Retrieved November 14, 2009, from http://www.provost.harvard.edu/institutional_research/factbook.php.

O'Gorman, J., and B. Trott. 2009. What will become of reference in academic and public libraries? *Journal of Library Administration* 49(4): 327–339.

Rainie, L., L. Estabrook, and E. Witt. 2007. *Information searches that solve problems.* Retrieved November 10, 2009, from http://www.pewinternet.org/Reports/2007/Information-Searches-That-Solve-Problems.aspx.

Report of the Committee on General Education, Harvard University, Faculty of Arts and Sciences. 2005. Retrieved November 10, 2009, from http://www.math.harvard.edu/chairmandocs/009_Report_of/general_education_nov_05.pdf.

Tyckoson, D. 2007. That thing you do. *Reference & User Services Quarterly* 47(2): 111–113.

ADDITIONAL READINGS

Bennett, S. 2009. Libraries and learning: A history of paradigm change. *portal: Libraries & the Academy* 9(2): 181–197.

Carlson, S. 2007. Are reference desks dying out? *Chronicle of Higher Education* 53(33): A37–A39.

Housewright, R. 2009. Themes of change in corporate libraries: Considerations for academic libraries. *portal: Libraries & the Academy* 9(2): 253–271.

Lewis, D. W. 2007. A strategy for academic libraries in the first quarter of the 21st century. *College & Research Libraries* 68(5): 418–434.

Mullins, J. L., F. R. Allen, and J. R. Hufford. 2007. Top ten assumptions for the future of academic libraries and librarians: A report from the ACRL research committee. *College & Research Libraries News* 68(4): 240–246.

4

THE INTEGRATED SERVICES MODEL: INFORMATION COMMONS IN LIBRARIES

Juliet Rumble

In his thought-provoking article "Conceptualizing an Information Commons," Donald Beagle reports on the emergence of a "new model for service delivery" in academic libraries (1999, 82). Often called an *information commons* (IC), this service model describes both "an online environment in which [a]...variety of digital services can be accessed via a single graphical user interface" and "a new type of physical facility specifically designed to organize workspace and service delivery around...[this] integrated digital environment" (Beagle, 1999, 82). While IC facilities have distinct features and organizational structures, certain key elements are typically present. The IC model brings together in one central location research resources, information technology (IT), and a combination of reference and IT staff to assist with both (Haas and Robertson, 2004).

Driving the construction of ICs is the recognition by librarians and other information professionals that research and computing are no longer separate, discrete activities. In the past, library users conducted research at the library but typically transported the resources they retrieved to home or office in order to use them. In today's integrated digital environments, library users can access information, process and manipulate that information, and create new knowledge products without leaving their computer workstations. The boundaries separating research from productivity have grown increasingly blurred. The aim of the IC service model is to ensure that users' access to the services that support these various activities is equally seamless.

To meet users' needs, ICs are integrating services that were once physically and conceptually separate. As Beagle observes, "The information commons is an expression of this particular period in history when two great long-term eras—the Age of Print and the Digital Age—are grinding against each other like huge tectonic plates" (Beagle, 2008, vi). Libraries that embrace the IC model of integrated services frequently reconfigure their organizational structures to align with this ideal. These organizational changes, in turn, affect the roles of library staff who work in these restructured units.

A number of academic libraries are broadening the integrated services model's scope to incorporate other aspects of research beyond information retrieval and manipulation. This includes support for broader institutional goals such as lifelong learning and information literacy. Library facilities with these characteristics are frequently referred to as learning commons. Learning commons provide reference librarians with exciting new venues in which to deliver reference and instruction services. These innovations are not without their challenges. Reference services built around print collections have had to adapt service delivery to rapidly changing digital technologies. As Beagle notes, "Even the most adaptive organization begins to show signs of strain as it attempts to cope with the relentless growth of services for which it was not designed" (1999, 84).

This essay examines reference services within the context of the IC environment. A discussion of motivating factors behind the development of the IC model of integrated services is followed by a selective review of IC organizational structures and staffing configurations. The essay concludes with an examination of various measures currently employed to assess the effectiveness of the IC.

THE CHANGING LANDSCAPE OF HIGHER EDUCATION

Technology has not been the only factor driving the development of ICs. From the beginning, ICs have always been about more than computers inside library buildings. Despite different physical layouts and service configurations, ICs share a common, guiding principle: Their services and physical spaces are designed around the library user. Rather than requiring users to adapt to library-centered policies and priorities, the visionary leaders who designed the first IC facilities set out to assemble resources and services that would support user needs. Significantly, this user-centered (or learner-centered) focus has been a guiding principle in higher education in recent decades. Increased attention to the user or learner has had a far-reaching impact on classroom pedagogies and learning support services.

During the 1990s, the focus in higher education shifted from teaching organized around content delivery to student-centered learning. According to Barr and Tagg, "the Learning Paradigm frames learning holistically, recognizing that the chief agent in the process is the learner.... Students must be active discoverers and constructors of their own knowledge" (1995, 21). Recognizing that students learned better when they were able to relate course material to their own lived experience, instructors sought to provide students with opportunities to make these connections. Knowledge was recognized as valuable not only for its own sake but also for its capacity, through critical thinking, to solve real-world problems.

Research into learning was also increasingly concerned with the social dimensions of knowledge acquisition. According to constructivist theories of learning, knowledge is fundamentally communal. It is acquired and applied in what Lave and Wenger termed "communities of practice" (1991, 29). "As an aspect of social practice," argued Lave and Wenger, "learning involves the whole person; it implies not only a relation to specific activities, but a relation to social communities" (53). According to Lave, individuals gain knowledge, skills, and expertise not through abstract, "out-of-context" ways but through acculturation into communities of practice located in real, not "contrived" or "academic," settings (Simons, Young, and Gibson, 2000, 125). Vygotsky's concept of the "zone of proximal development" further underscored the importance of learning communities, arguing that students progress from activities they can accomplish independently to more complex tasks through guidance from more knowledgeable teachers and mentors (including peer mentors). In short, "knowledge arises out of a process [that is] personal, social, situated and active" (Somerville and Harlan, 2008, 11).

As constructivist theories gained widespread acceptance, instructors began to apply these key principles to course design. Problem-based learning and collaborative group work became regular parts of many courses. Through these strategies, faculty sought to actively engage their students and to take advantage of students' abilities to teach and learn from each other.

LIBRARIES AS LEARNING SPACES

Research into learning also influenced the design of physical spaces in the higher education environment. While traditional pedagogies focused on the classroom as the primary arena for teaching and learning, contemporary learning theories have highlighted the narrowness of this understanding. If teaching and learning are not limited to what takes place in face-to-face interactions between faculty and students—if learning can occur outside the classroom with students working in groups and teaching each other—then any space that facilitates this type of collaboration can become a learning space. Learning spaces thus serve as logical extensions of the classroom (Freeman, 2005).

Since the 1990s, a growing number of campus building projects have involved the construction of innovative spaces designed to integrate academic and social activities. As campus planners and administrators have realized, libraries are ideally positioned to bring together scholarly and social pursuits. Libraries' interdisciplinary orientation and alignment with broad institutional goals contribute to the perception that they are inclusive community spaces. Library architect Geoffrey Freeman notes, "It [the library] is a place where people come together on levels and in ways that they might not in the residence hall, classroom, or off-campus location. Upon entering the library, the student becomes part of a larger community" (2005, 6). McKinstry echoes this sentiment, observing that libraries are "crossroads of ideas" where different ideas and perspectives converge in exciting ways (2008, 422).

Information commons are designed to enhance the role of libraries as communal learning spaces. As McKinstry observes, the focus in the 1990s was on getting technology into libraries, but, more recently, it has been on reinvigorating libraries as learning spaces where groups meet to work, socialize, and exchange ideas. Cafes, group study rooms, public presentation spaces, and furniture that is comfortable, portable, and modular have all become standard fixtures in today's ICs. But libraries are not simply social spaces. They are also places for individual study, research, and reflection. Library users require spaces that are multifunctional. Libraries that "get it right" have studied their users and actively sought their feedback on library spaces and services. Demas writes, "In recent years we have reawakened to the fact that libraries are fundamentally about people—how they learn, how they use information, and how they participate in the life of a learning community" (2005, 25). Library mission statements now focus on users as much as they do on collections. Boone suggests that it may be useful for librarians and others to view the library as an "environment rather than a facility—a place of interaction, learning, and experiencing rather than a place for storage and equipment" (2002, 392).

SERVICES AND ORGANIZATIONAL STRUCTURES IN THE IC

Information commons occupy a variety of physical spaces. Some commons are located on one floor of the library, others on multiple floors. Some occupy an entire building. Some commons are part of library renovation projects, while others are new construction. No single design has emerged as superior, but, in general, library commons are designed to be inviting to users, flexible and adaptable to multiple uses, and conducive to collaborative work and study. Just as important as the physical layout are the partners who share the commons space. When ICs first appeared on the scene, these partners were typically campus IT departments, but, in recent years, a variety of other campus units, including writing centers, tutoring services, academic advising and counseling services, adaptive technology units, and faculty teaching and learning centers, have joined forces with the library.

The collaborative relationships built around library commons influence the scope of services offered. There is a trend in the scholarly literature to distinguish between ICs and learning commons, a distinction that some view as representing a progressive movement or evolution. Beagle, for example, adapts terminology from the American Council on Education's primer on change to describe the dynamics that he views as characteristic of the evolution from IC to learning commons. These include "adjustment," "isolated change," "far-reaching" change, and "transformational" change (Beagle, 2006, 50–51).

According to Beagle's schema, the introduction of computer labs into libraries represents the IC as "adjustment"—an attempt by libraries to accommodate the convergence of information resources and computer technologies. Beagle notes that this change, while a welcome one, does not address a fundamental service issue: "Simply plunking down a computer lab in the reference room to provide digital resources... fail[s] to properly address the underlying problem," namely, that "the reference desk [is] fail[ing] to provide the scope of human resources needed to support the broader range of needs of students working in new online environments" (2006, 6). Regardless of where users are sitting in the library, they may require assistance with both research and productivity. Moreover, as Ferguson notes, library users are "exhibiting less and less patience with multiple agencies responsible for what seems to be one process" (2000, 303).

The IC with its integrated services and staff—its "one-stop shopping" service—is an attempt to address this issue. The IC's "continuum of service" (Beagle, 1999, 84) is an umbrella concept for a variety of IC service configurations and partnerships. The following examples, while by no means comprehensive, are intended to illustrate the range of services and organizational structures found in today's library commons.

At Indiana University Bloomington (IUB), the Information Commons is a joint partnership between IUB Libraries and University Information Technology Services (UITS). Management of the IC is addressed jointly by a governance group composed of administrators and managers from the libraries and UITS. On the first floor of the IC, library reference services and IT support staff share a large, central service desk. The sign above the desk reads simply: "Ask questions here." The joint service desk is designed to eliminate the need, on the user's part, to distinguish between research- and technology-related questions. The staff member at the desk either responds to the information need or directs the user to a staff member at the desk with the necessary expertise. Librarians, support staff, and School of Library and Information Science (SLIS) graduate students employed by the IC Undergraduate Library Services (ICUGLS) Department handle reference services at the desk. Upper-division undergraduates employed by the Student Technology Center help with printing and document formatting and also provide assistance with sophisticated multimedia and statistics software programs. In addition, there is a second, shared service point located at the entrance to the IC that is staffed by library circulation services and IT account support personnel. Here students can check out books and laptops and get help with computer hardware and connectivity issues (Dallis and Walters, 2006).

The Library West Commons (LWC) at the Georgia Institute of Technology is another example of a collaborative partnership between an academic library and a campus Office of Information Technology (OIT). The LWC's Information Services desk is located at the periphery of the commons area and provides reference services to users. It is easily accessible from the LWC's Productivity Cluster, which has computer workstations loaded with general productivity software as well as specialized software in engineering, chemistry, mathematics, statistics, and computer programming. User support for the Productivity Cluster is provided at a service desk located in the center of the area and staffed by the OIT. Student assistants assigned to the Productivity Cluster desk are expected to rove the space and provide assistance with desktop and printing issues. The LWC also houses a Multimedia Studio that offers high-end video-editing software and hardware. Staff hired and trained by the OIT provides user support for the Multimedia Studio.

Because of the LWC's extended hours of service, Library Information Services staff members also provide assistance in and supervise the Productivity Cluster and Multimedia Studio during nights and weekends when OIT full-time staff is unavailable. To address these staffing needs, Library Information Services has created a series of Information Associate positions that are jointly trained by library and IT departments to provide assistance with research and technology (Forrest and Halbert, 2009). Lippincott, citing Beagle, notes that the LWC embodies one of the ideals of the IC model: "The Information Commons creates a synergy between the user support skills of computer staff, the information skills of reference staff, and production skills of media staff" (2009, 25).

The Information Services desk also provides consultation space to student teaching assistants (TAs), who hold evening and weekend office hours. The TAs provide assistance with complex software programs such as MATLAB, a service that was requested by Georgia Tech engineering faculty (Stuart, 2008). This service has been a "big hit with students" (Stuart, 2008, 336) and highlights the benefits of "bring[ing] the teaching community into the library" (Whitchurch, Belliston, and Baer, 267).

While the ICs at Indiana and Georgia Tech involve partnerships with units outside the library, some ICs remain "library-centric." According to Beagle, these service models exhibit "isolated change." There is an effort to "integrat[e] functions formerly carried out by separate units within the library," but while this "better aligns the library with other campus priorities, it is still not intrinsically collaborative with other campus initiatives" (Beagle, 2006, 51). An important threshold is passed when the resources and services of the IC are organized in collaboration with the learning initiatives of other academic units. Beagle (2006), Somerville and Harlan (2008), and Bailey and Tierney (2008), among others, argue that this development marks the transition from IC to learning commons—an evolution that Beagle describes as "far-reaching change" (2006, 51). In the learning commons, there is an "integrating…[of] functions formerly carried out within the library with others formerly carried out beyond the library's purview. The service profile is no longer library-centric" and moves in the direction of true collaboration (51).

The evolutionary development of ICs into learning commons signals a growing recognition that libraries can—and should—be more fully integrated into the broader educational mission of colleges and universities. The changes in higher education alluded to earlier position libraries to play an influential role on campus. Achieving this potential requires that libraries cultivate partnerships with other units dedicated to student academic success and that they remain open and attentive to the evolving ways that students and faculty are utilizing library spaces, resources, and services. Simons, Young, and Gibson (2000, 124) describe "learning libraries" this way:

> The central idea of the learning library is that of integration: the library becomes an essential component of students' formal education and informal research needs. Rather than an external "add on" to the educational experience, the library, as information resource and gateway, is a primary catalyst for cognitive, behavioral, and affective changes in students—as they interact with information resources as directed by faculty, as they complete assignments and study with peers, as they extend their knowledge at multiple levels, seeking connections and making meaning in more self-directed ways. The learning library, rather than a repository of materials or a study hall, is therefore an agency of change in students' lives.

There are a number of outstanding examples of "learning libraries." The Information Commons at the University of Arizona is one such example. The IC is part of both the Main Library and the university's Integrated Learning Center (ILC), an underground facility that houses technology-rich classrooms and a variety of student support services, including academic advising and tutoring services focused on lower-division courses (Bailey and Tierney, 2008; Oblinger, 2006). The ILC serves as a home base for first-year students and was created to improve student retention at Arizona. Four campus units collaboratively manage the ILC: the University Teaching Center, the Office of Student Computing Resources, the University College, and the library. Within the library, the Undergraduate Services Team oversees the IC. The IC features three service points: a central service desk that handles reference and technology questions, a printing and photocopying center, and a multimedia center managed by the Office of Student Computing Resources. The IC and the ILC together provide support for multiple dimensions of undergraduates' academic experience. This is one of the aims of the learning commons model—namely, to provide an environment that encourages students to take ownership of their own education by facilitating their "orchestration of their own learning tasks" (Milewicz, 2009, 10).

Another example of a library partnership with academic support services is found at Loyola University at New Orleans. The Academic and Career

Excellence (ACE) Center is an academic "resource clearinghouse" housed adjacent to the reference room in Loyola's J. Edgar and Louise S. Monroe Library. What is noteworthy about the ACE Center is the level of collaboration between the library and the various academic support services (counseling, tutoring, career guidance, academic assessment, disability services, etc.). Peer tutors from each of the support services undergo an intensive period of cross-training so that they can make effective referrals between units. Orgeron writes, "While the core services retain their respective identities, the ACE Center creates an environment where old geographic boundaries are blurred and activities move smoothly across multiple departments." Armed with knowledge of the "nuts and bolts of each other's daily operations... the path to integrated services is clear" (2001, n.p.). In addition to playing an active role in the overall management of the ACE Center, librarians have incorporated research assistance into ACE clinics on paper writing, presentation creation, resume writing, and interview preparation.

At George Mason University, the Johnson Center Library is part of the Johnson Center, an example of a "campus commons" that, in addition to the library, houses computer labs and academic program offices as well as a bank, theater, bookstore, and a variety of dining facilities. The Johnson Center Library has developed a number of programmatic partnerships on campus. One of the most important collaborations is with the New Century College (NCC), a campus learning community. Librarians from the Johnson Center Library help team-teach an NCC interdisciplinary unit that combines content from traditional first-year courses in English composition, communications, and computer science. The NCC liaison librarian also manages a yearlong cultural biography research project, which is part of the NCC curriculum.

In addition to work with the NCC, the library's outreach programs extend to the English composition program, to University 100 (George Mason's freshman-year-experience program), and to the Writing Center. Among other projects, the library has worked with instructors in the composition program to better integrate library instruction into the program's curriculum and writing assignments. Working with the University 100 program, librarians have developed training sessions for instructors and undergraduate peer advisors. Training has focused on research basics and fostering "positive perceptions" of the library among new students. The Johnson Center Library has also hired a series of library graduate research assistants who serve as library liaisons to the Writing Center and hold office hours in the Writing Center (Simons, Young, and Gibson, 2000). These library initiatives lend support to Beagle's claim that the learning commons is "the framework of services and resources in which information literacy is the curriculum" (2006, 201).

The Learning Commons at North Carolina State University (NCSU) Libraries has all of the features of an "instructional testbed" (Beagle, 2002, 288). The Learning Commons (LC) is linked programmatically to the Libraries'

Learning and Research Center for the Digital Age (LRCDA), which, in turn, supports units that provide integrated services to faculty, staff, and students on all aspects of IT. Central components of the LRCDA include the Digital Library Initiatives department (supporting the Digital Media Lab and Usability Research Lab), the Digital Scholarship and Publishing Center, and the Learning Technology Service (supporting instructors and students who are engaged in instructional technology activities). While reference librarians do not interact with the LRCDA on a daily basis, they regularly collaborate with the LRCDA on faculty technology projects (Henning, 2005). LRCDA staff has also been involved in the design of the LC computing environment (Spencer, 2007).

As with other learning commons, the focus at NCSU is "not just on discovery and information seeking and retrieval but on the creation of information, the entire learning curve" (Spencer, 2007, 313). Large plasma screens throughout the commons area display information, announcements, and imagery related to the LC or to student and faculty work. Support for video games is also available. NCSU has strong programs in computer science, communications, and design that are involved in developing educational games in video format. The LC is a venue for testing and showcasing these projects—another instance of how learning and social activities often converge in the commons.

Significantly, the learning possibilities of the space are not limited to users. According to commons manager Joe Williams,

> I think it's going to be a real learning space for library staff as well. It's going to be a great place for us to learn how our users like to work and how we can support collaboration. I'm looking at the Learning Commons really as a class or seminar I attend and that the staff here will participate in every semester. Our goal will be to learn more about our users' preferences and how we can support them. (Spencer, 2007, 313)

To facilitate interaction between LC staff and students, the LC features a service area with low desks that students can easily move between. The combined reference and IT staffs at the service desk are encouraged to move out into the commons space to provide reference and assistance at users' workstations (Spencer, 2007, 313).

The LC at NCSU and the other information and learning commons profiled in this section have gained recognition for their innovative service models. In all likelihood, the featured services and organizational structures highlighted here will continue to evolve as these facilities adapt to stay current with new technologies and user needs. What makes these facilities exemplary is the robustness of the collaboration between their service units. As Lippincott points out, collocation is not the same as collaboration. Libraries have long shared space with other campus units, but these relationships have often been laissez-faire at best. Such associations are not true collaborations. According to Lippincott,

> In a genuine collaboration, there are a number of factors present in addition to the sharing of a physical facility. They include development of shared goals by the parties, joint planning, an awareness of and a valuing of the expertise of each partner, and pooling of resources. (2004, 148)

Lippincott is well aware that forging partnerships between service units with different missions, organizational structures, and service values is a challenging task. However, the benefits that can be realized—"seamless services to users, leveraging expertise, and pooling resources"—provide strong incentives for collaboration (2004, 152).

STAFFING THE IC

As the preceding case studies demonstrate, integrated services form the basis of the IC model. The combined skills and expertise of different service units have the potential to significantly enhance students' educational experience. Creating genuinely collaborative relationships is also arguably one of the biggest challenges facing ICs. The different units that share space in the commons bring their own staffs and service cultures into this arena. As the scholarly literature makes clear, personnel who work in the library commons can expect a period of adjustment (Church, 2005; McKinstry and McCracken, 2002; Mozenter, Sanders, and Bellamy, 2003). Not surprisingly, staffing arrangements have often been works-in-progress.

The Association of Research Libraries (ARL) survey on ICs indicates that, with few exceptions, libraries with ICs use a combination of full- and part-time staff, consisting of librarians, paraprofessional staff, student workers, and nonlibrary staff (Haas and Robertson, 2004). In 2004, about half of the ICs surveyed had a single service point; the rest had between two and four service points. Single service points typically consist of a desk combining research and technology support. The number of service points can be related to a variety of local factors, including the physical layout of the commons space and service partners. In some cases, the number of service points also reflects philosophical differences about appropriate staffing configurations.

Advocates of the single-desk model typically point to the convenience to users of the one-stop shopping experience. The IC at Lied Library at the University of Nevada, Las Vegas, was originally designed with multiple service points, which were later consolidated (Church, 2005). Librarians at Lied noted that the original model "provided too many specialized service points that required patrons to try and 'self-diagnose' before . . . receiving appropriate assistance. The subsequent bouncing from service desk to service desk resulted in frustration for users and staff" (Church, 2005, 77). Beagle provides another reason for the consolidation of service points, namely, that distributed service points risk "compartmentalization of expertise" and limit opportunities for "cross-fertilization of ideas" (2002, 291). However, the collocation of reference services and computing help at a single service desk does not in and of itself guarantee collaboration. As McKinstry and McCracken (University of Washington) reported about their shared service desk, "We envisioned that we would be sharing more of each others' worlds, but that has not happened.... We expected more of a one-team approach and it feels more like hands-off between two distinct, yet friendly, teams" (2002, 397). Nor is support for the single-service-desk model universal. For librarians at the University of Massachusetts Amherst's W.E.B Du Bois Library, the creation of a learning commons, with its "expert service providers," allowed the reference desk to "step back from its tech support role" (Fitzpatrick, Moore, and Lang, 2008, 233). Prior to the opening of the Learning Commons, the reference desk had operated with a combination of reference librarians, library support staff, and student workers, but librarians felt that "funneling questions to the right person did not always work efficiently.... Student assistants sometimes fielded questions beyond their training, providing incomplete or inefficient answers and occasionally failing to refer" (Fitzpatrick, Moore, and Lang, 2008, 231).

The mixed reviews about a single service point coordinating computing and reference work can be seen as participating in a larger discussion, dating from the 1990s, about "rethinking" the future of reference services (see, for example, Lipow, 1996). Part of this discussion focused on whether or not reference services would be more effective if there were different service points to address different kinds of information needs (Massey-Burzio, 1993; Whitson, 1995). For some, the growing complexity of the information environment called for a differentiated service model for libraries (Whitson, 1995). Reflecting on users' needs in IC environments, Martin Halbert posed this question: "Does effective service delivery in the Information Commons require a 'hybrid' 'mixed skills' support staff, or one with increasingly specialized skills?" (1999, 91). Halbert's response is "a little bit of both":

> Traditional reference staff [in the information commons] will require new training and skills to be effective. This is inescapable. The fact is also just as ineluctable that nobody can possibly know everything. Gaining additional knowledge broadly applicable to new technology must also be paired with relevant specialization in particular topics (both technical and subject-based) as well as an ability to make effectively targeted referrals. The model simply breaks down without a combination of these features. (1999, 91)

Halbert's assessment is widely shared, with the result that many ICs have adopted a tiered service model in which IC staff receives introductory-level training in reference and computing in order to guarantee a basic level of competence in these areas. To function properly, tiered service also requires effective referral, with first-tier staff directing users to specialists as appropriate. The general consensus appears to be that this system of triage works quite well, provided that staff are clear about "responsibilities, competency levels, and referral thresholds" (Ferguson, 2000, 306).

To ensure that these conditions are met, a number of ICs have instituted training programs to prepare staff for the demanding service requirements of the commons environment. At Colorado State University Libraries, staff developed a list of minimal technical competencies and a series of in-house training sessions taught by reference and library technology services staff (Cowgill, Beam, and Wess, 2001). Librarians at Atkins Library at the University of North Carolina at Charlotte developed training programs in database searching and reference basics (including instruction in the reference interview) for their paraprofessional staff. The instruction modules were later incorporated into WebCT, which facilitated easy updating of training materials and flexible, self-directed instruction to accommodate work schedules (Mozenter, Sanders, and Bellamy, 2003).

As each of these libraries discovered, effective training requires a serious, ongoing commitment of time and resources, but the benefits reaped are also substantial. Training increases awareness of the skills and expertise of other units and helps promote greater integration and collaboration between service units. Moreover, the presence of a well-trained first tier of assistance provides professional staff with more time for in-depth consultations in their areas of expertise.

Many ICs rely heavily on part-time student assistants to staff service desks. Budget constraints and the commons' extended hours of operation often necessitate this kind of staffing configuration. Libraries that employ students in their commons report both challenges and opportunities with this arrangement. Differences in professional demeanor and high rates of turnover are frequently cited as some of the challenges associated with student employees, although training helps address the former concern (McKinstry and McCracken, 2002). These issues aside, student workers often prove to be ideal employees for the IC environment. Typically, they have strong technology skills, and their fellow students often perceive them to be less intimidating and more approachable than professional librarians.

The University of Southern California's Leavey Library employs "student navigation assistants" who staff the IC service desk alongside reference librarians. These student workers provide first-tier assistance in reference and software applications. In addition to on-the-job training, student navigation assistants receive formal training in basic reference transactions, customer service, basic equipment repair, Web authoring, multimedia products, and network, e-mail, and connectivity issues, among other topics (Crockett, McDaniel, and Remy, 2002). Crockett, McDaniel, and Remy report that this "melded service" works particularly well for Leavey, given its status as a "gateway" library for freshman- and sophomore-level students (183–184).

At Dartmouth College, reference librarians, IT service staff, and writing center staff jointly train student peer tutors to work in the Student Center for Research, Writing, and Information Technology (RWiT) located in Berry

Library. The peer tutors provide instruction and feedback on writing, guidance with the research process, and assistance with software applications such as PowerPoint and iMovie. As Lippincott observes, Dartmouth (and Georgia Tech, as described earlier) are drawing on the talents of their students and leveraging the collocation and expertise of different units to provide innovative new services (Lippincott, 2006).

EVALUATING ICs

As Bailey and Tierney observe, assessment is a fundamental component of educational programs and is particularly essential for ICs, given their user-centered focus and needs-based services (2008, 19). To date, there are relatively few published studies assessing ICs, even though many of them carry out a variety of assessments. This situation is likely to change as ICs mature.

Given the diversity of IC environments, it is perhaps not surprising that no standardized instrument for assessing them currently exists. Certain standardized instruments do address aspects of IC services and resources implicitly, including, most notably, LibQUAL+. A number of LibQUAL+ 2004 questions that relate to information control, affect of service, and library as place pertain to ICs, and many ICs participate in LibQUAL+ (Bailey and Tierney, 2008). A number of library commons (including the University of Calgary, the University of Arizona, and the University of North Carolina at Charlotte) have also developed assessment instruments specifically geared to the commons environment (Bailey and Tierney, 2008). The latter are an important element of IC assessment, as they provide feedback about resources and services that are unique to ICs.

Library commons are multidimensional, which is another reason why assessing their impact is challenging. Many libraries employ a range of methods—formal and informal, quantitative and qualitative—to evaluate the effectiveness of their commons. Quantitative measures include gate counts, usage statistics (for instance, user log-ins, materials circulated, and electronic resources accessed), group study room reservations, and number of service point queries. Many libraries with ICs have reported dramatic increases in the number of students entering their buildings (Albanese, 2004; Bailey and Tierney, 2008; Dallis and Walters, 2006; Fitzpatrick, Moore, and Lang, 2008; Malenfant, 2006). If users vote with their feet, there is compelling evidence that the IC model is a success.

Focus groups, surveys, and interviews are other frequently employed assessment methods. Numerous case studies in the scholarly literature report enthusiastic user responses to library commons (Bailey and Tierney, 2008; Schader, 2008). Students at Georgia Tech voted their commons "the best improvement to campus" in 2004 (Forrest and Halbert, 2009, 93). In a 2006 Indiana University–Purdue University Indianapolis (IUPUI) survey, "convenience" and "group work" were listed as the top two reasons for visiting the commons—feedback that aligns with the mission statements of most ICs (Applegate, 2007, 169).

Data collected about the extent to which users are taking advantage of the integrated services offered by ICs are mixed. Carleton College reported that student appointments with subject liaisons combined with in-depth e-mail reference quadrupled during the space of several years following the construction of their commons (Bailey and Tierney, 2008). Westminster College (Salt Lake City, Utah) also reported an increase in demand for reference services (Malenfant, 2006). The University of Guelph Learning Commons reported an increase in students attending workshops and receiving individual consultations every year since the Learning Commons opened in 1999; in the 2004–2005 academic year, over half of all first-year students used one or more programs offered by the Learning Commons (Schmidt and Kaufman, 2007). The University of Indiana Bloomington, in contrast, experienced a decrease in reference questions after their IC opened (Dallis and Walters, 2006); likewise, IUPUI reported a decline (20 percent) in reference queries between pre-Commons and Commons pilot development periods (Applegate, 2007). Several surveys of IC users have recorded disappointingly low numbers of students taking advantage of the integrated services offered by their ICs. A 2003 survey of undergraduates at the University of Southern California revealed that only 12.6 percent of undergraduates came to Leavey Library with the intention of seeking research assistance (Gardner and Eng, 2005). Relatively low numbers of users seeking IC reference and computing services were also reported at IUPUI (Applegate, 2007) and at the University of Indiana Bloomington (Dallis and Walters, 2006).

It is worth noting, however, that students' actual use of services may be higher than student ratings suggest. At IUPUI, 40 percent of undergraduates had asked for information assistance in the commons, even though reference help rated a relatively distant third behind "convenience" and "group work" as reasons for visiting the commons (Applegate, 2007, 169, 171). A 2006 survey of Learning Commons users at the University of Massachusetts at Amherst found that 39 percent had asked questions at the reference desk, while 61 percent had used e-mail and chat reference, online subject guides, and after-hours basic reference help at other service points (Fitzpatrick, Moore, and Lang, 2008). While there was a decline in the number of queries at the Indiana University Bloomington reference desk, there was also increased usage of librarian-created class pages in the library's content management system, prompting library researchers to speculate that these figures might be related (Dallis and Walters, 2006).

Above all, the emergence of learning commons underscores the need for assessment directed at student learning outcomes. As Bennett observes, "We need to understand that the success of the academic library is best measured not by the frequency and ease of library use but by the learning that results from that use" (2005, 11). Assessing student learning will always be a challenging enterprise. Learning is multidimensional and requires multiple methods of assessment. Some library commons are using Project SAILS (Standardized Assessment of Information Literacy Skills) as a measure of students' information literacy. A small number of institutions are analyzing student work produced for specific course assignments in an attempt to gauge the impact that interaction with learning commons has on students' academic performance (Applegate, 2007; Bailey and Tierney, 2008). In a small-scale study conducted at IUPUI, preliminary results indicate a positive correlation between asking for help and information and technology usage scores (Applegate, 2007). More studies of this kind are needed. Assessment is most effective when it is iterative and focused on clearly defined learning outcomes.

CONCLUSION

Today's libraries are faced with what is simultaneously a challenge and an opportunity—namely, to rethink what it means to support learning and scholarly work in the digital age. Information commons are designed to support learning communities that have been fundamentally affected by tectonic shifts in how information is generated, accessed, manipulated, promulgated, and used. As the preceding discussion makes clear, ICs are not simply technological overlays to traditional library services. The core mission of the IC—to provide a collaborative environment that facilitates seamless access to information tools and resources—is transforming not only how libraries envision their services but also, ultimately, how they view their role in higher education. As Beagle notes, "What begins as the reconfiguration of an academic library ultimately becomes a reconfiguration of the learning environment" (2002, 289).

WORKS CITED

Albanese, A. 2004. Campus library 2.0: The information commons. *Library Journal*, April 15, 30–33.

Applegate, R. 2007. Build it and what? Measuring the implementation and outcomes of an information commons. In *Sailing into the future: Charting our destiny*, 167–173. Proceedings of the Thirteenth National Conference of the Association of College and Research Libraries, March 29–April 1, 2007, Baltimore, Maryland. Chicago: Association of College and Research Libraries.

Bailey, D. R., and B. Tierney. 2008. *Transforming library service through information commons: Case studies for the digital age*. Washington, DC: American Library Association.

Barr, R., and J. Tagg. 1995. From teaching to learning: A new paradigm for undergraduate education. *Change* 27 (6): 12–25.

Beagle, D. 1999. Conceptualizing an information commons. *Journal of Academic Librarianship* 25 (2): 82–89.

Beagle, D. 2002. Extending the information commons: From instructional testbed to Internet2. *Journal of Academic Librarianship* 28 (5): 287–296.

Beagle, D. 2006. *The information commons handbook.* New York: Neal-Schuman.

Beagle, D. 2008. Foreword. *Transforming library service through information commons: Case studies for the digital age*, by D. R. Bailey and B. G. Tierney, v–vi. Washington, DC: American Library Association.

Bennett, S. 2005. Righting the balance. In *Library as place: Rethinking roles, rethinking space,* ed. K. Smith, 10–24. Washington, DC: Council on Library and Information Resources.

Boone, M. D. 2002. Library design—the architect's view. A discussion with Tom Findley. *Library Hi Tech* 20 (3): 388–392.

Church, J. 2005. The evolving information commons. *Library Hi Tech* 23 (1): 75–81.

Cowgill, A., J. Beam, and L. Wess. 2001. Implementing an information commons in a university library. *Journal of Academic Librarianship* 27 (6): 432–439.

Crockett, C., S. McDaniel, and M. Remy. 2002. Integrating services in the information commons: Toward a holistic library and computing environment. *Library Administration & Management* 16 (4): 181–186.

Dallis, D., and C. Walters. 2006. Reference services in the commons environment. *Reference Services Review* 34 (2): 248–260.

Demas, S. 2005. From the ashes of Alexandria: What's happening in the college library? In *Library as place: Rethinking roles, rethinking space,* ed. K. Smith, 25–40. Washington, DC: Council on Library and Information Resources.

Ferguson, C. 2000. "Shaking the conceptual foundations," too: Integrating research and technology support for the next generation of information service. *College & Research Libraries* 61 (4): 300–311.

Fitzpatrick, E., A. Moore, and B. Lang. 2008. Reference librarians at the reference desk in a learning commons: A mixed methods evaluation. *Journal of Academic Librarianship* 34 (3): 231–238.

Forrest, C., and M. Halbert. 2009. *A field guide to the information commons.* Lanham, MD: Scarecrow Press.

Freeman, G. 2005. The library as place: Changes in learning patterns, collections, technology, and use. In *Library as place: Rethinking roles, rethinking space,* ed. K. Smith, 1–9. Washington, DC: Council on Library and Information Resources.

Gardner, S., and S. Eng. 2005. What students want: Generation Y and the changing function of the academic library. *portal: Libraries and the Academy* 5 (3): 405–420.

Haas, L., and J. Robertson. 2004. *SPEC kit 281: The information commons.* Washington, DC: Association of Research Libraries.

Halbert, M. 1999. Lessons from the information commons frontier. *Journal of Academic Librarianship* 25 (2): 90–91.

Henning, J. 2005. *Information commons study leave, October 2, 2004–March 31, 2005.* Retrieved September 15, 2010, from http://jhenning.law.uvic.ca.

Lave, J., and E. Wenger. 1991. *Situated learning: Legitimate peripheral participation.* New York: Cambridge University Press.

Lipow, A., ed. 1996. *Rethinking reference in academic libraries.* Berkeley, CA: Library Solutions Press.

Lippincott, J. 2004. New library facilities: Opportunities for collaboration. *Resource Sharing & Information Networks* 17 (1–2): 147–157.

Lippincott, J. 2005. Net generation students and libraries. In *Educating the net generation,* ed. D. Oblinger and J. Oblinger, 13.1–13.15. Boulder, CO: EDUCAUSE.

Lippincott, J. 2006. Linking the information commons to learning. In *Learning spaces,* ed. D. Oblinger, 7.1–7.18. Boulder, CO: EDUCAUSE.

Lippincott, J. 2009. Information commons: Surveying the landscape. In *A field guide to the information commons,* ed. C. Forrest and M. Halbert, 18–31. Lanham, MD: Scarecrow Press.

Malenfant, C. 2006. The information commons as a collaborative workspace. *Reference Services Review* 34 (2): 279–286.

Massey-Burzio, V. 1993. Rethinking the reference desk. In *Rethinking reference in academic libraries,* ed. A. Lipow, 43–48. Berkeley, CA: Library Solutions Press.

McKinstry, J. 2008. Beyond Facebook: Thinking of the learning commons as a social network. In *Learning commons: Evolution and collaborative essentials,* ed. B. Schader, 405–427. Oxford: Chandos.

McKinstry, J., and P. McCracken. 2002. Combining computing and reference desks in an undergraduate library: A brilliant innovation or a serious mistake? *Portal: Libraries and the Academy* 2 (3): 391–400.

Milewicz, E. 2009. Origin and development of the information commons in academic libraries. In *A field guide to the information commons,* ed. C. Forrest and M. Halbert, 3–17. Lanham, MD: Scarecrow Press.

Mozenter, F., B. Sanders, and C. Bellamy. 2003. Perspectives on cross-training public services staff in the electronic age: I have to learn to do what?! *Journal of Academic Librarianship* 29 (6): 399–404.

Oblinger, D. 2006. *Learning spaces.* Boulder, CO: EDUCAUSE.

Orgeron, E. 2001. Integrated academic student support services at Loyola University: The library as a resource clearinghouse. *Journal of Southern and Special Librarianship* 2 (3). Retrieved August 23, 2009, from http://southernlibrarianship.icaap.org/content/v02n03/orgeron_e01.htm.

Schader, B., ed. 2008. *Learning commons: Evolution and collaborative essentials.* Oxford: Chandos.

Schmidt, N., and J. Kaufman. 2007. Learning commons: Bridging the academic and student affairs divide to enhance learning across campus. *Research Strategies* 20 (4): 242–256.

Simons, K., J. Young, and C. Gibson. 2000. The learning library in context: Community, integration, and influence. *Research Strategies* 17 (2–3): 123–132.

Somerville, M., and S. Harlan. 2008. From information commons to learning commons and learning spaces: An evolutionary context. In *Learning commons: Evolution and collaborative essentials,* ed. B. Schader, 1–36. Oxford: Chandos.

Spencer, M. E. 2007. The state-of-the-art: NCSU Libraries Learning Commons. *Reference Services Review* 35 (2): 310–321.

Stuart, C. 2008. Improving student life, learning and support through collaboration, integration and innovation. In *Learning commons: Evolution and collaborative essentials,* ed. B. Schader, 325–358. Oxford: Chandos.

Whitchurch, M., C. J. Belliston, and W. Baer. 2006. Information commons at Brigham Young University: Past, present, and future. *Reference Services Review* 34 (2): 261–278.

Whitson, W. 1995. Differentiated service: A new reference model. *Journal of Academic Librarianship* 21 (2): 103–110.

5

LIBRARIANS IN SECOND LIFE AND FUTURE VIRTUAL WORLDS

Alexia Hudson

> And even the word "library" is getting hazy. It used to be a place full of books, mostly old ones. Then they began to include videotapes, records, and magazines. Then all of the information got converted into machine-readable form.... The number of media grew, the material became more up to date, and the methods for searching the Library became more and more sophisticated.
>
> Stephenson (1992, 22)

Reference librarianship in a virtual or online environment is by no means a new concept. In 1993, the possibilities of utilizing the Internet for library reference and instructional services were first addressed in *Crossing the Internet Threshold: An Instructional Handbook*, written by Roy Tennant, John Ober, and Anne Grodzins Lipow. The book highlighted pioneering thought regarding the use of e-mail reference and gave recommendations about Internet remote access for reference services.

Over the next decade, virtual reference librarianship incorporated a multitude of online tools that enabled real-time chat interaction services (often under the moniker "Ask a Librarian"). In the late 20th century, these services began to incorporate new synchronistic elements such as instant messaging and text-based delivery services compatible with mobile devices including personal digital assistants (PDAs) and cell phones.

The next phase of pioneering Internet-based virtual reference services to emerge in the early 21st century includes librarians inside virtual world technologies such as Second Life. An estimated 579 million users populated a virtual world technology as of the second quarter of 2009, an increase of

38.9 percent relative to the prior quarter according to a report from virtual world consulting firm KZero ("Virtual Worlds Popularity Spikes," 2009). Gartner Inc., a research analytics company, estimates that 80 percent of active Internet users will be involved in some form of virtual world technology by the end of 2011 (*Gartner Says 80 Percent,* 2007).

This chapter explores librarianship inside virtual worlds with a focus on the most popular virtual world technology, Second Life. A brief history of virtual worlds and the creation of the Alliance Second Life Library 2.0 and other libraries in Second Life are also covered. Additionally, this chapter reports on Second Life and virtual world technology in the graduate-level library and information science curriculum. Finally, future educational possibilities with children and teenagers under the age of 16 inside of virtual worlds and the Penn State Pilot Project in Second Life are also reviewed.

THE HISTORY OF VIRTUAL WORLDS, OR MASSIVE MULTIUSER VIRTUAL ENVIRONMENTS

A virtual world, also referred to as a massive multiuser virtual environment (MUVE) or a massively multiplayer online role-playing game (MMORPG), is best described as an Internet-based technology where users can engage and interact with others uninterrupted in real time (Mitchell, 1995). Virtual worlds are often grouped into the same category as video games. However, there are clear distinctions between the two. Whereas the primary objective of video games is to win by accruing points and prizes based on levels of mastery, virtual worlds simulate real-world engagement and interaction. Virtual worlds also tend to share six common features:

- A highly graphical user interface: The interface is usually either two-dimensional or three-dimensional.
- Persistence: The virtual world continues to function whether a specific individual user is logged in or not.
- Shared space: Multiple simultaneous users participate in the space without prescribed gaming rules.
- Immediacy: Upon entering the virtual world, engagement with other users can be instantaneous.
- Interactivity: Constant unscripted interaction that may or may not be activity based and that replicates real-world communication occurs with other users.
- Community: A sense of connectedness through shared interests fosters an active community of users. ("What Is a Virtual World?" n.d.)

Sophisticated digital content to enhance the user experience, such as the ability to create a customized digital persona (also known as an *avatar*), virtual land space, clothing, currency, and elaborate weapons for game play, is an essential part of the appeal of virtual world technology.

Prototypes of multiuser games were first piloted in the 1960s, primarily as U.S. government experiments to train pilots in virtual combat. The first computer-based virtual world was a game started in 1973 at the National Aeronautics and Space Administration's Ames Research Center in California, called Maze War. Multiple three-dimensional simulated avatars shaped like eyeballs chased each other in a maze. The game was played on the Arpanet, a predecessor to the modern-day Internet.

A few years later, the Programmed Logic for Automated Teaching Operations (PLATO) system was created at the University of Illinois's Control Data Corporation. Developed primarily for computer-based education, PLATO was the first multiuser virtual game environment that allowed up to 32 players at various internal locations to play one real-time game simultaneously. By 1978, PLATO's interface included various games including Airfight, dungeon games, star wars battles, and tank and air combat.

In 1979, the University of Illinois's PLATO interface led the way for the creation of a text- and graphic-based multiuser role-playing online game called Avatar. Created by Bruce Maggs, Andrew Shapira, and David Sides (who were high school students at the time), Avatar allowed for full rotation of characters and included an economy where players received gold and a store where players could purchase items (*Virtual Worlds Timeline*, n.d.).

Filmmaker George Lucas's company, Lucasfilms, developed Habitat in 1986; this was a two-dimensional gaming environment. Habitat is considered the first commercially marketed and fully functioning multiuser virtual world technology. Multiple participants were able to interact with each other via "humanoid" avatars on Commodore 64 home computers. Habitat was supported through the online service Quantum Link. Players were referred to as "residents" and allowed to establish their own rules and protocols so long as they did not hack into the system. Habitat quickly morphed into its own fully functioning world with unexpected outcomes. Residents independently established friendships and romantic partnerships and businesses, created governments, got divorces, and, at times, waged wars (Farmer, n.d.).

The Lucasfilms developers indicated that they learned that success in virtual worlds is driven more by individual participants' interactions than by the actual technology. Habitat was unique in providing elements of engagement and interaction in a computer-based environment that were not previously available to the general market. "Residents" were allowed to manage their own financial accounts, to purchase and store items, and to change the physical look and gender of their avatars. Habitat operated for only three years, briefly resurfacing as Fujitsu Habitat in 1990. The high costs of user participation and a series of technological barriers for both users and the company eventually resulted in a permanent end to Habitat (Morningstar and Farmer, 1990).

The 1990s saw the rise of more graphically elaborate multiuser online games with the development of Ultima Underworld in 1992. The first three-dimensional online game was received with enthusiasm in the gaming world (*Virtual Worlds Timeline*, n.d.). That same year, a science fiction novel was released that proved both inspirational and highly influential for future virtual world technology developers.

Neal Stephenson's 1992 novel *Snow Crash* envisions a successor to the Internet that is more interactive and participatory, called a *Metaverse*. The Metaverse is juxtaposed with "Reality," or the real world. Success in the Metaverse relies on one's access to often prohibitively expensive information. The central character (Hiro Protagonist) is guided through the Metaverse by an expensive software-generated reference librarian-avatar (The Librarian) programmed with materials from the defunct Library of Congress. The reference librarian-avatar operates as a seemingly independent entity with the ability to inject (rather) human emotions like humor and sarcasm into his reference interactions. Whether or not the Librarian is actually being powered by a human being is a part of the plot's intrigue (Stephenson, 1992).

In 1993, the first prototype of Cyberworld was released. It officially launched two years later. Over the course of the next decade, several virtual games and virtual worlds were developed and marketed to the general public. In 2002, The Sims online virtual game was launched, followed by several large-scale virtual world environments, such as There in 2003, World of Warcraft in 2004, and Metaverse in 2007 (*Virtual Worlds Timeline*, n.d.). But by far the most popular virtual world technology in terms of media attention, active participants, and educational usage is Second Life by Linden Lab, originally released in 2003.

THE HISTORY OF SECOND LIFE

Second Life began as a prototype called Linden World. It was developed in 1991 by Philip Rosedale, who spent his teenage years selling database systems to finance his college education. Inspired by Stephenson's *Snow Crash,* Rosedale, then RealNetworks' chief technology officer, spent years developing his vision of a virtual world where human beings could interact and transact in ways similar to the real world. Eight years later, in 1999, Rosedale left RealNetworks and founded San Francisco–based Linden Lab in an effort to focus full-time on his plans to create an Internet-based "metaverse" (Barnes, 2007). Although similar prototypes of several virtual world technologies, like LucasWorld's Habitat, existed nearly a decade before the founding of Linden Lab, Second Life founder Rosedale contends that the concept of Second Life is original.

In November 2002, the beta test phase of Second Life was launched and was opened to the general public in April 2003 with a small group of users referred to as "residents." Once users downloaded the Second Life software client available on the Internet, they were provided a basic avatar, or digital representation that they were able to customize based on their individual taste. The avatar could be any size, shape, color, animal, or gender and became the primary mechanism through which an individual would participate inside of Second Life (Rymaszewski et al., 2007).

Avatars were not bound to traditional relationships or societal norms but were expected to govern themselves based on a code of conduct. The purpose of this code of conduct was to ensure that all users could enjoy their individual Second Life experience without harassment or interruption from other residents. Avatars were given abilities such as text-based communicating, flying abilities, and a portable inventory to store items useful to their experiences in Second Life such as landmarks (portable teleporting shortcuts to favorite locations an avatar has visited in Second Life).

Participants also received starter items to customize their avatars (such as clothing, hair, eyes, skin colors, and shoes) in addition to building materials, such as virtual wood, tile, glass, and metal (Rymaszewski et al., 2007). On June 23, 2003, Second Life moved from the beta phase to an active stage. The active stage included major upgrades and new features, including enhanced land-management options, a copyright system that protected the users' creations, internal video filming capacities, and more advanced graphic enhancements to make the virtual world more visually appealing (Rymaszewski et al., 2007).

To subsidize the cost of maintaining the multiple servers required to run the technology, Rosedale enacted various user fees, or taxes on residents. This fee-based model included fees not only to maintain virtual space but also to allow users to navigate inside of Second Life (also referred to as teleporting fees). A large group of users, calling itself "Americana," responded negatively to continuous "taxation without full representation" inside of Second Life and launched a major online backlash. Americana held the first virtual world revolution, called the Tea Crate Rebellion of 2003. Rosedale quickly understood that the success of Second Life and the future growth of his company meant relinquishing some control (Rymaszewski et al., 2007).

Over the next three years, Rosedale updated Second Life to enhance the user experience. He introduced customized gestures and animations for avatars, the "Linden dollar" (which users purchase with their country's currency for a high exchange rate) in order to create an active economy of selling and purchasing, and a free basic membership for users (Rymaszewski et al., 2007). Individuals with premium memberships (which include a monthly base rate) are allowed to purchase unlimited virtual land, also known as *grids.* To provide the most robust technological experience in Second Life, Linden Lab provides free continuous software upgrades for all users.

Children and teenagers are banned from participation in Second Life. In response to a demand for a youth-targeted virtual world, Teen Second Life was launched in the summer of 2005. Teen Second Life is solely for youth ages 13–17 and is primarily marketed for educational purposes. Only educators willing to go through an external background check by Ascertain are allowed to manage and participate in educational activities inside Teen Second Life. Freedom of movement for adult educators is restricted to one location in an effort to ensure safety in the space. Additionally, teenage users are verified through methods such as landline phone calls and PayPal accounts. The National Center for Missing and Exploited Children also partners with Linden Lab to minimize inappropriate adult interaction with the users of Teen Second Life (Rymaszewski et al., 2007).

In the following years, Second Life experienced explosive user growth. Real-world businesses like American Apparel, Warner Brothers, Toyota, and Starwood Hotels began to enter Second Life as a means of engaging and capturing new consumers. Nonprofits like the American Cancer Society raised tens of thousands of dollars from Second Life fund-raising activities (Rymaszewski et al., 2007). Entertainers, including rappers Jay-Z and Talib Kweli and pop singers Justin Timberlake and Suzanne Vega, hosted concerts inside Second Life to promote new albums.

A May 2006 *BusinessWeek.com* cover story on avatar Anshe Chung, Second Life's most successful entrepreneur, exposed the possibilities of leveraging Second Life business opportunities for real-world financial gain (Hof, 2006). The "Virtual Rockefeller" owns thousands of dollars worth of virtual real estate in Second Life that she rents and "flips" for a profit. It is estimated that her annual real-world income for her Second Life business venture is $150,000 (Sloan, 2005).

Politicians also used Second Life as an inexpensive way to promote and share their political agendas in a virtual global environment. Former Virginia governor Mark Warner, former senator John Edwards, Senator John McCain, and former senator, now Secretary of State Hillary Clinton all maintained election sites in Second Life. President Barack Obama's Second Life location included campaign updates, parties, and an inaugural celebration.

In early 2008 Rosedale, then 40 years old, hired Mark Kingdon as his replacement in the role of chief executive officer of Linden Lab while electing to maintain his position as chairman of the board. Rosedale contends that "for broader sets of users like education, we need to keep making Second Life easier to use and get into" (Nino, 2009). Part of the process of making Second Life user-friendly for educational purposes includes the Second Life Library/Information Island.

LIBRARIANSHIP IN SECOND LIFE

> [The Librarian] can move through nearly infinite stacks of information in the Library with the agility of a spider dancing across a vast web of cross-references.... He is eager without being obnoxiously chipper.... The Library is his memory and he only uses small parts of it at once.
>
> Stephenson (1992, 100, 205)

History of the Alliance Second Life Library 2.0 Project

In *Snow Crash,* Stephenson first explored the figure of the Librarian as a necessary entity enabling one to successfully explore a virtual world. The Librarian serves as a technological and informational navigator while injecting a sense of humanism and civility into the virtual environment (Blackmore, 2004). The modern-day Second Life libraries also skillfully manage the multiplicity of librarianship inside the virtual world. Like Stephenson's Librarian in *Snow Crash,* Second Life librarians ensure that humanism is not sacrificed due to technology.

In January 2005, two years after Second Life's launch, the Second Life Library was created by an individual whose avatar name is Jade Lily. It closed its doors shortly afterward. Librarium, a project primarily developed and managed by librarian-avatar JJ Drinkwater, opened on March 25, 2006, and continues to exist, maintaining several collections, exhibits, and events.

The largest and most continuously active virtual world library was created on April 11, 2006, by Lori Bell, director of innovation for Alliance Library System; Kitty Pope, executive director of Alliance; and Barbara Galik, executive director of the Bradley University Library and member of the Alliance board of directors. A library in the youth-targeted Teen Second Life was organized by Kelly Czarnecki, teen librarian at the Public Library of Charlotte and Mecklenburg County in North Carolina, in 2006. Technical and creative support for both projects was provided by John Lester, Linden Lab leader of customer market development for education and health care, who uses the avatar name Pathfinder Linden.

A call for volunteer library participation was sent out via librarian-targeted discussion lists, mass e-mails, and general word of mouth. Almost-instantaneous international participation resulted in a large group of volunteers. The Second Life Library evolved into Information Island (or Info Island), which is a now a group of branch library locations including readers' advisory, a genealogy research center, mystery novel and science fiction branches, a science center, governmental resources, Health Information Island, and the 19th-century and Caledon literature–focused Jack and Elaine Whitehorn Memorial Library (Peters, Bell, and Gallaway, 2007).

Very early on in the development of the Second Life Library, a meta-management approach was adopted. Unlike many nonprofits and corporations that entered Second Life without a clear plan or strategy in place, the project leads of the Second Life Library 2.0 Project employed a strategic five-step approach. These steps included the following:

- Analyzing requirements
- Determining the manner in which requirements could be successfully satisfied
- Tracking resource allocation to ensure requirements were being fulfilled
- Maintaining and revising procedures
- Adjusting for optimality (Mowshowitz, 2002)

Unlike the traditional model of librarianship, meta-management within a virtual world ensures that the universes of possible options are engaged and empowers the librarian to make instantaneous creative decisions about the best way to serve patrons. This approach not only proved successful during the project's inception but also continued to generate long-term sustainable enthusiasm for subsequent years.

Part of the appeal of Second Life for many librarians is that it is the first cost-effective, easily accessible Internet-based technology that allows them to run various technological media simultaneously (including podcasts, PowerPoint presentations, and audio files). These items could be presented in an interesting and creative way that further engaged user interaction, such as having floating books that encouraged users to touch them for a brief synopsis and visual displays that incorporated audio files.

Avatar librarians in Second Life are qualified to work in their respective capacities by their real-life experience and educational background. Once certified to represent themselves as information professionals on Information Island, avatar librarians display their professional titles (such as librarian, reference librarian, cataloger, archivist) over their heads when working. Librarians with higher levels of technical proficiency were selected as officers of Information Island and have the ability to appoint additional librarian-avatars. Other highly skilled individuals were charged to head various large-scale functions, such as reference, collection development, and archives with staffing, scheduling, and training as a core part of their responsibilities. As of July 2009, internationally, 1,358 librarians and volunteers were a part of Information Island (Hudson, 2009).

Reference Services inside Second Life

Early participants in Second Life actively sought out qualified information and resources to make their user experience more valuable. As a result, Second Life reference services were launched immediately. The reference services were overwhelmingly popular. Reference services are coordinated by a librarian who works for the New York Public Library System and uses the avatar name Hypatia Dejavu. Reference services in Second Life are structured in the traditional manner with a reference desk staffed by 51 volunteer librarians for 80 hours per week. Each reference librarian-avatar works two-hour shifts and attends regular reference staff meetings where technical and avatar-to-avatar reference interview training is offered. Reference librarian-avatars are also trained to manage disruptive avatar patrons (known as *griefers*) and communicate in the primary language of the avatar patron by utilizing a Google translator tool. In addition, reference librarian-avatars provide tours of the Second Life library, offer instructional sessions, and attend conferences.

The reference librarian-avatar keeps several tools in her respective inventory file, which includes a litany of valuable resources for library patrons. Reference librarian-avatars create virtual note cards and landmarks to immediately transmit portable information to patron-avatars. This information can then be stored and organized by the patron-avatar for future reference.

Until mid-2008, all reference transactions were text-based. Communication between the reference librarian-avatar and the patron-avatar would appear on the computer screen in real time. Now, voice-enabled technology allows the reference librarian-avatar and the patron-avatar to directly communicate with each other by plugging a headset into the computer.

Partnerships and Collaborations

Early in the creation of the Second Life Library/Information Island, various companies approached the Alliance Library System about partnerships and collaborations to promote literacy and other activities of interest to Second Life library users. For instance, the library vendor EBSCO provided a free trial of the Consumer Health Database for avatars in 2006. The cable network Showtime, along with the Electric Sheep Company, worked with the Second Life Library to promote the launch of the television show *The Tudors.* From July 2006 to July 2007, the Online Computer Library Center (OCLC) QuestionPoint trial provided the Alliance Library System with its first vital reference transaction statistics. Reference librarian-avatars were able to answer questions directly in response to other avatars within Second Life in a QuestionPoint chat or e-mail. Approximately 30 percent of the questions from this trial were traditional reference questions, while another 30 percent were general questions about Second Life. The year 2007 also brought a sponsorship agreement from SirsiDynix to support the Second Life Library's "main branch" and the library in Teen Second Life (Peters, Bell, and Gallaway, 2007). Alliance Library System later partnered with Online Programming for All Libraries (OPAL) to provide Second Life's library to a wider audience.

Characteristics of Second Life Librarians

In a survey I conducted in 2007 of 59 librarians working in various capacities inside Second Life, the median age was 44.14 years old, with the oldest respondent being 70 years old and the youngest respondent being 30 years old. The librarians skewed older than the median average age of Second Life participants by 10 years, but they were 10 years younger than the median age of librarians. Their video gaming experience ranged from none prior to participating in Second Life to highly advanced or skilled gaming skills.

According to the survey, one common characteristic of Second Life librarians is their receptivity to multimodal literacy. Several respondents (anecdotally) mentioned that they perceived Second Life to be the merger of digital, visual, and information literacies. They also saw librarians as an integral aspect of the teaching and learning of technologically based multimodal literacy.

In my survey, Second Life librarians described themselves using the words "futuristic," "creative," "risk taker," "innovator," "interested in technology," "right brain-oriented," and "highly tolerant." A high tolerance level is vital to the success of virtual world librarianship. Beyond the learning curve and inevitable frustrations a constantly evolving technology can bring, colleagues' and residents' avatars can be anything the imagination can conjure; avatars run the gamut from human, to animal, to robot, to clouds of air, to plant life. Therefore, the reference librarian-avatar must work to eliminate any bias in interactions with library visitors or colleagues.

Tolerance is a core value inside Second Life, and in order to be successful, librarians must remove prejudices regarding what an appropriate avatar should look like. Interestingly, several of the librarians surveyed also indicated that they perceive themselves as champions of diversity in their real-world workplaces. Whether they were diversity supporters prior to their experiences inside Second Life or not was not ascertained in the 2007 survey. However, anecdotally several librarians indicated that the Second Life experience has made them more tolerant in their real-world reference interactions.

A few survey respondents indicated that Second Life strengthened their real-world reference skills. Respondents stated that Second Life "made me excited about being a librarian again" or "opened me up to the possibilities of exploring other technologies for virtual reference services." Another survey respondent added, "I am no longer intimidated to approach IT services about my library's technology needs. Second Life taught me that it's ok to stumble and fumble inside a virtual learning environment as that is a part of the learning process." Other librarians reported a sense of freedom in being able to explore other aspects of librarianship outside of their prescribed real-world roles and felt that this made them better real-world reference librarians. This sense of freedom from self-imposed and institutional limitations was part of the appeal of Second Life for this group of librarians.

Creating a Virtual Community of Practice

The concept of communities of practice organized for educational purposes was first introduced in 1991 by Lave and Wenger in *Situated Learning: Legitimate Peripheral Participation*. Throughout the 1990s, various articles emerged that explored the possibility of translating the community-of-practice philosophy to an online or virtual environment. In the article "Towards a Typology of Virtual Communities of Practice," a more concrete definition of a *virtual community of practice*, or VCoP, is given: a group of people who "rely primarily on information technology to connect their members...to establish a common virtual collaborative space...[using] a large array of traditional media and more sophisticated technological tools such as email, on-line meeting space [and] websites" (Dube, Bourhis, and Jacob, 2006, 69–93). The authors further elaborate that VCoPs are "multi-faceted" by nature and share characteristics like geographic dispersion, a selective membership process, membership stability, and cultural diversity.

By all accounts, the Second Life Library 2.0 Project meets the basic criteria of a VCoP. Second Life Library continues to remain one of the most heavily trafficked locations within Second Life, with an average of 5,000 visitors each day. Beyond the active VCoP of librarianship in Second Life is an interesting and unpredicted subset: the real-life relationships between Second Life librarians that were created as a consequence of their virtual work together. Upon meeting each other face-to-face for the first time at the Association of College and Research Libraries conference in 2007, many of the North America–based Second Life librarians physically embraced and exchanged work-related anecdotes no differently than if they were working together daily in a traditional brick-and mortar library. In-person meetings between librarians led to the creation of several task forces with the American Library Association and the Association of College and Research Libraries. A team of Second Life librarians now teaches courses on virtual world librarianship at the University of Illinois. Other librarians have published articles and how-to guides, including Lori Bell and Rhonda Trueman's *Virtual Worlds, Real Libraries: Librarians and Educators in Second Life and Other Multi-User Virtual Environments.*

A REVIEW OF THE LIBRARY LITERATURE ON SECOND LIFE AND VIRTUAL WORLD TECHNOLOGY

The library literature on Second Life and similar virtual world technologies is relatively limited in scope, primarily because Second Life is still fairly new. The literature tends to be largely anecdotal and generally promotes Second Life as viable means of extending library services beyond the traditional brick-and-mortar edifice. Second Life is also viewed as a new form of roving reference that synergistically combines virtual reference with visual information literacy (Godfrey, 2008).

In a number of ways, issues with Second Life mirror some of the same issues in traditional virtual reference services. The ability to instant message (IM), e-mail, and chat with patrons in Second Life is no different than standard virtual reference; however, all of these actions can transpire simultaneously. Therefore, the librarian working in Second Life must have the ability to work with multiple users who may engage in a variety of communication styles (Gerardin, Yamamoto, and Gordon, 2008).

Virtual reference services inside Second Life are perceived to be more personable than other forms of virtual reference service because avatars operate like humans inside Second Life. Avatars can gesture and provide guidance in ways that are not possible in a traditional virtual reference environment. For example, a librarian-avatar can walk a patron to a resource and provide a degree of visually based instruction that cannot take place in a chat or e-mail transaction. And no differently than in real-world reference interactions, librarian-avatars can distribute business cards to patrons, and patrons can seek out the same reference librarian for future assistance (Erdman, 2007; Gerardin, Yamamoto, and Gordon, 2008; Grassian and Trueman, 2007).

Second Life is not without its own unique set of challenges and disadvantages. Creating a library or developing reference services in Second Life can cause a significant amount of stress since the virtual world is often scrutinized as the "digital equivalent of the Wild West" (Joint, 2008, 420). This is largely because Second Life's general user environment is open source and therefore open to anyone. The majority of library locations that use virtual reference software, like Altarama VRLplus or QuestionPoint, require some form of user authentication. Incidents of harassment and destructive behaviors by individuals referred to as griefers (or problem Second Life patrons) are fairly common and can create extra angst when attempting to maintain a high quality of library services in Second Life (Luo, 2008).

Second Life users must possess a great deal of technical competence coupled with expensive hardware and software in order to participate successfully (Gerardin, Yamamoto, and Gordon, 2008). Also, since Second Life is developed via user-generated content, public services librarianship inside Second Life requires one to utilize resources at the librarians' disposal (Luo, 2008). This has the possibility of creating an even deeper digital divide, not just with patrons but also within the librarian community, as the majority of librarians do not have access to electronic databases and high-end gaming computers needed for Second Life.

Other concerns regarding reference services in Second Life include the lack of real privacy in the reference transaction (Gerardin, Yamamoto, and Gordon, 2008), Second Life's inaccessibility for individuals who are visually and reading impaired (Joint, 2008), and the limitations for international librarians working in the U.S.-dominated Second Life (Parker, 2008).

Nonetheless, Second Life is heralded by many librarians and library science educators as a transformative environment that assists in redefining the library as place and the role of the reference librarian. The librarianship focus in Second Life shifts away from librarians managing physical collections to "be[ing] managers of libraries as learning and social spaces" (Parker, 2008, 233). The virtual world offers a new access point for in-world patrons seeking qualified reference assistance, and "the reference desk is where all of these [reference] tools come together" (Erdman, 2007, 31).

SECOND LIFE AND VIRTUAL WORLD TECHNOLOGY IN THE MASTER OF LIBRARY SCIENCE CURRICULUM

Since the creation of Second Life in 2003, several graduate-level library science programs in North America and Europe have included Second Life education in continuing professional development courses, certificate programs, and core curriculum courses. In the fall of 2009, I conducted a quick survey of Second Life in the master of library science (MLS) curriculum. (I would like to thank colleagues who responded to my requests for information on discussion lists. I also thank Dr. Dolores Fidishun, who was kind enough to post my request on the JESSE discussion list.) These courses tend to focus on developing and providing reference services and user-centered instruction that enforce information literacy standards. Several of these courses explore connections between existing learning theory, pedagogy, and virtual world technology's role in current and future reference and instructional engagement with patrons.

The first institution to establish an in-world campus for graduate-level library and information science education inside Second Life was San Jose State University. Operating as a part of the Information Island "Archipelago" (a group of information services–based islands inside Second Life, including the Second Life Library), San Jose State University's MLS students are required to develop course-related presentations and meet within Second Life.

The University of Pittsburgh has included Second Life in various core curriculum courses since 2004. Their children's librarianship program provides information about educational uses of virtual worlds, and their academic librarianship programs have included Second Life exploration and education. Also, several noteworthy institutions offer Second Life as part of the standard MLS curriculum. The University of Hawaii at Manoa has forged a partnership with Texas Woman's University to provide Second Life–related courses for students there. The University of North Carolina at Chapel Hill and Greensboro, the University of Southern California, and the Pratt Institute all provide courses primarily focusing on Second Life. Other institutions that integrate Second Life into their standard MLS coursework include Dominican University, the University of Michigan, and Drexel University. Outside of the United States, the University of Western Ontario in Canada offers a course called Second Life and Other Virtual Worlds, and the University of Sheffield in the United Kingdom includes Second Life in their Educational Informatics course as a part of the master of arts librarianship program.

The field has responded to the need for virtual world professional development courses. Two institutions at the time of this writing offer either noncredit continuing education or full advanced certificate programs. The University of Illinois at Urbana-Champaign provides a popular continuing professional development program in virtual world librarianship. The courses include building, scripting, and managing virtual world collections, as well as building a virtual world library, and are taught by many of the principals of the Second Life Library. The University of Washington iSchool announced in the fall of 2009 that they will offer a three-course certificate program in virtual worlds focusing on virtual world selection, usage, design, and programming.

ON THE HORIZON

Several large colleges and universities, including the Pennsylvania State University, have begun exploratory librarianship work inside Second Life. The Penn State Virtual Worlds Project was conceptualized in 2005 by Penn State's lead instructional designer, Brett Bixler. Bixler was able to secure funding and developed an internal "Faculty Initiative Engagement Grant" for educational exploration inside Second Life for the 2007–2008 academic year. The timing of this grant was perfect, as our students' queries about the Second Life technology peaked a few weeks prior to the Thanksgiving holiday of 2006 (largely due to Second Life stories that appeared on the major television networks).

In February 2007, Dr. Peggy Daniels Lee (Management Department), Dr. Nortia Ahmad (Engineering Department), and I successfully submitted a proposal making the Penn State Great Valley School of Graduate Professional Studies the only Commonwealth Campus location within Penn State University to pilot Second Life across three divisions. The proposal was officially accepted on March 3, 2007, and I was designated lead faculty for the Penn State Great Valley Second Life project. Our preliminary work of organizing in-world and classroom activities started shortly thereafter.

Within a few weeks of our proposal being accepted, we held a series of meetings with the other lead faculty and instructional designers throughout the Penn State system in Second Life. We developed a Second Life etiquette document for our students that outlines behavioral expectations in-world. This document was essential to help students understand that while Second Life has a gaming interface, course-related activities and classes are treated as another form of distance education at Penn State University. After "terraforming" (reshaping) our virtual land space and purchasing a virtual building and furniture, we were ready to start the coursework.

I assisted in preparing students to successfully navigate inside Second Life by providing an in-class overview that outlined the expectations for students and opened the floor for dialogue to discuss concerns like privacy and time management. The campus's instructional designer and I worked with students to develop their avatars. In-world, my responsibilities as a reference and instructional librarian carried over to providing students with qualified Second Life resources and locations for them to explore.

Between the two courses from September 2007 to April 2008, 157 students participated in a combination of in-class and in-world instruction and projects. While several of them struggled with adjusting to this new form of instructional technology, the majority of the students found participating in Second Life courses a valuable experience. Future plans include the development of multiple Penn State libraries inside Second Life to reflect the diversity of Penn State's large library system.

Eastern University in Pennsylvania maintained what is believed to be the first library presence inside ActiveWorlds (another virtual world technology) from 2006 to 2008 (Eastern University Library Web site, n.d.). While many libraries have discussed creating spaces inside of other virtual worlds such as There.com, those projects remain in the conceptualization phase as of this writing.

As digital content is created inside virtual worlds like Second Life, other material is often deleted or abandoned. As a means of preserving the work occurring in virtual worlds like Second Life, the Library of Congress began the Preserving Virtual Worlds project in 2007 in partnership with the University of Illinois Graduate School of Library and Information Science. The project is implementing preservation methods, including capturing of Second Life reference transactions as teaching tools ("Digital Preservation Pioneer," 2009).

As was the case with Maggs, Shapira, and Sides (creators of the virtual game Avatar) and Rosedale (founder of Second Life), who envisioned and created virtual worlds before they were 18, youth continue to lead the way in virtual world technologies. According to eMarketer, a market research firm, approximately 10 million U.S. children and teenagers visit virtual worlds regularly. This number is expected to increase to nearly 15 million by 2013. This growth is partially driven by the 112 virtual worlds designed for users under the age of 18, like Webkinz, Club Penguin, and Barbiegirls.com. Another 81 youth-targeted virtual worlds are currently in development, which suggests that close to 20 million children will be members of virtual worlds by 2011 ("Online Playgrounds," 2009).

For librarians, the implications of increased use of youth-based virtual worlds are twofold: First, librarians should immediately educate themselves about virtual worlds, and second, further exploration and research into how to effectively deliver reference services to the next generation of "student-avatars" is vital to our long-term success in librarianship.

CONCLUSION

The work inside Second Life, and other potential virtual world technologies, demonstrates the connection between reference services and visual information literacy. In spite of repeated proclamations about the end of libraries, reference services, and virtual world technologies, there are approximately 136 active libraries and library organizations inside Second Life, including the American Library Association. Whether or not Second Life continues to exist, it is fairly certain that a successor is in development. The large number of young and teenaged virtual world users indicates that virtual worlds are not a passing fad. It is crucial that we as reference librarians acquaint ourselves with virtual world technology to prepare ourselves and each other for our emerging library patrons.

The past is prologue, and the future is present.

WORKS CITED

Barnes, B. 2007. Web playground of the very young. *New York Times* (December 31). Retrieved July 2, 2009, from http://www.nytimes.com/2007/12/31/business/31virtual.html?_r=2&oref=slogin.

Blackmore, T. 2004. Agent of civility: The librarian in Neal Stephenson's *Snow crash. Studies in Media & Information Literacy Education* 4 (4): 1–10.

Digital preservation pioneer: Jerry McDonough. 2009. *Library of Congress Digital Preservation Newsletter* (February). Retrieved July 23, 2009, from http://www.digitalpreservation.gov/news/newsletter/200902.pdf.

Dube, L., A. Bourhis, and R. Jacob. 2006. Towards a typology of virtual communities of practice. *Interdisciplinary Journal of Information, Knowledge, and Management* 1: 69–93.

Eastern University Library Web site. Retrieved September 29, 2009, from http://www.eastern.edu/library/about/Our%20Community1.html.

Erdman, J. 2007. Reference in a 3-D virtual world: Preliminary observations on library outreach in second life. *Reference Librarian* 47 (2): 29–39.

Farmer, F. R. n.d. *Social dimensions of Habitat's citizenry.* Retrieved July 1, 2009, from http://www.crockford.com/ec/citizenry.html.

Gartner says 80 percent of active Internet users will have a "Second Life" in the virtual world by the end of 2011. 2007. Retrieved July 30, 2009, from http://www.gartner.com/it/page.jsp?id=503861.

Gerardin, J., M. Yamamoto, and K. Gordon. 2008. Fresh perspectives on reference work in Second Life. *Reference & User Services Quarterly* 47 (4): 324–330.

Godfrey, K. 2008. A new world for virtual reference. *Library Hi Tech* 26 (4): 525–539.

Grassian, E., and R. Trueman. 2007. Stumbling, bumbling, teleporting, and flying . . . librarian avatars in Second Life. *Reference Services Review* 35 (1): 84–89.

Hof, R. D. 2006. Virtual world, real money. *BusinessWeek.com.* Retrieved September 29, 2009, from http://www.businessweek.com/magazine/content/06_18/b3982002.htm.

Hudson, A. 2009. Online access on July 30, 2009 to "Librarians of Second Life" Web group inside Second Life.com.

Joint, N. 2008. Virtual reference, Second Life, and traditional library enquiry services. *Library Review* 57 (6): 416–423.

Luo, L. 2008. Reference service in Second Life: An overview. *Reference Services Review* 36 (3): 289–300.

Mitchell, D. 1995. *From MUDs to virtual worlds.* Retrieved July 31, 2009, from http://www.mentallandscape.com/Papers_95vworlds.htm.

Morningstar, C., and F. R. Farmer. 1990. *The lessons of Lucasfilm's Habitat.* Paper presented at the First International Conference on Cyberspace, University of Texas at Austin, May 1990. Retrieved September 29, 2009, from http://www.fudco.com/chip/lessons.html.

Mowshowitz, A. 2002. *Virtual organization: Toward a theory of societal transformation stimulated by information technology.* Westport, CT: Quorum Books.

Nino, T. 2009. Massively talks with upbeat Second Life founder, Philip Rosedale. Retrieved July 9, 2009, from http://www.massively.com/2009/04/12/massively-talks-with-upbeat.

Online playgrounds: Virtual world for children. 2009. *Economist* (July 25): 62.

Parker, L. 2008. Second Life: The seventh face of the library? *Program* 42 (3): 232–242.

Peters, T., L. Bell, and B. Gallaway. 2007. *A report on the first year of operation of the Alliance Second Life Library 2.0 Project also known as the Alliance Information Archipelago, April 11, 2006 through April 18, 2007* (report dated August 10, 2007). Retrieved September 29, 2009, from http://www.alliancelibrarysystem.com/pdf/07sllreport.pdf.

Rymaszewski, M., W. J. Au, M. Wallace, C. Winters, C. Ondrejka, and B. Batstone-Cunningham. 2007. *Second Life: The official guide.* Hoboken, NJ: Wiley.

Sloan, P. 2005. The virtual Rockefeller: Anshe Chung is raking in real money in an unreal online world. *CNN Money.com.* Retrieved July 31, 2009, from http://money.cnn.com/magazines/business2/business2_archive/2005/12/01/8364581/index.htm.

Stephenson, N. 1992. *Snow crash.* New York: Bantam.

Virtual worlds popularity spikes. 2009. *Virtual Worlds News* (July 15). Retrieved July 30, 2009, from http://virtualworldsnews.com/2009/07/virtual-world-popularity-spikes.html#more.

Virtual worlds timeline: Origins and evolution of social virtual worlds. n.d. Retrieved September 29, 2009, from www.vwtimeline.org.

What is a virtual world? n.d. *Virtual Worlds Review.* Retrieved September 29, 2009, from http://www.virtualworldsreview.com/info/whatis.shtml.

ADDITIONAL READINGS

Thompson, S. 2009. On being a virtual world librarian: Experiences in offering live reference services in a virtual world. *Reference Librarian* 50: 219–223.

6

AN EXPLORATION OF THE HYBRID REFERENCE SERVICE MODEL: KEEPING WHAT WORKS

Marie L. Radford and Scott Vine

This chapter discusses the *hybrid reference desk*, defined here as a departure from the traditional reference configuration either through (1) a blend of traditional, face-to-face (FtF), virtual reference (VR; such as e-mail, instant messaging, and live chat), and other service types, such as phone, text messaging (also known as SMS, for *short message service*), and so on, in which staff handles different types of reference modes at one service point; or (2) use of tiered staffing models in which there may be up to three levels of service: "information desk, general reference desk and consultation services" (Cassell and Hiremath, 2009, 123). Four examples, two from academic libraries and two from public libraries, are discussed to exemplify successful hybrid initiatives that are currently in operation.

According to Numminen and Vakkari (2009, 1250), VR services are currently among "the most expanding services" in libraries. It is clear that to be able to serve on-site as well as off-site users who have a variety of preferences for how they want to access reference service, it is necessary to offer as broad a range of options as possible within FtF and cyber venues. For example, Radford and Connaway (2007) have found a generational preference for live chat among young members of the millennial cohort, who also enjoy FtF encounters with friendly librarians. These different modes can be combined to complement each other. For example, virtual encounters can lead to more in-depth research appointment-style interactions, while those FtF interactions can be followed up on virtually.

Critical challenges for most library reference departments involve determining which mix of traditional and virtual services is optimal for their particular range of users and what staffing model will work best. Human resources are frequently scarce in these times of shrinking funds, in which staff costs account for the largest proportion of the overall budget. Therefore, despite what librarians might consider to be the ideal array of services, the reality is that there is a finite amount of staff hours and energy. Burnout is a looming threat that is compounded when staff (who may already be stretched thin across different service points) may be pushed to multitask by juggling several services concurrently (Radford, 2009). Cassell and Hiremath (2009, 432) provide a highly useful table that contains a description with pros and cons for nine different models of reference service including the traditional reference desk, reference consultation model, tiered reference service, team staffing, integrated service point concept, roving, VR, outreach model, and no reference desk.

Kern (2009) delineates three types of reference staffing models and outlines the pros and cons of each. She refers to hybrid reference as the "one-desk" model in which "the library staffs all reference services from a single, public point... [which] encompasses all modes of communication" (73). The two other types she describes include the separate VR desk and staffing VR from the librarians' offices. Kern notes that in VR's early days, some librarians "voiced the opinion that it was not appropriate to staff synchronous virtual reference from the reference desk" (73). This thinking is being reexamined, especially for small institutions with limited staff or for libraries who consider the one-desk, hybrid model to be an "efficient use of resources that works with their reference workflow" (73). For libraries that have seen some decline in foot traffic to the FtF desk (see Library Statistics Program: Academic Libraries, 2008; Library Statistics Program: Public Libraries, 2008), it is possible that the hybrid approach may now work better to maximize reference staff time. Martell (2008) cites Association of Research Libraries (ARL) data that shows a widespread reduction in academic reference desk questions but an increase in use of VR service and online resources. Cassell and Hiremath (2009) agree that academic libraries' statistics show a decline in reference transactions but point out that public library use has continued to be stable, with a large demand for FtF services. According to Cassell and Hiremath, there has also been a shift in the types of questions posed: "Libraries have noted the decline in the number of ready reference questions and an increase in more complicated questions" (422).

To date, there has not yet been much research that directly focuses on the hybrid reference desk, although several articles have examined the changing nature of reference configurations (for example, see Bourne, 2005; Bracke, Chinnaswamy, and Kline, 2008; Brattin, 2005; Courtois and Liriano, 2000; Frey and Kaiser, 2008; vanDuinkerken, Stephens, and MacDonald, 2009). Some of these authors discuss the hybrid concept, offering perspectives that are based in experience and observation of practice. Hines (2007) and Kuchi, Mullen, and Tama-Bartels (2004) discuss reference "outposts" operating from locations outside the library building. Sonntag and Palsson (2007) have argued that the traditional reference desk should be eliminated and replaced by on-demand and course-integrated (embedded) reference librarians. Bahavar and Truelson (2008) discuss strategic planning for reference in a team environment and recommend using a "preferred futuring" model.

Kern (2009) reports that the hybrid model has several advantages: It uses existing staffing levels, increases staff utilization while at the service desk, provides proximity to print materials, and promotes marketing of all services. Cassell (2010) notes that economies can be realized by consolidating service points for "one-stop" service in which service standards require ongoing cross-training for all staff. However, Kern (2009) points out that there are also disadvantages to the hybrid model, including the possibility of librarian overload, increased juggling of users and multiple queries, and the potential need for extra staff during periods of high demand.

Ryan (2008) provides an argument for a tiered approach in a cost-effectiveness study that found that 89 percent of the questions posed to an academic reference desk could be answered by well trained paraprofessionals. It is interesting to note that the tiered model currently emerging as a solution for staffing shortages is a variation of the Brandeis Model (see Massey-Burzio, 1992; Nassar, 1997), a two-tiered approach that used a mix of personnel, including graduate students, to refer complex questions to reference librarians. Nassar (1997) found that the success of the two-tiered model relies on highly skilled librarians, a high number of questions, and suitable arrangement of the reference area to promote supervision of the front-line staff.

WHAT IS WORKING? SUCCESSFUL HYBRID DESKS AND STAFFING MODELS

To illustrate current desk and staffing practices that are working well within different environments, descriptions of several academic and public library examples are provided in the following.

Academic Libraries

The One-Desk Model at Franklin & Marshall College, Lancaster, Pennsylvania

Franklin & Marshall is a residential liberal arts college with about 2,200 students and 200 faculty; it has two libraries, one for the social sciences and humanities and one for the sciences. The main reference desk is open in the social sciences and humanities library for approximately 70 hours a week and offers FtF research and technology help, telephone assistance, and virtual help via e-mail, instant messaging using Meebo, and texting (http://library.fandm.edu). The virtual services are marketed under the Ask Us brand and logo. Nine reference librarians and two staff members take turns covering all of these services from the main reference desk, with help as needed from the adjacent reference office, as well as virtual help from colleagues in both libraries on e-mail and IM.

FtF queries run the usual gamut of directional, technological, reference, and research questions, answered by experienced librarians and staff with immediate access to about 150 subscription databases, a variety of e-reference collections, and a print reference and circulating collection exceeding 500,000 volumes. Beyond this walk-up service, users can also make research appointments with librarians, requesting a one-on-one consultation with a subject liaison librarian by filling out a paper or Web-based appointment request form.

Incoming e-mail questions go to nine librarians and seven library staff, but the person at the reference desk is expected to respond to as many queries as possible or to ask for backup, relying on others' subject knowledge or availability. When the on-site reference desk is closed, any of those 16 librarians or staff who is online can respond by e-mail, and answers are copied to all. The e-mail account can also receive text messages sent from cell phones, and responses of 140 characters or less can be sent back from the reference e-mail account to the user's phone number.

This hybrid arrangement developed over the last six years, initially because the number of e-mail questions rose and it became necessary to share the workload. As the technology continued to develop, the chat service and the ability to receive text messages (SMS) were added and have proved popular with users. The reference Meebo account is active whenever the desk is open, and it is also covered by staff in the science library from 10 P.M. until 2 A.M. during the semester. The change to Meebo in the fall of 2010 allowed for communication with a wider range of users, even those without a fixed IM account.

Offering this combination of services at one public service point has helped the organization focus on a rather straightforward delivery of services and has allowed users to easily identify where and when they can get FtF and virtual assistance. Challenges include instances when the librarian or staff member has too many FtF and online users to address simultaneously (though this is lessened during the day by backup help) and times when individuals fall behind on the rapidly evolving technological skills needed to provide good service. To alleviate this training lag, the information services librarian and reference services assistant offered updates to participating librarians and staff for new modes as they were rolled out and also gave refreshers each semester.

While there was some resistance to the hybrid model from librarians and staff—especially when VR services, such as live chat, were added to the spectrum—the delivery of quality reference and research service to faculty and staff through their preferred means is a key value in the liberal arts college environment. Eventually, all those involved came to see that providing FtF and

VR from the same public desk not only was possible but also had the positive effect of improving student and faculty perceptions of the library and its service quality.

All of the reference services provided are marketed around campus through various means. Librarians talk about them in instruction classes, and signs and flyers are distributed each semester in dorms, college houses, and gathering spaces. Online marketing occurs through the library and college Web sites and in the college's Blackboard course management system.

Conversations about reference services are also a staple of the library's House Calls outreach program. In the spring of 2004, out of curiosity about potential users in the various buildings and departments on campus, librarians started going from office to office around the campus, asking if anyone had library-related questions and joking that they were making librarian house calls. While many on campus didn't know what to make of this that first semester, some enjoyed the idea, and the next fall a two-week schedule of drop-ins by pairs of librarians was advertised. Librarians visited the departments for which they did instruction and collection development, and this outward projection of reference service had the added effect of strengthening some liaison relationships that had slipped over the years.

The House Calls efforts continued each semester, until faculty were responding to e-mail advertisements by asking for appointments; what had been brief conversations became lengthy give-and-takes about topics ranging from student work habits to study abroad programs to what faculty members could do to help the library argue for more financial resources from the college. Particularly useful interactions were rewarded with coupons to the campus coffee shop, which elicited enthusiastic responses and an increase in the number of appointments the next semester.

The Tiered Model at Cornell University, Ithaca, New York

The authors sought the input of Baseema Banoo Krkoska, reference and instruction coordinator at the Albert R. Mann Library of Cornell University, New York, to discover how a hybrid reference desk or tiered staffing model might be used in the library of a major research institution. In the fall of 2008, a tiered staffing model was implemented at Mann Library (http://www.mannlib.cornell.edu/) for a variety of reasons. Contemporary academic librarians perform a number of complex and time-consuming roles, such as managing projects and acting as liaisons to academic departments and faculty. In addition, there are limited human resources and the need to reach users in different settings. It is estimated that roughly 60 percent of queries are either directional or take less than five minutes and can therefore be handled by well-trained information assistants. Complex reference questions are received regularly but do not follow a predictable schedule. Users adopt different ways to contact reference services including the Web form, live chat, and walk-in assistance. Usually they approach the library after having exhausted their options and are generally amenable to waiting for a high-quality response or to scheduling an appointment with a librarian to discuss complex information strategies.

In the two-tiered model, the main reference desk is primarily staffed by a core group of four information assistants (staff and students), with librarians offering advertised walk-in research help Mondays to Thursdays from 11 A.M. to 5 P.M. and Fridays from 11 A.M. to 4 P.M. Librarians are called on for complex research questions that cannot be handled by information assistants.

The staffing model has helped use limited resources effectively. Recently, the Mann reference pool lost two librarians as they were needed to lead other functional areas in the library. With a shrinking number of librarians, it became crucial to evaluate the effective use of resources. A consistent quality of service is monitored and maintained because the pool of front-line information assistants is small. The four information assistants function as a cohesive team and have a sense of ownership, which is harder to accomplish with a larger group of staff members. The information assistants watch the turnaround time and ensure that library users' queries do not slip through the cracks. Information assistants post complex research questions to a collaborative wiki space in which librarians work on these questions and quickly e-mail responses to the user. In addition, the information assistants are the marketers of specialized services offered by librarians. They help to promote the walk-in research help model by frequently handing out librarian business cards. The tiered approach has been extended for a second year, and a full evaluation is planned for fall 2010. Feedback has been positive, and there have been no complaints from either users or staff.

As needed, adjustments have been made in the number of walk-in research hours librarians can offer and in the evening staffing levels for information assistants. Librarians do miss the experience of working at the bustling and stimulating reference desk. However, they are free to spend their walk-in research hour out at the desk with the information assistants as there are no restrictions except that they should be available when their expertise is needed. Librarians who are not embedded within their departments can compensate for front-line experience by reaching out to their departments and their users. When librarians reach out to users outside the building, the response has been overwhelmingly positive, creating even more demand for services.

Mann Library has an established organizational culture of innovation, creativity, and flexibility. New and promising solutions are tried without hesitation. If something does not work, this is acknowledged quickly, and alternatives are soon devised. The best staffing patterns mirror user traffic while responding continuously to transforming needs. Today, Cornell has moved to the tiered model, but the staff is constantly watching the information landscape. If its users alter their research behavior, staff will need to adapt as well, reflecting a strong, shared belief that the organization cannot afford to remain stagnant in service initiatives in this time of rapid change.

Public Libraries

The Combined Hybrid and Tiered Model at Arlington Heights Memorial Library, Illinois

The authors called on Bill Pardue, virtual services librarian at Arlington Heights, to discover how a hybrid reference desk and tiered staffing model might be applied in a heavily used public library environment. The Arlington Library is currently in limbo between a more traditional model and a true hybrid desk. It has a Welcome Desk, staffed by two to three library assistants who handle fiction queries, basic known-item requests, Internet sign-ups, and related tasks. The Answer Center (reference desk) is a separate desk nearby, staffed by one to three librarians and set up to handle more in-depth questions (see the first floor map: http://www.ahml.info/about/library-map).

Both desks handle phone calls appropriate to their functions, and the Welcome Desk staff is expected to forward calls that get into reference territory or escort users over to the Answer Center. The staff at the Answer Center also handles VR questions using QuestionPoint, using the Online Computer Library Center (OCLC) Qwidget on a number of their Web pages. They also use Trillian for a few IMs that come in through AIM, Yahoo!, and MSN and get an occasional SMS via IM request. Off-desk librarians have the first chance at VR questions (all reference librarians are logged in when at work), and phone calls go to the reference office after the third ring at the desk. IM monitoring, in contrast, is done only at the Answer Center desk.

This model has been around in some form for quite a few years, although the current Welcome Desk is actually a merger of the old Fiction, Music, and Movies desk and Catalog and Information desk. The Answer Center was moved about a year ago from a position further away from the center of the library, allowing librarians to more effectively encounter users as they enter the nonfiction area. Having off-desk librarians pick up VR sessions as they come in, as well as answer overflow phone calls, has worked well, reducing wait times for VR and the number of calls going into voice mail; this has taken some pressure off the desk. Still, as phone and VR use increases, maintaining a high level of service might require a call-center approach.

A large number of nonreference questions are still handled at the Answer Center as librarians look for opportunities to take on additional responsibilities, especially increasing outreach. There may be a move toward consolidation of the Welcome Desk and Answer Center in the next few years. Some members of the Answer Center staff believe that Welcome Desk assistants are handling reference questions that should be referred, but this impression has not been systematically evaluated.

The department head is looking at the data for FtF and phone reference sessions using DeskTracker to try and determine how well the staffing model works. DeskTracker allows data to be collected on the type of contact, purpose of visit, and equipment problems. It can be customized to temporarily track categories of interest, such as job seekers. Tracking days and times of high traffic has allowed recognition of those times when triple staffing works but also of others when it seems that single staffing will suffice. One consideration to take into account is that staff at the main library switchboard does triage of phone calls, in the way the Welcome Desk is expected to function for walk-ins, so personnel there will need to maintain and continue to hone already well-developed abilities to recognize different types of questions and to make appropriate referrals. VR, e-mail, and IM statistics are compiled and analyzed separately.

Arlington Public Library librarians are open to different models and seem to feel that having a presence in the Welcome Desk area would be a positive step. Moving forward, it will be increasingly important to involve the librarians closely in the planning process and to try to anticipate trends and emerging issues that may impact service excellence.

The Hybrid Model with Roving Reference at the Orange County Library System, Orlando, Florida

The authors asked Kathryn Robinson, division head of reference and information at the Orange County Library System (OCLS); Donna Bachowski, department head of reference central; and Gregg Gronlund, department head of Questline phone reference how their public library system has used a hybrid and tiered model to reach its users. The public service and collections area of the main library of the OCLS in Orlando, Florida, is approximately 200,000 square feet, spread over four floors. A variety of methods are employed to provide library users with great service, from the traditional desk model to the current Mobile Gamma model. Mobile Gamma's prime focus is to provide exceptional service at the user's point of need. To accomplish this, staff roves throughout the areas of the library, seeking opportunities to help people. They accompany customers from one area of the building to another as needed to fulfill their information requests. Providing this opportunity for personalized service has a positive effect—library users say it is unexpected and welcome. When people decline having library personnel accompany them, staff utilize Vocera, a wireless communication device, to advise the appropriate staff member that a client is coming to their area for information and what information the client has already been given. From time to time, staff is all busy assisting other users, so OCLS added assistance phones. Library users simply pick up the handset, and they are connected to a staff member, who is then able to provide assistance over the phone or who will meet them wherever they are in the building. Users also have access to OLIVE, a videoconferencing unit that enables audio and visual contact with a staff member who can also assist them with their needs.

Mobile Gamma is designed for continual refinement and improvement. Librarians are currently evaluating staffing levels in relation to the number of users seeking assistance during different parts of the day, trying out call shifts, and discussing how to use reference triage more effectively. They are discussing whether there needs to be a service point for staff and clients, as most users head straight into the collections and seek out a service point only when they are unable to find what they need. Utilizing new technology (such as mobile computing devices and netbooks) they feel they will be able to fully assist users wherever they may be in the building.

In addition, the OCLS has a call center, called Questline, which is located at the main library and was started in September 1994. As of December 2005, it became the call center for the entire system, so when clients call any library branch of OCLS they reach Questline staff. Questline averages 15,000 calls per month and serves as an all-around service desk, most commonly handling requests for account management, renewals, holds for pickup or delivery, information, meeting rooms and computer classes, computer assistance, and reference. For about 95 percent of calls, the service is completed while the user is still on the phone. The staff is a mix of full- and part-time librarians as well as two reference clerks who use e-mail, the circulation module, the Questline database, the Web, the library catalog and databases, texting, chat, and OLIVE to answer queries. Staff and library users have been delighted with the efficiency and effectiveness of Questline.

A variety of approaches are used for the suite of VR services including e-mail, live chat, and text messaging. Current statistics indicate an average of 270 e-mails and 270 chats per month. There has been a steady increase in texting (about 200 messages in January–July 2009). With more promotion planned, it is expected that this service will reach about the same level as that of e-mail and chat. One librarian is assigned one hour each day to answer electronic questions, mostly e-mail, but sometimes voice mail, mail, and fax. That librarian is responsible for continuing to work on e-mails throughout his or her work shift. Four librarians and the department head and assistant manager provide coverage for Florida's collaborative statewide chat service, Ask a Librarian, which OCLS covers for approximately six hours per week. Texting is covered by one Questline staff member, and InfoQuest (a collaborative text messaging service, started July 2009) is staffed one hour per week.

The OCLS is nationally recognized as an innovative public library that is known for its high level of service excellence. The OCLS blends traditional reference services with the roving model and collaborative virtual offerings, and it is continuing to seek out newer technological approaches to continuously expand the ways in which reference queries are received and answered.

CONCLUSION

This chapter has explored the burgeoning phenomena of hybrid reference desk and tiered staffing services, using four examples from different-sized libraries to illustrate current practice in academic and public libraries. The literature review revealed a scant amount of scholarship related to hybrid and tiered staffing models. It is clear that more experimentation in public and academic libraries, as well as research, is needed to help library managers become better informed to make the critical decisions involved in considering adoption of one or both of these approaches.

According to Cassell (2010), shifting use patterns and the tightening of library budgets are rapidly changing the way reference service is delivered:

> As a result libraries are evaluating and analyzing their own situations and trying out new arrangements and new technologies that will better meet the needs of their users and deal with their own budgetary limitations. Librarians understand that one model does not fit all users and that they must be flexible in order to meet user needs. (159)

The Reference and User Services Association (RUSA)'s "Guidelines for Implementing and Maintaining Virtual Reference Services" (2004) promote the idea that there can be no universal answer to the staffing quandary and recommend that "each library should examine staffing models to determine one that is appropriate for their organization. While there is not a 'one-size-fits-all' service model, a model should be chosen which would support quality reference interactions via all modes of communication" (12). The examples provided reflect the use of different desk and staffing models that work well at the respective institutions. This kind of flexibility and variance in the provision of FtF and VR services shows the diversity of users' needs and the willingness of librarians to move well out of their comfort zones to risk unprecedented change in modes and methods of service delivery to better meet these needs.

Disclaimer: The views expressed in the preceding examples are solely those of the respondents and do not reflect the views of their organizations or anybody else affiliated with these institutions.

WORKS CITED

Bahavar, S., and J. A. Truelson. 2008. Strategic planning for reference in a team environment: The preferred futuring model. *Reference & User Services Quarterly* 47 (4): 356–363.

Bourne, J. 2005. Reference by design: Technologies to enhance a new service model at Seattle's Central Library. *Library Mosaics* 16 (3): 10–11.

Bracke, M., S. Chinnaswamy, and E. Kline. 2008. Evolution of reference: A new service model for science and engineering libraries. *Issues in Science and Technology Librarianship* 53 www.istl.org/08-winter/refereed3.html.

Brattin, B. 2005. Reorganizing reference. *Public Libraries* 44 (6): 340–346.

Cassell, K. A. 2010. Meeting users' needs through new reference service models. In *Creating the reference renaissance: Current and future trends,* ed. M. L. Radford and R. D. Lankes, 153–162. New York: Neal-Schuman.

Cassell, K. A., and U. Hiremath. 2009. *Reference and information services in the 21st century.* New York: Neal-Schuman.

Courtois, M., and M. Liriano. 2000. Tips for roving reference: How to best serve library users. *College & Research Libraries News* 61 (4): 289–290, 315.

Frey, S. M., and A. Kaiser. 2008. Still evolving or facing extinction? Reference-as-place. *Indiana Libraries* 27 (1): 42–45.

Hines, S. S. 2007. Outpost reference: Meeting patrons on their own ground. *PNLA Quarterly* 72 (1): 12–13, 26.

Kern, M. K. 2009. *Virtual reference best practices: Tailoring services to your library.* Chicago: American Library Association.

Kuchi, T., L. B. Mullen, and S. Tama-Bartels. 2004 Librarians without borders; reaching out to students at a campus center. *Reference & User Services Quarterly* 43 (4): 318–325.

Library Statistics Program: Academic Libraries. 2008. National Center for Educational Statistics (NCES) reports. Retrieved from http://www.nces.ed.gov/surveys/libraries/academic.asp.

Library Statistics Program: Public Libraries. 2008. National Center for Educational Statistics (NCES) reports. Retrieved from http://nces.ed.gov/surveys/libraries/public.asp.

Martell, C. 2008. The absent user: Physical use of academic library collections and services continues to decline, 1995–2006. *Journal of Academic Librarianship* 34 (5): 400–407.

Massey-Burzio, V. 1992. Reference encounters of a different kind: A symposium. *Journal of Academic Librarianship* 18 (5): 276–286.

Nassar, A. 1997. An evaluation of the Brandeis model of reference service at a small academic library. *Reference Librarian* 27 (58): 163–176.

Numminen, P., and P. Vakkari. 2009. Question types in public libraries' digital reference service in Finland: Comparing 1999 and 2006. *Journal of the Society for Information Science and Technology* 60 (6): 1249–1257.

Radford, M. L. 2009. A personal choice: Reference service excellence. *Reference & User Services Quarterly* 48 (2): 108–115.

Radford, M. L., and L. S. Connaway. 2007. "Screenagers" and live chat reference: Living up to the promise. *Scan* 26 (1): 31–39.

RUSA guidelines for implementing and maintaining virtual reference services. 2004. *Reference & User Services Quarterly* 44 (1): 9–14.

Ryan, S. 2008. Reference transaction analysis: The cost-effectiveness of staffing a traditional academic reference desk. *Journal of Academic Librarianship* 34 (5): 389–399.

Sonntag, G., and F. Palsson. February 2007. No longer the sacred cow, no longer a reference desk: Transforming reference service to meet 21st century user needs. *Library Philosophy and Practice,* 1–12. Retrieved September 12, 2010, from http://www.webpages.uidaho.edu/~mbolin/sonntag-palsson.htm.

vanDuinkerken, W., J. Stephens, and K. MacDonald. 2009. The chat reference interview: Seeking evidence based on RUSA's guidelines. *New Library World* 110 (3–4): 107–121.

III

NEW AND REVISED ROLES FOR REFERENCE LIBRARIANS

7

THE EMBEDDED ACADEMIC LIBRARIAN

Susan Sharpless Smith and Lynn Sutton

As public service professionals, librarians constantly seek to provide better service to their clients. Key to providing optimum service is the ability to understand user needs and perspectives. Perhaps the ultimate in user understanding is the recent phenomenon of embedded librarianship, where librarians go native by living and working alongside faculty and students in the campus environment, not just in a single visit but for the duration of the course or learning experience.

In "A Strategy for Academic Libraries in the First Quarter of the 21st Century," Lewis urged librarians to act without delay to "reposition library and information tools, resources, and expertise so that they are embedded into the teaching, learning and research enterprises" (2007, 420). The classic notion of the library as a repository for materials must be superseded by the philosophy of the library as active partner in the information experience. Public service librarians have historically been closest to the user in their daily activities of reference, library instruction, and liaison to academic departments. They can, and should, play a leading role in the quiet revolution to position themselves as full partners in the academic enterprise. Embedded librarianship is one way to do that.

BACKGROUND

The notion of getting close to users is probably as old as librarianship. Many academic libraries arose from the Germanic model of departmental units that colocated (or embedded) librarians and subject materials with the students and faculty of the academic department. That model lost favor when electronic materials began to dominate, especially in the sciences, and many departmental libraries were consolidated back into the main library. Embedded librarianship may be seen as a return to these academic roots.

The idea of actively being present with the user at the point of need, rather than waiting passively for the user to come to the library, goes back at least to the 1970s when clinical medical librarians (CMLs) began to go on rounds with doctors in hospitals. The job of the CML was to listen to the cases being discussed at the bedside, identify points of information need, and then research and supply relevant information back to the medical team. Davidoff and Florance (2000) extended the CML concept to that of an "informationist," who was seen as another specialist on the clinical team. While neither the CML nor the informationist used the term *embedded* in their titles, the concept was there.

DEFINITION

Barbara Dewey was the first to coin the phrase *embedded librarian* in her seminal 2004 article. She borrowed the term *embedded* from the practice of placing journalists into field military operations in the Iraq War. U.S. military leaders hoped that media reports would be more favorable, or at least more sympathetic, if they came from journalists who experienced the action firsthand as part of the combat team. The term is particularly apt, as the dictionary definition of *embed* is to "make something an integral part of" (Merriam-Webster, http://www.merriam-webster.com/). Dewey explained that, in her view, "overt purposefulness makes embedding an appropriate definition of the most comprehensive collaborations for librarians in the higher education community" (2004, 6).

Dewey originally took a broad view of the concept of embeddedness, drawing analogies to a wide variety of situations in the campus environment, from colocation in collaborative campus spaces, to participation in research teams, to administrative involvement in high-level campus governance, and, most pertinent to the reference librarian, to integration into the teaching and learning experience. The underlying theme to all of these collaborations was the "library's transition from passive to active, reactive to proactive, staid to lively, and singular to social" (Dewey, 2004, 6). Following this manifesto, many librarians swiftly adopted the notion of embedded librarianship, with a number of creative spin-offs reported in the literature in the next five years and summarized in the following.

MODELS

We consulted existing literature to identify and define major models of embedded librarianship. Rather than a straightforward list of models, we discovered, as did Shumaker and Tyler (2007), that the topic is more complex.

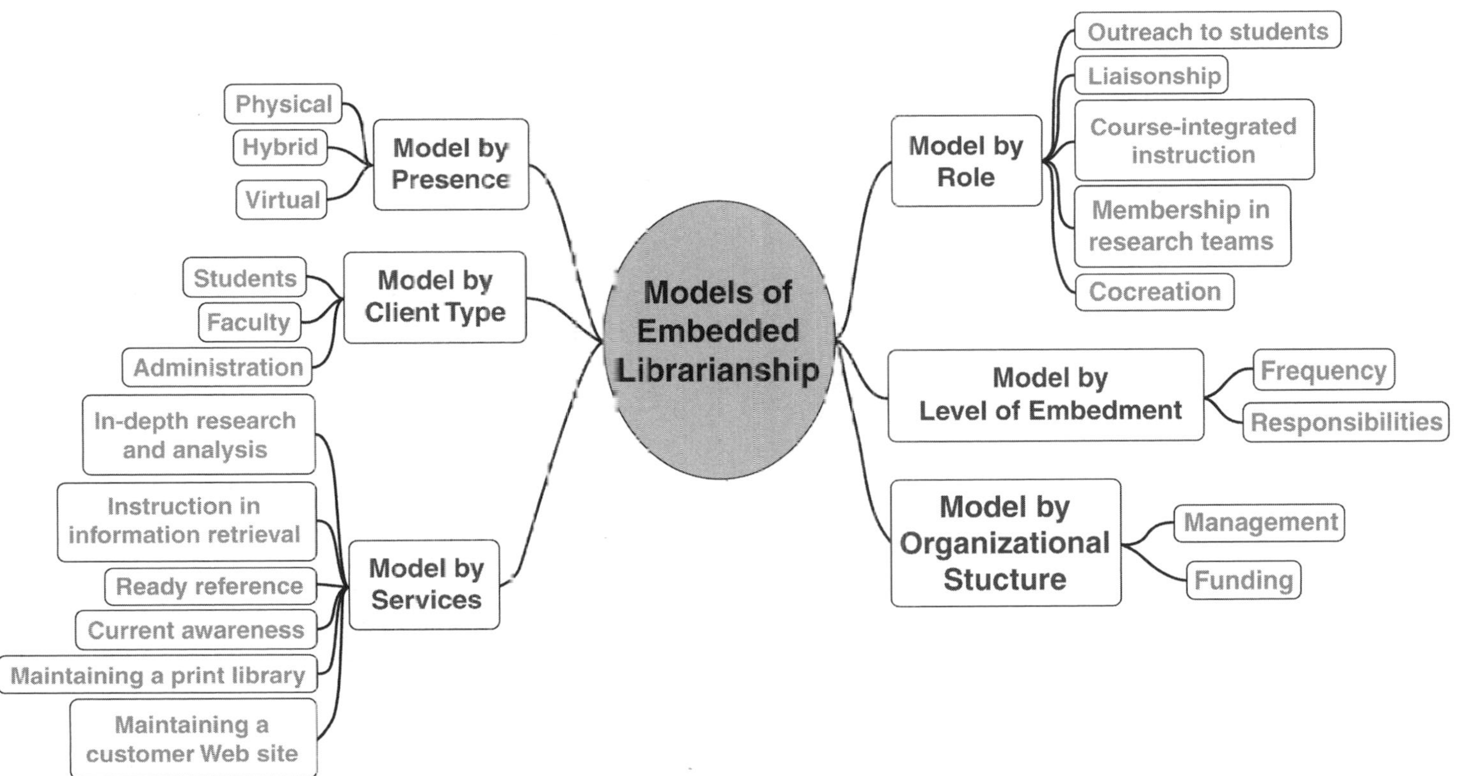

Figure 7.1. Models of Embedded Librarianship

The variety of approaches found in the literature suggests that embedded librarianship should be examined through a variety of criteria: physical versus virtual presence, librarian role and function, level of embeddedness, clientele category, types of services, and organizational structure. As might be expected with such an assortment of parameters, there are many possibilities for hybrid models to emerge. That the topic is an important one is demonstrated by the Special Libraries Association grant to Shumaker and Talley to research embedded librarianship, including identifying models (2009a). Figure 7.1 illustrates different models of embeddedness. A discussion of the various types and their characteristics follows.

MODEL BY PRESENCE

Physical

One of the most basic ways to identify embeddedness is by physical presence. One of the fundamental methods to increase interaction between librarians, faculty, and students is to venture out of the library walls and meet them in their spaces on campus. Two of the main options for accomplishing this are by finding regularly scheduled space for interactions or by establishing a permanent colocation arrangement.

Libraries have experimented with a variety of approaches to reach out to their clientele beyond the library. Many have looked around their campuses to identify high-traffic areas where they can establish a presence. Such locations include the student union, residence halls, and coffee shops. Rudin (2008) identifies this model as "outpost librarianship." However, selecting the correct location can be problematic, as some libraries have discovered that types of interactions may be directly related to the service location. For instance, Rutgers librarians, who established an Outpost Service at the Busch Campus Center, found that 82 percent of their questions were directional in nature, most in reference to the campus center. Simon Fraser University librarians took a different tack, establishing their remote locations in two faculty buildings. The majority of their questions were reference-related rather than directional. A comparison of the two approaches suggests that question types are related to the normal function of the building where a service is located (Rudin, 2008).

Colocation refers to space that is carved out in the customer's workplace for a librarian to inhabit, on either a part-time or a permanent basis. In the first instance, regularly scheduled office hours may be established, with the librarian assigned an academic department office during those hours, to facilitate accessibility for consultation with the faculty. In the second, the librarian becomes a permanent occupant in the academic department. Although the part-time model is more common in academia (Shumaker and Tyler, 2007), permanent colocation offers the most promise for true integration into the fabric of daily faculty activity. It retains the best features of former departmental libraries with the economic and logistical advantages of managing the print and electronic collection from the central library. Through this type of physical immersion a librarian has the opportunity to truly join the departmental conversations that take place both formally and informally.

A third model of embeddedness relating to physical space can be found through service-oriented collaborative campus spaces. Although there are many examples of these types of spaces located in the library, there are also innovative examples of collaborative spaces located outside the library with strong library connections, through combined services and staffing. Dewey (2004) cites examples of strategic collaborative spaces, including Washington University's Nancy Spirtas Kranzberg Studio for the Illustrated Book. This space is a partnership between the University Libraries and the School of Art. The studio is dedicated to the study of the art of the book, and Olin Library's Special Collection librarians are involved with influencing curriculum in the Arts and Sciences' Writing Program (Rogers, 2007).

A fourth model of embeddedness relating to physical location is for librarians to follow faculty and students to remote locations away from campus for both course-related instruction and/or service learning. Smith and Sutton (2008) describe a two-week road trip to the Deep South with a sociology class to study social stratification. Course-integrated instruction, technology management, and service learning in a Katrina-damaged library were integral parts of the unique, experiential course.

Virtual

Embeddedness is not limited to a physical presence. With the explosion of online learning environments in higher education, librarians have investigated ways to embed their services virtually. The most common example of virtual embedding is libraries' and librarians' presence in the course management systems (CMSs) that are standard on many campuses, such as Blackboard, Sakai, and Moodle. As use of these systems has become the norm, faculty and students have demanded that library support be integrated to provide "one-stop shopping" (Washburn, 2008). Whether through a built-in module (such as Blackboard's building blocks) or a result of local customization, use of library integration tools lends itself to librarian involvement. A minimal level of integration can take place through an automatically generated default link to library resources inserted into every class in a course shell. More ambitious approaches include the addition of course-specific links to resources, participation in discussion via e-mail and discussion boards, and the adoption of an instructor's role through writing and administering quizzes (York and Vance, 2009). York and Vance's review of the literature reveals a number of roles that librarians play in the CMS: course librarian (providing research assistance), lurking librarian (monitoring course discussion and initiating communication in response to perceived needs), technical innovator (enhancing delivery of information within the CMS through customized additions such as an RSS feed), and instructional designer.

Developments in virtual social environments have expanded embedment opportunities beyond the traditional CMS. Today's social networking technologies offer a myriad of possibilities to support reference and information literacy instruction, as well as research collaboration, by putting librarians where their users are. Over the past few years, wikis and blogs have become popular venues to establish collaborative environments for research and study. In addition to using these environments to provide services and establish a library presence, librarians have been early proponents of social networks such as Facebook and of Web 2.0 applications such as Flickr (image sharing) and Twitter (microblogging). These technologies have current functionality that facilitates library embedment (such as the ability to insert chat, RSS, library catalog, and database searching into a local or external Web site). At Wake Forest University, librarians have successfully partnered with professors in collaborative ventures to leverage the interactive capabilities of these technologies (Smith and Sutton, 2008). Facebook groups and pages have also been used effectively by the Wake Forest University librarians to serve as de facto course frameworks to promote student-driven participation and interaction within their own social spaces (Mitchell and Smith, 2009).

Library presence in virtual worlds can take embedment to the next level by providing a three-dimensional environment for communication and collaboration that reaches out to users beyond a library's defined clientele. Second Life was established in 2003; by 2006, the Alliance Library System (a consortium of Illinois libraries) created the first virtual library using avatars to provide reference services. Other libraries have followed to establish virtual facilities there as well. Those who are experimenting with this paradigm believe that there is value in establishing a presence but acknowledge technical and resource barriers to maintaining effective services (Godfrey, 2008).

MODEL BY ROLE AND LEVEL OF EMBEDMENT

A second way to define a model of embedment is to examine librarians' specific roles. As already discussed, librarians fill different roles depending on client needs and expectations. One theme that appears in the previous section is the role of research outreach to students. A subsequent librarian role has developed from a model familiar to academic librarians—that of liaison to an academic department. Traditionally, a liaison librarian interacts with the department in matters affecting collection development activities, including acquisitions of print and electronic resources. In the age of embedment, this relationship is expanding to include a more comprehensive integration into the department, thus promoting a higher degree of involvement in a department's activities. Such activities range from attending departmental meetings to serving on departmental committees (Rudin, 2008).

Kesselman and Watstein (2009) defined two types of librarian embeddedness in the academy: course-integrated instruction and membership in research teams. Course-integrated instruction is the most prevalent form of embeddedness for academic librarians and can take place in-person, virtually, or in a hybrid environment. The defining components are that the focus is on student services and that instruction is designed to address specific course content and assignments. Of course, specific roles within this model will vary depending on negotiations with the course professor. These variations can result in a different experience and level of effectiveness that is defined by the level of embedment. How frequent is contact with the students? Does the librarian interact throughout the course, or is there limited contact? What level of instruction occurs? Does the librarian provide links to resources, participate in discussions, or help design the instruction and teach the class? In a 2008 article, Bowler and Street report on their local study to determine whether different levels of librarian embedment correlated with improvement in undergraduate students' information literacy skills. They found significant improvement in students' scores when a librarian was conspicuously embedded in the classroom.

Team membership can take different forms as well. An early model of embeddedness is clinical librarianship, an idea conceived by health science librarians in the early 1970s. The model was established to meet doctors' need for quick access to the professional literature and information (Lappa, 2004). The clinical librarian's role is to provide immediate responses to information requests related to patient care. The librarian is a member of the clinical team and provides research support. An update to this model is known as the clinical informationist. These librarians work outside the library and are on the clinical department's payroll (Kesselman and Watstein, 2009). Membership as a partner in research and its outcome requires a different level of librarian specialization. In addition to their expertise in searching and evaluating information, clinical informationists need a higher level of subject expertise and increased knowledge of the faculty research process (Dewey, 2004).

A new role has emerged in recent years, that of the librarian as academic cocreator. In this model, students, faculty, and librarians are all cocreators in the research and learning process (Dewey, 2004). As scholarly communication becomes a growing focus on many campuses, so do the opportunities for collaboration between librarians, faculty, students, and administrators. It requires teamwork on the part of all stakeholders to build an infrastructure that supports knowledge creation, copyright compliance, scholarship dissemination, local and open-access publishing, and institutional repositories.

MODEL BY CLIENT TYPE

In the preceding sections, we have described various models of librarian embeddedness with regard to client type. In the academy, there are three main groups with which libraries can develop embedment opportunities: students, faculty, and administration. The group not yet detailed, but one that is key to finding acceptance and developing opportunities for leadership roles on campus, is the administration. Dewey (2004) calls the librarian in this role the "campus librarian." In this model, librarians proactively embed themselves in projects beyond the library and in the governance of the university. By involving themselves in campus-wide projects, they are able to understand campus agendas and interject the library's strategic needs into the larger university picture. Administrative departments will quickly discover the insight that the library staff can bring to the table. Some important units with which to embed include the faculty senate, campus advisory groups, university committees, the department of institutional research, the development office, information systems, academic departments, and the central administration, including, of course, the chief academic officer's office (Dewey, 2004).

MODEL BY SERVICES PERFORMED

In this model, embedded librarians are defined by the kinds of services they provide. In a 2007 survey, Shumaker and Tyler asked embedded librarians to rate the importance of the services they provided. Academic librarians rated "in-depth research and analysis projects" and "instruction in information retrieval" equally as most important. These were followed in descending importance by "ready reference," "current awareness," "maintaining a library of print materials," and "stewarding or maintaining a website for the customer group." Further research is necessary to correlate user ratings with those of librarians. Do users value the same vital services as librarians?

MODEL BY ORGANIZATIONAL STRUCTURE

Organizational embedding refers to how the embedment arrangement is funded and managed. These arrangements are variations on the traditional concept of departmental and branch libraries. In some cases, the librarian is colocated in an academic department but still reports to the central library. In others, the librarian is supervised and funded by the customer group. In academia, at the time of the 2007 survey, 88 percent of the academic librarian respondents reported to their parent central library, and only 15 percent were funded by their customer groups (Shumaker and Tyler, 2007, 26). Freiburger and Kramer's account of the Arizona Health Sciences Library's decentralized service (where librarians assigned to four academic departments were maintained on the library payroll) may convey a common rationale: "Keeping the librarians on the library payroll serves to reinforce the fact that the liaison service is a library activity and serves a common good" (2009, 140).

TRENDS AND THE FUTURE

The essence of librarianship is to identify user information needs and find ways to meet them. Both Dewey (2004) and Lewis (2007) have urged librarians to leave the library and embed themselves and their skills as deeply into the fabric of the campus environment as they can, to become equal partners in the teaching and learning experience. Embedded librarianship may be seen as the culmination of many years of movement in this direction. Academic institutions started out with numerous branch and departmental libraries on campus and then consolidated back in a central movement when digital materials became prevalent. However, the move to digital libraries had the unexpected consequence of reminding students that the library was more than a place for materials. It was also a place for help, support, and guidance in the use of those and other information materials. So, the "library as place" movement began concurrently with the migration from print to electronic materials. Similarly, as soon as departmental libraries were consolidated back into the main library or other groupings, the research began to recommend moving back into the domain of faculty and students.

Public service librarians have taken this advice to heart and introduced all the creative examples of embedded librarianship found in this chapter. They have ensconced themselves in the classroom, the lab, the student union, the dorm, the hospital bedside, the Web site, and the CMS, and they have even boarded the bus for a two-week living experience. With the inevitable march toward the digitization of the entire scholarly record, those librarians who have embedded themselves as a vital and necessary component of the user experience will make themselves indispensable.

In times of economic hardship, librarians (or administrators) who are new to the embedded experience might think it is a luxury that can be dropped to conserve resources when things get tight. Similarly, Shumaker (2009b) asked who picked up the duties that embedded librarians left behind when they boarded the bus or attended every class. With no new resources (and sometimes far fewer resources), it is difficult to maintain new programs like these. However, librarians and administrators need to look closely at which programs best meet user needs. Long-established but little-used traditions, like staffing the reference desk with professional librarians every hour of the day, might be better candidates for elimination than embedded services that prove indispensable to faculty and students. The librarian who is deeply embedded into the fabric of the campus and defines success by the accomplishment of user goals will be best equipped to survive higher education's continuing evolution, even in the most difficult economic times.

WORKS CITED

Bowler, M., and K. Street. 2008. Investigating the efficacy of embedment: Experiments in information literacy integration. *Reference Services Review* 36 (4): 438–449.

Davidoff, F., and V. Florance. 2000. The informationist: A new health profession? *Annals of Internal Medicine* 132 (12): 996–998.

Dewey, B. I. 2004. The embedded librarian: Strategic campus collaborations. *Resource & Sharing Information Networks* 17 (1–2): 5–17.

Freiburger, G., and S. Kramer. 2009. Embedded librarians: One library's model for decentralized service. *Journal of the Medical Library Association* 97 (2): 139–142.

Godfrey, K. 2008. A new world for virtual reference. *Library Hi Tech* 26 (4): 525–539.

Kesselman, M. A., and S. B. Watstein. 2009. Creating opportunities: Embedded librarians. *Journal of Library Administration* 49 (4): 383–400.

Lappa, E. 2004. Clinical librarianship (CL): A historical perspective. *Electronic Journal of Academic and Special Librarianship* 5 (2–3). Retrieved July 27, 2009, from http://southernlibrarianship.icaap.org/content/v05n02/lappa_e01.htm.

Lewis, D. 2007. A strategy for academic libraries in the first quarter of the 21st century. *College & Research Libraries* 68 (5): 418–434.

Mitchell, E, and S. S. Smith. 2009. Bringing information literacy into the social sphere: A case study using social software to teach information literacy at WFU. *Journal of Web Librarianship* 3 (3): 183–197.

Rogers, B. 2007. Studio speaks volumes. *Washington University in St. Louis Magazine.* Retrieved July 27, 2009, from http://magazine.wustl.edu/Fall07/StudioSpeaksVolumes.htm.

Rudin, P. 2008. No fixed address: The evolution of outreach library services on university campuses. *Reference Librarian* 49 (1): 55–75.

Shumaker, D. 2009a. Good news: Embedded librarian research funded. *The embedded librarian: Exploring new, embedded roles for librarians in organizations of all types.* Retrieved July 27, 2009, from http://embeddedlibrarian.wordpress.com.

Shumaker, D. 2009b. Who let the librarians out? *Reference & User Services Quarterly* 48 (3): 239–242.

Shumaker, D., and L. A. Tyler. 2007. *Embedded library services: An initial inquiry into practices for their development, management, and delivery.* Paper presented at the Special Libraries Association Annual Conference, Denver, Colorado, June 6, 2007. Retrieved July 27, 2009, from http://www.sla.org/pdfs/sla2007/ShumakerEmbeddedLibSvcs.pdf.

Smith, S. S., and L. Sutton. 2008. Embedded librarians: On the road in the deep south. *College & Research Libraries News* 69 (2): 71–74, 85.

Washburn, A. 2008. Finding the library in Blackboard: An assessment of library integration. *MERLOT Journal of Online Learning and Teaching* 4 (3): 301–316.

York, A. C., and J. M. Vance. 2009. Taking library instruction into the online classroom: Best practices for embedded librarians. *Journal of Library Administration* 49 (1–2): 197–209.

ADDITIONAL READINGS

Callison, R., D. Budny, and K. Thomes. 2005. Library research project for first-year engineering students: Results from collaboration by teaching and library faculty. *Reference Librarian* 43: 93–106.

Cochrane, C. 2006. Embedding information literacy in an undergraduate management degree: Lecturers' and students' perspectives. *Education for Information* 24 (2–3): 97–123.

Dugan, M. 2008. Embedded librarians in an ag econ class: Transcending the traditional. *Journal of Agricultural & Food Information* 9 (4): 301–309.

Foutch, L. J., B. Griffith, L. A. Lannom, D. Sommer, and S. Weiner. 2007. How to embed a librarian. In *Uncharted waters: Tapping the depths of our community to enhance learning: Thirty-fifth National Library Instruction Conference Proceedings*, ed. B. Sietz, 51–56. Ypsilanti, MI: LOEX Press.

Gordon, R. S., and M. Stephens. 2007. Embedding a librarian in your web site using Meebo. *Computers in Libraries* 27 (8): 44–45.

Grassian, E., and R. B. Trueman. 2007. Stumbling, bumbling, teleporting and flying… librarian avatars in Second Life. *Reference Services Review* 35 (1): 84–89.

Hall, R. A. 2008. The "embedded" librarian in a freshman speech class. *College & Research Libraries News* 69 (1): 28–30.

Hearn, M. R. 2005. Embedding a librarian in the classroom: An intensive information literacy model. *Reference Services Review* 33 (2): 219–227.

Hightower, B., C. Rawl, and M. Schutt. 2008. Collaborations for delivering the library to students through WebCT. *Reference Services Review* 35 (4): 541–551.

Kearley, J. P., and L. Phillips. 2005. Embedding library reference services in online courses. *Internet Reference Services Quarterly* 9 (1–2): 65–76.

Kelly, R. 2008. Team teaching with an embedded librarian. *Online Classroom* (October): 7–8.

Kinnie, J. 2006. The embedded librarian: Bringing library services to distance learners. In *22nd Annual Conference on Distance Teaching and Learning*. Retrieved July 27, 2009, from http://www.uwex.edu/disted/conference/Resource_library/proceedings/06_4327.pdf.

Kresh, D. 2005. Going where the users are: We'll get there only if we want to. *Advances in Librarianship* 29: 133–158.

LaBaugh, R. T. 2008. Embedded library, embedded librarian: Strategies for providing reference services in online courseware. In *The desk and beyond: Next generation reference services*, ed. S. K. Steiner and M. M. Leslie, 53–64. Chicago: Association of College and Research Libraries.

Lampert, L. 2005. "Getting psyched" about information literacy: A successful faculty-librarian collaboration for educational psychology and counseling. *Reference Librarian* 43: 5–23.

Love, M., and S. Norwood. 2007. Finding our way as "embedded librarians." *College & Undergraduate Libraries* 14 (4): 87–93.

Manuel, K., S. E. Beck, and M. Molloy. 2005. An ethnographic study of attitudes influencing faculty collaboration in library instruction. *Reference Librarian* 43: 139–161.

Matthew, V., and A. Schroeder. 2006. The embedded librarian program. *EDUCAUSE Quarterly* 29 (4): 61–65.

McGuinness, C. 2006. What faculty think—Exploring the barriers to information literacy development in undergraduate education. *Journal of Academic Librarianship* 32 (6): 573–582.

Mitchell, E., and S. B. Watstein. 2007. The places where students and scholars work, collaborate, share and plan. *Reference Services Review* 35 (4): 521–524.

Owens, R. 2008. Where the students are: The embedded librarian project at Daytona Beach College. *Florida Libraries* 51 (1): 8–10.

Owusu-Ansah, E. K. 2004. Information literacy and higher education: Placing the academic library in the center of a comprehensive solution. *Journal of Academic Librarianship* 30 (1): 3–16.

Partello, P. 2005. Librarians in the classroom. *Reference Librarian* 43: 107–120.

Ramsay, K. M., and J. Kinnie. 2006. The embedded librarian. *Library Journal* 131 (6): 34–35.

Seamans, N. H., and P. Metz. 2002. Virginia Tech's innovative college librarian program. *College & Research Libraries* 63 (4): 324–332.

Shepley, S. E. 2009. Building a virtual campus: Librarians as collaborators in online course development and learning. *Journal of Library Administration* 49 (1–2): 89–95.

Smith, N. M., and P. Presser. 2005. Embed with the faculty: Legal information skills online. *Journal of Academic Librarianship* 31 (3): 247–262.

Stewart, V. D. 2007. Embedded in the blackboard jungle: The embedded librarian program at Pulaski Technical College. *Arkansas Libraries* 64 (3): 29–32.

Wheeler, A. 2008. Teaching old dirt new tricks. *College & Research Libraries News* 69 (2): 80–81.

8

COMMUNITY REFERENCE WORK

James LaRue

> The question once was, "What can a library be?" Today the question is, "What can a library do?" Formerly it was a question of resources, of number of books, of wealth, of material. Now, it is rather a question of effectiveness, of vitality, of influence in the community.
>
> John Cotton Dana, 1898 (in Hadley, 1943, 40–41)

The library profession grapples with a few questions again and again. How can we best serve the people in our community? How can we secure their support through an incontrovertible and compelling demonstration of our value? And now, in a time when Google and the Kindle are on the rise and newspapers are falling, how do libraries discover or invent a sustainable business model?

There are several public library trends that I believe will carry us well into the 21st century. Among them are swiftly responsive collection development and merchandising that focuses on what people actually want; expansion and deepening of children's storytelling that consciously connects to research on emergent literacy; and marketing to grow not just library use but also library support.

But what of reference? The trend is clear: If reference librarians were once the second place people looked for "information" (after consulting a friend or family member), we are now third—or worse (Rainie, Estabrook, and Witt, 2007). Our patrons go first to Google, then to the Web at large, a place so diverting we may never see them again. Google has had at least two interesting effects. First is the commercialization of information through attendant advertising. A second is the trivialization of information. It used to be hard to find facts. Now it's easy, or at least Google's interface is far more immediately satisfying than most interactions with our catalogs or staff. That leaves reference librarians looking, to the average person, a little less rare or necessary.

But I believe that our reference librarians may be part of a strategy to make the public library indispensable to its community. Our communities *need* reference librarians. Here is my thesis: Reference librarians can bring essential problem-solving skills to important community issues. Investing our time in this strategic direction is not only worthwhile in its own right but also good for libraries and good for librarianship.

FROM COMMUNITY PROJECT TO COMMUNITY ASSET

Since the inception of public library reference services, most of our tasks have been, in Greer and Grover's terms, either *passive* (the acquisition and organization of resources) or *reactive* (the staffing of public service desks, from which we await mostly individual requests for information).[1] Moreover, most of our reference transactions fall pretty low on the information hierarchy (where that hierarchy moves from random data, to more contextualized information, to more comprehensive or new knowledge, to wisdom). We compete with Google at the lowest level of information—answering trivia questions ("What is the capital of North Dakota?").

On occasion we get meatier questions. Library users may be seeking a larger context, something approaching real information ("Given the lifestyle preferences of the region, what new business might I establish that would be likely to do well here?"). Even then, librarians tend to compile resources and hand them over. We provide information, but we do little to help make it useful for decision making or learning.

Greer and Grover pose a model for a more *assertive* style of library reference service that closely parallels the emerging process for what we have come to call "community reference projects" at the Douglas County Libraries. These projects have far more in common with true *research* (a systematic approach to the development of new knowledge) than the more ready-reference model of today's libraries. If handled with true professional competence, such projects have the power to add significant value to, or indeed transform, our communities.

AN EXPERIMENT

As a county-wide library director, I attend a lot of meetings. I began to notice that one topic came up almost everywhere I went: the development of a thriving downtown. The questions were often very pointed: How many blocks long must a business district be to "work"? How tall should the buildings be? What kind of parking (parallel, angled, structured) best generates pedestrian activity? What architectural styles were "native" to the area? The motive was clear: These business people wanted to make more money but also wanted to coordinate with the larger cultural concerns of their communities to ensure that capital projects (road improvements around water system upgrades and the like) actually improved the larger social environment. There was some urgency: Such capital projects were already underway.

At about this time, a recent graduate of a local library science program, working as a reference librarian, came to talk to me. Given all that was going on at our system, she wondered, was there even a future for reference librarianship? I said I thought there was and invited her to come to the next meeting of the still-developing Downtown Development Committee (DDC), mainly composed of business property owners in one of our municipalities. I explained that they were working on some things that were of interest to our entire community, and I thought they needed some assistance.

When I introduced this librarian, Colbe Galston, the business people were friendly but unimpressed. "My wife and kids love the library!" they said. It was obvious that they couldn't think of any way in which the library had relevance to their own concerns. When I said that the work they were doing was so important that I was assigning a reference librarian to it, they were baffled.

A year later, things had changed. Colbe was a valued member of the team. That group of business people eventually spearheaded a library funding campaign, raising over $100,000 for us. Not to put too fine a point on it, the end result of our process was not just increased respect for librarians. It was a demonstrable success in generating significant financial commitment and support.

THE PROCESS: CASE STUDY 1

Environmental Scan: Cataloging the Community

More formal planning models may begin with community analysis: demographics, surveys, lifestyle trends, and geographic information system layers. Our DDC project process at this stage was more casual. It leveraged existing community contacts. While I believe more formal methods have their place, a great deal of insight can be gathered far more simply by just asking some group of people to identify community leaders, then interviewing those leaders.

This process might begin as a staff or board meeting, where people brainstorm a list of other people believed to be important. Ideally, the board, director, and staff *are* community leaders. But even people who aren't leaders know about them, at least some of them. Probably, it's the library director or senior staff who facilitates this discussion. This information can then be handed over to reference staff to work up contact information. This is the beginning of a catalog of the community: identification of key information resources that just happen to be people. Who are the players?

A related list of contacts might be organizational. That is, which *groups* are working on important community projects? Then reference librarians might visit those groups and, through observation, identify key leaders within them. Yes, this means leaving the building, and yes, it means paying librarians to do so.

The Reference Interview

The follow-up is, ultimately, a reference interview. But this time, the reference librarian makes the appointment. Then she asks the identified leaders, perhaps over lunch, a few straightforward questions: What are you working on? What else is hot right now? What do you think are the emerging issues in the community? Who else should we be talking to? A deeper level of interviewing might probe what kinds of information needs are holding up important decisions. For instance, "What do you wish you knew about this issue?" Another librarian might come along to record the answers and push for any follow-up questions.

There is great power in this approach. Community leaders are steeped in the concerns of their contacts. While there may be issues not on the radar, and maybe some efforts are not as significant as leaders believe them to be, leaders "make meaning"—boil down and interpret a lot of facts into remarkably succinct statements of community need.

There is a secondary effect. Interviewing important people, listening carefully to their concerns, is tremendously flattering to them and so captures their attention. Through this kind of interview, I have seen leaders begin to think of the library in a different way—as a community asset that may have been overlooked. Sometimes, questions come the other way: How many people visit the library in a day? What kind of effect is the Internet having on library use? How many people does the library employ? It is often wise to take along some marketing information—an annual report or quick facts brochure. It's human nature to be interested in the people who are interested in us.

While my focus is public libraries, I believe this approach is adaptable to other library types. Academic environments have their own leaders. They, too, constantly assess the significance of trends, threats, and opportunities around them. The same is true in a school or corporate environment. Surely, identifying and evaluating such leaders is at least as significant a professional task as the creation of a bibliography.

As an aside, one of our internal leadership development groups recently suggested that instead of buying another reference database, we create our own, combining aspects of customer relations management software with the information retrieval and reporting options of library catalogs. It would be useful, they thought, to be able to see who had been interviewed and what issues had been raised.

Assigning and Researching the Questions

In the case of the DDC, the series of interviews with business leaders yielded something a little surprising to staff: some clearly identifiable reference questions. The branch manager met with her reference staff to talk about them. For instance, were there any other significant downtown redevelopment projects in towns of similar size that local leaders could learn from? Then the manager asked who had an interest in the various topics. There were ready volunteers. Reference librarians, already wired to respond to the thrill of the chase, enjoyed the challenge. This was something they understood, a good match for their existing professional skills. Because they had some lead time, the reference librarians were really able to do some digging. It didn't take long to come back with heaps of material.

The Executive Summary

In fact, our librarians found too much material. Quickly, they realized that walking back into the DDC meeting with a grocery cart full of paper simply wasn't helpful. What the business people wanted was not an undigested pile of information. They wanted to know not what the librarians *found* but what it *meant.*

The library manager asked an intelligent question: "Has anyone ever written an executive summary?" One of our reference librarians, a former medical librarian, had indeed. The skill is far more common in special libraries than in public libraries. This librarian then worked with the librarians who had done the research to reduce the pile to the core ideas, a two-page report per question that weeded out fluff and redundancy and focused on what mattered.

Delivering the Answer

Further reflection demonstrated that even an executive summary wasn't enough. The business people hoped to hear a presentation. The library manager again asked for volunteers. Colbe was more than happy to work with her colleagues and our community relations department to put together and practice a PowerPoint package that summarized the summaries. She wowed them.

The business people, to whom it would never have occurred to take such questions to a librarian, were stunned. You mean, they asked, I can ask a big question, and for no charge, the library is able to provide such comprehensive, focused, and digestible answers? Not exactly, we said. Your business taxes have prepaid for this service already.

The information we provided (also posted on our Web site[2]) profoundly influenced the priorities of the group and were used to lobby the town. The result was a far more attractive, inviting, and successful downtown than would otherwise have been the case. The research made a difference in people's lives. Colbe went from "mascot" status to valued partner. The telling detail: Meetings did not begin until Colbe arrived.

Two points should be made about this. First, some librarians will be terrified by the prospect of delivering the answer. But not every librarian has to. Some may be better at interviews, some at research, some at summarizing, some at preparing presentations, and only a few need to stand in front of a large group and present the package. At the same time, forward-thinking libraries may want to start advertising for, and hiring for, a full range of such skills as a new definition of professional expectations. Second, the library answer, the library resource, may not always be research. Responding to a community need might call, instead, for making professional staff available to facilitate a group or plan a conference, providing meeting space after hours, teaming up to work on a grant, or loaning some equipment. The answer varies with the question.

Evaluating (and Ending) the Project

A caveat: Having your own librarian is a very nice thing for a group. The DDC went from being baffled about what they might do with one to assuming that they now had this highly prized asset on permanent assignment. But the community reference project is not open-ended. It should be rigorously managed. When the answer has been delivered, a formal evaluation should be conducted. That might take several forms: an online survey, a follow-up interview with key leaders, or a group evaluation. Several messages are conveyed: We approached you because you were doing something important; we added value to your project; with your help, we can be even more effective in the future; and most important, *the project is done,* and we wonder if you have any thoughts about other pressing community needs.

Here's what I observed: Announcing that the project is done reminds everyone of just how significant the role of the library may have been. As one business person told the group, our involvement added enormous credibility to their efforts, particularly when talking with town officials. Then it was fun to see canny business people trying to secure library staff for their own pet projects, to which we replied that we would allocate our resources on the basis of projects where we thought we could really make a difference and those that reflected significant community impact. In fact, such a dialogue with leaders not only underscores the desirability of making sure the library has a seat at the table for anything important but also broadens the whole arena of civic engagement, beginning the shared process of better coordinating community-wide leadership around a real agenda of improvement.

Repeating the Process

Then, I believe, the whole process starts over: an annual scanning for significant projects, follow-up to zero in on the real needs, assignment of staff to research, summarization of the information, delivery, and evaluation.

BOTTOMS UP: CASE STUDY 2

Staff Time: Use It or Lose It

The most frequent objection to this model comes from librarians: I don't have time for this! But recent technological innovations may well transform staffing models from the bottom up, freeing a significant number of professional hours. Over a decade ago now, I set up a staff committee to answer a deceptively simple question: What can we stop doing? In other words, what do we spend a whole bunch of time doing now that, if we stopped, would give us time to do more important things?

It didn't take long to find an answer. At that moment in our library's history, we were still telephoning our patrons to say that the materials they placed on hold had come in. Even with volunteer labor, this was becoming extraordinarily time-intensive. A software package, sold by our integrated library service (ILS) vendor, seemed expensive—but not when we realized how much human capital we were dedicating to the task. So we bought and installed the software.

About a month before that happened, I spoke to our branch managers. "We are about to receive a gift," I said. "This gift is the most precious thing we have: staff time. But there's a danger. If we don't immediately redirect that time to other things, we will lose it." We talked about what we wanted to do with that time—improve the quality of our service. We suspected that a lot of people who came to the library never had that conversation at just the right time to make sure they found what they needed. We were going to lose our staff, recently liberated from the telephone, into the stacks. They were to become friendly ambassadors and guides.

It didn't happen. Perhaps there just wasn't enough lead time to think this through. Perhaps the managers didn't really think we would gain so much time. Perhaps it is human nature to gear up for a crisis but to take the luxury of too much help in stride. Perhaps I just didn't convince anybody that we had to seize the moment.

In the short run, the immediate reduction in work, in frantic busyness, was obvious. And when there was a vacancy, there was no great need to hurry about a replacement. Eventually, of course, the volume of library business grew. Staff discovered a host of endlessly fascinating and time-intensive tasks that really deserved attention. Just one year later, we were surprised to find ourselves short-staffed. Again.

SELF-CHECK

For about a decade, our library was fortunate enough to see its revenues grow along with demand. But eventually we found ourselves faced with a new business problem: We were out of space, and the circulation process had become an expensive bottleneck both for staff-assisted checkout and back-room check-in. We needed three to five people at the circulation desk; we needed five to six people in the back room. And it was starting to take us almost two days to get returned materials back on the shelves. The solution we'd used before—build a new and bigger library—wasn't going to happen in a time of new fiscal constraints. It was time for a change in the business model.

My then–associate director of information technology, Bob Pasicznyuk, went on several jaunts to look at RFID-enabled self-check and automated material-handling systems. He put together an internal task force that looked at products from various vendors. This time, we did it right. We didn't want to just install a new machine and keep the same number people hanging around to watch it. Our analysis suggested that these new technologies, if accompanied by the radical redesign of work flow they made possible, could reduce the number of people required for checkout and check-in by almost two-thirds. How were we going to manage that? That is, how were we going to, in fact, make sure that we captured the benefit of that staff time?

I'll condense a two-year story to two sentences: We rolled out a project timeline to weed and re-barcode our collection and install the self-check and automated material-handling units throughout the system. At the same time, we launched a human resources and training program to redefine the job description of the circulation clerk to something new: a paraprofessional who worked more closely with the reference staff.

Our circulation staff were naturally concerned that they would simply lose their jobs. But we promised them something else: Yes, jobs would certainly be eliminated as people left. As clerks left through attrition—not forced layoffs—we said we'd take the money and apply it to the new job description. The people who remained, the people who took the training for the new paraprofessional job, were getting raises, paid for by the folks who left. And so a large pool of library clerks became a smaller pool of a new category of library worker.

As it happens, we really did need far fewer people to manage the circulation process. What used to take two days to shelve was reduced to less than two hours. The new paraprofessionals loved their jobs, which involved far more merchandising, book talking, and more interesting, more *meaningful* interactions with patrons. In short, it worked: We used technology to solve a real business problem, managed to create new and more engaging opportunities for our staff, and, in the process, improved service from every angle.

DING-DONG, THE DESK IS DEAD

It shortly became clear that we hadn't just reduced the size of the circulation department. Self-check stations took up surprisingly little space. Since our big honking circulation desk was redundant, we realized we could get rid of it. It will surprise no one to learn that initially there was strong staff resistance to this. When we pulled out the circulation desk, we freed up more space for displays. That display eventually turned into the "power wall"—an ever-changing display as fresh as yesterday's book returns. We saw a big jump in use—which our new systems enabled us to absorb with ease.

When you reduce the circulation staff, then take away the fortress of the desk, when you start intermingling the floor supervision and patron contact of former circulation clerks and reference librarians, you've fundamentally changed both the social and administrative structure of the library. You have, in fact, dismantled the circulation department and taken a step toward a more integrated staffing model. I don't think we realized that when we invested in self-check.

INTEGRATED TEAMS (HOW MANY OF WHOM?)

Another objection to this model might be summed up like this: "Who is minding the store while the librarians are away?" Indeed, we began to detect a significant source of friction in what was rapidly becoming a one-stop staff desk, the former reference desk. The friction had several sources:

- While over 90 percent of circulation was now handled by our self-check systems, 10 percent still needed some staff intervention. Not surprisingly, the former circulation clerks were better at that than the reference librarians.
- The workload of the combined desk had a higher number of circulation-related issues than reference questions, making the reference librarians feel like overpaid (and undertrained) clerks.
- Two independent studies (one through an analysis of phone calls through our central telephone system, called the Contact Center, and one conducted by University of Denver master of library science [MLS] students observing the desk) determined that 85 percent of the questions received could be easily handled by our new paraprofessionals; an MLS was necessary just 15 percent of the time.

- The new paraprofessionals, proud of their new skills, were eager to use them. Sometimes, the reference staff felt that the paraprofessionals got in over their heads, offering incomplete or incorrect information and failing to hand the patron over to someone more qualified.

To put it another way, the reference librarians now felt just as threatened as the circulation clerks once had. The fortress of the reference desk—once a haven for degreed professionals—was besieged by pretenders. There was some jousting for status and some hurt feelings on both sides. Some paraprofessionals felt belittled and mistrusted; some professionals felt devalued and humiliated.

We have made great progress in building newer, stronger teams. That took pointed training in the art of the "handoff." It took some crucial conversations with staff. It took managerial attention to the most productive use of professional staff and the results of "off-desk" time. It took structural changes in supervision. It took time.

This drama will be replayed in many of our libraries over the next few years, and it needs thoughtful preparation and focus. It is good that we have replaced a clerical job with a more interesting paraprofessional position. Professional jobs need to get more interesting, too. While in-library patron contact with professionals still has enormous value, the plain truth is that there are bigger problems to be solved and questions to be answered.

I want to emphasize something I addressed at the beginning of this piece: Librarians have been trying for a long time to demonstrate their value to society. I began to notice that this quest for value was concentrated within our own buildings, among our own staff. But that's wrong, isn't it? Library workers shouldn't be fighting for status among themselves. The people whose perceptions we need to change are outside the library. That status is best secured by unified teams who respect the contributions of all and work together to answer questions that nobody would have walked in our doors to deliver. We must leave the building and thoughtfully identify, and assist in solving, *other people's* problems.

CONCLUSION

Next, Douglas County Libraries is attempting not only to synchronize the management of our projects with the budget cycle but also to investigate community projects that tie into strategic priorities for the library: early childhood literacy, a strong response to the current recession through a contribution to economic development, and the general investigation of positive community outcomes as a measure of library efficacy. There are many potential partnerships.

In addition to this larger example, our librarians have also done a number of smaller community reference projects (researching foreclosure trends for another nearby town, for instance) and find that our perceived value grows with each one of them. I am pleased to report that the shift to larger concerns, more group contacts, and a fuller range of professional services is of particularly keen interest to our newer librarians.

John Cotton Dana announced the need for a new kind of library over 100 years ago. We still don't have it. But with the right kind of reference librarian, we can.

NOTES

1. For more information on Roger C. Greer and Robert J. Grover's use of the phrases *passive, reactive, and assertive reference* see R. C. Greer, R. J. Grover, and S. G. Fowler's 2007 book *Introduction to the Library and Information Professions* (Westport, CT: Libraries Unlimited), pages 142–143.

2. Much of the information is posted on our Web site. See http://www.douglascountylibraries.org/Research/iGuides/DDC.

WORKS CITED

Hadley, C. 1943. *John Cotton Dana: A sketch.* Chicago: American Library Association.

Rainie, L., L. Estabrook, and E. Witt. 2007. *Information searches that solve problems.* Pew Internet & American Life Project. Retrieved November 14, 2009, from http://www.pewinternet.org/Reports/2007/Information-Searches-That-Solve-Problems.aspx.

9

CONTEMPORARY AND FUTURE ROLES FOR READERS' ADVISORY IN PUBLIC LIBRARIES

Barry Trott and Neil Hollands

As reference librarianship enters the 21st century, there continues to be a great deal of discussion over and concern about the future of both reference work and the reference librarian. The traditional model of reference work, in many minds, is no longer relevant to the needs of users. In many academic and public libraries, reference statistics are declining, which is a concern for librarians and library administrators (O'Gorman and Trott, 2009). In light of these concerns, many libraries are reemphasizing readers' advisory (RA) services in order to remain relevant to their users. While the renaissance of RA has primarily been a public library phenomenon, academic libraries are also exploring the value of expanding RA services in light of declining reference statistics (Elliott, 2007). RA service offers librarians the opportunity to connect with users and to remain vital to their user communities.

Since the earliest days of librarianship in the United States, there has been an emphasis on connecting readers with books. In 1876, Samuel S. Green noted that "the more freely a librarian mingles with readers, and the greater the amount of assistance he renders them, the more intense does the conviction of citizens, also, become, that the library is a useful institution " (Green, 1876, 81). Over the last century and a quarter, the emphasis on working with readers in libraries has waxed and waned with professional and cultural changes. Since the 1980s, though, RA has had an increasingly prominent role on the public services side of librarianship. That decade saw three events that would mark the beginning of the revitalization of RA services and that continue to influence the library profession in the 21st century. These events were the publication of the first major print tool for readers' advisors, Betty Rosenberg's *Genreflecting* (1982); the establishment of the first group of librarians who shared an interest in and a passion for RA, Chicago's Adult Reading Roundtable (ARRT), in 1984; and the publication of the first guide to working with readers, Joyce Saricks and Nancy Brown's *Readers' Advisory Service in the Public Library* (1989). Saricks and Brown were the first to define the concept of "appeal" as a major tool in connecting readers with books. These events served as models for the development of RA services in terms of the creation of print, and later online, resources; the coming together of librarians to discuss and refine both the theory and practice of RA services; and the continuing emphasis on developing skills as a readers' advisor.

Over the past 25 years, interest in RA services has grown exponentially. Dozens of print tools for readers' advisors offer assistance in connecting readers with books. Online subscription databases offer librarians and readers access to vast amounts of book and author information. There has also been a proliferation of free Web sites devoted to genres, authors, and reading. It is a rare library conference that does not have at least a session or two on some aspect of readers' services. RA services have also expanded into the area of nonfiction RA, and titles continue to be published that address the theory and practice of RA.

As librarianship enters the second decade of the 21st century, RA services seem to have a firmly established role in library public services. However, in difficult budget times, RA services must still compete for resources to remain viable. With this in mind, it is useful to reexamine the value that RA services bring to the library, especially when collection budgets are reduced and fewer new books enter the library.

THE BENEFITS OF RA

The practice of RA is good for patrons, good for collections, and good for librarians. RA occurs at any place where those three elements—librarians, patrons, and collections—combine in library practice. Consider the many important results that RA can achieve: RA retains a personal touch in an increasingly impersonal world. While automated methods of advisory exist online, the best RA can occur only when a skilled practitioner listens carefully to a reader, asks questions to further understand the reader's needs, compares that reader's preferences with a broad base of knowledge about books, and shares possible suggestions. Whether completed in person or online, this is a complex interpersonal transaction requiring both art and skill. What results builds relationships between readers and librarians. When practiced well, it creates a bond between the user and the library institution.

Without the added value of advisory practice, a library collection has little more to offer than those collections found in bookstores or on Web sites. While the library collection has the advantage of being free, there are the downsides of longer waiting periods for desirable items, aging and sometimes dirty materials, and limited periods of use. Developments on the Internet, in electronic books, and in the growth of print-on-demand publishing will continue to make access to new materials ever easier. To remain relevant, libraries must make themselves into more than distribution points. We must add value to the process of getting books and other materials.

RA creates this added value. By advertising and practicing RA, libraries create a special place for readers, a place that welcomes them as individuals and as a community. Readers learn not only that they can find books at the library but also that they can get help in finding the books that are most likely to educate and entertain them. Instead of being treated as parts of a supply-and-demand equation, they can get individualized service that provides them with fitting reading, regardless of which demographics they inhabit.

Maintaining collections of older books is a double-edged proposition. These collections provide ready access to materials that may be difficult to obtain in stores, where new and popular items get most of the attention. Lacking media promotion, and gathered into daunting stacks, these books can confuse experienced readers and completely baffle new readers. How does one begin to make selections? In libraries where advisory isn't practiced well, the answer is that one generally doesn't and that lovely collections turn into moldering museums where some of the greatest treasures suffer from disuse. RA provides the solution, connecting readers with older books and midlist authors, creating entry points into a library's carefully selected collection. Whether through book lists, displays, or direct suggestion during discussion, RA methods provide a means for advocating books that the mass media largely ignore.

The proof that RA is a welcomed, value-added service can be found at any public library service desk. In an era when Google searches and other online tools are driving down the overall number of reference questions (Applegate, 2008), the demand for RA is increasing. Libraries that practice advisory well have seen the number of reference transactions hold steady, an important benefit in times when money is tight and reference jobs are among those on the line. Libraries that don't invest energy in advisory may find the extent of their reference departments difficult to justify to cost-cutters.

In addition to improving circulation of older materials, RA also benefits the collection by informing collection decisions (Orr, 2008). We make the best decisions when we know our readers, and the easiest way to know them is to talk with them. Where RA is practiced well, librarians become aware of local reader interests, of key books that have quietly left the collection, even of worn copies. They become cognizant of forthcoming books and of community demands that might make certain unexpected items locally popular.

Finally, the practice of RA builds librarian skills, providing on-the-job continuing education. It's no coincidence that in public libraries, many of the happiest, most productive librarians are RA specialists. Interacting regularly with readers, researching materials across genres and collections, keeping up with authors, and learning to use all the tools necessary for good RA service provides challenging but rewarding work that reminds librarians and other library staff of their profession's value and keeps a job fresh that could become stale if practiced passively.

TRADITIONAL ELEMENTS OF RA SERVICE IN THE PUBLIC LIBRARY

Many different practices fall under the umbrella of RA. Traditionally, these have been divided into *passive* and *active* RA, but these terms aren't accurate, as there is nothing passive about proactively creating displays, lists, and reference tools and taking them to readers who might never approach a desk. In search of better terminology, we borrow from the model of distance learning and divide RA into *synchronous*, or face-to-face transactions in which both librarian and reader engage in dialogue in a common place and time, and *asynchronous* transactions, those in which the advisory takes place without direct, real-time contact.

Face-to-Face RA

The most fundamental practice of RA still occurs when a reader encounters a librarian and receives help in finding books (Saricks, 2005; Wright, 2008). In a process that somewhat mirrors a reference interview, the librarian asks questions that summarize the patron's reading history and help the patron identify the appeal factors that he or she enjoys in books. Then, sometimes heading directly to the stacks and other times employing the catalog, lists, RA books, or databases, the librarian introduces a reasonable number of relevant book suggestions from which the reader can choose.

This kind of synchronous RA is a complicated and delicate process. The best practitioners of face-to-face RA (1) are nonjudgmental, (2) listen actively, (3) have wide book knowledge and the curiosity and reference skills to supplement that knowledge on the fly, (4) balance subtlety and enthusiasm, (5) seek out potential customers, and (6) find ways to follow up and build the relationship with the reader.

One of the most difficult skills of RA is remaining nonjudgmental. The goal of the RA transaction is not to provide the reader with books that the advisor thinks are the best but to match the reader with books that she or he will find enjoyable and useful. This means creating a mix of suggestions, both those that are down the middle of the reader's interests and those that offer opportunities to make tentative explorations into related work, if the reader is so inclined. Many librarians become frustrated with the popularity of a few best sellers when they are aware of underappreciated authors and books across the genres—books that they may consider superior. When practicing advisory, though, they must balance the desire to educate with an ongoing commitment to getting readers books that they want and that will keep them coming back for more.

To achieve this balance, good advisors listen actively. Instead of jumping for the first suggestion that comes to mind, they continue to ask questions, paraphrase reader's responses to confirm understanding, help provide readers with the vocabulary to describe their preferences, and ask for feedback to ensure that suggestions are on the right track. While time pressure may constrict this ability to fully measure reader preferences, the advisor should never forget to balance listening with advising.

The most confident advisors have wide book knowledge. This may require reading in, or at least about, genres and subjects that do not appeal to them personally, particularly if requests for advice in these genres consistently create a stumbling block in practice. Since the list of books and authors is forever expanding, the search for such knowledge will remain rewarding and challenging across an advisor's career. The best advisors retain curiosity about new books after years of research and make use of a suite of research tools that they can employ quickly when gaps in knowledge leave them unable to provide suggestions.

RA requires both subtlety and enthusiasm. Some promotion of suggested books is usually welcome. Enthusiasm is contagious, and readers who are accustomed to advertising and sales will expect a little persuasiveness behind suggestions. Particularly when backed by solid reasoning and an explanation of why a particular title may be of interest, an enthusiastic pitch may be all that is needed to get a reader to try a new author who may become a favorite. This should not, however, turn into pressure to take books that the reader doesn't really want. Subtlety is needed for many reasons—to avoid invading the patron's privacy, to draw out important but previously unconsidered preferences, and to introduce a common vocabulary when the reader does not know book terminology or uses it unconventionally—to name just a few.

As new readers' advisors quickly learn, waiting for RA questions to come to a service desk is not enough. Whether because of negative prior experiences, shyness, a misunderstanding about which questions are appropriate, an assumption that a particular librarian will not share their reading interests, or a plethora of other possible reasons, many library patrons will not ask reading questions at a desk. In addition to employing the asynchronous RA methods listed in the next section, the best advisors learn productive ways to approach readers in the stacks, to engage them in discussion of books, and, ultimately, to lead them to be receptive to advisory help.

Finally, RA is best thought of as a long-term relationship, not just a single discussion. Skilled advisors encourage follow up, document their transactions with particular readers, pursue feedback, and build on past suggestions. One knows a special success has been achieved when give-and-take between the advisor and the reader reaches equilibrium, and book knowledge begins to pass both ways.

Asynchronous RA

Even librarians who practice face-to-face advisory with art and skill will reach only a fraction of their library's readers. Other readers will rarely approach desks, may decline direct assistance, will use the library primarily at a distance, or will otherwise slip out of the advisor's reach. To serve these readers, libraries must also employ asynchronous RA.

Asynchronous RA includes many methods, including building book displays, booklists, and RA Web sites; offering or supporting book groups; and providing access to books and databases that feature advisory information. Asynchronous RA must not be neglected. It is the only means to reach the many library patrons who rarely ask questions at service desks or engage with librarians. In a world where quick use and privacy are key concerns, such patrons may well be the majority of library users.

Displays are a keystone of library practice. They make library buildings visually interesting and create variation in the building for regular visitors. They highlight collections or suggest connections between books that do not usually sit on adjacent shelves. Displays simplify the complex act of selecting materials from a large collection and result in higher circulation figures. Most important for RA, displays provide a means of suggesting some of the best titles and authors that may be hiding in the stacks.

Booklists serve a similar function but are especially important in promoting groups of materials for which there is regular, ongoing interest. Libraries should develop lists that go far beyond the latest best sellers. Book genres and subgenres, items of local interest, in-demand subject matters, and readalikes for popular authors should all be promoted. Lists create handy tools that allow librarians without knowledge of or interest in particular genres, subjects, or authors to provide quick and relevant service as their own skills develop. Adding short annotations that identify the appeal factors of the listed books gives readers the information to make their own educated decisions.

The number of users who access libraries primarily through the Internet is growing. Such users browse and make most of their decisions online, place holds electronically, and stop at the physical building only briefly to pick items up. Because librarians don't see these patrons, it's easy to underestimate their numbers. It's important to meet this electronic demand with asynchronous RA tools. Start with an advisory Web site. This Web site should, at a minimum, include electronic versions of booklists distributed within the building and links to Web sites that provide reviews, book sales, and detailed genre information. Content must be kept up-to-date to maintain patron interest over time. With hundreds of good models located on library sites around the Internet, there is no reason why any library should forgo this online advisory presence. This is a minimum presence: Methods of "2.0"online advisory are discussed later in this chapter.

Book groups provide another RA forum (Smith, 2008). This can be done asynchronously for groups that are not affiliated with the library, through means such as bags of books, discussion guides, readalike lists for group favorites, or lists of books that result in good discussions. If a library staff member leads the group, face-to-face advisory opportunities will be plentiful.

A common element of contemporary RA, whether used together by patron and librarian in synchronous transactions or accessed by the user alone in asynchronous transactions, are RA books and databases. Publishers such as Libraries Unlimited and ALA Editions have produced dozens of books on nearly every conceivable genre or subject of reading. These books typically contain topical lists and annotations, and subcategorize the literature in question; they make a fine starting point for those researching books. In addition, many public libraries subscribe to databases such as Novelist, Readers' Advisor Online, Booklist Online, or Books and Authors, all of which provide keyword searching of extensive information about books. Along with the core database, each of these products provides other original value-added content: readalikes, lists, training materials for RA, and more (Towner, 2008).

ENHANCING TRADITIONAL RA METHODS

Before we begin to discuss the many new methods of RA that creative practitioners are using, it behooves us to consider modifications to traditional RA methods that can make them more successful or help them reach a broader audience. First, librarians should become more cognizant of opportunities to include RA in other reference interviews. There are many opportunities to ask patrons if they would be interested in reading nonfiction or even fiction related to their reference queries (Moyer, 2007). Every request to place an item on hold, particularly when the reserve list is long, should be viewed as an opportunity to introduce a readalike or other alternatives to the original desire. The same is true when a patron requests purchase or interlibrary loan of an item. It's a perfect time for a librarian to ask what the reader enjoys about the author or book in question. There are many such opportunities to practice reference and RA in unison, many good justifications for providing both services from the same desk.

In a similar vein, advisors might consider reviving more classical approaches. Originally, the term *readers' advisory* was applied not to pleasure reading but to self-education programs in various disciplines that were built through carefully selected and sequenced lists of materials. The current practice of RA that emerged in the 1980s was motivated by the lack of support for pleasure reading and the need for guidance among fiction readers. It was, in some ways, a reaction to the education-focused RA of earlier eras, particularly the derogatory views of popular fiction that some librarians of those eras held (Crowley, 2004). While contemporary RA has filled this important niche admirably, the two different modes of RA are not mutually exclusive in practice. They can coexist quite well. Particularly in an era when many library users are trying to improve their lives at the same time that they are forced to tighten their belts, some revival of the old self-education programs is probably in order. Increased emphasis on nonfiction advisory somewhat reflects this opportunity, but we can go further, applying the methods of advisory to all nonfiction reading, not just narrative works.

As Internet searching has reduced the traffic at many reference desks, the last five years have seen much discussion of "roving" reference: service provided away from a central desk. This practice is easily combined with more aggressive approaches to RA. When patrons are reluctant to engage with a librarian perching behind a monolithic desk, they may be willing, even anxious, to ask reading questions or simply discuss books when surrounded by many interesting but confusing choices in the stacks.

Another adaptation to traditional RA service is to offer it not just to individuals but also to targeted groups, particularly groups that we know are using our libraries. In addition to building readalike lists for individual patrons, we can supply them to groups that meet in our buildings or are listed in local organizations' directories. We should deliver lists or carts of appropriate materials to patrons who visit our buildings for programs but remain unaware of related resources in our collections. We can suggest readalikes to book groups. We should think of delivery of books to homebound patrons as a kind of RA. We can coordinate with teachers to work with their classes. Any group that uses the library presents an RA opportunity.

Finally, in an era when there are so many different formats in which people obtain information, we must get better at reusing and recompiling the information we create for RA, not just using it in one context. Anytime a book annotation is written, it should be collected in a format that can be easily pasted into other materials. Lists generated for the Web should be made available in print format in the building and vice versa. The tools exist for librarians at many institutions to collaborate in building shared databases and archives of information, no longer passively waiting for products created by publishers and vendors. When librarians everywhere struggle to find enough time to provide good RA service and create quality resources for readers, the solutions ultimately lie in collaborative efforts and better propagation and reuse of similar materials that are now produced separately in many different institutions.

NEW APPROACHES TO RA

In addition to traditional face-to-face RA and asynchronous RA, creative thinking and new technologies are blending the personal and the automated to create new methods of reaching readers (Hollands and Moyer, 2008; Trott, 2008). The first of these is RA provided in response to reader profile forms, a practice pioneered at Williamsburg Regional Library (Hollands,

2006). Readers fill out a form, either on paper or online, that documents their reading history and interests in various appeal factors. The form uses scales, check boxes, and options that can be circled and crossed out to collect the maximum amount of information with the least difficulty for the reader.

Once the form is received, a librarian claims it and responds with an annotated list of personalized reading suggestions. By saving annotations in a common archive, a library can soon collect a large archive of reusable material for future readers, reducing response time as the service becomes established. Because librarians can respond at any time convenient to them, the profile forms allow detailed, timely service in institutions with busy staff schedules. Because anyone in the building can respond to a form, knowledgeable staff who don't normally work with the public can become involved, and readers with different interests can be routed to the specialists most able to serve them. Because it is easier to use other resources when responding at a distance with a slight time gap, profile-based RA is an excellent training ground for new advisors. Form-based RA results in better documentation of all parts of the advisory transaction, enabling more accurate counts of the amount of service provided and better information for ongoing work with readers.

LIBRARY 2.0 AND RA

Since at least the 1980s, librarians have been providing digital services to users. At that time, e-mail reference services were being developed in academic libraries to increase user access to information (Bankhead, n.d.). Digital reference services continue to be a growing part of the interaction between librarians and library users. However, as Bankhead notes, "Readers' advisory service is almost invisible in the literature regarding digital reference service" (n.d., 2). In her chapter on RA and the Internet in *The Readers' Advisor's Companion,* Roberta S. Johnson cites three uses of the Internet for RA librarians: "for answering challenging patron requests, as a source of information on authors and their works, and as a collection development resource" (2001, 192). These three uses reflect the traditional use of Internet tools in what has become known as the Web 1.0 world. Here, digital tools are used to locate information and to push it out to potential users.

The past five years have seen a seismic shift in the digital world, most commonly referred to as Web 2.0. In 2005, Tim O'Reilly of O'Reilly Media attempted to define Web 2.0 in terms of businesses (O'Reilly, 2005). From a library, and RA, perspective, three points that O'Reilly makes seem particularly pertinent. He defines these as being part of the core competencies of Web 2.0:

- Trusting users as codevelopers
- Harnessing collective intelligence
- Leveraging the long tail through customer self-service

These three principles are at the core of RA work (which has been 2.0 since before the term was coined). RA work has always been user centered. It does not matter what sort of material the librarian personally likes or does not like to read. Rather, the advisor works with the reader to come up with suggestions based on that reader's interests. The entire RA encounter is based on developing trust: If the reader does not trust that the librarian will take her request seriously, there can be no useful discussion. Sharing reading interests puts the reader in a position of vulnerability, and she must feel that her reading tastes will not be called into question. At the same time, readers' advisors have to be willing to set aside personal likes and dislikes and trust that the reader really knows what she wants. Additionally, RA work requires that the librarian/advisor give up a certain level of authority and work in partnership with readers. Readers' advisors are not infallible oracles who tell the reader what he ought to be reading. Instead, the reader and the advisor work together to develop a reading list that fits the user's interests, while at the same time opening up new possibilities.

RA services have always been a model of collaborative work, "harnessing the collective intelligence" (O'Reilly, 2005). The most successful advisors rely not only on their own knowledge but also on that of their colleagues. Since the beginning of the contemporary RA movement, this idea has been consistently reinforced. In the early days, this collaboration was often limited to locally created reading lists and other in-house resources for assisting readers. The development of the Adult Reading Roundtable in 1984 was just the first in what has become a long line of organizations bringing together readers' advisors. The growth of the Internet has enabled this collaborative work to expand globally. Discussions groups such as Fiction-l (http://www.webrary.org/rs/flmenu.html) bring together the collective knowledge of RA librarians across the country and have helped to shape the practice and theory of working with readers. More focused groups such as Dorothy-l (www.dorothyl.com/) for mystery lovers, RRA-l (http://groups.yahoo.com/group/rra-l/) for romance readers, and others bring together readers and librarians to discuss specific genres or reading interests.

While these discussion forums offered librarians and readers the chance to interact in new ways, by the early 21st century, new technology was expanding the possibilities for readers' advisors and their libraries. Weblogs, commonly called *blogs,* began to proliferate on the Internet in the late 1990s. Originally a mechanism for keeping an online diary, open to the world, blogs soon became a major tool for individuals and organizations to share information ranging from the personal to the professional. Blogs offer the opportunity for any reader to review materials that he or she is reading and make those reviews available to a wide audience. Thousands of new voices are thus available to librarians working with readers. Often these voices discuss lesser-known titles, new authors, or older works that are not being reviewed in what remains of the traditional print book review media. While the quality of these reviews varies widely, the sheer volume of titles being covered means that readers are now able to locate materials that they might not otherwise have come across. It also means that readers' advisors need to keep an eye not only on what is on best seller lists and in professional review journals but also on the books that are mentioned on blogs that their users follow. Reading these nonprofessional reviews provides insight into how average readers view their reading—what appeals to them and how they talk about books. All of this information helps advisors to develop a more comprehensive picture of reader response that should prove helpful when working with an individual reader.

In addition to expanding the portrait of the reading community, blogging also offers libraries new ways to reach out to that community. Many libraries have incorporated blogs into their Web sites. These blogs may be used to promote library programs and services or to keep the local community informed of library news. From an RA perspective, blogs enable librarians to promote library resources and collections to those readers who may not ever come into the library. Library book review blogs such as Seattle Public Library's *Shelf Talk* (http://shelftalk.spl.org/) or the Williamsburg Regional Library's *Blogging for a Good Book* (http://bfgb.wordpress.com) present reviews of library materials that readers might otherwise not come across, expanding readers' perspective beyond the best seller lists. These blogs act as virtual displays, incorporating cover art and providing a visually attractive collection of materials for readers to consider. By linking from the blog post to the library catalog, libraries enable readers to quickly locate and place reserves on materials that they might wish to read.

Successful review blogs all share some similarities. They must be updated consistently, preferably daily, encouraging readers to come back on a regular basis. It is also important for blogs to identify and maintain a focus. Including program information, news updates, or other nonreview posts will tend to dilute the blog's effectiveness and discourage regular readership. Review blogs also offer the opportunity for libraries to expand their institutional culture of RA. Writing posts for a blog need not be limited to RA librarians or even to public services staff. There are passionate readers and avid writers in all divisions of the library, and a library review blog will benefit from including these voices. Book review blogs create an opportunity for libraries to enter into a conversation with their readers. Enabling open commenting on blog posts gives libraries a chance to hear what readers think about the materials being reviewed, good and bad. Readers can use the comments to ask for and propose reading suggestions, to offer their own responses to titles, and to connect with librarians and with each other.

The online discussion of books and reading extends beyond e-mail lists and blogs. Reader reviews in Amazon.com (http://www.amazon.com) and social networking sites that focus on reading such as LibraryThing (http://www.librarything.com), Goodreads (http://www.goodreads.com), and Shelfari (http://www.shelfari.com) allow readers to connect with each other in new ways. As readers incorporate these tools into their habits, it becomes essential for libraries to understand the appeal of these sites. Reviewing titles is a major part of each of the sites mentioned, but another important piece that they offer is the opportunity for readers to tag books with identifiers that have meaning for the reader. These tags are central to the social networking concept of "folksonomy" as opposed to the traditional taxonomic model that uses a controlled vocabulary (Spiteri, 2007). These tools are part of O'Reilly's concept of "harnessing collective intelligence" (O'Reilly, 2005). An understanding of how readers rate, review, and tag titles allows RA librarians to make better reading suggestions to their users. Relying on this sort of information does require a certain relinquishing of authority on the librarian's part. However, as the process in RA is to offer suggestions rather than to tell the reader what they should be reading, this usually is not a problem.

In addition to individual librarians incorporating tools such as LibraryThing and Amazon reviews into their individual practice, libraries are adapting their technology to these same ends in a variety of ways. LibraryThing for Libraries allows libraries to incorporate information from the LibraryThing database into the online catalog. These added tags and readalike suggestions from LibraryThing users enrich the catalog content for specific titles, allowing readers to locate titles that are similarly tagged and thus might have some similar appeal to the reader. Integrated library systems (ILS) are also being modified to allow users to enter their own reviews, ratings, and tags for library materials. In all of these cases, the end product should be an expanded conversation between the reader and the library that enhances the reading experience.

THE FUTURE OF RA

The RA renaissance of the past 25 years has proven successful for both libraries and readers. Attention to readers enhances the status of the library in its community as well as increasing circulation of materials and building a community of readers. Enhanced services for readers, both direct and indirect, allow them to find reading suggestions that meet their needs and interests. The expansion of access to fiction, the focus on popular genre reading, and the inclusion of nonfiction into RA practice all have been important parts of the renewed interest in readers' services in libraries. The future offers a number of challenges for RA services. These items will no doubt be part of the RA discussion in the coming quarter century, and this discussion will shape the practice of RA in the 21st century.

- *The future of genre:* Within genres, there have always been ebbs and flows as new forms develop and older ones go out of style. Using genre when working with readers has always been a complex process. As increasing numbers of writers are blending genres, such as romance and mystery or literary and science fiction, it becomes more and more difficult to use genre as a defining tool in working with readers. Additionally, new genres or reading interests are developing that have their own set of appeals. To be successful in the future, readers' advisors must be able to easily move among these shifting tides and continue to develop their understanding of how readers respond to books.

- *The future of appeal:* As noted earlier, Saricks and Brown defined the concept of appeal in 1989. Their definition has proven remarkably resilient, but, recently, librarians have begun to look at ways to expand the concept of appeal to better incorporate new ideas of reading theory and to develop a more useful vocabulary of appeal (Wyatt, 2007).
- *RA for non-English speakers:* As more and more libraries are seeing their user communities expand demographically, it will become increasingly important for readers' advisors to look for ways to reach out to readers who are not reading titles in English. Reader demand for materials in languages other than English raises a number of issues regarding collection development and RA that libraries will need to address.
- *RA services in academic libraries:* While public libraries have been the center of the RA revival, there have been some efforts to promote and support extracurricular reading on college and university campuses. Here, RA services offer an opportunity to reach out to users in a new way, building new avenues of support for the library.
- *Format-based RA:* The success of working with readers raises the question of how these tools and practices can be applied to working with listeners and viewers as well. The areas of film and music advisory seem to offer opportunities for expanding services beyond print and audiobooks.
- *Technology and RA:* A continuing challenge will be for readers' advisors to develop best practices for incorporating technology into their work. One of the most pressing issues will be how to continue to preserve the human touch that is central to RA services.
- *Marketing RA services:* One of the weakest points in readers' services continues to be marketing RA services to readers. Practitioners need to look for ways to reach readers other than waiting for them at the public service desks. As libraries must compete with other resources for readers' attention, the more that can be done to make library RA tools and services easy to access and use, the more likely it is that users will take advantage of them.
- *Quantifying RA services:* As RA tends to be a very personal service, it can be challenging to measure its success. While anecdotal evidence can be collected on the use of RA services, the long-term success of RA will depend on the development of more quantifiable methods of tracking these encounters between librarians and readers. As statistical measures for RA services are developed, librarians must look at the entire range of services offered, not just the one-on-one encounter between the reader and the advisor. Book discussion groups, author visits, book blogs, displays, outreach services, reading lists, and all the other means of connecting readers with materials need to be included.

It is difficult to predict the future of any library service. Technological developments over the past decade have brought huge changes to the library profession in general and to the provision of reference services in particular, and they no doubt will continue to do so in the coming decades. However, regardless whether a user is taking a print copy of a book from a library shelf, listening to an audiobook version on her iPod, or downloading a digital version to his e-reader, they will continue to need assistance in navigating the literary waterways in search of a new book or author. If readers' advisors continue to focus on readers' needs and remain flexible in their use of technology, then RA services will continue to be an essential part of reference librarianship in the future.

WORKS CITED

Applegate, R. 2008. Whose decline? Which academic libraries are "deserted" in terms of reference transactions? *Reference & User Services Quarterly* 48 (2): 176–189.

Bankhead, H. n.d. *Digital reference services, not just Q and A: An inclusive examination of digital reference services.* Retrieved October 31, 2009, from http://www.webjunction.org/c/document_library/get_file?folderId=441705&name=DLFE-12020.pdf.

Crowley, B. 2004. A history of readers' advisory service in the public library. In *Nonfiction readers' advisory*, ed. R. Burgin, 3–25. Westport, CT: Libraries Unlimited.

Elliott, J. 2007. Academic libraries and extracurricular reading promotion. *Reference & User Services Quarterly* 46 (3): 34–43.

Green, S. S. 1876. Personal relations between librarians and readers. *Library Journal* 1 (2–3): 81.

Hollands, N. 2006. Improving the model for interactive readers' advisory service. *Reference & User Services Quarterly* 45 (3): 205–212.

Hollands, N., and J. E. Moyer. 2008. The future of readers' advisory. In *Research-based readers' advisory*, ed. J. Moyer, 242–260. Chicago: American Library Association.

Johnson, R. S. 2001. The global conversation about books, readers, and reading on the Internet. In *The reader's advisor's companion*, ed. R. Burgin and K. D. Shearer, 191–206. Englewood, CO: Libraries Unlimited.

Moyer, J. E. 2007. Learning from leisure reading: A study of adult public library patrons. *Reference & User Services Quarterly* 46 (4): 66–79.

O'Gorman, J., and B. Trott. 2009. What will become of reference in academic and public libraries? *Journal of Library Administration* 49 (4): 327–339.

O'Reilly, T. 2005. *What is Web 2.0: Design patterns and business models for the next generation of software.* Retrieved October 31, 2009, from http://oreilly.com/web2/archive/what-is-web-20.html.

Orr, C. 2008. Collection development and collection management. In *Research-based readers' advisory*, ed. J. Moyer, 219–241. Chicago: American Library Association.

Saricks, J. G. 2005. *Readers' advisory service in the public library.* Chicago: American Library Association.

Smith, A. 2008. Book groups. In *Research-based readers' advisory*, ed. J. Moyer, 111–133. Chicago: American Library Association.

Spiteri, L. F. 2007. The structure and form of folksonomy tags: The road to the public library catalog. *Information Technology & Libraries* 26 (3): 13–25.

Towner, M. W. 2008. Tools for readers' advisors. In *Research-based readers' advisory*, ed. J. Moyer, 172–196. Chicago: American Library Association.

Trott, B. 2008. Building on a firm foundation: Readers' advisory over the next twenty-five years. *Reference & User Services Quarterly* 48 (2): 132–135.

Wright, D. 2008. Readers' advisory interview. In *Research-based readers advisory*, ed. J. Moyer, 154–171. Chicago: American Library Association.

Wyatt, N. 2007. An RA big think. *Library Journal* 132 (12): 40–43.

10

LEISURE READING COLLECTIONS IN COLLEGE AND UNIVERSITY LIBRARIES: HAVE ACADEMIC LIBRARIANS REDISCOVERED READERS' ADVISORY?

Anne Behler

Collection development at the collegiate level has always boiled down to this one-sentence mantra: Support the curriculum. Indeed, in a chapter in the 2003 publication *Collection Development Policies: New Directions for Changing Collections*, authors McGuigan and White make the argument for subject-specific collection policy statements. Of these policy statements, the authors note, "By presenting a detailed level of description of the content of the collection, these documents aid users who benefit by being able to determine the appropriate scope of a collection for a particular research need" (2003, 18).

However, as students' research habits and needs change and as the library shifts from a monument of knowledge to a place, it stands to reason that the way we approach collection development should change as well. One of the most obvious changes has been from physical to electronic collections—from traditional Web pages to mobile ones. In turn, the purpose of library collections, and the services associated with them, has also changed. As general library services have become more user centered and information literacy focused, collections services have followed suit. This is not to say that the traditional "support the curriculum" mantra has flown the coop—it's very much alive and well—but many libraries have begun to incorporate portions of collections and services that focus on the promotion of reading as a lifelong habit rather than simply a research stop along the way.

GOING BACK IN TIME: THE CHANGING ROLE OF LIBRARIES

Literacy has long been the cornerstone of libraries and librarianship. However, the 21st century has brought changes that have challenged this foundation, and the focus has shifted from reading literacy and comprehension to online literacy. At the same time, America's young adults are indeed reading less, particularly once they enter high school and college. In November 2007, the National Endowment for the Arts published *To Read or Not to Read: A Question of National Consequence*. This study confirmed what many had believed to be true—Americans are doing less and less voluntary reading (Office of Research and Analysis, 2007). The data showed that only 22 percent of 17-year-olds read for pleasure frequently. Perhaps of more concern, the demographic that has seen the greatest decline in reading is the 18–24 age group—reading does not resume when teenagers enter college and/or the workforce. Rather, this college-age constituency decreased their reading of nonrequired texts by 12 percent between 1992 and 2002 (Office of Research and Analysis, 2007).

Not surprisingly, incoming college students' reading comprehension skills are also suffering. According to the long-term trends assessment of the National Assessment of Educational Progress, average reading scores for 17-year-old students declined significantly over the last 20 years, with 2004 scores below the minimum for "proficient" reading skills (Office of Research and Analysis, 2007). These trends are reflected in SAT scores, which have shown a 35-point drop in critical reading scores between 1970 and 2007 (U.S. Census Bureau, 2009).

These statistics mandate an increased academic library focus on developing students' traditional literacy skills. This newfound focus on encouraging reading and literacy represents a change that has not come about overnight. In fact, it's more of a resurrection of tenets and practices that have lain dormant for the last 50 years. A review of literature on the topic reveals that there was a great deal of concern about college students' reading habits in the 1940s and 1950s. Many academic libraries engaged in studies of their students' reading behaviors and preferences. In 1946, the College of Saint Francis in Joliet, Illinois, published the results of a student survey that sought to determine how much of its collections were indeed used by the students and, furthermore, how many books the students read and whether any of the books they read were nonassigned reading. Students were also asked about their genre preferences, and the data were sorted by class level (Elvira, 1946). Similar studies were carried out at many other academic libraries, including a focus group exercise at the University of Illinois in 1951 (Chapin, 1951) and a student leisure reading study at the University of Idaho in which the author stated that "the library is interested in determining student tastes in reading for guidance in the development of these tastes" (Waldron, 1952, 99). Other universities, such as Delaware State College, went beyond studies and actually required their students to read recreational or leisure reading titles, an effort spearheaded by the libraries (Josey, 1959).

Literature on this topic nearly disappeared through the 1960s to early 1990s, but in more recent years the discussion of reading promotion has re-emerged. In 1994, Morrissett carried out a survey of 120 academic libraries from 12 southeastern states. Of the 75 respondents, 45 percent had some form of leisure reading collection in place, and 42 percent of those collections employed some form of book leasing program. As Morrissett concluded, this early study illustrates "a significant interest and investment in leisure reading collections" among institutions in the region surveyed (1994, 124). While the interest may be present at many institutions, a disconnect between the existence of a leisure reading collection and the act of reading promotion, or readers' advisory, often remains. Dwyer notes that "reading continues to be a popular public activity, book sales are increasing, book discussion groups are popular in many communities, and reader's advisory function is experiencing resurgence in public libraries. One would scarcely guess this was the case, though, if his or her experience were limited to academic libraries" (2001, 62). Dwyer goes on to challenge academic librarians to consider the bookstore model of operation (that of Barnes & Noble in particular)—offering a shelving arrangement that guides book selection, frequent and stimulating book discussions, and so on. Such a model can work to build a "community of readers" (Dwyer, 2001, 73).

Literature from the last two years illustrates that Dwyer's vision for a reader-engaging academic library is beginning to gain traction. A 2004 study of collection development policies regarding leisure reading and/or textbook collections revealed that as academic libraries have become more user centered, the collections statements have also. A growing number of university libraries have adjusted their statements to include collection of leisure reading materials (Hsieh and Runner, 2005). In addition, a recent readers' advisory column by Elliott (2007) highlights many of the methods academic libraries are using to promote both reading in general and leisure reading collections specifically, including partnering with their local public libraries and creating comfortable spaces for patrons who want to read in the library. In many cases, these institutions have harnessed prevalent technologies, such as blogs and Web spaces, to present their message in the medium most of their patrons prefer (Elliott, 2007). And reception of such efforts has been positive, from both students and the academic community, reinforcing the importance of establishing some form of collection and space to promote reading as a lifelong activity.

THE LEISURE READING COLLECTION AS READING PROMOTER

Many academic libraries have established front-and-center shelving areas for new and/or popular books that arrive with their firm orders. Circulation for these collections is generally higher, due to visibility and appeal—these books usually still have their original covers attached, unlike the boring sea of black, blue, red, and green in the main library stacks. Some libraries have taken a step beyond the feature-shelf model and have created permanent leisure reading collections. From community colleges like the Waubonsee Community College, whose library is using Twitter, to large research libraries like the Penn State University Libraries, there are many examples of libraries innovating in the area of leisure reading promotion.

A permanent leisure reading collection not only serves as a draw into the library's book collections but also provides a space and structure for the promotion of reading for personal enjoyment and intellectual growth. This ideology aligns with the goals of the rest of the library's collection development program, which focuses on supporting the academic curricula. When administration at the Virginia Commonwealth University adopted a strategic plan that included the goal of "find[ing] a way to integrate an institutional focus on research, scholarship and creative activity with a decided focus on the student experience" (Bosman, Glover, and Prince, 2008), the library administration took the mandate seriously. It became the impetus for hiring undergraduate services librarians, who in turn implemented several reading services—including a readers' advisory blog, a book swap, and a summer reading program—that were designed to "improve the undergraduate library experience" (Bosman, Glover, and Prince, 2008). The leisure reading collection at Penn State University answered a similar focus in the university's strategic plan, which called on faculty and staff to "achieve greater student-centeredness" (Pennsylvania State University, 2009).

In addition, many leisure reading titles are now crossing over into the academic curricula, creating several sources of demand for the collections, as well as an integration with the rest of the library's titles. Adaptations are one such example that help to build a bridge between leisure and academic titles. One such title is Jane Austen's *Pride and Prejudice,* which alone serves both academic and pleasure reading audiences and has inspired many spin-offs geared toward popular audiences, including *Pride and Prejudice and Zombies,* by Jane Austen and Seth Grahame-Smith, and countless sequels by various authors. Librarians from West Carolina University's Hunter Library note that they see many graphic novels and mainstream nonfiction titles being checked out for use in class as well as for pleasure reading (H. Buchanan, personal communication, August 25, 2009).

A leisure reading collection also provides users with a collection that is constantly refreshed with new and popular titles, as opposed to the main library stacks, which can much more easily become a warehouse for older, underused titles. In addition to moving popular books front and center, leisure reading collections offer the chance to experiment with new collection development models, including primarily lease plans but also book-swap racks or carts or a hybrid of firm orders and one of these two other acquisitions models.

Book lease plans carry with them the clear benefit of allowing the collection to be constantly refreshed—orders for new titles are submitted monthly, and titles that lack appeal can be returned. This model also allows for the easy acquisition of multiple copies of titles with short-lived popularity. Imagine being able to order 25 copies of the latest *Harry Potter* or *Twilight* and then gradually send back the copies that are no longer needed to meet patron demand. From the patrons' perspective, this cuts down immensely on wait time for holds when a new blockbuster is released. From the selector librarians' perspective, it prevents needless expenditure on multiple copies that will become dead weight in a relatively short amount of time. Lease plans come in all sizes and price ranges, so libraries that want to test one out can sign up for allotments as small as 50 books per month or as large as 250 books per month. The vendor works with librarians to customize their order preferences—options available are protective covering, shelf-ready service, catalog record downloads, and custom labeling. Other perks associated with book lease plans include the ability to permanently retain a portion of the books ordered through the plan (this may vary slightly from one contract to another) and to firm-order additional books at a very low price.

One of the downsides of working with book lease vendors—at least for now—is that their primary clientele is public libraries, and they lack a sense of an academic setting's unique needs. For example, most lease plans will not send paperbacks, even if it's the only format available for a title. This often excludes great books like cookbooks, crafting books, and reissues of titles that reemerge due to newfound popularity via films, the Oprah Winfrey Show, and so on. Firm-order vendors for academic libraries also tend not to carry very many of these titles. On the plus side, lease plan vendors realize that this is an up-and-coming market for them and are often willing to work with the selector to make exceptions to the rule, amend contracts, and so on. Another issue to be aware of when considering lease plans is simply the attention and upkeep that they require. Because orders are often submitted monthly and title selection is driven by popularity—which is fleeting—rather than academic relevance, significant energy must be spent on making selections, inputting orders, and processing receipts and returns on a regular basis. Selectors often seek assistance from staff in making title selections and inputting orders for this reason.

HOW DO WE FIND OUT WHAT OUR USERS WANT?

Readers' advisory at the academic level is often something of an act in divination. It's not often that a student will request a title for the academic library, unless perhaps it's a textbook that she is hoping not to buy. Students' time is ever at a premium, and university libraries are not stereotypically associated with any sort of books that fall outside of the serious research sphere of topics. So how do we provide a service that our students will actually value?

Before embarking on creating a leisure reading collection in their University Park library, Penn State librarians gathered data at their annual library open house, through the feedback survey that most participants take. Though the survey was primarily about the students' experiences at the annual orientation event, it included a question about what students thought would improve facilities and services at the library that they had just toured. Votes for a leisure reading collection were overwhelming, with 40 percent of the 2,672 respondents in support. Additionally, the number one response to that question was "comfortable areas to relax," with 48 percent of the vote. Given the data, the Penn State librarians proceeded to create a space and collection with an eye toward meeting both of those desires. Initially, no new space was constructed; however, the area chosen for the collection was filled with soft seating and coffee tables, and the shelving purchased for the collection was wooden and at browsing level, providing a warm, comfortable feel to the area. The library has further plans to move the collection to an area just inside the library's main entrance, which will create both a wow factor and an inviting atmosphere for students. When the University of Northern Colorado's James A. Michener Library established its leisure reading collection in 2003, librarians surveyed the students once the collection had opened. The feedback they received was unanimously positive and reinforced that the collection met a need for the users (Rathe and Blankenship, 2005).

In addition to taking polls about demand for library services (sometimes students don't know what they want until it's in place), librarians who are implementing leisure reading collections and services can do a lot with use statistics to determine future title selections (and deselections). Sorting use data by call number, patron type served, and current holds can all be helpful in determining whether librarians are selecting titles that meet the demands of the target population(s). It is also important to create as many opportunities as possible for patrons to give ongoing feedback on the collection and make title recommendations. One way to do this is to create and advertise an e-mail address for that purpose. Many libraries have also created blogs related to their collections, providing an outlet for many librarians to contribute their reading recommendations and continue to pique readers' interests about what the collection holds for them. West Carolina University's Hunter Library employs a blog to share reviews of interesting leisure reading titles. Any librarian involved in selection of titles for that collection is invited to contribute as he or she is able. Librarian Heidi Buchanan (personal communication, August 25, 2009) notes that the blog allows for easy content versatility: "The blog can feed into our webpage, our Facebook pages, people can subscribe to the RSS, etc."

Other libraries are experimenting with Twitter and other social networking tools to encourage online interaction with their collections. When it comes to Twitter, some libraries are authoring individual tweets, while others, such as the Waubonsee Community College's Todd Library, are using a tweet generator to announce new arrivals and interesting checkouts from the collection. Facebook has proven itself another great ground for encouraging students to find and share their favorite books. The Penn State University Libraries' Facebook Application now includes a catalog search box that enables users to recommend titles of interest in their profiles by simply clicking a button that says "Share." The users can then insert a review or comment before posting the recommendation to their profile for all of their networks to see. In fact, many online catalogs are including this type of functionality. Interactive features such as this will likely become more prevalent and are wonderful ways to promote reading and informal interaction with a community of readers.

LEISURE READING COLLECTIONS AS CENTERS FOR ENGAGEMENT

An emerging trend in the 21st-century library is engagement. Libraries nationwide are shifting from an inward focus as a repository of collections and knowledge to an idea of the library as a center for engagement for the entire campus community. In keeping with that trend, leisure reading collections provide the opportunity for far more than reading lists and inviting spaces. They also provide the perfect platform for offering programs to engage students with both literature and their campus community. This is a tradition that has a long history in public libraries, and one way to begin building a programming element is to partner with the nearest local library to do so. Many public libraries have participated in a "One Book, One Community" program. Begun in Washington, D.C., in the late 1990s, these programs, which encourage participants to read and discuss one common book as a community, have spread across the nation like wildfire. The National Endowment for the Arts followed with a similar type of event called "The Big Read," which began in 2006. "The Big Read" is also focused around community-engaging book discussion and includes many events, such as film screenings, to accompany the reading and discussion experience (http://www.neabig read.org/about.php). Both "One Book" and "The Big Read" programs can be adapted to the campus environment, either alone or in partnership with the community libraries that are already participating. One way to explore the possibilities is to seek out an existing community reading program and sit on the planning committee in order to foster partnership between the public and college libraries and to glean valuable ideas about how to make a reading program work.

Engaging college students in already-established book discussion groups can bring an entirely new and unique dimension to these groups. Students represent many diverse backgrounds—from ethnicity to class to age—and can provide a fresh perspective on topics from which book club members from the college community can surely benefit. In addition, the college students who participate will find themselves becoming active members in the community in which they now live, allowing them to feel more connected to their new home.

Not all book clubs must be community or library conceived. In 2008, the Penn State University Schreyer Business Library and leisure reading selectors were approached by students who wanted to form their own business book club and needed both a location to meet and support for titles acquisition. The leisure reading collection's lease plan model proved the perfect way to support such a group. This initiative was entirely student driven but presented a wonderful way for the library to support ongoing reading and discussion. Library staff at Penn State have also shown great enthusiasm toward the collection, and the leisure reading lease plan has supported several library-wide book discussions as part of the annual staff in-service day and other professional development initiatives.

KEEPING UP

One of the most challenging aspects of both managing a leisure reading collection and creating features and programs that support readers' advisory is simply keeping up. The academic librarian who is teaching, providing research assistance, and participating in committees is pressed for time when it comes to keeping up with popular reading and providing relevant programming. Thankfully, readers' advisory is not a wheel that needs to be reinvented. Many resources are available to assist the college librarian in selecting books and developing marketing and programming ideas.

The Collection Development and Evaluation Section (CODES) of the Reference and User Services Association (RUSA) provides a wonderful forum for keeping in touch with what's happening in readers' advisory. CODES launched the Readers' Advisory Research and Trends Forum at the 2009 American Library Association Annual Conference. This forum provides a venue for the exchange of ideas and best practices for providing readers' advisory service, and it seeks to advance these practices to meet changing user needs (American Library Association, 2009). Another helpful resource that RUSA offers is an online course in readers' advisory practices. This regularly offered course addresses selection tools, marketing, review writing, and many other helpful topics for establishing an effective program in your library (http://www.ala.org/ala/mgrps/divs/rusa/development/readersadvisory101/index.cfm).

When it comes to title selection, there are many guides to help librarians get started on a path to collecting both popular and thematic titles. CODES is responsible for awarding an annual Notable Books Award for adult literature in the categories of nonfiction, fiction, and poetry (http://www.lita.org/ala/mgrps/divs/rusa/awards/notablebooks/index.cfm). In addition, they maintain the *Reading List,* which compiles noteworthy adult fiction by genre (http://www.lita.org/ala/mgrps/divs/rusa/awards/readinglist/index.cfm). The American Library Association also gives several annual book awards to excellent works of popular literature, by audience age and by genre. And while it is a commercial site, Amazon.com is probably one of the most useful resources for title selection, as it continuously publishes its best-selling titles, by theme, genre, relationship to films, and awards. Finding out what students would like to read can be as simple as placing a blank piece of butcher paper near the leisure reading collection and inviting them to graffiti the paper with suggestions of favorite titles, authors, and genres. Librarians may also solicit comments about the space and the collection in general—students will not be shy about what they'd like to see in their space.

CONCLUSION

No matter what the approach, leisure reading collections serve as the ideal vehicle for promoting the lifelong practice of reading on the college campus. If academic libraries are to combat declining literacy head on, re-invigorating readers' advisory in the library's goals is essential. Establishing collections and associated programs that respond to student preferences and campus and community issues, and that encourage engagement with reading and discussion, is an exciting step toward breaking the declining reading trend among young adults. These collections enable students to connect with their academic libraries and the greater university community in a way that they have not been encouraged to before, and rather than sitting on the sidelines, libraries are playing a very important role meeting the student-centered strategic goals of their universities and bringing reading back to campus.

WORKS CITED

American Library Association. 2009. *Readers' advisory trends subject of RUSA President's Program.* Retrieved December 15, 2009, from http://www.ala.org/ala/newspresscenter/news/pressreleases2009/march2009/rusapresprogram.cfm.

Bosman, R., J. Glover, and M. Prince. 2008. Growing adult readers: Promoting leisure reading in academic libraries. *Urban Library Journal* 15 (1). Retrieved December 15, 2009, from http://ulj.lacuny.org/index.php/past/36–151/62-growing-adult-readers-promoting-leisure-reading-in-academic-libraries.

Chapin, R. 1951. The recreational reading of University of Illinois students. *College & Research Libraries* 12 (2): 155–157.

Dwyer, J. 2001. Books are for use? Keeping the faith in reading. *Acquisitions Librarian* 25: 61–79.

Elliott, J. 2007. Academic libraries and extracurricular reading promotion. *Reference & User Services Quarterly* 46 (3): 34–43.

Elvira, M. 1946. How much do college students read? *Catholic Library World* 17: 271–276+.

Hsieh, C., and R. Runner. 2005. Textbooks, leisure reading, and the academic library. *Library Collections, Acquisitions, & Technical Services* 29 (2): 192–204.

Josey, E. J. 1959. Encouraging reading by incoming freshman. *Library Journal* 84 (16): 2571–2573.

McGuigan, G. S., and G. W. White. 2003. Subject-specific policy statements: A rationale and framework for collection development. In *Collection development policies: New directions for changing collections,* ed. D. Mack, 15–32. Binghamton, NY: Haworth Press.

Morrissett, L. A. 1994. Leisure reading collections in academic libraries: A survey. *North Carolina Libraries* 52 (Fall–Winter): 122–125.

Office of Research and Analysis. 2007. *To read or not to read: A question of national consequence.* Washington, DC: National Endowment for the Arts. Retrieved July 1, 2009, from http://www.nea.gov/research/ToRead.pdf.

Pennsylvania State University. 2009. *Penn State University—Strategic planning at Penn State.* Retrieved on November 23, 2009, from http://strategicplan.psu.edu.

Rathe, B., and L. Blankenship. 2005. Recreational reading collections in academic libraries. *Collection Management* 30 (2): 73–85.

U.S. Census Bureau. 2009. SAT scores and characteristics of college-bound seniors: 1970–2007. *Statistical Abstract of the United States 2009.* Retrieved November 12, 2009, from http://www.census.gov/compendia/statab/tables/09s0258.pdf.

Waldron, R. 1952. Student leisure reading—1951: A report and an analysis. *Bookmark* 4: 99–101.

11

LIBRARIAN AS MARKETER: LEARNING TO PROMOTE REFERENCE AND OUTREACH SERVICES

Elisabeth Leonard

Imagine that you, the head of reference, instruction, and outreach, have just been charged with marketing for Lake Joyful's Above Average Library. Your library director has asked you to take complete control and expects you to have a report ready for her when she returns from an extended vacation, saying that all her peer directors have some kind of marketing plan, whatever that is, and she wants one too. Where will you start? Why is this something you should do, in addition to everything else you do? In this chapter, I use the fictional case of Pat, the head of reference, instruction, and outreach at Lake Joyful's Above Average Library, to illustrate what marketing can do for libraries in general and for reference, instruction, and outreach units in particular. This essay presents marketing fundamentals for libraries, including marketing strategy, marketing communications, and marketing plans.

WHAT IS MARKETING AND WHY SHOULD YOU CARE?

Marketing is not new to libraries. At Lake Joyful, multiple small promotional efforts are underway, most managed either by individual reference librarians or by the Outreach Committee. After all, it often falls to the public services staff to promote not just their own services but also the entire library's products and services. At academic libraries, subject librarians often are responsible for promoting the library's services to the faculty and students in their discipline, while an outreach committee is responsible for larger efforts, like freshman orientation or new faculty orientation. At a public library, this can be done very similarly; for example, business community outreach is often managed by the business librarian, while youth outreach is managed by youth services librarians. In some libraries, there is a marketing librarian or a public relations staff member, but Lake Joyful does not have either.

What *is* relatively new to libraries is what the Above Average Library's director is asking for: a consistent, holistic, and systematic approach to marketing. This approach to marketing is a response to a greater understanding of what marketing is and to requests from our patrons that we respond more directly to their needs, as well as mandates from our funding agencies to prove that our products and services are needed in our communities.

So what, then, is marketing? *Marketing* is the "activity, set of institutions, and processes for creating, communicating, delivering, and exchanging offerings that have value for customers, clients, partners, and society at large" (American Marketing Association, 2007). For marketing to occur, you must understand your library's mission, know how much your library sees customer relationships as part of that mission, and know what your customers want and need. Traditionally, this is determined via developing a marketing mix, which is defined by either the four Ps (product, price, promotion, and place) or the four Cs (customer wants and needs, cost to satisfy, convenience to buy, and communication). However you approach the marketing mix, the point of the exercise is the same: to answer the questions of what products and services you should offer, how you should price the goods or services, what your value proposition is, and how you will communicate with your consumer. In short, the marketing mix is a key component to creating a winning marketing strategy. More recently, the marketing mix is being combined with a broader notion of customer relationship marketing, as there is a sense that focusing solely on the marketing mix can lead to a myopic view of what marketing can do for an organization and its stakeholders (Gronroos, 1994). In this context, library staff must make decisions about how to foster long-term relations rather than focusing on isolated events that create a momentary splash.

THE MARKETING PLAN

To make strategic, long-term decisions, it is best to create and follow a marketing plan. A marketing plan is a one- to three-year plan for how the library will provide and promote products and services; it includes goals, a timeline, a budget, and an assessment plan. Anyone in the library can create the marketing plan. In some libraries, it is done by a marketing committee, a public relations committee, or an outreach committee. In other libraries, there is a marketing or outreach librarian who is charged with creating and implementing the plan. Whoever takes ownership of the marketing plan should have the authority to do so, a full understanding of the plan's purpose and the library's mission, and a willingness to obtain input from all the stakeholders, including patrons and library staff.

For Pat, the marketing plan was a mandate, but in other libraries, having a marketing plan can be a way for a unit head to demonstrate to administration both why a marketing budget is needed and how the library's resources will be spent for the benefit of the library and its patrons. A marketing plan can also be shared with other staff as a way to educate the staff about patrons' needs and how the library plans to serve and reach them. In addition, when it is clear just how much is being done, it is easier for staff to understand that interrupting the scheduled workflow on a whim is not desirable. Instead, if the staff is asked to provide feedback on a draft plan, the final plan can include all the necessary outreach events, without surprises for the staff or the manager.

Ideally, the marketing plan is for the entire library, but a marketing plan can also be for a department or for a product or service. For example, when the Above Average Library launched its chat reference service, the library could have created a marketing plan just for that service. This is especially useful when the service is a collaborative effort with another library or when the service is so new to the staff that they are unsure how to promote it inside or outside of the library. However, a marketing plan is most effective when it is part of the process of planning products and services, rather than intended solely to promote a new or existing service. Why? Because marketing, at its best, is a long-term approach to creating lasting and meaningful relationships. An unfocused or mixed message can result in patrons misunderstanding everything the library has to offer or what the library should mean to them, which can damage relationships with patrons. For a reference department, this can be seen in terms of what level of service the department has agreed to provide. Is the purpose of reference at the Above Average Library's Reference Department to instruct patrons in how to find answers, or is it to provide the answers? If one service is promoted as a way to get answers and another service is promoted as a way to get coached in finding information, the department needs to discuss why different reference services serve different purposes and whether that difference is intentional. If everyone in the department is clear about what levels of service exist where (and why), then that can be communicated to the patron. If, however, the differences are not intentional (and perhaps are a surprise to the reference staff), the reference department should expect that patrons will be confused about why they receive different levels of service, especially if the reference staff has communicated with patrons only about the newest reference service. Decisions about which services to offer, and how to promote them, should be documented in the marketing plan but decided through the marketing mix.

MINDING YOUR Ps AND Cs

The marketing mix is a combination of product, price, promotion, and place. However, service-based organizations often turn to the Cs (customer wants and needs, cost to satisfy, convenience to buy, and communication) when deciding their marketing mix, rather than relying on the Ps. Under the four Cs, "product" becomes "customer wants and needs," "price" becomes "cost to satisfy," "promotion" becomes "communication," and "place" becomes "convenience." The Cs concentrate on the relationship the library should have with its customers, but when done properly, the four Ps combine consideration of what is best for the customer and what is best for the organization. What follows is a discussion of the four Ps, using the example of Lake Joyful's Library. Remember, either the Ps or the Cs can be applied to the benefit of any library and its patrons; what matters here is reaching an understanding of managing, via marketing, a suite of products and services.

- *Product:* Like almost every library, Above Average Library's most obvious product is the collection, with individual products like a popular reading collection, textbooks, DVDs, and CDs forming a range of product extensions. Think of the collection as a product line, similar to how Suave has an entire product line devoted to various hair-care items like shampoo, conditioner, hair spray, hair gel, and so on. Extending the Ps into services, library products can include instruction, one-on-one reference consultations, mediated searching, circulating laptops, photocopying services, document delivery, and consultation with faculty on assignments.
- *Price:* Price is not just what the consumer pays for a product. In the nonprofit world, price extends to opportunity costs for the library and the patron. For example, Pat must consider what it costs the Above Average Library (mostly in staff time) to provide multiple forms of reference services (text, e-mail, instant messaging, physical desk, one-on-one consultations), as well as what it costs the patron (what else could the patron do with the time it takes to ask a librarian for help). At what point is it worth it to the patron to ask a librarian for help via any one of the multiple access points, and at what point is it worth it to either get an answer another way or never get an answer at all? Think about it this way: How many times has a patron said, "I've been looking for an answer for weeks and finally decided I should ask you"? The level of frustration was high enough, or the deadline close enough, that asking for help was worth the cost to the patron (maybe the patron must overcome pride, fear, or a disbelief that asking will help).
- *Promotion:* This is perhaps the least understood of the Ps, especially given how widely promotion is used. Promotion refers to how the library communicates with its patrons, with the intention of getting their attention, increasing their interest in a service, activating a desire for that service, and motivating the patron to take action and use the service. Some marketing communications are aimed at only one of these areas, and sometimes an entire long-range campaign is designed that is intended to move the consumer through the span of attention, interest, desire, and action (AIDA).

  For AIDA to work optimally, Pat and her fellow librarians must know their potential patrons well. Pat initially will want to look at her entire target population before deciding whether she should reach them as an entire community with a single campaign or whether she should divide each of these populations into even smaller segments before designing a campaign. In an academic library, this means she might find that transfer students need reference services for different reasons than seniors, that science majors respond to a different message than business majors, and that new faculty members are not interested in hearing from the library until the second semester they are on campus. In a public library, this means she might find that services appeal differently to mothers of newborns than to empty nesters or to male teenagers. Deciding which population to target and how specifically a population needs to be defined is critical.

Timing, demographics, media, language, and type of service need to be carefully matched before a campaign is released across the targeted population. This is one reason why every library needs to consider its own population before launching a campaign, rather than simply replicating a winning campaign from another library. Your patrons and your services can be very different than those at a nearby and seemingly similar library.

Marketing communication can include word of mouth, communication between an individual librarian and her target audiences, and ads on the radio, in the newspaper, or on social networks like Facebook. Promotion should not be done in isolation from the other areas of the marketing mix. Librarians must look at everything they are offering before attempting to promote a single service or a range of services. Marketing communications should be done in concert to avert any mixed messages. If there are too many messages, each simply adds to the noise the patron receives from all directions, both inside and outside the library.

- *Place:* The library must decide what the best way to reach potential patrons is; in business speak, what are the appropriate channels for distribution? Pat must ask herself: Is it worth setting up a table at the local coffee shop or at the YMCA? Or adding an "Ask a Librarian" area in Blackboard? Where will the patrons want to receive reference services? Remember that these decisions regarding "place" are not about *promoting* the service but instead about *accessing* the service. It matters if you think that a link is a way to promote a service (like a link to your chat reference service in an online newspaper) or that a Web site is a place to offer a service (like embedding the chat service into the online newspaper). The approach you take guides your decision making and how you evaluate your decisions.

  At this point the Above Average Library should consider its relationships with others in the community and with its vendors. Will the database vendor allow the library to link to the reference service on the database page? Would the bookstore want to partner with the library on an outreach event? Would faculty be willing to serve as a distribution channel (via class Web pages and the syllabus)? Are there any clubs or social groups with which the library could partner? For example, for academic libraries, if there is a study night for the fraternity, maybe they would like having a librarian talk to them about research methods. For public libraries, if there is an investment club, they might like to have a librarian talk about resources for financial research, or if there is a gardening club or local extension office, a librarian could talk about resources to help a garden grow.

MARKET RESEARCH

To make decisions about the marketing mix, market research is necessary. Market research is often done as part of the strategic planning process; even if the library has just done market research for the strategic plan, additional research is necessary for marketing. What follows is a discussion of primary and secondary market research sources and techniques. Primary research is done to discover what your patrons want and need, what they are likely to respond to, and how they would like for the library to communicate with them. Secondary research involves using published reports and statistics about your target audience, such as reports about Generation X. The best market research uses a combination of methods and sources, as each provides a different piece of the puzzle.

Primary Research

There are many ways for librarians to find out what their students, faculty, and staff think about the library and its services. In addition to the quantitative data that libraries keep (door count, circulation statistics, reference statistics, interlibrary loan statistics, etc.), the most popular qualitative market research methods are focus groups, interviews, surveys, and observation. Before you conduct your research, think about who you want to reach and what you want to know. Are you trying to attract new patrons? Existing patrons? Is there a particular segment of your population you need to reach? Do you want to know about beliefs, behaviors, or attitudes? Also, on some campuses, any human subject research is considered to be under the purview of an institutional review board, so before conducting this research, consult your campus policies.

A focus group consists of gathering 3 to 10 people in a room where they are asked about their opinions, beliefs, and attitudes. The focus group can be for a single niche group, like business students, or can represent every target group. Often, focus groups begin with a wide range of population types and narrow as the library determines more about who they are trying to reach and what the library needs to know. Sometimes focus groups are conducted by an outside interviewer who is trained in the method. If the library cannot afford this, the staff should find someone who is able to remain neutral no matter what the group says about the library, someone who is good at asking probing questions. Focus groups last one to two hours and are recorded so they can be analyzed later.

Interviews allow the library to delve more deeply into opinions, behaviors, and attitudes than focus groups or surveys can. Interviews are typically between a single librarian and a single patron. They can be done as follow-ups to information gained from surveys and focus groups. Interviews range in length but rarely last longer than two hours and are recorded so they can be analyzed later.

Surveys are a terrific way to get a lot of information from a mass of people quickly. Unlike focus groups or interviews, respondents can remain anonymous. The biggest drawback to a survey is that the questions are fixed and may not allow your patrons to tell you everything they want you to know. If you conduct a survey, make sure there is at least one comments field.

Observation is done to determine behaviors that patrons may be unwilling to verbalize or unaware that they have. Observation is something every reference librarian does, even though it is rarely intentional. Ask a librarian how patrons use the catalog, and every librarian will have an answer, often based on what she observes at the reference desk. Observation illustrates how people use the library and can inform you about when and how people are getting frustrated, as well as illustrate what they find easy to use. Observation is often conducted as part of a usability study.

Secondary Research

There are many ways for a librarian to get information about her target population, including articles and presentations done by other librarians, market research reports available through library databases, and research conducted by organizations such as the Online Computer Library Center (OCLC). Commercial market research reports can help librarians to understand general consumer behavior, such as when and why Generation Xers use cell phones or why and how people use bookstores.

VALUE PROPOSITIONS

Once Pat has a sense of what products and services she wants to concentrate on, and knows which target groups she is trying to reach, she needs to craft different value propositions for different patron groups (market segments) and for different services. It is rarely true that every market segment wants the same thing from the same service. Writing multiple value propositions will remind Pat what value the library can provide to each market segment. Each value proposition should communicate the most important benefits to the patron. It is key to remember to write these from the patron's point of view and not try to force organizational values onto her. For example, imagine that Pat knows that the library has always promoted the reference desk as a way for students to get quality information. However, she discovers that students are overwhelmed in general by the transition from the local high school to Lake Joyful University and that they feel neglected by both the public library and the university library. This problem is compounded by the fact that students who are admitted in January do not receive an orientation to the university, and thus there is no easy way for the academic librarians to reach them. After conducting several focus groups, interviewing a few outspoken students, and looking at the demographic information the registrar provided, Pat discovers that more than anything, the students need to feel welcomed by the library. She needs to convey to them that the library is there to help them and that individual assistance is available. Once she writes her value proposition about this, she can then use that value proposition to inform the marketing campaign that includes these students. Pat's final value proposition? *The Above Average Library. Wherever you have a question, we're here with the answer.* Why *wherever* rather than *whenever*? When Pat tested the message of 24/7 help, her transfer-student focus groups did not respond favorably. The students wanted to know that they could get help both on- and off-campus; they were not interested in when that help was available. Knowing what mattered to these students helped Pat distill the value proposition into the essence of what the library needed to communicate to the students. She was able to communicate that same message to the other public services staff as well so that they, too, were aware of what mattered to this market segment.

TIMELINE

A timeline not only establishes what work needs to be accomplished and when but also illustrates whose responsibility that work is. The timeline should include the information for any work that will be accomplished, not just list the marketing communications (events, advertising, etc.). This helps make sure that no staff person will suddenly become overwhelmed by her part in the marketing plan and helps remind those involved of what work needs to be done so that they can manage their time effectively. Once the timeline is established, a manager like Pat can see whether the reference staff is trying to do too much in one month, with no marketing efforts in another month. Pat can then spread out the work more evenly so it is easier to accomplish and so that in no single month will any target audience be overwhelmed by the marketing messages from various members of the reference staff.

BUDGETS

Once Pat has determined what she hopes to accomplish with her marketing plan, she will ask her director for feedback. Knowing that her director will want to know how much Pat's marketing plan will cost before agreeing to it, Pat will establish a realistic budget. Even though her director may seem enthusiastic about marketing, it is unlikely that Pat will have an unlimited budget at her disposal. For the draft budget, Pat will need to know who is doing the work for each part of the plan and provide costs for the work. For example, because there is no staff member capable of designing graphics, she will estimate how much it will cost to hire a graphic designer to create brand images. She also will find costs for promotional materials for various community events and catering for several receptions. Because her patrons want new services, Pat will need to think about how the reference department could respond to those desires. She will consider if there is money to begin a new service and how much time and money might be saved by ceasing a service that she has discovered no one wants.

Once Pat's director is ready to move forward, Pat can discuss how much time and money it will take to implement that plan. Pat is mentally prepared that her director may want to spend less money and do less, but she also hopes that by having facts she can demonstrate what will be accomplished by spending the time and money on marketing. Her director is a great fund-raiser and may be able to provide more money than Pat ever needed. The director may also know of ways to partner with other agencies and departments to leverage shared resources to create enough savings to fund additional efforts.

ASSESSMENT

Assessment is perhaps the hardest area of marketing. There is no single measurement to apply to any particular marketing goal. Instead, there is a large suite of measurements that can be used based on your needs. For example, if your goal is to increase use and you have designed a marketing campaign intended to do that, then you may want to not only track use before and after the marketing campaign but also determine if any of the use is *because* of the marketing campaign. In this section, I describe several different metrics and how they are used.

If your goal for an event is to have a certain number of people in the audience, measuring success is quite easy. You simply set your target audience size and count heads. This is not an example of strategic marketing, however, so as you grow your efforts, your goals should indicate a more direct tie to the library's mission or to the larger goals of your marketing plan. What exactly is your event intended to do? Are you trying to raise community awareness about an issue, such as literacy? Are you trying to create a relationship with a target audience? Your goals should be set before you plan and host an event, and your evaluation should be based on those goals.

Libraries keep innumerable statistics about use. If any of your marketing goals are about increasing use, then take a close look at what statistics you already keep. You may not need to create a new measurement and instead can use the tools that are already in place. Some of those statistics may be harder to obtain than others. Circulation statistics can often be gathered that illustrate by market segment (undergraduate, graduate student, alumni, faculty, staff) how often and what type of materials are circulating (travelogues, political commentary, biographies, romances, graphic novels, audiobooks). Depending on what integrated library system your library has, generating the data can take time. Be sure that you really need the data before you ask someone to run the report.

It may seem odd to think of LibQUAL as a marketing metric, but given that libraries are in the service business and marketing is about customer relationships, LibQUAL can be used as a measurement of patron satisfaction with your current services. This measurement can be used as part of your market research, rather than as a way to measure the impact of a marketing plan. However, it also can be extended in terms of measuring current marketing efforts. Adapt the questions you would ask in LibQUAL to measure perceptions of service before and after you implement a campaign, then measure the change in perception after your marketing campaign.

Advertising effectiveness is one way to measure the success of marketing. Advertising can include for-fee and free media, such as a video on YouTube, a banner on your library's Web page or in Blackboard, a poster on campus buses, or a traditional ad in the student paper or on the radio. Popular metrics include impressions, click throughs, response rate, and recall.

- *Impressions:* Impressions are the number of times the marketer assumes that a message has been seen. The premise of using advertising this way is based on AIDA, where part of what a marketer wants to do is get the patron's attention. Thus, if the goal for your advertising campaign is simply to have the message be seen, impressions can be used to help determine how many people you have reached.
- *Click throughs:* Click throughs became all the rage as an advertising metric in the 1990s when Internet advertising became popular and cheap. Advertisers use click throughs to determine not just if someone has seen your message but if she is interested enough in it to click and find out more or to use the service.
- *Response rate:* Response rate is similar to click through in that you are measuring whether your patron is taking action on your message. This measurement can be used if you have sent out mailers or have coupons for services (like if you had an ad for a free research consultation that the patron needs to bring in with her). If so, you can collect the coupons and use those to see how many were used in conjunction with the service. If you do not require the coupon to be brought in, you would need to ask at the point of use how the patron had heard about the service.
- *Recall:* Recall measures how many people were able to remember your advertising or how many people can say that they have heard of your service. This can be a useful baseline for establishing your advertising's impact throughout the duration of an advertising campaign.

MARKETING IS ESSENTIAL FOR LIBRARIES

The *culture of assessment* is a frequently touted phrase in libraries. It is used to convey the message that, for a library to succeed, not only does assessment need to be consistent, but every member of the staff must be aware of how what she does helps the customer. The same is true for marketing. Libraries must arrive at a culture of marketing, where there is an understanding articulated among everyone on staff of what relationship the library wants to have with its patrons and how the library is working on those relationships. Marketing is a cyclical process for quantifying patron needs, creating services and products based around those needs and the library's mission, determining value propositions, communicating those value propositions, and monitoring to see if the promised value was noticed by the patron and delivered to the patron. Marketing should be embedded into the daily work of the library and its staff. Our patrons change every year, and our products and services are not stagnant, and therefore neither should our efforts at promoting them be. A library that implements the full promise of marketing will find itself a ubiquitous and integral part of its patrons' lives.

WORKS CITED

American Marketing Association. 2007. *Definition of marketing*. Retrieved August 9, 2009, from http://www.marketingpower.com/AboutAMA/Pages/DefinitionofMarketing.aspx.

Gronroos, C. 1994. From marketing mix to relationship marketing: Towards a paradigm shift in marketing. *Management Decision* 32 (2): 4–20.

ADDITIONAL READINGS

Alire, C. 2007. Word-of-mouth marketing: Abandoning the academic library ivory tower. *New Library World* 108 (11–12): 545–551.

Anderson, J., J. Narus, and W. van Rossum. 2006. Customer value propositions in business markets. *Harvard Business Review* 84 (3): 90–99.

George, W. 1990. Internal marketing and organizational behavior: A partnership in developing customer-conscious employees at every level. *Journal of Business Research* 20 (1): 63–70.

MacDonald, K., W. vanDuinkerken, and J. Stephens. 2008. It's all in the marketing: The impact of a virtual reference marketing campaign at Texas A&M University. *Reference & User Services Quarterly* 47 (4): 375–385.

Osif, B. 2006. Branding, marketing, and fund-raising. *Library Administration & Management* 20 (1): 39–43.

Siess, J. 2003. *The visible librarian: Asserting your value with marketing and advocacy.* Chicago: American Library Association.

Wallace, L. 2009. Gaming in academic libraries: Collections, marketing, and information literacy. *Journal of Academic Librarianship* 35 (4): 391–392.

12

REFERENCE QUALITY: A PRIMER ON METHODS AND TOOLS FOR ASSESSING REFERENCE SERVICES

Julie A. Gedeon and Joseph A. Salem, Jr.

Reference services are a significant investment in library human resources. Reference services are often staffed for most, if not all, of the hours a library is open, and in the case of 24-hour virtual reference, services are even provided beyond library hours. In addition to the time commitment, reference services often represent the highest concentration of professional positions within the organization. Because of the significant investment, it is essential for public service librarians to assess reference services for their quality and accuracy, and to determine user needs and satisfaction. With the various modes of delivery of reference services, methods applicable for in person and virtual contact must be considered.

This chapter describes the most common assessment methods as well as standardized tools available to assess reference services. All except one may be used to evaluate a variety of aspects of both in-person and virtual reference. The one exception, the Wisconsin-Ohio Reference Evaluation Program (WOREP), is appropriately applied to in-person transactions only. Another standardized tool not usually thought of initially when considering reference evaluation, LibQUAL+, may be customized to focus on some aspects of reference service quality.

In addition to describing each method and tool, this chapter presents pros and cons and offers suggestions for implementation. Before describing tools and methods that assess quality and impact of reference services, it is necessary to discuss the most common and basic form of reference data collection—use data.

USE DATA

Although not an assessment technique per se, the gathering and analysis of reference service use data are almost ubiquitous and can be effective in making staffing decisions, setting service hours, determining the questions that other assessment methods can answer, measuring the effectiveness of outreach and marketing efforts, and gauging the utilization of new services or resources. In addition to their value for planning and assessment, use data are often required to fulfill local, regional, and national reporting requirements. For example, the Association of Research Libraries (ARL) requires all member institutions to report reference service use data on an annual basis. ARL reporting guides usage data collection by adhering to the National Information Standards Organization (NISO) standards (NISO, 2004). ARL statistics are available at no cost on the association's Web site (ARL, 2009) so they can be used as benchmarks to put one's use data in context.

It has become much easier to collect use data since the advent of the Web. Hash marks on paper have been replaced with Web forms and mouse clicks to gather data and generate reports for a given period. The convenience of collection and tabulation makes it easier to gather use data on a continuing basis rather than sampling. If sampling is done, ARL suggests gathering data for a typical week and extrapolating to the annual number of transactions based on those data (ARL, 2007).

Several options exist for gathering use data using already-developed tools. DePauw Libraries provides an example of using the Google Docs suite to set up a form for collecting use data and storing them in a spreadsheet (DePauw Libraries, 2009). Libstats (http://code.google.com/p/libstats/) is a free program for collecting data; however, assistance from a Web programmer is needed to take advantage of the code to run the program. Hosted commercial services are available as well. Two in current use that allow the gathering of reference statistics, along with questions asked and answers given, are Gimlet (http://gimlet.us) and SiteScripter (http://www.sitescripter.com). The advantage of using these tools is that users can build a local knowledge base, enhancing the usefulness of the data collected.

STANDARDIZED TOOLS

Although use data can offer guidance in planning and staffing decisions, their application is limited. Counts can provide a sense of busy times and staffing needs; however, the level of expertise necessary to meet those needs can be difficult to ascertain from use data alone. By gathering not only counts but also information regarding the level of effort expended to complete each reference transaction, the Reference Effort Assessment Data Scale can enhance use-data collection and reporting.

The Reference Effort Assessment Data Scale

The Reference Effort Assessment Data (READ) Scale (http://www.dom.edu/library/READ/index.html) was developed in 2003 by librarians at Carnegie Mellon University. It is a six-point scale tool for recording supplemental qualitative statistics gathered when reference librarians assist users. It was devised as an expansion of the traditional hash mark system of merely counting the number of reference transactions, and as such it provides a way for librarians to indicate their own level of effort and perceived difficulty for each transaction. Staff assign rankings from 1, for the answers that require the least amount of effort and no specialized knowledge, skills, or expertise, through 6, for those requiring the most effort and time.

The purpose of the READ Scale is to document perceived effort on an individual and departmental level. It is a qualitative instrument that relies on individual personal assessment (Gerlich and Berard, 2007). The numbers in the scale are defined, and examples are provided. Because subject specialists would find it easier to assist users with more intensive, subject-specific needs, it is possible that staff who help someone outside of their area of expertise could assign a higher scale point than a subject librarian responding to the same question would. This can make comparisons within and across institutions difficult, a fact that has been acknowledged by the READ Scale developer (Gerlich and Berard, 2010). Careful training within a reference department prior to implementing the READ Scale will help minimize this effect.

READ Scale data recording can use a library's existing paper or online form to capture day, hour, and approach type (walk-up, telephone, virtual) for both directional and reference questions, both on and off the desk. The difference is that staff record a number instead of a hash mark, thus adding value to the recording of reference transactions. At least one commercial service for collecting reference statistics, SiteScripter, offers an option to implement the READ Scale method, with READ Scale definitions and examples included. A free Web tool is also available for creating online forms (http://creator.zoho.com/?home).

The READ Scale is useful in determining staffing needs for a particular service, such as in person reference, or for an institution's reference service program overall. If used to record data for all services, the READ Scale can help determine if different difficulty levels for questions occur at the public desks or via other media, which can facilitate a tiered reference approach. For example, if lower-level questions are asked via instant messaging, it may be possible to staff that service with students rather than with librarians. The READ Scale can also identify training needs and outreach opportunities. At the very least, it can be used to fulfill requirements for reporting to library administration, the institution overall, or any institutional affiliations.

Requirements for Administration

- Local coordinator
- Staff training and orientation to ensure consistent data recording
- Consistent method for recording data
- Willingness to share data, results, and experiences with scale developer

Advantages

- Is simple and quick to complete
- Allows for inclusion of effort and skills used during each reference transaction
- May be localized by adding sample questions typical of library's inquiries
- Includes a detailed instruction manual
- May be implemented into existing system for recording reference transactions (paper and pencil, network, Web-based)

Disadvantages

- Benchmarks not yet established
- Levels can be interpreted subjectively and specific to the staff member responding
- Requires commitment to local training and discussion before data collection begins

The READ Scale is one of the newest standardized tools available to assess reference services. Descriptions of two other standardized tools, WOREP and LibQUAL+, follow. WOREP is designed exclusively to evaluate reference services. Because of LibQUAL+'s broader focus on service quality in all areas of the library, it provides less information targeted to reference services.

WOREP

WOREP (worep.library.kent.edu) was developed in 1984 by researchers at the University of Wisconsin–Madison and the Ohio State University. This paper-and-pencil tool is used to gather information from both the user and the reference staff member upon completion of an in-person transaction. Each transaction is evaluated by both parties, who complete a scannable form, and only transactions where both customer and staff forms are submitted are analyzed.

WOREP looks at each transaction from the point of view of the patron and the staff. The purpose is to determine customer satisfaction and gauge whether customers got what they sought. In the report, satisfaction is defined as the patron getting exactly what she wanted and being completely satisfied with the transaction. Because satisfaction alone may have little to do with actually obtaining the correct or useful information or source but could be influenced by effort and courtesy on the part of the reference staff, the WOREP definition of satisfaction provides more rigor and a higher standard by combining the feeling of being satisfied with the obtaining of required information or materials.

Questions asked of the patrons include if they were satisfied with the service; whether they obtained what they had sought; how they found the information or materials; if the staff appeared knowledgeable and courteous; if the staff appeared busy; how important the transaction was; if they received enough time, help, and explanation; and if they learned something as a result of their interaction with the librarian.

Questions asked of the staff include the type and difficulty level of the question, the amount of time spent, the nature of the transaction (directional, help, instruction), their level of busyness, the number of sources used, the subject area of inquiry, any special factors, and the outcome of the transaction. Demographics collected are type of staff (librarian, library assistant, other), patron status (class rank, faculty/staff, visitor), and patron major or teaching/research area.

Reports provide institution-specific details about reference service during the survey administration period, as well as benchmarks to other libraries that have participated in WOREP. Comparisons are provided to all other libraries of the same size (small, medium, large, based on total collection), to the top scoring library of the same size, and to all libraries in the data set.

Within a single WOREP administration, an institution can use the results to plan professional development opportunities for reference librarians. Because it associates user satisfaction and service accuracy with factors such as the subject matter of the transaction, the types of resources consulted, the level of activity in the reference center, and the level of assistance provided by the librarian, areas of lower satisfaction can identify professional development needs. For example, low user satisfaction associated with statistics questions can lead to a refresher session on statistical resources. As benchmarking is provided, problem areas can be placed in context, which helps to set realistic expectations for improvement.

WOREP is also useful for capturing a snapshot of the activity at the reference desk, including the level of activity and at least the subject areas of the questions being asked. Repeated administration provides a better understanding of reference service trends at an institution over time.

Requirements for Administration

- On-site administrator
- Preplanning to determine appropriate sampling method
- Brief orientation for staff to ensure reliable data collection
- #2 pencils
- $1.25/form
- A recommended minimum of 50 responses

Advantages

- Is easy to administer
- Is low in cost

- Has short forms
- Includes a detailed user manual
- Allows for a flexible time period
- Focuses on single in-person reference transactions from the point of view of both patron and staff
- Includes comparison to benchmarks of all libraries that have participated in WOREP, all libraries of the same size, and the top scoring library of the same size (130 libraries in benchmark and more than 20 years of data gathering)
- Results in detailed reports that are provided within two weeks of forms being received by Kent State
- Measures patron satisfaction with reference transactions and factors that influence it

Disadvantages

- Because of scannable forms, requires special handling and completion with #2 pencils
- May be obtrusive (staff may consciously or unconsciously provide better service knowing they are participating in evaluation)
- Evaluates only in-person reference transactions
- Does not provide raw data to institutions

LibQUAL+

LibQUAL+ (www.libqual.org) was developed by researchers at Texas A&M University and the ARL beginning in 2000 and is now administered by the ARL. This Web-based tool is used to collect quantitative and qualitative information from users regarding their perceptions of overall library service quality. The tool measures user satisfaction on three levels: quality of service provided by staff, extent and quality of information resources available, and quality of the physical space. Demographic information is collected, including age, sex, status (undergraduate, graduate, faculty), and discipline, as well as how often and how the respondents use the library. The survey consists of 22 core items written to assess in the three dimensions, some general satisfaction items, and demographic questions about respondents. The 22 core items require participants to answer, on a nine-point scale, three times about each item: What is my minimum expectation? What is my desired expectation? What is my perceived level of service? There is one open-ended general response item at the end. Participating institutions define their user populations and usually include staff as well as students and faculty.

Once the survey administration window is closed for the specific term, the ARL begins processing the data to provide detailed reports. Participants receive reports describing their own users' desired, perceived, and minimum expectations of service. Raw data are also available in SPSS and Excel formats.

Norms tables are available for the 2001 through 2005 surveys on the Web site. It is also possible to view other libraries' reports for the specific year(s) an institution participated. LibQUAL+ Analytics is a tool that permits participants to dynamically create institution-specific tables and charts for different subgroups and across years. The current interface grants access to data from 2004 and later. Additional features are in development.

It should be noted that LibQUAL+ would not be the first choice if a library is interested in assessing reference services exclusively, as its purpose is more broadly focused on overall library service quality. However, if a library is planning to use LibQUAL+ as part of an overall service assessment, the reference department can get some data on reference service quality. In addition to the core questions, some of which address reference-related issues, there is an option to select five custom questions. These may be selected to be specific to reference services.

LibQUAL+ can be used to identify areas where services and resources do not meet user expectations. Because it is a standardized tool, institutions can administer it repeatedly over time to determine the efficacy of efforts to close the gap between user expectations and user perceptions of service and quality. Within a single administration, results can be compared with results at similar institutions, which may help set realistic goals for improvement. For example, if most institutions do not fare well with graduate students with regard to reference and research resources, it may not be realistic to expect vast improvement with that group over time. As it breaks down results by undergraduates, graduates, and faculty, LibQUAL+ also provides opportunities for additional assessment and outreach opportunities.

Requirements for Administration

- On-site administrator
- E-mail invitations and reminders to selected sample
- $3,200 base registration fee (as of 2010)

Advantages

- Is Web-based and also allows for paper administration
- Allows the user to select up to five optional questions, which allows for an increased focus on reference services
- Includes a detailed user manual
- Yields detailed reports
- Provides raw data to institutions
- Allows access to other libraries' reports available within same administration year
- Collects data from a large number of people
- Provides breakdowns by user groups

Disadvantages

- Has a moderate cost
- Gathers information not only about reference services but also about the entire library
- Solicits information from customers and potential customers only, without staff input

LOCALLY DEVELOPED TOOLS

Standardized assessment tools cannot always meet needs at the local level. Cost and lack of applicability to a specific service may prohibit their use. The rest of this chapter focuses on techniques that can be used to develop reference service assessments. When designing an assessment instrument or study at the local level using the methods in this section, it is important to note the need to pilot the instrument and methods before gathering data. A primary advantage of using standardized instruments is that they have already been validated. Locally designed instruments and study protocols must be tested before they are deployed on a large scale.

For studies requiring members of the target audience to respond to questions (surveys, focus groups), the questions should be pretested with a subsample of the population. For observational studies, the checklists and protocols developed should be tried out in the field by those who will be doing the observations. Careful preparation prior to data collection will ensure more useful study results.

Observational Methods

Observational methods have traditionally been used to evaluate in-person reference service quality (Crowley, 1971; Weech and Goldhor, 1982; Whitlatch, 1989). The techniques may be adapted for assessing other modes of reference delivery. Observation is often used to assess reference service quality by focusing on accuracy of the reference service transaction, behavioral aspects of the service, or both.

Data may be gathered obtrusively or unobtrusively. Each has its pros and cons, and the debate over their uses is worth noting. Obtrusive evaluation is often criticized for its perceived lack of efficacy due to the effect of the presence of the evaluator on the behavior of those being evaluated. Unobtrusive evaluation is often criticized on ethical grounds, as participating librarians are unaware that they are being evaluated.

Unobtrusive Observation

Unobtrusive observation can be used to gather data on reference service quality and accuracy. Studies employing unobtrusive methods use one of two strategies. Those seeking to evaluate service accuracy often employ the "secret-shopper" strategy where anonymous users ask questions of the reference librarians and record data on the accuracy of the response, resources consulted, and behavioral characteristics of the librarian. Assessment projects interested in service quality often employ observational studies that focus on recording behavioral characteristics of reference service providers.

Unobtrusive testing was the source of the oft-cited "55 percent rule." Hernon and McClure (1986) used unobtrusive methods to assess service quality in federal depository libraries. Anonymous patrons asked librarians questions for which the patrons knew the answers and which resources to consult. Librarians were scored on their ability to answer the questions. The researchers found that only 62 percent of the questions were answered correctly. When Hernon and McClure reviewed other similar studies, they discovered that the percentage of questions answered correctly ranged from 50 to 62 percent, leading them to conclude that, on average, 55 percent of questions asked at reference desks receive correct responses. The methodology of the Hernon and McClure study is a good example of unobtrusive assessment of reference service.

Many unobtrusive studies go beyond a simple right/wrong scoring and gather data on other aspects of the transaction, including time for transaction completion, resources consulted, and behavioral characteristics of the librarian providing the service. The Reference and User Services Association (RUSA) publishes behavioral guidelines that can be used to assess the performance of librarians providing reference services (RUSA, 2004). Using the RUSA guidelines in reference service assessment helps to standardize even locally developed instruments. Gatten and Radcliff (2001) provide a sample form, based on the RUSA guidelines, used in the Ohio Reference Excellence Initiative project.

In addition to the secret shopper approach, the same behavioral guidelines can be used in another form of unobtrusive assessment, the nonparticipant observational study. Unobtrusive observational studies can evaluate service accuracy; however, it is often difficult to do so in an effective way due to environmental obstacles in the reference department. Because behaviors can be observed from some distance, many observational studies assess this aspect of reference services. Even if the evaluation is to be unobtrusive, it is best to share the standards upon which librarians will be assessed in advance. Another key to reliable data gathering in observational studies is the use by all observers of a standard form to record the degree to which librarians meet the standards.

Obtrusive (Peer) Observation

The most common use of obtrusive observation in reference is in peer evaluation. Obtrusive observation often resembles the studies already described, the difference being that librarians are aware that they are being evaluated. Many of these evaluations focus on behavioral aspects of the reference transaction. One benefit is the ability to offer immediate suggestions for improvement or tips for successfully completing the reference transaction. One way to make these evaluations successful professional development opportunities for the librarian being evaluated is to have peers assess each other. Like the unobtrusive observational studies described earlier, it is important to share the criteria for evaluation and use consistent instruments to record observational data so that the evaluation can assess not only the individual librarians but also the service overall.

While peer assessment can be employed for evaluating in-person reference, it is also an effective way to assess virtual reference services. Virtual reference assessment offers a unique opportunity to evaluate the accuracy of the service while ensuring the anonymity of individual librarians. Although virtual reference can be assessed through the secret-shopper strategy described earlier, it can also be evaluated *post facto* through the analysis of chat transcripts. If librarian anonymity is important, any identifying information, including login credentials or the time and date of the transaction, can be removed before transcripts are analyzed. Transcript analysis has become a standard method for evaluating virtual reference services. A study by Pomerantz, Luo, and McClure (2006) is a good example. The authors used peer review of chat transcripts to evaluate the NCknows project. Their study simply asked whether each question was answered accurately and completely, finding a generally high level of quality in the service provided.

Requirements for Administration

- Training for "secret shoppers" or observers to ensure objectivity and consistency
- Data-gathering instrument; rubric or checklist of behaviors for observers to use; or questions to be asked
- Opportunity for librarians to familiarize themselves with standards to be assessed

Advantages

- Gathers data on authentic behaviors and service provision by librarians
- Provides opportunities for professional development during review with each librarian
- Provides immediate feedback (peer evaluation)

Disadvantages

- Can be time- and resource-intensive
- Raises ethical issues
- Creates potential for resistance by librarians being observed

- Creates potential for subjectivity among observers
- Creates potential for interpersonal dynamics to affect the assessment

Surveys

Surveys are commonly used to measure user satisfaction with reference services. They can also be used to assess user needs, which is particularly useful when planning for physical enhancements or reorganization of the reference center or when gauging the types of services and reference resources to provide. The key to effective surveys is the questionnaire's design. Survey mechanics are easy to focus on, especially with the advantages of online survey tools; however, the questionnaire is the focal point of any survey.

It is important to ask only questions with a productive or helpful array of responses. This helps to keep the questionnaire as short as possible and aids in data analysis. It is difficult enough to recruit respondents for a survey, and even more difficult to get them to complete the questionnaire. It is also important to limit open-ended questions. Although the data gathered will often be worth noting, the information can often be generalized only to a limited extent and can be easily disregarded as anecdotal. With the emphasis on the questionnaire, it is vital to pilot the survey before disseminating it. The pilot survey should gather feedback from members of the target audience regarding the questions to ensure that the study gathers the data desired and that the questions are clear to the respondents. The survey pilot should also test the survey mechanics.

Survey mechanics include the distribution of paper questionnaires or the setup, promotion, and gathering of data via online questionnaires. Both paper and online questionnaires can be promoted through library resources. Paper surveys can be distributed at the reference desk or other service desks in the library. Online questionnaires can be promoted through e-mail, on the library's Web site, and through paper promotional materials distributed at library service desks. Survey options are often built directly into many commercial software packages used to provide virtual reference services. If using a free instant messaging service, a link to the survey can be provided as part of the conclusion of the transaction.

A good example of a locally developed survey to gather users' and providers' perspectives at the close of a reference transaction is presented by Miller (2008). This tool was developed to build on LibQUAL+ survey data; similarly to WOREP, it asks about outcome and satisfaction with individual interactions. Miller provides the questionnaire and encourages other libraries to modify and use it locally.

Requirements for Administration

- Access to members of the target audience for piloting
- Incentives to aid in recruitment

- Staff expertise in question development and data analysis
- Tools for developing and delivering the survey

Advantages

- Can gather data from a large number of respondents
- Is relatively simple to administer

Disadvantages

- Can be difficult to recruit participants
- Can be time-intensive for data analysis and result reporting

Focus Groups

While the other methods discussed can be used to evaluate individual reference transactions, focus groups are useful for gathering more general information regarding user satisfaction and needs. Focus groups are interview sessions with small groups from the target audience. The ideal focus group includes between 8 and 10 participants. If possible, a focus group study would include at least three sessions with each target audience group. This requires strong recruitment efforts. Incentives are often key to recruiting participants.

Before conducting the session itself, planners will need to create discussion prompts to keep the conversation going. Sessions typically last 30 to 60 minutes. In a 60-minute session, 10 discussion prompts can be covered. A key to focus groups is flexibility. Even if the original prompts are not addressed in a session, discussion among participants should be encouraged as long as it is related to the issue central to the focus group study.

Every focus group should be conducted by a moderator who will use the prompts to facilitate discussion among participants. At least two additional colleagues should take notes and, when necessary, help facilitate. The sessions can also be recorded, but recording should not replace note taking. The notes taken during a focus group session can be useful in adjusting prompts from one session to another or in documenting nonverbal cues among participants that would be missed on an audio recording.

Focus groups can be used to determine user satisfaction with existing reference services, facilities, and information resources; assess needed services and resources under consideration; or brainstorm new services or resources that can be provided as part of the library's reference program. These need not be exclusive. A focus group assessment of reference services can ask questions related to all three aspects.

Requirements for Administration

- Skilled moderator
- Note takers
- List of prompts and forms for taking notes
- Private conference room or other similar comfortable setting
- Subgroup of the target audience for piloting prompts and mechanics
- Incentives to aid in participant recruitment
- Audio recording device
- Transcriptionist

Advantages

- Allows gathering of data not only on desired discussion items but also on related issues
- Explores user satisfaction, needs, and new ideas for services or resources

Disadvantages

- Generates large amount of data
- Can be time-intensive to prepare and facilitate the session, transcribe recordings, and analyze data
- Can be costly to provide incentives

TURNING DATA INTO INFORMATION

As reference continues to evolve, it is increasingly essential to assess the commitment to providing user assistance in library facilities and beyond through reference services and Web-based reference resources. The standardized instruments and assessment techniques discussed in this chapter are the most commonly used methods for reference service evaluation. No one tool is perfect for any assessment project. A comprehensive assessment of reference services can use many of the methods described to gather a variety of types of data.

The most important aspect of any assessment is data use. Many people do well at data collection and even analysis. When planning reference service evaluation, consider what will be done with the data collected. For example, if changes to facilities are not possible, do not address them in a survey or focus group.

Assessment results should also be shared widely. Even seemingly bad news should be shared with stakeholders in general and study participants in particular to highlight the importance of their involvement as well as the library's commitment to improvement. Assessment is useful only as part of a cycle that includes data gathering, data analysis, and the implementation of changes based on the data. Once changes are made, the assessment cycle begins again. As a significant commitment in every library, reference services should be included in the assessment cycle to ensure the highest quality of service and the best use of increasingly scarce resources.

WORKS CITED

Association of Research Libraries. 2007. *ARL statistics questionnaire, 2007–08: Instructions for completing the questionnaire.* Retrieved July 28, 2009, from http://www.arl.org/bm~doc/08instruct.pdf.

Association of Research Libraries. 2009. *ARL statistics.* Retrieved July 28, 2009, from http://www.arl.org/stats/annualsurveys/arlstats/index.shtml.

Crowley, T. 1971. The effectiveness of information service in medium size public libraries. In *Information service in public libraries: Two studies,* by T. Crowley and T. Childers, 1–71. Metuchen, NJ: Scarecrow Press.

DePauw Libraries. 2009. *Spring 2009 reference @ DePauw Libraries.* Retrieved July 28, 2009, from http://spreadsheets.google.com/viewform?key=p2m2zWermdR722xhkinbXHQ.

Gatten, J. N., and C. J. Radcliff. 2001. Assessing reference behaviors with unobtrusive testing. In *Library evaluation: A casebook and can-do guide,* ed. D. P. Wallace and C. Van Fleet, 105–115. Englewood, CO: Libraries Unlimited.

Gerlich, B. K., and G. L. Berard. 2007. Introducing the READ Scale: Qualitative statistics for academic reference services. *Georgia Library Quarterly* 43 (4): 7–12.

Gerlich, B. K., and G. L. Berard. 2010. Testing the viability of the READ Scale (Reference Effort Assessment Data) ©: Qualitative statistics for academic reference service. *College & Research Libraries* 71 (2): 116–137.

Hernon, P., and C. R. McClure. 1986. Unobtrusive reference testing: The 55 percent rule. *Library Journal* 111: 37–41.

Miller, J. 2008. Quick and easy reference evaluation: Gathering users' and providers' perspectives. *Reference & User Services Quarterly* 47 (3): 218–222.

National Information Standards Organization. 2004. *Information services and use: Metrics and statistics for libraries and information providers—data dictionary.* Retrieved July 28, 2009, from http://www.niso.org/dictionary.

Pomerantz, J., L. Luo, and C. R. McClure. 2006. Peer review of chat reference transcripts: Approaches and strategies. *Library & Information Science Research* 28: 24–48.

Reference and User Services Association. 2004. *Guidelines for behavioral performance of reference and information service providers.* Retrieved July 28, 2009, from http://www.ala.org/Template.cfm?Section=Home&template=/ContentManagement/ContentDisplay.cfm&ContentID=26937.

Weech, T. L., and H. Goldhor. 1982. Obtrusive versus unobtrusive evaluation of reference service in five Illinois public libraries: A pilot study. *Library Quarterly* 52 (4): 305–324.

Whitlatch, J. B. 1989. Unobtrusive studies and the quality of academic reference services. *College & Research Libraries* 50: 181–194.

ADDITIONAL READINGS

Fink, A. 2003. *How to conduct surveys: A step-by-step guide.* 3rd ed. Thousand Oaks, CA: Sage.

Gerlich, B. K., and E. Whatley. 2009. Using the READ scale for staffing strategies: The Georgia College and State University experience. *Library Leadership and Management* 23 (1): 26–30.

Glitz, B. 1998. *Focus groups for libraries and librarians.* Chicago: American Library Association.

Hoseth, A. E. 2007. We did LibQUAL+—now what? Practical suggestions for maximizing your survey results. *College & Undergraduate Libraries* 14 (3): 75–84.

Hubbertz, A. 2005. The design and interpretation of unobtrusive evaluations. *Reference & User Services Quarterly* 44: 327–335.

Jones, S., and J. Kayongo. 2008. Identifying student and faculty needs through LibQUAL+TM: An analysis of qualitative survey comments. *College & Research Libraries* 69 (6): 493–509.

Kayongo, J., and S. Jones. 2008. Faculty perception of information control using LibQUAL+ indicators. *Journal of Academic Librarianship* 34 (2): 130–138.

Kuruppu, P. U. 2007. Evaluation of reference services—a review. *Journal of Academic Librarianship* 33: 368–381.

Novotny, E., and E. Rimland. 2007. Using the Wisconsin-Ohio Reference Evaluation Program (WOREP) to improve training and reference services. *Journal of Academic Librarianship* 33 (3): 382–392.

Parker, J. D. 1996. Evaluating documents reference service and the implications for improvement. *Journal of Government Information* 23: 49–70.

Paster, A., K. Fescemyer, N. Henry, J. Hughes, and H. Smith. 2006. Assessing reference: Using the Wisconsin-Ohio Reference Evaluation Program in an academic science library. *Issues in Science and Technology Librarianship* 46 (Spring 2006). Retrieved September 7, 2010, from http://www.istl.org/06-spring/article2.html.

Pomerantz, J., L. Mon, and C. R. McClure. 2008. Evaluating remote reference service: A practical guide to problems and solutions. *portal: Libraries and the Academy* 8: 15–30.

Powell, R. R., and L. S. Connaway. 2004. *Basic research methods for librarians.* 4th ed. Westport, CT: Libraries Unlimited.

Radcliff, C. J., and B. F. Schloman. 2001. Case study: Using the Wisconsin-Ohio Reference Evaluation Program. In *Library evaluation: A casebook and can-do guide,* ed. D. P. Wallace and C. Van Fleet, 89–102. Englewood, CO: Libraries Unlimited.

Roszkowski, M. J., J. S. Baky, and D. B. Jones. 2005. So which score on the LibQual+ tells me if library users are satisfied? *Library & Information Science Research* 27 (4): 424–439.

Saunders, E. S. 2007. The LibQUAL+ phenomenon: Who judges quality? *Reference & User Services Quarterly* 47 (1): 21–24.

Stalker, J. C., and M. E. Murfin. 1996. Quality reference service: A preliminary case study. *Journal of Academic Librarianship* 22 (6): 423–429.

Thompson, B., M. Kyrillidou, and C. Cook. 2007. On-premises library versus Google-like information gateway usage patterns: A LibQUAL+ study. *portal: Libraries and the Academy* 7 (4): 463–480.

IV

OLD TOOLS / NEW TOOLS: THE ROLE OF TECHNOLOGY IN REFERENCE SERVICE

13

TELEPHONE REFERENCE AS THE PAST AND THE FUTURE OF LIBRARY SERVICE

M. Kathleen Kern

The telephone was invented over 130 years ago. Documented use in libraries dates back to 1876 (Wilson, 1876). Given the long history, how does a chapter on the telephone fit into a book on breathing new life into reference? Cell phones, and smartphones in particular, have opened up new ways of communicating, such as texting. Even if we limit our examination to traditional telephony, voice communication has been dramatically changed by Internet technologies such as voice over IP (VoIP) and voice chat. In the United States 270 million people, 86 percent of the population, own a wireless telephone (Central Intelligence Agency, 2010; CTIA, 2009). These figures do not even delve into mobile communication's prevalence worldwide and the enormous impact on telephony in the developing world. After all this time, the telephone still holds great potential for both voice and text communication; what is old is new again.

AN ENDURING MEDIUM

Even though telephones in libraries are documented as early as 1876, telephone reference as a service did not really become popular until the middle of the 20th century. After World War II, the number of businesses and households with private telephone lines increased, making telephone reference a popular service. The necessary catalyst was *access* to the technology. Today, an unprecedented number of people have telephones, not only in the United States, but around the world. For mobile telephone owners, access is at hand all the time. This increased access could dramatically increase our telephone reference inquiries if libraries strategically market the service.

Mobile telephones have revolutionized the world of telephony. In developing nations, cellular service has allowed populations to leap over inadequate networks of telephone lines and cables, especially since access to cellular telephone services is more widespread and staggeringly less expensive than Internet service (International Telecommunications Union, 2009). Now, services such as Question Box (http://www.questionbox.org) use telephones (particularly cell phones) to provide vital information, such as up-to-date agricultural prices to farmers in areas of Africa and India who previously would have had to wait for this news by mail or word of mouth.

That telephone reference has been a mainstay in libraries attests not to tradition but to the continued popularity of the telephone as a way to communicate. People communicate with each other through newer technologies, but the proliferation of technologies has resulted in more communication rather than just a shift from one mode to another. In our eagerness to embrace new communication technologies, are we risking leaving behind the obvious?

The New York Public Library has a famous telephone reference department that was organized into a separate unit in 1968. This department now answers patron inquiries received by telephone, e-mail, and text message. A *New York Times* article (Ramirez, 2006) notes, "While the number of telephone calls has declined over the years to fewer than 150 a day from more than 1,000, they still made up two-thirds, or 41,715, of all inquiries to the staff last year (the rest were by computer)." This dramatic drop in overall question volume is a discussion for a different place, but the impressive statistic is that the telephone is chosen more often than e-mail and online chat combined.

People have a personal, even emotional, attachment to their cell phones because they carry them with them all of the time and rely on them for maintaining personal connections with others (Vincent, 2006). This creates the opportunity for a new level of connection between the patron and the library. Librarians can encourage patrons to program the library's phone number into their mobile address books. First, however, people must be aware that they can call the library not only for book renewal but also for research questions. Patrons need to know that there is a service that they can use to answer questions from wherever they are. Telephone reference is taken for granted by librarians and has not been promoted in the ways that new services such as instant messaging (IM) have been. We should not assume that people (library users and nonusers alike) know the range of services that we offer. Radford (2007) has an entertaining blog post on using in-class library instruction time to have students enter the library reference number into their mobile phones. If libraries find it odd or awkward to promote a service that has become so mainstream, they can use a new hook by cross-advertising with more recently added services such as IM and SMS (short message service, or text messaging).

MOBILIZING THE TELEPHONE

Libraries are using telephones to make their reference librarians more mobile and responsive. A few libraries have done this extensively and creatively and can serve as examples for offering truly "roving" reference. Cordless phones, wireless Internet, and mobile telephones all mean that librarians do not need to be at a desk to assist patrons. Instead, librarians can walk around to find patrons in need of assistance. This makes for more visible librarians and means that we can work with people where they need us, which is often at a computer where they can conduct database searches rather than having librarians search for them. With the increase in patrons bringing their laptops to the library, these computers can be far from the reference desk or any other type of library service desk.

The Orange County Library System (OCLS) in Florida started using the Vocera mobile device in 2003. This device uses the library's wireless network to allow librarians to talk to one another, with the push of a button and a voice command to connect. The telephone device itself is very small and can be clipped onto a lapel or worn on a lanyard. The Vocera system can be connected to a telephone number, allowing patrons using other telephone systems to reach librarians through their Vocera devices. Librarians can work away from the reference desk, going to where patrons or materials are located throughout the library; it enables the staff to move through the building but remain reachable, and it supports reference teamwork even when staff are dispersed in one building or across several branch locations (OCLS, 2003).

During the first decade of the 21st century, many libraries closed their reference desks, often in response to declining numbers of questions received, changes in types of questions asked, and budget woes. A triage model developed at these libraries in which circulation or help desk staff would answer directional questions and basic questions about finding library materials and refer more in-depth questions to librarians. Often there would be librarians on-call so that patrons would not need to wait to obtain in-depth assistance. The on-call librarian would work from a location away from the circulation desk (such as her office) but remain available to come out to the public area to work with patrons. Questions received via telephone in the library were similarly triaged through front-line staff and transferred to librarians as needed. The telephone, particularly cordless and mobile models, has provided librarians with the mobility to move from office to public space quickly, but only when they are needed. Librarians no longer have to wait at a fixed location for patrons to arrive with questions that may sometimes require expert reference help but often could be answered by well-trained circulation staff. By equipping librarians with cordless or mobile telephones, reference assistance can be easily located without the physical presence of a reference desk.

The telephone is not just for incoming calls from patrons with questions. It is itself a powerful reference tool. Telephones can connect librarians with other librarians within their organization or beyond. It can make available expertise from our colleagues and expertise from other fields. It can be a timesaver to call a business or association to ask for information we are sure they have rather than to search through large or poorly designed Web sites. It is important to remember that sometimes another person is the best resource for answering a question.

NEW MODES OF VOICE COMMUNICATION

VoIP is another way of using technology to convey voice communication. Services like Skype and Google Voice use the Internet to deliver sound and video. Videoconferencing is now within reach of anyone with a fast Internet connection and a computer with sound and video. In addition to the video feature, these VoIP services have another advantage over the telephone: They are usually free. With Skype, for instance, calls are free as long as you are communicating with another user on Skype, but if you want to use Skype from your computer to call a non-Skype number, then there are charges. Since Skype accounts are free to register for, friends can arrange together to join the service. Unlike mobile telephones, VoIP and videoconferencing have the disadvantage of requiring proximity to a computer, which limits physical mobility during the conversation.

Libraries have several opportunities to take advantage of VoIP and videoconferencing technologies. VoIP services often have a text-entry or IM component, to allow users to shift between typed and voice communication. Thus, an IM communication about a reference question can become a voice interaction if it becomes clear that this would be a more effective way to communicate. This does require that both the librarian and patron have sound enabled on their computers and that they are in locations where they can talk without disturbing others. Using VoIP and online video could be useful to reach students and researchers studying or living in different countries as these services can make it free to place a call.

Librarians differ in their opinions about using video for online reference interviews, and no study of patron preferences has yet been done. From a communication standpoint, using online video would reintroduce some of the nonverbal communication that is lost with telephone and online communication. As with the telephone, if online video becomes popular for personal and business purposes, then patrons will be ready for it from the library. Using videoconferencing in the library might complicate staffing logistics by limiting how many patrons an online librarian can help at once. With text-only online reference it is not obvious to patrons when a librarian is assisting more than one person, but video reference might make it more difficult to handle simultaneous interactions.

MOVING BEYOND VOICE: TEXT (SMS) FOR REFERENCE

The telephone has become so much more than a tool for voice communication. Text messaging is a popular use of mobile phones now gaining popularity as a library service. Libraries are right to heed this trend in popular culture, because text messaging is huge. According to CTIA (2009), 1.35 billion text messages were sent in the United States during June 2009. While some librarians have raised concerns over the limitations of communicating in phrases of fewer than 160 characters, others see text messaging as a way to connect with busy, on-the-go patrons.

One of the earliest adopters of text messaging for library reference was the library at South Eastern Louisiana University, which first piloted this service in 2004. Hill, Madarash Hill, and Sherman (2007) report that while the service had very few users the first year, they presciently envisioned the trend and persisted. Six years later, reference via text messaging is an active topic of conversation on library e mail lists, and several companies support SMS for use by libraries. There are different ways for librarians to offer a text reference service. Some libraries use a mobile phone for sending and receiving texts, while others use software that allows text messages to be received in the same interface as IMs or e-mails. A growing list of libraries, both public and academic, have adopted this service. Since the vendors for this software and the list of libraries using SMS for reference are changing rapidly, the best way to find out more is the Library Success Wiki (http://www.librarysuccess.org) under the section "Online Reference."

Text messaging uses a protocol called SMS to transmit typed messages of fewer than 160 characters from one mobile device to another. Any messages over 160 characters are split into multiple messages. To use text messaging, users must have a subscription to a mobile phone service that allows it. Text messaging is not free for the user (nor is use of a mobile phone for voice), but with the popularity of texting, many people have subscription plans that allow them to send and receive hundreds of texts a month or plans that have unlimited texting. It is probably safe to assume that someone texting the library has sufficient texting paid for to receive at least one or two texts from the library in response. However, librarians should keep in mind that sending twelve 160-character messages in response to a query could be unexpected and also may be difficult for the patron to follow. As with any reference interaction, following the patron's lead is a good starting point. If the patron wants to engage in a conversation via text, then you can do so. You can also suggest that another mode of communication might be easier (faster?) for the patron's particular question. If the patron is texting, she has a phone and could possibly call. Or she may be near a computer and able to IM, or even in the library and able to come talk to you at the desk. Suggesting another mode of communication is a professional judgment based on your experience, but be prepared for the patron to be comfortable with her chosen mode of communication.

With the limit on the length of response, some librarians wonder what types of questions can possibly be answered effectively. To some extent, the situation recalls the early days of virtual (chat or IM) reference when librarians believed that this form of communication was limiting and should be used only for short, factual questions. Today, virtual reference is a widely adopted service used to answer all sorts of questions, from brief factual inquiries to guidance about in-depth research topics. Nonetheless, 160 characters is a physical limitation that might structure patron expectations of the service as well as the ways that libraries can effectively employ it for reference. Since texting is a relatively new service for libraries, I believe this is something we will find out over time, through experience.

Text messaging for reference service has even caught the attention of commercial ventures such as ChaCha (http://www.chacha.com) and kgb (http://www.kgb.com). These information service providers employ people (generally not librarians) to answer inquiries received by text messaging. ChaCha provides answers for free, but the number of questions is limited and they send links to advertising targeted to your question. In contrast, kgb charges per question (at the time of this writing, the cost was 99 cents per question). Both services provide a single answer in response to a question and do not support the back-and-forth texting of the reference interview process.

The "About us" page at http://www.kgb.com is interesting. Read the following once. Then read it again substituting *library* for *kgb:*

> In a world that runs on knowledge, kgb is a better way to get answers. Our goal is to deliver information to all those who seek it across multiple business platforms. Anywhere there are questions, kgb will be there with answers.

kgb spends much more on advertising than most libraries do (really, any library that I am aware of); they have national television ads during prime hours. As relatively new companies—ChaCha launched in 2008 and kgb started in 2009—it remains to be seen if these companies will experience the levels of use that they need to continue to operate as profit-making businesses by doing what libraries do as a no-cost, unlimited, advertisement-free service: To quote ChaCha's mission statement, "Providing the easiest way to access information while on the go."

CONCLUSION: REACH FOR THE POTENTIAL

Innovative use of the telephone could potentially increase the visibility and usefulness of library reference service. When we advertise one mode of reference communication, we promote our reference service as a whole by raising awareness. Where are patrons using their telephones that they might have questions? I've called my library from the bus and texted from a restaurant. Our own computer labs and even our book stacks are places where people have used their phones to call and text us with questions. Connecting over the phone means that the library can be located anywhere in our communities where our patrons are. We just need to be creative.

The telephone, in all of its current incarnations, is a powerful and timely tool for reference. It can connect us to our patrons; it can connect us to each other. We can use it to both provide and find information. It extends our reach by enabling us to move to where a patron is in our buildings but remain within reach of other patrons and staff. As we become part of patrons' contact lists, we become more present in their minds. The telephone makes librarians ubiquitous as we are only as far away as the patron's pocket or bag.

WORKS CITED

Central Intelligence Agency. 2010. Country comparison: Telephones—mobile cellular. In *World Factbook*. Retrieved February 3, 2010, from https://www.cia.gov/library/publications/the-world-factbook/rankorder/2151rank.html.

CTIA. 2009. *Wireless quick facts: Mid-year figures*. Retrieved February 3, 2010, from http://www.ctia.org/consumer_info/service/index.cfm/AID/10323.

Hill, J. B., C. Madarash Hill, and D. Sherman. 2007. Text messaging in an academic library: Integrating SMS into digital reference. *Reference Librarian* 47: 17–29.

International Telecommunications Union. 2009. *Measuring the information society: The ICT development index*. Retrieved March 1, 2010, from http://www.itu.int/ITU-D/ict/publications/idi/2009/material/IDI2009_w5.pdf.

Orange County Library System (OCLS). 2003. *OCLS finds multiple uses for wireless technology, VOCERA and WiFi*. Retrieved January 9, 2010, from http://www.ocls.info/Programs/Press_Releases/PDFs/2003/Wifi031009.pdf.

Radford, M. L. 2007. Back to the future: Phone reference OnCall OnDemand OnSite. *Library Garden* (September 25). Retrieved March 1, 2010, from http://librarygarden.blogspot.com/2007/09/back-to-future-phone-reference-oncall.html.

Ramirez, A. 2006. Library phone answers survive the Internet. *New York Times* (June 19). Retrieved March 1, 2008, from http://www.nytimes.com/2006/06/19/nyregion/19answer.html.

Vincent, J. 2006. Emotional attachment and mobile phones. *Knowledge, Technology, & Policy* 19: 39–44.

Wilson, J. 1876. From the president's address. *Library Journal* 2: 22.

ADDITIONAL READINGS

Kern, M. K. 2003. Have(n't) we been here before? Lessons from telephone reference. *Reference Librarian* 41: 1–17.

Lippincott, J. 2010. Mobile reference: What are the questions? *Reference Librarian* 51: 1–11.

Pavincich, M. 2007. *Information central: Not just a call centre*... Paper presented at Information Online, Sydney, January 30–February 1. Australian Library Association. Retrieved January 9, 2010, from http://conferences.alia.org.au/online2007/Presentations/30Jan.A2.information.central.pdf.

14

RECONFIGURING REFERENCE SERVICES FOR MOBILE DEVICES

Jim Hahn

Mobile computing technology's widespread use and popularity with library patrons represent an opportunity for ubiquitous reference service. Ubiquity of access is the ability to retrieve information anytime, in any place, on any device. Recent Pew Internet and American Life reports indicate that as a result of mobile access, users of information and communication technology accelerate their engagement with online content (Horrigan, 2009). This research signifies a trend among a portion of American Web users to engage with online content everywhere. Mobile devices offer an additional tool for continuing the conversation between patron and librarian. Mobile-service design requirements call for short intervals of interaction. The current state of handheld technology is not positioned to replace a desktop-based computing experience. However, if deployed strategically, with attention to leveraging handheld computing attributes, reconfigured mobile services will enhance the desktop-based and in-person reference experience.

Devices such as the iPhone, Droid, and the iPod Touch are essentially handheld computers that offer new ways to access information. These devices are distinct from desktop information access in important ways. They offer the ability to connect the users with information at their point of need. Handheld access to information is essentially personalized access delivered in sufficiently sized proportions (Traxler, 2007). The hardware and infrastructure properties of handheld computing devices include Wi-Fi, global positioning system (GPS), and picture and video creation and sharing. The combination of these attributes in mobile-device software applications offers users access to data in previously unavailable ways inclusive of context-aware services, such that users gain a broader understanding of their surrounding world and connect to information in a mode that has no analog or desktop-based equivalent.

This chapter begins with a review of mobile-mediated access to information (short message service, or SMS). A treatment of mobile Web design follows; due to the small screen size of mobile devices there are best practices for mobile delivery of Web-based content. Web sites designed for desktop presentation will display poorly on mobile devices because images and text may not be marked up in sufficiently accessible format. Mobile Web design practices are based on World Wide Web Consortium (W3C) standards. Adherence to XHTML specifications will ensure basic content accessibility across a multitude of devices and reader systems. Research databases available in mobile-accessible format are increasingly being developed. These beta services are reviewed in the second section. Vendors who have not simply reformatted their Web-based tools for small screens will be successful in this domain. The final portion of this chapter reviews mobile applications as reference tools. Software is the most significant development in reference sources for mobile computing. The proliferation of application stores by mobile developers is indicative of a profound shift in information access.

To reconfigure reference services for mobile devices is to view the reference encounter as an opportunity to include a mobile phone application as reference material. The use of such an application may help users explore more about their information needs. The application suggested may be a traditional reference work that has been remediated for the device, or the new application may make use of a variety of hardware, software, and infrastructures, lending the user a new manner of exploring her surroundings. The field of m-libraries moves very quickly. A wiki reference source available in the Library Success Best Practices wiki (www.libsuccess.org/index.php?title=M-Libraries) will help librarians stay current with the changes in service provision, be they interactive SMS-based or Web design–based or within the offerings of software applications.

MEDIATED REFERENCE SERVICE: SMS REFERENCE TRANSACTIONS

Librarians have developed mobile computing service through text (SMS) reference. New York University (NYU) Library has a dedicated BlackBerry for reference transactions, staffed by members of its reference team. Reference transactions from the BlackBerry may last for a time interval that spans many hours, if not days, depending on when the user responds to the text and when librarians respond to a patron text message (Pearce, Whatley, and Collard, 2009). The transaction logs at NYU indicate that questions are directional as well as traditional reference, with the reference encounters mirroring questions a user may ask in person. The service providers at NYU have found that virtual reference service does not mean they are not helping patrons in the building. In fact, text services do see queries from users who are in the building but not at the desk. This underscores the way in which reference services for mobile devices help to fill patron requests at their point of need. This point of need may not always be a dedicated reference desk. This device-based model is utilized at Yale's science library, which staffs an SMS service with a dedicated iPhone.

The University of California at Los Angeles (UCLA) partners with a vendor to provide a desktop interface for answering SMS reference queries. Yale and UCLA are both early innovators with SMS reference services (Jacobs, Smith, Murphy, and Amstrong, 2009). Regarding UCLA question types, the transaction logs report answering questions relating to hours, off-campus access, research, directions, and inquiry, including questions from non-UCLA users; their use data from three semesters indicate research and inquiry as the most frequent question types (Jacobs, Smith, Murphy, and Armstrong, 2009).

Reference models for SMS include device-based staffing and using a desktop for SMS answers. Types of questions a librarian may see can be the traditional, more in-depth queries, or users may understand that they should ask short, factual questions of the service. Hill and coauthors (2007) describe a service at Southeastern Louisiana University in which the typical questions are these short factual queries. The medium (with a limit of 140 characters per message) does not entirely shape the question type, but the *user group* will be the variable that shapes the type of reference transaction any given library will field from SMS service. It should not strike any librarian as surprising that user queries from disparate institutions and the communities in which they exist will lead to different conversation types. Further study should inquire into how SMS reference service best suits particular communities and users. Also of interest for virtual library service researchers will be to study how a user community's service requirements change as a result of SMS service availability. A service's ability to adapt and reshape to fit technology and user needs will ultimately be most useful. Those involved in coordinating reference services will be concerned with how SMS-based reference can be integrated into their suite of virtual reference offerings, and how that service is contextualized within reference services and library services generally. Mobile computing for reference services is accelerating. Depending on available staffing and institutional user preferences, an additional mobile device at the reference desk may seem outside of the reference tool kit; consequently, integration with desktop-based tools will alleviate the demands of staffing device-based tools.

ACCESSING CONTENT ON THE WEB WITH MOBILE TECHNOLOGY

The W3C develops standards for resources on the Web. These standards help to ensure accessibility and interoperability across platforms. Mobile Web best practices available from the W3C include schemes that verify mobile-device accessibility. These documents include the *W3C mobileOK Scheme 1.0* (www.w3.org/TR/mobileOK/), which acts as a conformance checker, and the *Mobile Web Best Practices 1.0* document, which is designed to assist Web designers to deliver compelling mobile Web-based experiences (www.w3.org/TR/mobile-bp/).

Important considerations for content viewed on mobile devices include attention to the screen size of handheld computers. As indicated in the *Mobile Web Best Practices 1.0* document, "because of the limited screen size and the limited amount of material that is visible to the user, context and overview are lost" (Rabin and McCathieNevile, 2008). The best workaround for viewing pages that have not been encoded for mobile devices includes a view of the page in which users must take a high-level view and magnify a section of the page for closer viewing. In the worst-case scenario, plug-ins such as Flash and images with high bandwidth demands may not display or format properly. With regard to device limitations, section 2.6 of the *Best Practices* document states, "Mobile browsers often do not support scripting or plug-ins, which means that the range of content that they support is limited. In many cases the user has no choice of browser and upgrading it is not possible" (Rabin and McCathieNevile, 2008). The user with a smartphone such as the iPhone will fare better than those with basic entry-level market phones when attempting to view pages that have not been designed for accessibility.

Mobile devices allow only limited input of lengthy text strings. Users cannot input long URL strings; similarly, they cannot easily complete forms. The *Mobile Web Best Practices 1.0* document explores user requirements more fully. It regards *user goals* for mobile technology as significant:

> Mobile users typically have different interests to fixed or desktop devices. They are likely to have more immediate and goal-directed intentions than desktop Web users. Their intentions are often to find out specific pieces of information that are relevant to their context. An example of such a goal-directed application might be the user requiring specific information about schedules for a journey they are currently undertaking. (Rabin and McCathieNevile, 2008)

It is also critical to understand what content users will access. As noted in *Mobile Web Best Practices 1.0,* "the ergonomics of the device are frequently unsuitable for reading lengthy documents and users will often only access such information from mobile devices as a last resort, because more convenient access is not available" (Rabin and McCathieNevile, 2008).) As research database development for mobile formatting becomes more widespread, this "last-resort" mode of access may attract special user groups, such as medical professionals who need to access documents with their phone as they lack any other means of access to information.

Ensuring basic accessibility across devices and e-book readers requires attention to the information modeling of Web-page markup. The classic summary of markup systems, contained in an article by Coombs, Renear, and DeRose (1987), is instructive and valuable for all Web developers, particularly with regard to the concept of descriptive markup. A short, simplified account of the history of markup is as follows: The development of HTML did not separate content and presentation markup. This led to the use of HTML as a markup language in which the underlying structure could not readily be processed by other systems. HTML was not completely descriptive. It contained elements of procedural markup. HTML styled the page as much as it held the content for what was to be displayed. With the advent of XML, a meta-markup language or a language that can encode other markup languages, XHTML was developed and led to Web pages with markup of content separated from presentation, and the ability for Web pages to be processed by their descriptive markup, thereby allowing for greater interoperability by other information systems. More on the markup languages and e-book reader systems and associated specifications can be found in a chapter by Renear and Salo (2003). Sample XHTML for a mobile Web site can be found in the book *The Anywhere Library: A Primer for the Mobile Web* (Greene, Roser, and Ruane, 2010, 48–50).

Adherence to XHTML standards is a related strategy to ensure basic Web content accessibility across a number of devices. The XHTML specification and checker are available from the W3C Web site (http://www.w3.org/TR/xhtml1/ and http://validator.w3.org/). While best practices in the current acceptable markup standard will shift, the foundational concept of data independence will not. Data independence is the ability to separate the data in a system sufficiently so that global changes to system resources are not noticeable for the end user. The objectives of interoperability (a feature of data independence) are not met when using HTML as a markup language. Data independence and data abstraction are well-researched cost-saving principles of general database design. The availability of research database access through mobile computing is a topic of considerable interest and beta implementation.

MOBILE DATABASE ACCESS

Beta trials of access to research databases and licensed content represent experimentation with mobile service delivery. User needs and device capabilities guide the development of these access tools. Emerging best practices include a paired mobile–desktop experience. Additionally, certain features of desktop-based databases are not included in the mobile versions, such that they function differently and will not provide the same search forms. Design choices aim for simplicity. These choices affect the users' ability for recall and the precision of database content.

Consider the following product. The popular bibliographic citation management tool RefWorks is available in a mobile-accessible version RefMobile (www.refworks.com/mobile/). The creators of this software designed their mobile interface for the small screen size of mobile devices and used XHTML mobile (XHTML Mobile 1.2) for markup as well. This service is a good example of the ubiquitous interplay among content accessed through a desktop interface as well as mobile devices; those users who have saved citations in their standard RefWorks account are able to access their folder and citations in the RefMobile version. The mobile layout does not replicate the exact navigation of a desktop-based system; rather, the design features minimum content and simple layout where users are able to access their folders and saved citations easily through mobile Web browsing.

There are four basic options for using the bibliographic data in a user's RefWorks account: *search, folders, all,* and *smart add. Search* allows the mobile user to search the contents of items already saved. The *folders* icon lists the user's previously saved folders. With attention to the small-screen-size constraints, the display will list only 10 folders at a time. The *all* function lets the user scroll through all saved data while taking care not to overwhelm the user; this display is broken up into manageable pieces. Finally, the *smart add* feature allows the user to add by identifier like DOI and ISBN (ISBN input being suited especially for smartphones), or by author and publication year, or by partial title. Advanced database users may want to request the development of a "help" page for this mobile database that would tell the user where these data are pulled from.

The IEEE Xplore Mobile Digital Library is one example of a research database that is experimenting with optimized mobile access (http://ieeexplore.ieee.org/mobile/). The interface here is simple, showing a Google-like single search box. The interface does not provide the user with feedback about what she has searched. This search style does not allow the user to improve the result returned from an initial search. Additionally, it is not possible to know how the search is used to determine relevancy. After searching, the user can view the abstract of the article returned in the search. Included in this beta release is also the ability to e-mail the abstract for future use. This kind of experimental research database offers partial access to the content of the desktop-accessible version.

Worldcat Mobile (www.worldcat.org/m) is an example of a database that leverages the benefits of being a mobile user. The mobile user of this database can input her location so that search results can guide her to the library nearest her. Another use of this service would be simply using this database to identify the nearest library. The book search allows for interactive and quick results after searching. Once the user has entered a search query, she is shown the results organized by different format types (books, Internet resources, sound recordings). After selecting the book, the user can view the libraries the book is in and, scrolling down, is able to view various ways to cite the item.

These are examples of emerging applications for database access through mobile devices. While these applications may be convenient for users on the go, they may not be powerful enough to replace a desktop-based experience. As with the RefMobile, a paired mobile–desktop experience is recommended. Prior familiarity with how RefWorks, or other research databases, functions will help in making the mobile versions usable while on the go. A first-time RefWorks user may not want to start with the mobile version. In summary, mobile user needs should be given further sustained inquiry in understanding best practices for mobile database use. User requirements for mobile access should be the guiding principle of mobile database interface design and functionality.

MOBILE-COMPUTING REFERENCE MATERIAL: APPLICATIONS FOR SMARTPHONES

Mobile phone applications (commonly referred to as *apps*) are software components added by the user after she has purchased the phone. Devices beyond phones can have aftermarket software added. In the case of the iPod Touch device, users can add software from an application store. Access to device-specific stores is integrated into the phone, such that the user can explore what can be added on the phone itself. These virtual storefronts for postpurchase software additions can be explored from the desktop-based browser as well. With the popularity of the App Store by Apple, nearly all smartphone manufacturers have followed suit with their own versions of application stores: Nokia has an online market, Ovi (http://store.ovi.com), and BlackBerry has an application store, the BlackBerry App World (http://na.blackberry.com/eng/services/appworld/). The Android operating system by the Open Handset Alliance, currently (2010) running on the Droid and many other new phones has an application store as well—Android Market (www.android.com/market/).

Many libraries have also begun to produce apps specific to their collections. Duke University (www.medu.com/duke.index/) recently released an iPhone app that has as a component access to images in their digital library collections. Another example is the University of North Carolina's digital-delivery application Wolfwalk (www.lib.ncsu.edu/dli/projects/wolfwalk/). This application is an example of how mobile technology can make use of geographically specific information to explore digital library content. This tour is designed to show the user content from digital collections based on geographic position on campus. Access to the online public access catalog is provided though an application developed by the D.C. Public Library (http://dclibrarylabs.org/projects/iphone/).

The following applications are new types of reference material. The organization of application types within application stores includes a category of reference applications. Traditional reference tools such as dictionaries and encyclopedias reformatted for mobile access are also available.

Dictionary.com (iPhone and iPod Touch)

http://dictionary.reference.com/apps/iphone

Drawing from the *Random House Dictionary,* this reference source will not replace comprehensive dictionaries but will provide a quick on-the-go definition. For those learning English this can be a useful study tool with an added pronunciation function.

Wikipanion (iPhone and iPod Touch)

http://www.wikipanion.net/index.html

The contents of Wikipedia are a great starting place for learning more about a topic, especially for computing research. This application is an improvement over visiting Wikipedia because it uses a mobile browser. Mobile viewing is enhanced by allowing the user to understand where she is in the document with an overlaid table of contents listing.

White Pages Mobile (iPhone, iPod Touch, and Android phones)

http://www.whitepages.com/tools

This application has many functions, including reverse phone number lookup, designed to address the perennial question mobile users have: Who is the person behind this unknown number? Users of this application can avoid costly 411 number lookups by using this White Pages database to look up personal and business phone numbers.

Shazam (available on the iPhone, Android phones, and BlackBerrys)

http://www.shazam.com

Many librarians have had a patron who would like to identify the lyrics to a song, or a song title. Frequently such a reference transaction will include the patron humming the song as well. Now the librarian can suggest a tool so that the user can identify songs while listening. One of iTunes's most popular applications is the Shazam app. All users need to do is activate the app as the unknown song is playing and hold the phone microphone to the sound source. After the app has sampled the song, it informs the user of the song title and artist and enables the user to purchase the album or song.

GoogleMobile application (iPhone, Android, and BlackBerrys)

http://www.google.com/mobile

This Google mobile application allows the user to perform a Google search by voice. The user states her search query, and Google's application will enter this as a Google search. Search by voice is still being refined, yet it is an excellent use of smartphone voice-input capabilities.

Weather Channel application (iPhone, iPod Touch, Android Market)
http://www.weather.com/mobile/pda/iphone/
The popular *Weather Channel* Web site is configured for mobile viewing by using tabs formatted for small-screen viewing. Features include saved locations and severe weather alerts delivered to the phone.

Sky Map (Android Market)
http://www.google.com/sky/skymap.html
The user can learn what constellations she is looking at by simply pointing the phone at the night sky.

MobileMe (iPhone and iPod Touch)
http://www.apple.com/mobileme/setup/iphone_ipod.html
The popular MobileMe productivity software that allows access to users' data from Mail, Calendar, Contacts, and Bookmarks across platforms now offers access through mobile devices. Users can even use this application to locate lost iPhones with the Find My iPhone feature.

SUMMARY AND FURTHER STUDY

Computing best practices have general application to mobile services. The principle of data independence is significant in appreciating why XHTML should be used for basic content accessibility across devices. A typology of services for mobile devices includes mediated reference, such as SMS, and unmediated services, such as software and database access. Software applications do not require direct librarian interaction yet are useful as reference material. The use of mobile is by design a personalized service; librarians can recommend applications, databases, or Web sites that the user will utilize for ubiquitous access.

New developments in mobile technology for library service can be tracked by consulting conference proceedings, special topical journal publications, blogs, and online discussion forums. The most practical way to stay current about applications for mobile devices is to periodically monitor the most popular applications in the Apple iTunes App Store or the Android Market.

For further individual study, consider reading the collected papers from the two international m-libraries conferences (Needham and Mohamed, 2008; Needham and Mohamed, 2010). The Handheld Librarian Conference, convened online in July 2009, is an additional source for practical information by librarians. The Spring 2011 (vol. 52, no. 1) issue of *Reference Librarian* will feature selected presentations. The 2009 Library and Information Technology Association (LITA) National Forum conference theme is "Open and Mobile." Interest groups within LITA, such as the Mobile Computing Interest Group, are focused on bringing together presentations of mobile-computing research and opportunities for professional development at annual conferences of the American Library Association. Try connecting with the community through ALA Connect (http://con nect.ala.org/).

Special topical journal publications include a *Reference Services Review* m-Services in Libraries issue from 2010 (vol. 38, no. 2), a May 2009 issue of *Computers in Libraries* (vol. 29, no. 5), and *Library Journal*'s special Net Connect issue from Fall 2008 (vol. 133). The American Library Association's report on libraries and mobile technologies (Kroski, 2008) is another useful publication. Look to these publishers to continue to put out special reports as mobile technologies become increasingly sophisticated and service offerings proliferate.

Blogs to follow include the *Handheld Librarian* (www.handheldlib.blog spot.com/) and the *Mobile Libraries* blog (http://mobile-libraries.blog spot.com/). The Google Group on m-libraries (http://groups.google.com/group/mobilelibraries) and the Yahoo group on handheld libraries (http://tech.groups.yahoo.com/group/pda-ebook/) are great places to discuss mobile initiatives and learn more about upcoming conferences.

The International Association for Mobile Learning (http://mlearning.noe-kaleidoscope.org/) plans the annual m-learn conference. An additional general conference on mobile technology is the practice-oriented conference Handheld Learning (www.handheldlearning.co.uk/). For a review of mobile-learning literature and conferences, consult the article by Traxler (2007) that appeared in the *International Review of Research in Open and Distance Learning*.

Innovators in the field of m-libraries must be cognizant of mobile technology's quick rate of obsolescence and anticipate future hardware possibilities. Pilot services must be designed to accommodate future hardware and software advances. Strategies to future-proof systems include designing for portability, being concerned with data abstraction, deploying systems using open formats, and utilizing standards promulgated by the W3C.

WORKS CITED

Coombs, J., A. Renear, and S. DeRose. 1987. Markup systems and the future of scholarly text processing. *Communications of the ACM* 30: 933–947.

Greene, C., M. Roser, and E. Ruane. 2010. *The anywhere library: A primer for the mobile web.* Chicago: Association of College and Research Libraries.

Hill, J. B., C. M. Hill, and D. Sherman. 2007. Text messaging in an academic library: Integrating SMS into digital reference. *Reference Librarian* 47: 17–29.

Horrigan, J. 2009. *The mobile difference.* Pew Internet & American Life Project. Retrieved July 22, 2009, from http://www.pewinternet.org/~/media//Files/Reports/2009/The_Mobile_Difference.pdf.

Jacobs, M., B. Smith, J. Murphy, and A. Armstrong. 2009. *UCLA and Yale science libraries data on cyberlearning and reference services via mobile devices.* Paper presented at the Second International m-Libraries Conference. Retrieved July 22, 2009, from http://ocs.sfu.ca/m-libraries/index.php/mlib/mlib2009/paper/viewFile/18/17.

Kroski, E. 2008. On the move with the mobile web: Libraries and mobile technologies. *Library Technology Report* 44 (5): 5–47.

Needham, G., and A. Mohamed, eds. 2008. *M-libraries: Libraries on the move to provide virtual access.* London: Facet.

Needham, G. and A. Mohamed, eds. 2010. *M-libraries 2: A virtual library in everyone's pocket.* London: Facet.

Pearce, A., K. Whatley, and S. Collard. 2009. *Say what? An SMS transcript analysis at New York University.* Paper presented at the Second International m-Libraries Conference. Retrieved July 22, 2009, from http://ocs.sfu.ca/m-libraries/index.php/mlib/mlib2009/paper/view/28/26.

Rabin, J. and C. McCathieNevile, eds. 2008. Mobile web best practices 1.0: Basic guidelines. *W3C recommendation 29 July 2008.* Retrieved September 13, 2010 from http://www.w3.org/TR/mobile-bp/

Renear, A., and D. Salo. 2003. Electronic books and the open ebook publication structure. In *The Columbia guide to digital publishing,* ed. W. F. Kasdorf, 455–520. New York: Columbia University Press.

Traxler, J. 2007. Defining, discussing and evaluating mobile learning: The moving finger writes and having writ . . . *International Review of Research in Open and Distance Learning* 8 (2). Retrieved July 22, 2009, from http://www.irrodl.org/index.php/irrodl/article/view/346/882.

ADDITIONAL READINGS

Kent, W. 1978. *Data and reality: Basic assumptions in data processing reconsidered.* Amsterdam: North-Holland.

15

USING ONLINE SOCIAL NETWORKING TOOLS FOR REFERENCE AND OUTREACH

Emily Rimland

Libraries that want to remain relevant need to focus on providing both excellent customer service and valuable services. With all the chatter about social networking tools, it is impossible to ignore these venues as another conduit to help libraries deliver services. Libraries can easily harness the power of the social Web to reach users and create an online library as place that extends the reach of the physical library. While social networking sites may have received much negative attention at their advent, they have since proven themselves influential tools that allow libraries to effectively connect with patrons.

Definitions of online social networking tools abound. As Cathy De Rosa points out in the introduction to the Online Computer Library Center (OCLC)'s report *Sharing, Privacy, and Trust in Our Networked World*, "today, the term social networking is being used in new ways, but the concepts behind it—sharing content, collaborating with others, and creating community—are not new" (OCLC, 2007, ix). For the purposes of this chapter, online social networking tools are considered according to Agosto and Abbas's definition: "A social networking site has a unique community of registered users who read other people's profile pages, create profiles describing themselves and their interests, and communicate with each other electronically" (2009, 32). With this definition in mind, this chapter primarily explores sites like Facebook, MySpace, Ning, and Twitter as social networking tools. Other social software, such as blogs and wikis, may share some characteristics with this definition but are not the main consideration, although some of the techniques discussed here may be applied to these tools as well.

WHY SHOULD LIBRARIES CARE ABOUT SOCIAL NETWORKING TOOLS?

Social networking tools provide many benefits, the most important of which is allowing for the easy creation of an online library as place. As the dialogue around the future of reference continues, one thing is clear: Excellent customer service will need to be a defining factor in what sets libraries apart from other services. In what is rapidly becoming an experience-based economy (but still holding fast to a service-based economy), users want to be engaged in customized interactions with real people—something libraries have a long history of offering but may need to extend to new online realms through channels like social networking tools. Author and business consultant Joseph Pine (2004) describes a service-based economy as one in which goods are commoditized, or, in other words, when a good becomes inexpensive and indistinguishable from its competition. However, through customization or personalization, a good can be transformed into something new: a service. This customization can be done on demand and for a particular person or purpose. This customization makes the service noteworthy (e.g., Southwest Airlines).

Services have been the world's primary economic model for the last few decades, but, more recently, services have also become commoditized (consider outsourced information technology support). Pine suggests the solution is, once again, customization. Customizing a service takes it to another new level—this time it becomes an experience. The world is now seeing a shift to where experiences are becoming the "predominant economic offering" (Pine, 2004). In an experience, a service is tailored to a user's needs at that very moment and "can't help but make them go 'Wow!'" according to Pine. Some familiar experience providers might be Las Vegas, Disney, theme restaurants, or boutique hotels, or an experience can simply be a meaningful place or enjoying a bottle of wine (Pine, 2004). Libraries, too, need to play a part in the experience arena. Our long tradition of providing services to users is ripe with opportunities to take services to the next level and provide customized services, or experiences, for users. One area where this is possible is the online environment, and social networking sites can help to facilitate this.

A tenet of creating an experience, according to Pine, is to provide something that is authentic. An example of a familiar service is dialing an 800 number and attempting to navigate a company's phone menu, only to give up in frustration and exclaim, "I just want to talk to a real person!" This kind of encounter may seem very inauthentic to a customer, especially after witnessing the company's promotions that boast how much the company cares about its customers. In other words, the company's phone service is not authentic and detracts from the company's reputation. In contrast, Land's End has turned an otherwise-commoditized type of service into the experience of landsend.com, offering live chat or phone help (they call you) from a customer service representative when and if you need it. Sound familiar? In an online environment, there are also ample opportunities to provide customized and personalized reference service to patrons using the power of social networking sites. By maintaining a presence on social networking sites, librarians and libraries have more opportunities to showcase their services and provide positive, authentic experiences for patrons.

It is easy to assume that social networking sites are primarily used by teens, and indeed they are. However, social networking sites are increasingly popular with adults: "The share of adult internet users who have a profile on an online social network site has more than quadrupled in the past four years—from 8% in 2005 to 35% now" (Lenhart, 2009). Adults tend to use social networking sites in much the same way as other age groups—to connect and engage with people they already know. Although the sites are primarily used for social interactions, they are also used for other purposes, such as to collaborate on school projects, with more than 50 percent of middle school and high school students using them in this way (Project Tomorrow, 2009).

Users of social networking sites are spending a lot of time there. In 2009, a monumental year for social networking sites, time spent using them jumped 73 percent, and use of social networking sites exceeded the use of Web-based e-mail for the first time (*Online Engagement,* 2009). Not only are these sites in high demand, but audience preferences are also quite capricious. MySpace peaked early as the dominant social networking site in the United States, but, more recently, "time spent on Facebook soared 699% since April 2008, compared to a 31% drop in time spent on MySpace" (Goldman, 2009). And while Facebook is gaining users throughout the world, other sites like Orkut and Mixi still lead in popularity in other countries (*Online Engagement,* 2009).

With so many users spending so much time on social networking sites, it is only natural that libraries should want to boost their online presence by using these tools as well. As the library as place becomes increasingly important, it only stands to reason that the online library as place should at least mirror, if not extend, what libraries do in the real world. Social networking tools thus allow libraries to quickly and easily position themselves as online community hubs for users.

Online social networking sites provide opportunities to help libraries enhance the user experience, both as a gateway to an online library as place and as a way to customize users' experiences. This is a ubiquitous experience for all online users. "The Internet remains a place of continuing innovation, with users finding new ways to integrate online usage into their daily lives. In recent years the Internet has changed dramatically as people seek more personalized relationships online. In particular, time spent on social networks and video sites has increased astronomically" (*Online Engagement,* 2009). Thus, users are becoming more engaged with their online experiences, which adds a new value to these tools for libraries. But before libraries dive right in, there are, of course, advantages and disadvantages to consider when using social networking sites.

PROS AND CONS OF SOCIAL NETWORKING TOOLS

Clearly, online social networking sites provide opportunities for libraries, the biggest ones being that they provide a space for the online library as place and a chance to provide personalized services to users. However, it's not a given that every librarian and library should automatically have a profile on every site or use every tool. Rather, the pros and cons of these tools should be taken into consideration first, followed by each tool's potential application and the degree to which each tool aligns with patron use and needs.

While online social networking tools help us to meet users where they are, in some online communities or instances libraries may not be welcome. For example, it's not recommended social networking etiquette for a librarian or library to randomly initiate friending of community members without some kind of face-to-face experience to ground it. Otherwise, users tend to experience the "creepy treehouse effect" and view this behavior as an invasion of their space. Overall, it's best to let the users come to you first, and giving them a reason to do so is the most effective technique. As Farkas (2007) points out, "A big difference exists between being where our patrons are and being useful to our patrons where they are. A profile should be designed to offer something to patrons so they will keep coming back to it" (122).

Social networking tools are a great way to stay abreast of user trends and needs in the community. Knowing what users need and want helps libraries to stay relevant in their communities, and social networking tools help to improve the communication between the library and patrons. Sometimes Twitter's and Facebook's live feeds make it seem like events are taking place faster than they do in real life. However, this concentrated dialogue around the community's interests can be valuable for anticipating reference questions and proactively answering them, making strategic purchases for the collection (based on local speakers or new media releases), and reaching out to organizations with customized resources.

Third-party social networking tools are almost always free, but the tradeoff may be control of information. Be sure to examine the tool's terms of service and privacy policy, and be aware of what control the provider has over your content. If the company goes belly up tomorrow, what will happen to your information? Are you able to erase your information if you abandon the service? Early in 2009, Facebook attempted to change its terms of service in such a way that would give it control over its users' content in perpetuity. Bending to the backlash of user outrage about the new terms, Facebook reverted to its original terms and returned intellectual property control to users. While this seems to be the popular attitude at the moment with similar sites, don't assume so on every site. Librarians should also become familiar with a site's privacy controls and become comfortable with the settings. Thankfully, social networking tools are increasingly offering finer granularity to allow users to tailor settings to best suit their needs (remember, they're providing an experience too).

While there may be a bit of a learning curve with each new social networking tool, it is generally moderate, and there tends to be significant overlap of features from site to site. For example, those trying to wrap their heads around Twitter need only make a small mental leap to recognize its similarities to Facebook's live feed feature. And in some cases libraries may not even need to learn how to use a new social networking tool in order to take advantage of its features. For example, many sites allow the creation of links that enable syndication of content between sites, like between a Facebook page and a Twitter account, so that updating one site automatically updates the other. While maintaining these sites may seem like more work for busy libraries, syndication between tools can help to minimize upkeep.

Social networking sites have received a negative rap for being unsafe; however, these claims are often overhyped by the media. While this may have held libraries back from condoning social networking sites both for patrons and themselves, (obviously) there is also much more to gain in terms of increasing the library's reach and visibility among users. Additionally, libraries have an opportunity to help teach patrons how to stay safe and maintain privacy while still enjoying social networking sites.

After considering these tools and knowing how powerful they can be, you or your library may be ready to set up accounts on some choice sites. However, simply adding a profile to social networking sites does not a cooler library make. Rather, there are some tips and tricks to keep in mind to make these sites work best for libraries and librarians in reference and outreach contexts. In the following section selected tools are examined for ways they might currently be employed. Since these sites change so frequently, it's best to remember the basic ways these tools can add value: by creating an online community hub for the library and by providing a gateway to the library for patrons to access customized services.

SELECTED TOOLS AND PUTTING THEM INTO PLAY

Facebook and MySpace are currently the two heavy-hitting social networking sites; with a majority of users already familiar with these sites, it might make sense for a library or librarian to first build a profile using one or both sites. Most of the activity that takes place on these two sites revolves around the profile, and investing a small amount of time in adding pictures, contact information, and news and events will be well worth it. Facebook offers a choice of two kinds of profiles. The first is the traditional type of profile that is intended for individuals to use to represent themselves. The second type is called a page and is intended for an entity (like a library), business, product, or group to use to highlight itself. If you are using a personal profile to offer services, don't feel obligated to include a lot of personal information about yourself, but do include some information so as not to seem fake or impersonal. You may also want to create two accounts—one for personal and one for professional information.

Once a page or profile is created on either site, the creator has the option to add more features in the way of applications, or "apps"—tools that perform a certain task inside the social networking site. An app may be as simple as a discussion board that enables patrons to leave feedback or something more complex such as a specific library application that allows users to search the online public access catalog (OPAC) and place holds on books. In most cases, libraries will need to develop their own custom apps or draw on open-source outlets if they would like one specific to their library. There are many library-related apps to choose from to enhance a profile, including apps to feature collections (for example, Shelfari), survey an audience, and access specific library resources (for example, WorldCat, JSTOR). MySpace offers more flexibility than Facebook when it comes to profile design. MySpace allows the use of cascading style sheets to create the desired look and feel of the profile (perhaps to match the library's Web site, or purposefully not to match), whereas Facebook does not allow this level of freedom. In both cases, choose the apps and provide information consistent with the level of interaction and feedback your community expects or that you want to espouse in an online environment. Once your profile is up and running, market it in any way you can by providing a URL or "badge" for your profile on business cards, handouts, library literature, Web sites, and your online catalog.

These sites are clearly marketing tools and can be used to let users know what libraries have to offer and how libraries can help. Using them as reference and outreach tools will require only a little bit of extra effort. Another way to market a social networking site is through word of mouth; this is often a good approach if you want to begin using the profile as a portal for reference services. Casually telling patrons after an interaction or instruction session that they can Facebook you is a simple way to get started and puts the control in the users' hands so they don't feel pressured to friend you. Additionally, all they need to remember in order to locate your profile is your name. They can choose from the site's internal messaging system (private) or your wall or discussion board (public) to get in touch with you. Keep in mind that a certain etiquette is used on these sites that you will want to be aware of, such as not friending people you don't know in person. However, the reverse is not always true, and it's acceptable for the library to confirm requests from patrons or "fans" of the library that the librarians may not know by name. It also behooves the library to reciprocate any feedback or questions you receive on these sites, as this dialogue contributes to raising your visibility and creating an online presence.

It's easy to reach out to your community to publicize library events by way of social networking sites. In most cases, you just need to fill in the details about the event on the site's prebuilt forms, then add pictures and friends, and your event is ready to go. Facebook allows the event organizer to create open or closed events depending on the type of event. Leaving events open may promote a viral marketing approach to maximize attendance.

Twitter is currently the hottest social networking tool on the block. At its simplest, it is a "real-time short messaging service that works over multiple networks and devices" and asks users to answer the question "What are you doing?" in 140 characters or less (*About Twitter*, 2009). While at first blush the uses of Twitter may seem obtuse or only for people with a lot of extra time, many businesses and libraries alike have started to see the value in it as an outreach tool. Twitter has some similarities to Facebook and MySpace. In particular, Twitter resembles Facebook's news feed, which provides real-time updates in a reverse chronological timeline; Twitter allows users to interact with each other's tweets by commenting on them or by tagging other users. While the central part of Twitter is not the profile but rather a steady stream of tweets, libraries can use Twitter in similar ways by building a network of interested followers and tweeting events, resources, and information pertaining to their core user group.

Not to be overshadowed by its high-profile social networking cousins is Ning.com. If the one-size-fits-all social networking sites are not a direction you want to go, Ning allows users to create custom, on-the-fly social networks. Ning's easy-to-use social service allows libraries to create networks around any topic, whether specifically about the library, book clubs, or other interests. The features of Ning are similar to those of Facebook and MySpace, but it offers the advantage of customization around a central theme, with a blend of Facebook's clean look and MySpace's flexibility.

FUTURE TRENDS AND ASSESSMENT

Social networking sites are in a constant state of flux and will require constant monitoring and maintenance by libraries to remain relevant tools to the community. What the future holds is anyone's guess as peripatetic users switch tools, new developments in technology and privacy evolve, and social networking savviness increases. As users' tastes become more sophisticated, specialized social networking sites may gain more popularity. This is especially true if standards like OpenID, which allows users to access multiple sites using one login, become the norm for unifying users' preferences and allowing greater ease of integration between sites. Sites like LibraryThing have achieved surprising success by giving users the power to catalog their own books and then build a social framework around their collections. Google Wave is on the horizon, an online communication and collaboration tool that may disrupt social networking sites as we know them now by creating a media-rich environment where users can share maps, videos, and photos with even greater real-time ease.

Whatever platform you choose, you should evaluate the tool's effectiveness regularly, both formally and informally. Libraries should constantly monitor whether or not they are reaching targeted audiences and if those audiences are happy with the information they are receiving. As audiences change, and as social networking sites themselves change, so too should libraries adapt their online presence to meet their community's new needs. For example, researcher danah boyd has discovered that the popularity of a social networking site tends to fall along social lines like race and class: "You have environments in which people are divided by race, divided by class, divided by lifestyle. When they go online they are going to interact in the same way" (quoted in Sydell, 2009). In the online world, this translates to higher use of MySpace by lower-income and Latino users but also artists and musicians, since MySpace allows for greater expression via customization of the site. However, this is a current snapshot of the state of social media, so it's important to keep a pulse on what's happening with your community. Conducting your research could be as simple as talking to your users about their preferences or drawing on other surveys done in your community as to the community's demographics and preferences. Because social networking sites are relatively new, formal assessment tools are only beginning to surface, such as Mashable.com's how-to guide for measuring social media return on investment through metrics and analysis tools (Warren, 2009). Libraries should monitor Web sites and spaces outside the library to both gauge which ones users are frequenting and gain insight into what's important in other areas of their lives. Oftentimes these types of casual observations can be more informative than a formal assessment such as a survey, although both approaches will give libraries valuable feedback to inform future developments and directions.

With all the buzz surrounding social networking sites now and into the future, it may benefit libraries to proactively consider social networking policies or, more broadly, social media policies, to ensure responsible use among libraries, patrons, and library employees. Because these tools are so easy to use and can be so powerful, questions may arise very quickly: Who will be responsible for monitoring, updating, and responding to questions on these sites? How, if at all, should they be used in a professional context by librarians? Should patrons be allowed to use Facebook when other patrons need computers for other tasks? Having a policy in place will help to guide the library and its patrons in the use of these tools. The American Library Association (ALA)'s Reference and User Services Association (RUSA) has published *Guidelines for Behavioral Performance of Reference and Information Service Providers,* which addresses best practices for approachability, searching, privacy, and other areas of information service; however, this document does not mention the use of social networking tools for these purposes as of its most recent (2004) revision. However, many of the guidelines for remote service can be applied to encounters using these tools, and the guidelines are good to review before embarking on a social networking campaign. Developing a social media policy may also be a good time to consider the introduction of social networking mentors into the equation. While younger generations may feel more comfortable in these environments, other generations may actually have fresher approaches to applying their library wisdom to a new interface. This type of symbiotic relationship can contribute to the librarians' wisdom and benefit users with better service.

As the studies and reports referenced in this chapter demonstrate, a large percentage of users—our library users—maintain a presence on social networking sites and spend vast amounts of online time there. Commercial businesses have long been savvy to the idea of leveraging social networking sites as places to market their services. Although some libraries were early adopters of social networking sites, all libraries need to consider this new approach. As integral community resources, libraries can use these tools to build an online presence and meet users where they are: online. Doing so integrates libraries more firmly into users' social worlds—exactly where libraries want to be.

WORKS CITED

About Twitter. 2009. Retrieved October 18, 2009, from http://twitter.com/about#about.

Agosto, D., and J. Abbas. 2009. Teens and social networking. *Public Libraries* 48 (3): 32–37.

Farkas, M. 2007. *Social software in libraries: Building collaboration, communication, and community online.* Medford, NJ: Information Today.

Goldman, D. 2009. Facebook is king but Twitter makes waves. *CNNMoney.com* (June 2). Retrieved July 2, 2009, from http://money.cnn.com/2009/06/02/technol ogy/social_network_growth/index.htm.

Lenhart, A. 2009. *Adults and social network websites.* Pew Internet & American Life Project. Retrieved October 5, 2009, from http://www.pewinternet.org/Reports/2009/Adults-and-Social-Network-Websites.aspx.

Online Computer Library Center. 2007. *Sharing, privacy, and trust in our networked world.* Retrieved August 25, 2009, from http://www.oclc.org/reports/sharing/default.htm.

Online engagement deepens as social media and video sites reshape the Internet, Nielsen reports. 2009. Retrieved June 12, 2009, from http://en-us.nielsen.com/main/news/news_releases/2009/april/online_engagement.

Pine, J. 2004. *Joseph Pine on what consumers want.* New York: TED Conferences. Retrieved October 6, 2009, from http://www.ted.com/talks/lang/eng/joseph_pine_on_what_consumers_want.html.

Project Tomorrow. 2009. *Selected national findings: Speak up 2008 for students, teachers, parents and administrators.* Retrieved August 25, 2009, from http://www.tomorrow.org/speakup/pdfs/SU08_findings_final_mar24.pdf.

Reference and User Services Association. 2004. *Guidelines for behavioral performance of reference and information service providers.* Retrieved June 12, 2009, from http://www.ala.org/ala/mgrps/divs/rusa/resources/guidelines/guidelines behavioral.cfm.

Sydell, L. 2009. Facebook, MySpace divide along social lines. *NPR Topics: Digital Life* (October 21). Retrieved October 22, 2009, from http://www.npr.org/templates/story/story.php?storyId=113974893.

Warren, C. 2009. *How to: Measure social media ROI.* Retrieved November 6, 2009, from http://mashable.com/2009/10/27/social-media-roi/.

ADDITIONAL READINGS

AFP News. 2009. *AFP: No Facebook at work in most companies.* Retrieved October 9, 2009, from http://www.google.com/hostednews/afp/article/ALeqM5g46V1qCXwiXcfAP9LXT5kAnXuA9w.

Kroska, E. 2009. Should your library have a social media policy? *School Library Journal* (October 1). Retrieved November 2, 2009, from http://www.schoollibraryjournal.com/article/CA6699104.html.

Stone, B. 2009. Is Facebook growing up too fast? *New York Times* (March 28). Retrieved June 12, 2009, from http://www.nytimes.com/2009/03/29/technology/internet/29face.html.

16

WHAT'S NEXT? TRACKING TECH TRENDS

Michael Stephens

Tracking technology trends should be one of the most important duties of librarians, including reference librarians. In fact, *not* monitoring how technology is changing the ways people use and access information and responding to those changes with different service models and new library initiatives is a surefire way to become irrelevant.

Monitoring blog posts, checking in with tech trend panels at conferences, and reading technology-centric periodicals outside our field are all ways to stay in the know. This chapter, which began as a blog post at *Tame the Web* in January 2009, explores some recent trends gleaned from doing all of the preceding and from tapping into the wisdom of all the library and information science (LIS) folk sharing in the biblio-blogesphere, Twitterverse, and Facebook realms.

THE UBIQUITY OF THE CLOUD

Cloud computing is a tech buzzword term that describes the creation, storage, and use of data on servers out on the Internet—not on someone's desktop computer hard drive. Storing documents in the cloud means they have the potential to be accessed from anywhere. Right now, I'm using the cloud in various ways. My photo collection resides in Flickr's cloud of image data. I store presentations and chapter drafts at a service such as Dropbox. I work in Google Docs with students and colleagues to create documents, spreadsheets, and presentations—all created and stored in the cloud. This points to a fascinating future of data, information, and media accessible from anywhere because it is not stored on one specific hard drive on one specific computer.

This future was predicted in *The Future of Music: Manifesto for the Digital Music Revolution* (Kusek, Leonhard, and Lindsay, 2005). In their vision of 2015, music streams to you via Wi-Fi wherever you are. Your "TasteMate" remembers your favorites and keeps those songs in rotation in your personal playlists. News and entertainment are available as well. Raining down from the cloud, music, news, and any other type of user-selected information will be available 24/7 via broadband into home media centers, personal media devices, the car media receiver, work computers, and so on. In 2009, we're seeing these advances in the form of streaming music to phones, among other innovations.

Cloud computing, via services offered by Google, Amazon, Dropbox, Mozey, and similar socially focused networks like Facebook, broadens the scope from music and media to everything. The potential is there for some people to store and archive all of their data in the cloud and to do their work in the cloud as well. In "Stranger Than We Know" (2008), Jason Griffey, assistant professor and head of library information technology at the University of Tennessee at Chattanooga's Lupton Library, describes a "radical shift" for libraries:

> Library buildings won't go away. . . . Buildings will move more fully into their current dual nature, that of warehouse and gathering place, while our services and our content will live in the cloud, away from any physical place. The idea that one must go to a physical place in order to get services will slowly erode. (12)

Griffey's forecast rings true with available data and current shifts in service models. The reference desk of the future may well be in the cloud.

What does this mean for libraries and librarians? Here are a few points to ponder and to put into practice. Allow unfettered access to the cloud. Locked-down personal computers won't help users get to their data. This means offering multiple browsers, providing the fastest connections you can, and establishing security measures that do not block access to what users want. Hardware access is important too: I sometimes carry a 160GB portable drive with my presentations, videos, and documents. I may need to plug it into your library computer someday to sync data to the cloud. Please let me.

Understand that the cloud may also be a valuable information resource in its own right. How many times have we answered a reference question via Facebook, Wikipedia, blog posts, a Flickr picture, and so on? These are all viable means to get answers. Tap into user-generated data as a resource. It may become one of our most important mechanisms.

Utilize the cloud to save time and money. Be aware that Google Docs and similar tools will only get more share of the application market. Maybe offering access to Google Docs and instruction on how to use those applications would be a useful way to save time and money in the long run by preventing the frustration of users who lose documents on library computers. Maybe only a few computers in your library will need MS Office in the future. OpenOffice and some future online version of the same will allow us a lot more freedom to spend our dollars and time on other improvements.

Useful Links

"The Future of the Desktop": http://www.readwriteweb.com/archives/future_of_the_desktop.php

Will Richardson, "Is My Head (and My Life) in the Clouds?": http://weblogg-ed.com/2008/is-my-head-and-my-life-in-the-clouds/

Robin Hastings's presentation "Collaborating in the Cloud" at Slideshare: http://www.slideshare.net/webgoddess/collaborating-in-the-cloud

Jenny Levine, "We're Not All Ready for the Cloud Yet": http://theshiftedlibrarian.com/archives/2009/01/14/were-not-all-ready-for-the-cloud-yet.html

THE PROMISE OF MICROINTERACTION

At IDEA 2008, a conference sponsored by the Information Architecture Institute, social media expert David Armano presented a paper entitled "Micro Interactions in a 2.0 World." His presentation highlighted the power of social technologies to enable connections between people and brands or companies on even the smallest scale. In an online article for *Advertising Age* he defines microinteractions: "Micro-interactions are the everyday exchanges that we have with a product, brand and service. Each one, in and of itself, seems insignificant. But combined they define how we feel about a product, brand or service at a gut emotional level" (Armano, 2008). The little things mean a lot. Twitter is a perfect example of Armano's microinteraction concept. Twitter (www.twitter.com) is a microblogging site that allows status updates of 140 characters. Growing exponentially and becoming steeped in popular Internet culture, the uses and abuses of Twitter in 2009 are staggering. Sharing little updates—called *tweets* in the Twitter vernacular—and engaging in tweeted conversations is currently a popular pastime for the digitally connected.

A few months ago, I bought a new Subaru and tweeted about passing on the $250 Subaru charity donation promotion money to the American Society for the Prevention of Cruelty to Animals (ASPCA). That tweet yielded a reply from the ASPCA within minutes—a perfect example of a little connection, a little interaction, meaning a lot. The organization had set up a monitoring search for mention of the charity, and my tweet must have popped up in the search feed.

Libraries are following the lead of companies in this microinteraction space. It is not unheard of in some progressive institutions for librarians to monitor Twitter through various search tools and RSS feeds for mentions of the library or for users asking questions. This may be another new frontier for reference librarians—just as the phone, e-mail, and interactive chat were before.

Twitter has also broken down barriers to global interaction. I experimented with Twitter and taking conference notes in the fall of 2008. At the Internet Librarian International conference in London, I sat on a panel discussing next-generation library services. I was also tweeting some of the other panelists' thoughts and the audience's reaction. Librarian David Kemper was following the conference tweets and asked a question over Twitter. He writes,

> The point was not necessarily to receive a response or to even debate the statement. . . . To my surprise, however, Stephens and Casey both replied to my tweet and panel members started to discuss the question I had asked, revealing once again the power of Web 2.0 in general and Twitter in particular. How cool is that? While the statement regarding librarian attitude and education and the question I had asked still require more thought (and perhaps a dedicated blog post), I was pleasantly surprised to see that Twitter leveled the field, whereby someone in Canada could influence the direction of a conference in London. (Kemper, 2008)

The conversation between librarians via Twitter has exploded at conferences and in our day-to-day work. A librarian can ask a question of the Twitterverse, and if he or she has a large number of followers, the responses may be many and useful. I use Twitter to share information, articles of note, and more with my technology classes. Groups for student presentations used the site to stay in contact between class meetings. It's a way to keep a little bit of contact going, a little bit of "hey, I'm thinking about class stuff, are you?" Anecdotally, students inform me that they appreciate the connectedness during the semester.

So much of what we do in the library world comes down to this type of interaction: questions, pointing people in the right direction, troubleshooting. It's an extension of human contact and feeling, offering both something useful and ease of use. Twitter—and microinteraction online in whatever form it may take—is a perfect example of those things coming together.

What does this mean for libraries and librarians? Interaction and engagement at the microlevel can influence your library users. The microlevel might also be where they are looking for answers. For example, I recently did a talk in Schaumburg, Illinois. Afterward, I wanted to stop at the nearby World Market to get some wine. Heading to the store, I became confused because it wasn't where I thought it was supposed to be. I pulled into a parking lot, grabbed my iPhone, and asked the Twitterverse, "Did the Cost Plus World Market close in Schaumburg?"

Within minutes I had an answer. It had closed! I did this mostly as an experiment, but I am sure I'm not the only one seeking information via Twitter, or Facebook, or any number of the Q&A sites available on the Web and via mobile devices. My first thought was not to find a library but to ask the question within my personal network and the spaces that I visit. Reference librarians would be wise to explore this emerging question-space and see what their users are doing—and asking.

Library staff could use microinteraction tools to get things done as well. These tools can be used for easy communication and project updates. Additionally, there are excellent examples of libraries using Twitter in time- and money-saving ways. Consider the *workstream,* defined by *Wired* as "a live updated record of work you've completed. When doing group work with remote colleagues, it allows you to keep track of what everyone else is doing. When working solo, it helps you keep track of your own productivity" ("Workstreaming," 2008). How could a workgroup benefit from such technologies at your library?

Useful Links

David Armano's "Micro-Interactions in a 2.0 World": http://www.slideshare.net/darmano/microinteractions-in-a-20-world-v2

"State of the Twittersphere": http://blog.hubspot.com/blog/tabid/6307/bid/4439/State-of-the-Twittersphere-Q4–2008-Report.aspx

"Twitter for Internal Communication": http://tametheweb.com/2008/12/10/twitter-for-internal-communication-a-ttw-guest-post-by-mick-jacobsen/

"Why Is Twitter Exploding?": http://darmano.typepad.com/logic_emotion/2007/12/why-is-twitter.html

THE TRIUMPH OF THE PORTABLE DEVICE

Cell phones are everywhere! iPods, netbooks, and other devices are on the move as well. To spot this important trend, just look around in any crowded public space. You'll see mobile devices of all kinds. Currently, the library technology literature is filled with articles, conference presentations and books about mobile technology and library services. This may be one of the most important trends for libraries highlighted in this chapter.

Smartphones, including the iPhone and Google's phone, have become affordable and commonplace. Every new feature that extends our devices' capability impacts libraries. What were once simple devices created to make and receive calls are now an integral part of one's personal information space—handling e-mail, text messages, images, Web browsing and search, access to social tools, and so on. Librarians should watch the adoption and use of converged devices in everyday life, education, and business in order to understand how people access information. For example, Abilene Christian University (ACU) proactively encourages student use of mobile technology. Incoming students are given iPhones and iPod Touches as part of a university-wide initiative to create a connected 21st-century campus. "Mobile technology is shaping the way we live, work and learn. Since education can now take place in the classroom or virtually anywhere, ACU is committed to exploring mobile learning technology that makes sense for our students and their future" (ACU, 2009).

Students utilize the devices to stay in touch with each other and with faculty. The ACU Web site reports on the connect-campus initiatives, including these facts:

> The devices are being used campus-wide both in and out of the classroom; Implementation team has created a suite of web applications for mobile learning involving classroom management, file storage, university information, polling, and community information.
>
> Teacher training classes are ongoing and cover iPhone basics and integration in the classroom. (ACU, 2009)

Other libraries are experimenting with "Text a Librarian" services, using the short messaging service (SMS) built into mobile phones as a way to answer questions or provide information. Southeastern Louisiana University (SELU) was one of the first libraries to offer such a service, receiving a start-up grant in 2005. SELU is nestled between New Orleans and Baton Rouge and has a student population of 15,000.

At ALA's TechSource blog, I interviewed two of the SELU librarians responsible for the service. Angela Dunnington, coordinator of library science, and Beth Stahr, interim head of reference, presented at the Mississippi University Libraries Library 2.0 conference and chatted with me afterward. Dunnington reported that the library receives various types of questions over SMS including short-answer reference questions, nonserious questions, library questions, and sometimes more complex questions. She reiterated, "It was an easy thing to do—both to set up and to train staff." Many of the librarians learned to use text messaging in a time of crisis. After Hurricane Katrina, when Stahr was without a home phone for two months, she realized how easy it was to learn to text. It was the only communication option available to many of the SELU librarians at that time. "The librarians learned to text message when everything else was down," she said (Stephens, 2007).

Other libraries offering text message services include Yale Science Libraries, College of Charleston Libraries, and Denton Public Library in Denton, Texas. For an up-to-date list, see the Library Success wiki at http://www.libsuccess.org/index.php?title=Online_Reference.

Another innovation finding its way into online catalogs is the addition of an option to text the citation to a phone. Mobile users could collect all of their needed bibliographic information in their cell phones and then find the materials in the stacks. Look for this option to appear in more online catalogs.

Consider also the impact of Quick Response codes, those squarish, two-dimensional barcodes you may have seen in stores or at conferences that can store data and are readable by mobile devices. The librarians at ACU are using them to share information about various materials in the library.

A Flickr set displaying images of the codes, uploaded by the ACU librarians, includes this explanation of use:

> An example of a QR barcode (mobile tag). When a library patron takes a picture of this code in their mobile device, it takes them automatically to our library catalog where it executes a dynamic search. They get a list of more books on the topic, see book jackets and reviews, have the option to check out or request titles, etc. Scanning the QR code is much easier that typing in a complicated url. Users get a pre-formatted tailored search constructed by a librarian that delivers information right to their hand. ("Mobile Tag," 2009)

Creating connections via a converged device in a library setting is a huge step forward for using technology for education and access. I applaud the forward thinking and sense of innovation that went into these initiatives.

What does this mean for libraries and librarians? Understand that converged devices are everywhere and that people use them. The days of "No Cell Phone" policies and signage in the library are long gone. Courteous cell use in our libraries is very important to emphasize, but banning cell phones—a user's window to his world—is no longer an option. Converged devices are much more than just phones. They are Web, text, e-mail, Twitter, camera, and video machines that can also be used to store data and manage information. How can we deny the use of someone's personal information manager?

Don't ignore the channels and spaces that mobile devices access. Reach out to users this way, such as with cell phone–enhanced Web sites or a mobile device application (app). The District of Columbia Public Library's recently developed iPhone application enables easy access to library information and catalog searching.

Useful Links

DCPL iPhone App: http://dclibrarylabs.org/projects/iphone/

Mobile Libraries Blog on QR Codes: http://mobile-libraries.blogspot.com/2009/07/library-instruction-on-your-iphone-you.html

SELU Text a Librarian: http://www.selu.edu/library/askref/text/index.html

THE IMPACT OF LOCALIZATION

These trends build on each other. Data stored in the cloud and accessed via mobile devices points to a third important trend: localization. Global positioning systems built into smart devices are creating a new landscape of information based on location. Many of the new social networking apps on the iPhone tap into using my location in various ways:

- I can find nearby dining places with Urban Spoon.
- I can share my current location with trusted friends on Loopt or Brightkite.

- I can search for nearby shops and services with the Google Maps app.
- I can find nearby Twitter users with Twinkle—always good for a laugh in airports because of the tweeted frustrations of travelers.

These examples are messy, weird, and kind of silly, but they speak to the promise of what could come. I might easily find three vegetarian restaurants within a mile of a conference hotel via a localized search on my device. I might benefit from the wisdom of three other hikers while exploring a national park through services like "Find Twitter Users Near Me." In the future, I might selectively broadcast my location to trusted friends—"hey, I'm at the café come join me." And I might also tap into these nearby friends for my information needs. Traveling with a device that can tell me I am near attractions, services, favorite stores, and more is not out of the realm of possibility. Where does the library fit into these activities?

This is also the point where issues of privacy become so important. We need to understand how much is too much and how much is too little ("No photos in the library! It's a privacy thing!"). We also need to understand what it means to share location or status updates with others. Understanding privacy settings in apps, Web sites, and so on is of the utmost importance for librarians and for everyone. Translating that understanding to helping our users understand how to share—and not share—will assuredly become part of the duties of the training librarian.

Michael Casey and I found ourselves on either side of the spectrum of social tools and privacy in a piece we wrote for our column, "The Transparent Library" (Casey and Stephens, 2008), in which we discussed our use of social tools and the consequences of doing so:

MS: I embrace a lot of it. I use Facebook to interact with students as well as with LIS colleagues and friends. I use Flickr to share the way I see the world—though I'm still surprised when someone at an American Library Association conference tells me they saw what I had for dinner the night before. The benefits outweigh the costs right now, though I also believe those of us of a certain age or awareness self-edit their life streams to a certain degree.

MC: And how do we manage this personal/professional divide? Should we be worried that supervisors "friend" subordinates on Facebook and can look into their personal lives while at the same time they must evaluate their performance? Do we go to someone's Flickr stream or Twitter status to check on them when they call in sick? Ethical questions surround what we can now "find out" about coworkers, job applicants, potential friends, etc.

MS: Indeed! Our location-aware iPhones and applications like Loopt make it very easy to follow someone's movements. I am both excited about broadcasting my whereabouts to trusted friends/colleagues and a little rattled when I see how easily the "nearby" functions in iPhone apps reveal one's location—if people choose to be public with their data. Friending and un-friending is a tough call. I've deleted contacts in many of my networks but not others because of the transparency of the tool; I don't want to send the wrong message.

What does this mean for libraries and librarians? This may be a crucial trend to embrace. What happens when people are asking questions and finding their information using a location-aware device within their trusted, or even not-so-trusted, circles of contacts because it's so easy? What does it mean when services like Layar present a view of city streets overlaid with information, links, and more, all within a portable device? Stephen Abram, vice president of innovation at SirsiDynix, pondered these questions in "Evolution to Revolution to Chaos? Reference in Transition" (2008):"When question space is localized to cities or city blocks, how will the librarian be present? This will be one of the most interesting things to watch in the next few years and I'll applaud the library that innovates into this realm." As an exercise, ponder for a few moments how you could extend the librarian's presence into localized areas such as town, campus, and neighborhood. What challenges are there? What benefits? And what happens if you don't extend your work into this space?

Useful Links

Layar, the Mobile Augmented Reality Browser: Layar video: http://www.youtube.com/watch?v=b64_16K2e08

A FOCUS ON HUMANITY AND THE HEART

Seth Godin's *Tribes* was a touchstone for me in 2008. He took discussions of social tools to a much higher level and expertly pulled out the connection to humanity behind the technology. Humans, Godin writes, "need to belong" (2008, 3). We want to contribute, collaborate, and feel a part of something. "Give us the tools and make it easy," Godin writes, and folks will continue to join the tribe (3).

In "What's Your Tribe?" (2005), Jonathan Ford brings together the concept of the tribe with microinteraction and localization:

> Brands need to think small and act small; maybe by scaling down to look at the individual towns and cities—even the streets—where the tribes are living and working to provide brands that are very local and specialized to that market. Alternatively, brand owners could look at brand and product options that allow the consumer to collaborate in the creation process of the brand, like providing them with the means to customize the packaging to create something as unique and individual as they are.

What we may find at a future reference desk is a librarian receiving a question from a nearby user via some location-aware service. She accesses the required information in the cloud and shares that data with the user, who may in turn contribute more information back to the cloud, customizing and personalizing it for future use or the use of others.

Today, interactions between people and librarians can and do play out on blogs, Twitter, and Facebook, with varying degrees of success. The possibility is there—as is the probability that technology-enhanced connection in real time will only increase as devices, networks, and batteries get better and stronger. These tools are new. Each day it seems there are new social networks to join, but the underlying connections between humans have always been there.

If the conversation at your institution hasn't already shifted from the "using the shiny technology of the day" type to thinking about what it actually means to interact with another human being, it needs to now. These interactions just happen to be electronic. As we go forward into this new landscape of connectedness, with new avenues for learning and entertainment, and always available information, I hope that we encourage the heart in everything we do, every item we provide, and every reference transaction we conclude.

How can we inspire curiosity in our users? How can we be the community center of town, of campus, of the school? In my mind, this is very important—everything we do should encourage our users to think of us when they need help, an escape, or a road map in an ever-changing world. Sure, snazzy technology in a beautiful space is sexy and alluring, but the purpose behind it should be deeply grounded in a highly refined service ethic with the mission of putting information into the hands of those who need it. Art. Music. Space. Technology. Gadgets. Shiny new toys. Rather important as well. Collaboration. Service. Connection. These are the foundations that make everything work so well. Caring and empathy? They are a given if we want to encourage the heart.

How will your library's humanity shine through today? Will it be a connection made in person or virtually? Will it inspire someone's curiosity? Will it lead a tribe of passionate users who care about the institution? Tapping into the power and insight of the tribe is important. It's outreach in a way but more than that. It's also "marketing" in the new world—without big money for billboards and ads and without the phony public relations talk. As Godin notes, the tribe is listening. The tribe wants to follow. So ponder how you will encourage your library's tribe, continually wow and engage them with service innovations, and let them share as much or as little as they'd like while participating.

TREND WATCHING

The trends identified in the preceding are all ones to watch in the next few years. But also do not lose sight of the road farther ahead because you never know what is waiting just over the horizon. A useful resource for this is Trendwatching.com. A recent article at the site ("Trend Briefing," 2008) shared ways to become a better trend watcher. Although aimed at business, the suggestions speak directly to our field:

Acquire a point of view about the world around you.

Be curious and be open minded.

Your professional interests should be broader than your personal interests.

Aim to become a generalist. Yes, we all need to be a specialist in something. However, we also need to be generalists, to understand the big picture.

Library administration should take note of these tips and charge librarians with trend watching as part of their duties—and then give them time to do it. Emerging-technology groups are one way to get people discussing trends. Then see how the trends impact your technology plan and long-range planning documents for services and new initiatives.

To conclude, the skills and mindset of a forward-thinking trend spotter are what I want my students to have when they leave the Dominican University Graduate School of Library and Information Science program, and I want this for any librarians in the field, too. There are great opportunities for libraries and librarians in this ever-changing world. I wrote about this on *Tame the Web* (Stephens, 2008) and offer an updated version here:

If we **learn to learn,** it doesn't matter that this week's shiny new tool is Twitter and next week's even shinier tool is something else. We can still play around with it, figure it out, use our foundational knowledge to make sense of it, and decide if it works in our situation. Not every tool will work for every library, but learning to experiment and explore will help us spot those that will fit well.

If we **adapt to change,** we aren't thrown every time the world shifts. There's no knee-jerk "I don't need to know anything about that" or "that doesn't really have anything to do with me" response, or some other excuse that essentially means "I can't think about the future so I'll just point out some more reasons why it just won't work." We use point one and dive in and figure it out, and then get ready for the next change. Trend watching makes the shifts less scary.

If we **scan the horizon,** we're trend spotting for the future. We are pondering, for example, what the popularity of a certain technology might do to library service, or what bigger trends will mean to libraries in the next 10 or 20 years.

If we make sure to **be curious about the world,** it makes all of the preceding super-easy.

Finally, please remember to **focus on encouraging the heart.** This is important as we move into a more emotionally rich, experience-based world. Social networks enable us to extend the heart across cyberspace. User-centered planning, engaging and exciting spaces, and opportunities to follow one's curiosity are all part of the heart of libraries. The library should encourage the heart.

In a nutshell

Learn to Learn
Adapt to Change

Scan the Horizon
Be Curious
Encourage the Heart

WORKS CITED

Abilene Christian University. n.d. *ACU connected: Mobile learning*. Retrieved July 24, 2009, from http://www.acu.edu/technology/mobilelearning/index.html.

Abilene Christian University. n.d. *Our progress with mobile learning*. Retrieved July 24, 2009, from http://www.acu.edu/technology/mobilelearning/progress/index.html.

Abram, S. 2008. Evolution to revolution to chaos? Reference in transition. *Information Today, Inc*. Retrieved July 24, 2009, from http://www.infotoday.com/searcher/sep08/Abram.shtml.

Armano, D. 2008. Brand interactions are the future. *Advertising Age*. Retrieved July 20, 2009, from http://adage.com/digitalnext/post?article_id=126579.

Casey, M., and M. Stephens. 2008. The transparent library: When worlds collide. *Library Journal* 133 (15): 21.

Ford, J. 2005. What's your tribe? *STEP Inside Design*. Retrieved July 24, 2009, from http://www.stepinsidedesign.com/STEPMagazine/Article/28539.

Godin, S. 2008. *Tribes: We need you to lead us*. New York: Portfolio.

Griffey, J. 2008. Stranger than we know. In *netconnect* (Fall 2008): 10–12, supplement, *Library Journal* 133 (17).

Kemper, D. 2008. From Canada to London: How Twitter opens (conference) doors. *The DIGITAL Archive*. Retrieved July 24, 2009, from http://digitalpermanence.blogspot.com/2008/10/as-twitter-matures-and-empowers-people.html.

Kusek, D., G. Leonhard, and S. G. Lindsay. 2005. *The future of music: Manifesto for the digital music revolution*. Boston: Berklee Press.

Mobile tag closeup—Flickr—photo sharing! Retrieved July 24, 2009, from http://www.flickr.com/photos/aculibrary/3011082552/.

Stephens, M. 2007. Can U TXT the LBRY? *ALA TechSource blog*. Retrieved July 24, 2009, from http://www.alatechsource.org/blog/2007/06/can-u-txt-the-lbry.html.

Stephens, M. 2008. Meme: Passion quilt or what I want for new librarians. *Tame the Web*. Retrieved July 24, 2009, from http://tametheweb.com/2008/04/26/meme-passion-quilt-or-what-i-want-for-new-librarians/.

Trend briefing (November 2008 briefing covering top 15 trend questions). 2008. Retrieved July 24, 2009, from http://trendwatching.com/trends/top15questions/.

Workstreaming with microblogs. *Anywired—wired self-employment tips*. 2008. Retrieved July 24, 2009, from http://www.anywired.com/2008/01/workstreaming-with-microblogs/.

V

REFERENCE COLLECTION DEVELOPMENT

17

FROM PRINT TO E-REFERENCE

David A. Tyckoson

If you have been a reference librarian for any length of time, there are certain reference books that you have come to know and love. My top 10 list would probably include the following:

- *The World Almanac*
- *Encyclopedia of Associations*
- *Who's Who in America*
- *Statistical Abstract of the United States*
- *Handbook of Chemistry and Physics*
- *Webster's Collegiate Dictionary*
- *Roget's Thesaurus*
- *Goode's World Atlas*
- *Facts on File*

And last, but certainly not least . . .

- *Encyclopaedia Britannica*

Your list may vary, but each of these titles is a traditional source that reference librarians have come to rely on. We know what they contain, how they are indexed, and how they are organized. We know their quirks and foibles, from the table-number instead of page-number indexing in the *Statistical Abstract* to the entry numbers surrounded by stars in the *Encyclopedia of Associations.* We even know what color they are, from the dark blue of *Facts on File* to the pretty maroon of *Who's Who* to the classy faux-leather brown of the *Encyclopaedia Britannica*. And, of course, the *Encyclopedia of Associations* is red and blue, except for the international volumes, which are green and blue.

These are old friends that we know intimately and love passionately. They have shared our triumphs as we sought out the answer to some obscure question, making us look like geniuses and never taking away our glory. They have helped us understand the breadth of human knowledge, including history, economics, literature, and science. They have told us who won the Super Bowl and the biographies of the presidents. They have told us what happened on July 5, 1956, and have displayed the geography of Iraq. They have shown us the Mexican flag and told us the difference between *nuclear* and *nucular*. They have even explained the meaning of life.

Reference librarians know each of these print sources well. Each of these titles represents a classic reference source—one without which no library could function. These standard reference tools are contained in almost every reference collection, from the most scholarly academic research library to the smallest of public libraries. They are tools that generations of librarians have used to find information for their users. They are indispensable to any, representing the core sources in every library. And no one uses them anymore.

The use of reference books—traditional print on paper—is clearly in decline. Sources that reference librarians used to consult on a daily or weekly and sometimes hourly basis are sitting on our shelves collecting dust. And since the most popular sources are not seeing any use, those that were used less frequently are sitting there as well. Sources such as the *Dictionary of Scientific Biography*, the *Macmillan Encyclopedia of Religion*, and the *Palgrave Dictionary of Economics* contain some of the most scholarly and comprehensive information on their respective subject fields, but most of their pages have not seen the light of day for several years. When sources of that quality are no longer being used, what is happening to the rest of the collection? Will we stop purchasing—and will publishers stop publishing—standard reference books? Will Google and Wikipedia become the new standard reference tools? Will librarians no longer be able to offer familiar, reliable sources to our users? Is this the end of reference service as we know it? The short answer is yes—and no. To understand the long answer, we need to look back at why reference collections were developed, how they were used, and how new technologies have affected that use. Only then can we make sense of our current confusion—and understand reference collections' future path.

THE ORIGIN OF REFERENCE BOOKS AND REFERENCE COLLECTIONS

Like the yellow brick road, it is best to start at the beginning. The first widely read English-language reference book was the *Encyclopaedia Britannica*. Although a few similar works were published during the times before the

Britannica, none had the scope, the distribution, or the audacity of this first encyclopedia—and none is still being published today. First published in series format for subscribers from 1768 to 1771, the *Britannica* was a landmark in concept and scholarship. Inspired by Diderot's *Encyclopédie,* it attempted to compile the 18th-century world's knowledge into one single published work. Given Britain' and France's domination of Europe and colonization of much of the rest of the world at that time, it is not surprising that a group of authors and editors in each nation felt that they could collect the knowledge of the world and publish it for their respective king and country. The Enlightenment concept that humans could understand the world through reason had as one of its outcomes the idea that understanding could be compiled and published for all to read. The English-language reference work that attempted to achieve this ideal was the *Britannica.*

The original *Britannica* was of decidedly mixed success. Eventually published in three volumes, the contents were very uneven in nature. Volume 1 (A–B) provided in-depth articles on a wide variety of topics. Volume 2 (C–L) demonstrated a significant drop in both the number of articles and their comprehensiveness. Volume 3 (M–Z) continued that decline as the project ran out of funding and needed to be completed quickly and cheaply. Needless to say, readers of that first set received much more information about anatomy, Australia, and botany than about philosophy, Russia, and zoology. Fortunately, there was enough interest—and sales—to continue the project. Later editions were better funded, had more editorial assistance, and were able to explain the world and its knowledge more evenly throughout the alphabet. Over decades and centuries, *Britannica* evolved to become the authoritative and comprehensive source that is still published today.

The goal of this early tool was to summarize knowledge, providing students, researchers, and readers with a basic background on any and every topic. Readers seeking more in-depth information would begin with the *Britannica* and then consult more specialized resources. That role of summarizing and abstracting the world's knowledge was soon adopted by other publishers. These early reference books did not publish original research findings but summarized the knowledge of others. However, at the time of publication, none of these publications were called *reference books.* That name did not come about until the development of the modern public library in the mid-19th century. With such large numbers of readers coming to the library, the librarian needed to somehow differentiate this type of book from the rest of the collection. Since these books were not sources that users read from cover to cover but ones that they referred to for specific facts or other information, they were segregated from the rest of the library's collection. These books that users would *refer* to began to be called *reference* books—and the name stuck.

Reference books became very popular with library users. For the average citizen, access to information in the 19th century was difficult. All books were relatively expensive as compared to family income, resulting in households with very little available reading material. Due to their scholarly nature and smaller print runs, reference books were, then as now, more expensive than other books. At the same time, the advent of universal public education caused the literacy rate to soar. Newly literate readers wanted to exercise that skill, but access to reading material was difficult. In many homes, the Bible and the *Farmer's Almanac* were the only books available—elevating each to a more revered status for its accessibility as much as for its content. As more and more of the population became literate, a national thirst for reading material ensued. When public libraries became established, citizens naturally turned to their local library as a source of new knowledge. At the time, the concept of the public library as the "people's university" was very real. Readers turned to the library as a source of literacy, knowledge, and enlightenment. The public library had the books, the staff, and the mission to improve the lives of its community members. And it did.

When all books had to be used within the physical library building, the status of a reference book was no different than that of any other tome. As circulating collections became popular, most reference books were excluded from circulation and remained available for use in the library only. Although several factors contributed to this decision, including format and price, the primary reason for making reference books noncirculating was access. Keeping reference books in the library provided access for all library users—and for the librarian—so that they could serve a larger segment of the user population. Sacrificing high access for one user (the person who would have checked the book out) provided on-demand access for everyone else. In this common scenario, limiting access for one provided greater access for all. Soon it became almost universal among libraries that reference books did not circulate.

By the 1880s, the number and use of reference books had grown tremendously. Reference collections had become standard components of most libraries, and specialized staff who could help members of their community use reference books to find information—reference librarians—were beginning to appear. Over 100 years after the publication of the first reference book, libraries began to employ the first reference librarians. By 1886, Melvil Dewey himself called the reference department the most important single department in the library at Columbia College (Rothstein, 1972). In 1891, *Library Journal* published the first article to use the term *reference work* in the title ("Reference Work in Libraries," 1891). So-called reference departments became very popular in public and academic libraries. By the end of World War I, almost every library that employed more than one librarian had one or more staff designated to serve as the reference librarian(s).

Interestingly, at this same time the *Encyclopaedia Britannica* became the single most comprehensive reference source in the English-speaking world. The 11th edition, published in 1910–1911, is widely recognized as the most complete, scholarly representation of the knowledge of its era—more so than any other encyclopedia. Almost a century and a half after its beginnings, it had come as close to achieving the Enlightenment idea of capturing the world's knowledge through reason as any reference work would ever get. Although it is outdated, quaint, and somewhat biased when viewed from our perspective a century later, the publication of the 11th edition of the *Britannica* reestablished it as the world's premier English-language reference source.

REFERENCE SUCCESS

Users flocked to reference departments. Whether to consult specific reference resources, to get assistance with a general information query, or just to engage with a knowledgeable reference librarian, community members came to view reference as a standard service in almost every library. Reference departments had two things that users desired: reference books and reference librarians. Three factors contributed to making reference collections critical to the community:

- Reference books were generally not available in the home, making the library the only source of this type of information for the average citizen or student.
- Reference books did not leave the library, so they were always available when needed.
- Reference librarians were available to help users find relevant reference materials and to show them how to use those materials.

These three factors combined to place the library—and especially the reference collection—at the center of information for the community. The popular image of the reference librarian as the "answer person" grew out of this arrangement. People came to the library and told the reference librarian what they needed; the librarian then either provided them with an answer (usually after a few minutes of searching) or took them to sources to search on their own. The absence of other alternatives for finding this type of information resulted in an elevated status for the reference collection within the community. When they needed information, people either used the books in the reference collection or did without.

As communications technology improved, the requirement that a user had to go into the library to access reference sources was relaxed. While in-person service was still considered the primary means of using reference materials, by the mid-20th century most libraries began offering reference information over the telephone. Telephone reference was especially useful for short, factual questions, such as statistics, directory information, and trivia. Telephone reference did not work as well with in-depth research questions, where a significant amount of searching and analysis is required. In many urban areas, telephone reference became a huge business for the local public library, with hundreds or even thousands of queries per day. Users who did not want to take the time to visit the library in person were able to receive basic information from their homes, their offices, or their social clubs (anecdotes abound about librarians being called to settle bar bets). The expansion of reference service to the telephone brought the library—and the information that it contained—one step closer to users' homes.

Over the years, this configuration for the provision of reference service varied little. Print collections became larger as more and more reference books were added. In some research libraries, the reference collection became larger than the entire collection of many small public libraries. In order to allow librarians to find information more quickly, ready-reference collections were developed. These were the super-reference books that were used frequently or that needed to be placed in a special area nearest the reference librarian. As a result, ready-reference books were usually segregated further from the reference collection and often kept behind the desk with the librarians. Many of the titles at the beginning of this paper would have been part of most ready-reference collections. As the reference librarian's reference collection, these works were some of the most heavily used titles in the library.

Reference librarians built collections to meet the needs of their local users. Materials were selected and purchased because they met the needs of the local community, whether those needs were for Egyptian archeology or automotive repair. Users came to the library—or called on the phone—and the librarian would help them find what they needed. Although the collection slowly changed over time, as new materials were added and old sources withdrawn, its status as a reliable core information resource for the community rarely changed. The Enlightenment ideal of summarizing and capturing the knowledge of the world, which could no longer be done in one single reference work, was filled by the reference collection as a whole. The reference collection was the physical embodiment of solid, accurate information. The relationship of the reference collection to the community was established—and that relationship remained unchanged for most of the 20th century.

However, the progress of knowledge marched on. By the 1970s, the editors of *Britannica* realized that the body of human knowledge was far too complex to continue to be organized in simple alphabetical format. With the publication of the 15th edition in 1974, they introduced a radical new approach to the process of summarizing human knowledge. According to Robert M. Hutchins, chairman of the board of editors, this was no less than "a revolution in encyclopedia making" (1974, ix). Under the leadership of Mortimer J. Adler, the editors organized the encyclopedia around the "circle of knowledge." Rather than a single alphabetical list of topics, they provided an outline of knowledge (the *Propaedia*) that linked to short entries on specific topics (the *Micropaedia*), which were then further related to more lengthy treatises on major subject areas (the *Macropaedia*). The idea was that users would start with the outline in the *Propaedia,* link to relevant articles in the

Micropaedia, and link again to the relevant information in the *Macropaedia*. At each level, the user would learn more and obtain greater context about the information being sought.

This design was genius. It recognized the interrelations between all human knowledge and attempted to present that concept in the design of the encyclopedia itself. It was intended to draw the reader further and further into a topic and relate it to the other subjects within the encyclopedia. In many ways, it presaged the concept of the World Wide Web, where users link back and forth between related yet different information pages as their primary means of finding information. Unfortunately, it is much more difficult to link through print on paper than it is online. As a result, users found this organization difficult and tedious. For librarians, it lacked the important feature of a central index that would lead us directly to the information we sought. While it taught the reader about the complexity of the world's knowledge, often diverting the reader to related—and even unrelated—topics along the way (very much like the World Wide Web), it was just too difficult to find specific information quickly in the *New Encyclopaedia Britannica*. As a result, this revolution in encyclopedia making sat on the shelf while we all used the *World Book* instead.

DECLINING NEED FOR REFERENCE COLLECTIONS

Several factors combined over a long period of time to erode the print reference collection's elevated status. Many of these changes occurred so slowly as to be almost invisible in most libraries. Others happened very quickly, changing the role of the reference collection almost overnight. However, each played a role in modifying the nature of the reference collection for the community. The cumulative effect of these changes was to eliminate the dependency of users on traditional print reference collections, resulting in the lightly used reference collections we see in our libraries today.

Technology

The first and most obvious element leading to the decline in our dependence on print reference collections is technology. When computing power was applied to information resources, our reliance on print reference sources was profoundly shaken. In today's reference environment, almost every reference transaction starts by searching an electronic information source—and most end there. Whereas reference librarians a century ago relied on catalogs, indexes, and bibliographies to help them find solutions to a user's query, today's reference librarians go directly to the computer. Today's tools are faster, more comprehensive, and more current than anything imaginable even a few decades ago. It is no wonder that the use of traditional print reference tools declined—they simply cannot compete with their electronic equivalents.

The application of information technology to reference started slowly. The earliest general use of computing in reference was in the 1970s through online subscription services such as Dialog, SDC, and BRS. These services allowed librarians to conduct Boolean and keyword searches of large databases such as *ERIC, MEDLINE,* and *Psychological Abstracts.* Because the economics of these tools was built on pay-per-use agreements, they were very expensive as compared to their print equivalents. As a result, they tended to be used only by high-end users who had the funds available to cover the costs. Typically, they were adopted primarily in academic libraries where researchers could use grants—and graduate students their own meager funds—to pay for a comprehensive search of their specific research area. To minimize the time online, librarians conducted searches for users rather than letting the users search on their own. The economic disadvantage of this technology meant that it was adopted only by the elite who had sufficient funding to take advantage of its benefits. Like the first edition of the *Britannica,* which was sold only to a few wealthy subscribers, these first electronic reference tools reached only a small percentage of potential users. However, those users did prove that electronic search techniques would vastly improve results. It was economics, not performance, that prevented electronic search techniques from being more widely adopted.

That situation changed in the 1980s when CD-ROM technology became available. CD-ROM products eliminated the pay-per-use disadvantages of the subscription services. Libraries could subscribe to—or purchase—a source for a fixed price and search as often as desired. Although most of the early CD-ROM products were still relatively expensive, there was no additional cost based on usage. Once open-ended, usage-based pricing was replaced with a known fixed cost, libraries could decide which electronic products fit their users' needs. Since users saw no direct cost, these resources became extremely popular. The number of searches of each database increased 1,000-fold over the same product as a fee-based service. Economics had finally caught up to technology—and the future would never be the same.

CD-ROMs also brought us the first replacements for traditional print reference sources in electronic form. In 1985, the *Grolier Multimedia Encyclopedia* became the first traditional print encyclopedia to be released in CD-ROM format. That first version included the same text as the print equivalent—and that was all it included. Although it provided keyword and Boolean searching, it was not a success. When answering questions, it took longer for reference librarians to load and search the CD-ROM than it did to look up the same information in the print. Besides, the source on which it was built was just not that good an encyclopedia. The technology's benefits could not overcome the content drawbacks in this first electronic reference tool.

Good content did come along in CD-ROM format over time. The *World Book* was released on CD-ROM in 1990 and the *Britannica* in 1994. In 1993, Microsoft got into this market with its *Encarta* product, which was based on the print *Funk and Wagnalls Encyclopedia.* Microsoft's low pricing and mass production put electronic encyclopedias directly into many homes and workplaces. The stage was set for widespread adoption of electronic information tools. And another new development—the introduction of the World Wide Web in 1991—was about to make CD-ROM technology obsolete and change reference service forever. However, before examining how the Internet changed the reference environment, it is important to examine another longer-term trend that contributed to the decline in the use of reference books.

Access to Information

The second—and much more subtle but equally important—reason for the decline in the use of print reference collections is related to the public's access to information. A century ago, people came to the library for the same reason that criminals robbed banks—because that is where the information was. There was very little access to authoritative information in the home, and only limited access in most workplaces. Books were expensive, and people had very few other choices for obtaining quality information. As a result, the library's investment in reference sources became a shared community investment. The reference collection became the information utility for the entire community.

During the course of the 20th century, access to reference information outside the library increased dramatically. As the cost of books dropped in comparison to family income, more and more families purchased reference books for the home. The dramatic rise in home encyclopedia sales after World War II reflected many families' desire to have reliable information available immediately. Dictionaries, almanacs, atlases, and encyclopedias became part of many home libraries, forming literal in-house reference collections. *Funk and Wagnalls* could be purchased on a weekly basis, volume by volume, at the supermarket; the *World Book* could be ordered through the schools; and even the *Britannica* was sold door to door. As more and more homes acquired these reference works, children working on homework assignments or parents seeking background information for something they heard on the radio or television no longer needed to go to the library for basic reference information—it was now available 24/7 on a bookshelf, only an arm's length away.

It took a long time for home access to translate into reduced use of library reference collections. While home libraries had a few basic reference works, users still came to the library for more specialized materials. Use of the *Britannica* may have dropped somewhat, but use of specialized subject encyclopedias and indexes rose. Ready-reference tools continued to be librarians' favorites. For several decades, home reference sources may actually have increased the use of the same titles in the library. Since users tend to start with tools that are familiar, they often used the library copies of those same sources when they were in the building. In addition, the library copy continued to be the starting point for those who did not have reference works in the home. As part of libraries' democratizing effect, those who could not afford access at home relied on the library even more. These factors combined to continue relatively high use of library reference collections. However, in the early 1990s, something new came along that changed everything.

The Rise of the Network

With the Internet's arrival, technology and access to information merged into one. In a matter of only a few years, the World Wide Web grew from a network linking a bunch of geeky physicists into a phenomenon that swept the world. Within a decade, it became the standard communication medium for education, business, and government. As a technology, it was very simple to develop and even simpler to use. As an access tool, it provided free and immediate access to information from any source on the network to anyone with a computer attached to that network. The Internet soon became the first source for anyone seeking information, including librarians and library users. And it delivered the final blow to the use of most reference books.

The Internet is the great equalizer in providing societal access to information. Over the Internet, every citizen has access to more information than used to be contained in the largest library. No matter where someone is located, she has the same expectation that the Internet will provide her with information that will be fast, free, and final. Of course, not all information available on the network is accurate, and one of the biggest problems that users have is differentiating the good from the bad. However, with the advent of Google, Yahoo! and other search engines, most of the time people can find useful information easily and quickly by themselves. And since they can find that information on their own, they no longer need to rely on library reference collections.

The network has had a few other interesting impacts on reference collections. Publishers have attempted to use the network as a means for selling and distributing their reference tools. Oxford, Gale, and many other publishers of traditional reference works sell e-book versions of the same titles that they publish in print, and many libraries make these products available to their users. However, like the previous generation of reference books on CD-ROM, the use of reference e-books has never reached initial expectations. The process of identifying that a book is available, authenticating as a user, and then searching that title for the information desired takes a lot longer than simply using the free, open Web. Even though e-books provide higher-quality, professionally written and edited information resources, most users simply collect the same information from less academic sources. Although many libraries do purchase some of these reference e-books, they have yet to be used and accepted by the public.

Famously, *Britannica* tried the opposite approach to providing reference information on the Internet. In 1999, the editors decided to make *Britannica*'s content available for free, creating a Web portal that would fund its ongoing revision and development through advertising. They also announced that no more print versions would ever be published. It appeared that the oldest and most prestigious English-language encyclopedia would become a leader in the Web-based economy for distributing information to the public. Unfortunately, they discovered the same reality that affected many Internet-based businesses of that era—there was no money to be made in such an open-access model, and they were losing their corporate shirts. Within two years, the *Britannica* was back in print, and the online equivalent was available only to subscribers. Giving the content away free may have been popular, but it was not a sustainable business model.

The Internet was much more than just a new technology—it presented a significant societal change. It not only affected how people accessed information but also led to the creation of totally new kinds of information sources. For example, the most consulted encyclopedia in the world today is not *World Book* or *Britannica* but Wikipedia. Wikipedia presents a completely new design concept for encyclopedias. Written not by scholars but by average citizens, it can be updated and changed by anyone who has knowledge to add and wants to take the time to do so. It is a truly collectively composed and edited information resource, reflecting the socially connected environment in which it was conceived. While there have been many criticisms, one of the most significant being that it is not entirely accurate, those complaints can also be made about the traditional print resources that it is replacing. It is extremely current, with changes often being made while events are occurring. No traditional reference source is able to adapt to changing events as easily and quickly as Wikipedia. In the few short years since it debuted in 2001, Wikipedia has become the starting point for students, librarians, researchers, and the rest of the information-seeking public. In many ways, it has achieved the goals set forth by the editors of that first *Britannica* back in the 18th century. It comes closer to an accurate, comprehensive, and current collection of the world's knowledge than any publication in human history. The ideals of the Enlightenment remain alive in Wikipedia and other information sources like it.

THE FUTURE OF REFERENCE COLLECTIONS

The external influences that led to the creation of reference collections have changed significantly since such collections were first developed in the 19th century. Information that once was available only in expensive reference books within a library collection inside a library building is now available immediately, anywhere and everywhere, at no cost. Finding information has become fast, easy, and cheap. Unfortunately, reference collections remain slow, difficult, and expensive.

One reason that the use of reference books is in such great decline is that the nature of reference service has shifted. With so much information available to so many people so quickly, library users are able to answer many questions on their own and no longer need the intervention of a librarian. The popular image of the reference librarian as someone who provides answers to factual questions (think Katharine Hepburn in *Desk Set*) was never entirely accurate and is now totally misplaced. Reference is not about the *answers* but about the *questions*. People find answers to the easy questions on their own—they come to the library only with their difficult queries. Most of the time, those queries do not have simple answers but are part of a more complex search. From the student writing a paper on global warming, to the business owner trying to increase sales, to the teacher trying to improve student learning, to the politician trying to increase voter participation, the questions that librarians receive are not likely to have specific factual answers. Instead, they are complex questions with hundreds of potential answers. The librarian serves not as a fact-giver but as a consultant who advises the user on search strategies and potential resources. What is important to the librarian is not a comprehensive knowledge of the contents of the reference collection but the ability to interact with the user to identify—and help shape—the nature of the question being asked. Being able to conduct an effective reference interview has replaced knowledge of sources as the single most important factor in reference success.

As a result, reference collections have seen a tremendous decline in use. A study in my own library at California State University, Fresno, demonstrates that fact. Since January 2008, all use of the collection has been tallied through the statistical package included with the online public access catalog (OPAC). Every book that circulated was counted through the circulation system, and all in-house use was measured through count use data. Users were told not to refile materials, and every book was wanded by staff or student assistants before it was reshelved. Since we had already implemented an RFID system, counting was fast and easy. All materials were counted, no matter whether they were used by a librarian, student, faculty member, or someone from the community. If a book made it off the shelf, it was counted as having been used.

Results of this study were staggering. We have always had a fairly large and comprehensive print reference collection that covers the wide variety of subject fields taught on campus. As such, it contained the basic encyclopedia, dictionaries, and similar reference genres in all subject areas. It also had a significant collection of older abstracting and indexing services (including *Chemical Abstracts*) and a sizable legal collection. The total number of items in the collection varied over time, but at the date that the usage snapshot was taken for this study, it was slightly over 30,000 items (30,182, to be precise).

We knew that it was probably larger than necessary, but we had no idea how much larger. Total measured use over the period of the study was 6,121. Of that use, 2,837 was circulation and 3,282 was in-house. Dividing the total use by the total collection size indicates that only 20 percent of the collection was used. However, actual use is overstated by that simple calculation. In reality, reference book usage was concentrated among a very small number of items. Those 6,000+ measured uses were of only 2,770 total items. Of the over 30,000 items available, only 9.2 percent received any use at all. But wait—there's more. Only 923 titles in the collection were used. Many of the items that received at least one use represented multiple volumes of a single work.

High-use items represent an even smaller portion of the collection. Using even a moderate indicator of high-use items (five or more times during the period of the study) results in only 256 items that are identified as high use, or less than 1 percent of all the items in the collection. Even looking at all of the items used more than once leads to a disappointing result. Out of 30,182 total items in the collection, 1,167 were used two or more times, representing less than 5 percent of the total collection.

These data clearly show that the reference materials in our collection are not being used. Yet we had built this collection over decades specifically to meet the information needs of our users. Yes, there is definitely some deadwood—but that is true in any collection. Although the size of the collection might have been inflated by the legal materials and the backfiles of indexing and abstracting services (the volumes that predate the online databases), most of the collection contained materials appropriate for our user community. And while we knew that it had been used heavily (or so we thought) in the past, it became obvious that it was not being used much at all now.

Reference librarians everywhere still select, catalog, and shelve reference books. However, the cost per use of reference materials has become very high. People in the community that the library serves simply do not use print reference collections as much as they did decades ago. With library users—and librarians—relying on electronic resources to respond to most queries, what is the future of reference collections? Is there still a need or desire for print resources? If so, what can be done to increase usage of reference materials? Should libraries still be investing in this format? Do reference books—and reference collections—have a future in today's libraries?

PROMOTING THE USE OF PRINT REFERENCE

The primary problem with most traditional print reference materials is that they are not being used. They are good information sources, but they sit on the shelf collecting dust, silent sentinels to the fact that the world of knowledge has changed around them. At the same time, our users sit at computers, searching the Internet to find the same information contained within those dusty reference books. If librarians are going to continue to purchase reference books, we need to find a way to promote their use. Otherwise, we are just throwing the collection funds used for reference down a dark blue, buckram-covered hole. Fortunately, there are several techniques that can be used to promote reference materials.

Use Studies. The first step in increasing the use of traditional reference collections is to determine what is currently being used, what is not being used, and how those figures relate to the rest of the collection. The easiest way to determine use is to tally the frequency with which items are pulled from the shelves, as we did in our use study mentioned earlier. Every major OPAC vendor provides a count-use feature, where usage data can be tallied by wanding the barcode or RFID tag included in the book. The system can then generate reports of use by item, call number, or collection. By scanning every item before reshelving, a library will get an accurate assessment of what is being used and how often. Alternatively, it will quickly become obvious what materials are not being used. While using the statistics in the OPAC is the simplest means of gathering these data, the same information could be compiled by entering titles into a spreadsheet, marking the books themselves, or simply writing down the titles that get used. No matter how the data are collected, compiling reference book use data over a period of time will provide librarians with the information required to make intelligent decisions about what belongs in the reference collection and what does not.

Circulating Reference Collections. Historically, reference materials have had a noncirculating status. The reason behind that status was the counterintuitive concept that noncirculation promoted access. Since users came to the library to find reference information, a noncirculating collection increased the chances that a particular item would be available when a user wanted to consult it. By restricting access for borrowers, we increased access for all other users. This model is still prevalent in reference collections today. In most libraries, reference books do not circulate.

Given the current low state of demand for these reference materials, one means of promoting their use would be to change them to a circulating collection. If reference books are allowed to circulate, access will be increased for the few people who are using them because those users will be able to take them out of the library and use them for a longer period of time. This is exactly the practice that we have adopted in my library. There are always a few reference titles in any given collection that need to be kept in the library so that users will be able to consult them when needed—a ready ready-reference collection. However, 99.9 percent of the books in most reference collections would be able to circulate without creating access problems for other users.

Libraries that have made reference books circulate have found that users greatly appreciate being able to take them home and have them available for a longer period of time. Loan periods for circulating reference collections range from overnight, to three days, to one week, to the standard loan period for the regular circulating collection. Local needs will determine the loan period, and not all reference books may need the same loan period. What is clear from libraries that circulate reference books is that use of the collection increases, user satisfaction increases, and there is little effect on access to information for others.

Integrated Reference Collections. Taking the concept of user access to reference materials one step further, some libraries have decided to shelve their reference materials with the main library collection. Many users view the books in the reference collection as belonging to the staff, whereas they see the circulating collection as their portion of the library. By shelving the reference books in the main collection, a user who is seeking information on a particular topic would find the reference books on that topic and the "regular" books all in one place. Placing reference items alongside the circulating collection increases the chances that they will be discovered through browsing. If the reference books also circulate, users are able to take out any of the materials they find on their topic. If the reference books do not circulate, then in-house use should increase as a result of increased exposure in the main library collection. No matter which policy is adopted, users can find all the library's materials on a topic in one place, which is not a bad model.

One downside of this philosophy is that filing reference books into the main collection decreases access for the librarians, who generally would have to go much further to find a book when needed. In larger libraries, this can mean having to go to a different floor or wing of the building to get information that used to be located only a few feet away. For that reason, the high-use ready-reference materials should remain close to the service point and only the low-use majority of the reference collection should be moved. However, in my case, that low-use majority would be over 90 percent of the collection. Integrating reference books into the main collection makes it easier for the user to find information, makes it more likely that she will find the reference tools the library has, and, combined with a circulating reference policy, makes it more likely that she will check them out. In general, the benefits of easy access for users clearly outweigh the inconvenience for the staff.

PROMOTING E-RESOURCES

It is not just the print collection that needs promotion. Many libraries have high-quality electronic resources that also receive relatively low use. These materials are often e-book equivalents of print reference books, such as those available through *Oxford Reference Online* or the *Gale Virtual Reference Library.* They might be individual reference works such as the *New Grove Dictionary of Music and Musicians,* or they might even be encyclopedias such as the *Britannica Online.* No matter how they relate to print reference books, they contain information that has undergone the same scholarly editorial processes but also see less use than expected. We pay for most such resources and want our users to find them, but we often place too many roadblocks in the way. If our users are not touching the print equivalents, we can at least try to get them to use the online versions. There are many techniques for increasing the use of reference e-books, including the following:

Add Bibliographic Records to the Catalog. We always tell our users that if they want to see what books are in the library they should check the catalog. This is as true for e-books as for print books. The catalog should tell a user when a title is available in electronic form and should provide a link directly to that title or database. If the catalog lists only print books, catalog users will find only print books.

Highlight E-Resources on Library Web Pages. Many users are simply unaware of the variety and scope of electronic reference sources available through the library. Placing bibliographic records in the catalog will help a few users find these materials, but we can also provide links from other sections of the library's Web pages. We can even put them on display by highlighting various topics or titles on the Web page. Rotating the display will make the Web page more interesting and will drive users to try out some of our electronic reference books. Once users are aware of these materials, they are more likely to return and use them again.

Minimize Authentication Barriers. Sometimes users try to get into an e-book but are inhibited by the process of authenticating as a valid user. While we must all follow the access requirements of our contracts with vendors, it is in our best interest to make access as simple as possible. For example, requiring users to create individual accounts in order to access e-books will inhibit some from doing so, whereas simply logging into the system with a barcode or ID number creates less of a barrier. Review access to electronic resources with an eye toward a first-time user, and get rid of any unnecessary steps that can inhibit use of these materials.

SENSIBLE COLLECTION DEVELOPMENT DECISIONS

While use of reference collections has dropped considerably, most libraries continue to select and purchase reference books as if little has changed. Although we have made the transition from print to electronic access for some select genres of reference sources, especially indexing and abstracting services, most librarians continue to collect reference books at the same rate as in the past. Given the always-difficult economic realities of collection budgets, we simply cannot afford to buy reference materials this way any longer. It is important to select materials that will enhance the other resources in the collection, including those available on the Internet, rather than continue to purchase titles just because they are good works or we have always had them. Simply stated, most libraries spend too much on print reference materials.

The purchase of traditional print reference materials should not be eliminated. New reference books that belong in library collections are published every day. However, their selection should be based on user demand and staff utility. There is no point in buying a reference book just because it has always been a good reference book or is one that every collection should have. If neither users nor librarians will read it, all it does is waste collection funds and take up space. Fortunately, there are several techniques that librarians can use to tighten up the collection while saving collection funds.

Buy What Will Get Used. This is an obvious recommendation but one that cannot be overstated. New reference books are published every day on every topic imaginable, from nanotechnology to numismatics and poetry to putting. Six recent reference books that were added to my own collection include the *Biographical Dictionary of Central and Eastern Europe in the Twentieth Century, Sage Handbook of Action Research: Participative Inquiry and Practice, Architectural Graphic Standards, Encyclopedia of Police Science, Biographical Encyclopedia of Astronomers,* and *Merck/Merial Manual for Pet Health.* Whether any of these titles will be used by our librarians or our users is unknown, but my personal guess is that three will be used and the other three will not. None will become a best seller—or circulator—and some probably should not have been purchased for the collection at all.

As the reference collection's role as an access point diminishes, we need fewer reference books in the collection that fulfill that role. Some genres of reference titles may disappear completely, such as directories or collective biographies. That type of information is easily available for free on the Internet, with neither librarians nor users looking for it in print. We should certainly buy the reference books that meet our users' demands but not purchase those that supported the old just-in-case-someone-asks model. The reality is that when someone does ask, we will use our electronic resources to answer rather than traditional reference books. Saving funds on print reference materials allows us to spend more on other areas of the collection, where use is higher. It is simply good economics to buy less.

Purchase Less Frequently. By their nature, reference books are frequently updated. And as new information is produced, new editions of standard reference works are published. In the past, libraries needed to purchase the newest books to ensure that the collection was as accurate as possible. That was how we kept the reference collection current—and how publishers made a profit. With the advent of the Internet, that is no longer necessary. In most cases, background information that is found in a reference book can be updated with information found online. As a result, those reference books that we continue to purchase need not be purchased as frequently. For example, an encyclopedia that might have been ordered every year could be reduced to a once-every-three- or once-every-five-years cycle. The reality is that last year's *Britannica* is not all that different from this year's. Most users will be satisfied with a relatively recent set and do not necessarily need the absolutely most recent. Similarly, titles that have been purchased quarterly or annually could be reduced to annual, biannual, or a less frequent rotation. Reduced frequency saves money without significantly altering the use of the collection.

Review Standing Orders. Many reference titles arrive in our libraries as a result of standing orders. Standing orders were set up to ensure that titles that we knew we wanted would arrive as soon as they were published without a lot of labor in the acquisitions process. This was a logical step in acquiring those books that we knew that we all wanted every time they were updated. Primarily used for annual or other regularly scheduled publications, they were also used for books in series, multivolume sets, and other continuing publications. Most libraries have added standing orders over time but have done very little to revise those orders. The books keep coming and get updated on the shelves, and the librarians are happy. The orders are easy to continue, so we do. But a hard look at standing orders can result in a significant savings to the library. A recent review in my own library, which was conducted with the use study mentioned earlier, resulted in the cancellation of over $40,000 in standing orders. This does not mean that we will no longer buy many of the titles that used to be on standing order—just that we will no longer buy them automatically every time they are published. While our reduction may be more dramatic than those of some other libraries, it is representative of the savings that can be made by a thorough standing-order review.

Eliminate Supplements and Other Publishing Extras. When reference books needed to be updated regularly, another means by which publishers were able to support that need was by selling supplements. For example, the annual *Encyclopedia of Associations* had a quarterly supplement that included entries for new organizations, lists of associations that folded, and changes to key information for others. When print reference was the only means of finding this information, some libraries found the supplements useful for providing accurate and up-to-date information. However, that information came at a cost. These supplements were often a separate subscription—and in this example it still is. In fact, for those libraries that want this information, Gale will sell you that supplement at a current subscription price of $693.00 per year (2009 pricing). However, that same information is available at no cost over the Internet for nearly every organization in the world. There is simply no reason to pay for updates for materials that do not need updating.

Even the *Britannica* has the *Book of the Year* series that chronicles events during a given calendar year. We all buy these but never look at them. The current price is only $59.95/year, but there is little reason for libraries to continue subscribing to these materials if neither the librarians nor the public will use them. Other supplemental material may consist of CD-ROM disks or even online access to updates. No matter what format, we often buy them but never use them. Eliminating supplements is another means of saving money and reducing the size of the collection with very little impact on our users.

CONCLUSION

Reference collections play a very different role in today's society then they did a century or even a few decades ago. Once the pinnacle of access to information for the community that the library served, they now mainly supplement access available in many other ways. Reference librarians are still busy answering questions, but dispensing facts has evolved into consulting about research methods and search strategies. Reference books still have a place in the overall structure of information, but that place has been diminished by free access to innumerable other information resources over the Internet. For reference collections to become useful, they need to be more refined in scope, selected to meet the specific needs of the community, and made as accessible to users as possible.

Returning to the *Encyclopaedia Britannica,* the first line of the preface of the first edition (1771, v) sums up the role of reference books well: "*Utility ought to be the principal intention of every publication.*" What the editors of this first reference book understood almost 250 years ago was that such a publication had to meet the needs of its users or it would not survive. That is as much or more the case today. People in our communities sometimes still turn to reference librarians for information, but they now have much greater access to that same information themselves. They also have the technology to access that information no matter where they are located. It is time to reduce reference collections to the core that our users and our staff find helpful. Making utility the primary intention of our collections will keep them viable. Otherwise, the collections—and the librarians—will find themselves out of print in very short order.

WORKS CITED

Hutchins, R. M. 1974. Foreword. *New Encyclopaedia Britannica. Propaedia.* 15th ed. Chicago: Encyclopaedia Britannica.

Preface. 1771. *Encyclopaedia Britannica: Or, a dictionary of arts and sciences, compiled upon a new plan in which the different sciences and arts are digested into distinct treatises and systems, and technical terms &c. are explained as they occur in the order of the alphabet.* Vol. 1. Edinburgh: A. Bell and C. Marcfarquhar.

Reference work in libraries. 1891. *Library Journal* 16: 297–300.

Rothstein, S. 1972. *The development of reference services through academic traditions, public library practice and special librarianship.* ACRL Monographs 14. Boston: Gregg Press.

18

DIGITAL VISIBILITY: CREATING USABLE INTERFACES SO USERS CAN FIND RESOURCES

Jody Condit Fagan and Meris A. Mandernach

Library reference collections are in a transition period. While many traditional reference questions can now be answered through public search engines, others require sources still available only through the library. However, without attention to the digital visibility of these sources, the depth and relevance of library reference resources may remain hidden from users.

Digital visibility of the reference collection is the key factor for good stewardship of both print and online titles in the 21st-century library. Though librarians will not always be present to guide users to resources, they can set up online environments and interfaces to enable unmediated access.

PREPARING FOR DIGITAL VISIBILITY

Preparing for digital visibility starts with a fresh look at the reference collection. As libraries have added online reference titles, adjustments to the collection as a whole may have been haphazard. Rather than seeing print and online reference as separate, librarians would do well to reenvision the collection as a hybrid, using information such as use studies, usage statistics, and collection portfolios to provide a big-picture perspective. Libraries also need to consider new definitions and terminology for reference and to revisit cataloging procedures and metadata standards so that interfaces display reference resources effectively.

Seeing Your Reference Collection with New Eyes

The size, scope, and balance of reference collections are no longer immediately visible as collections are split between the physical and virtual realms. When it comes to physical visibility, the print reference collection still wins. A print reference collection is viewable at a glance. Its size and basic organization, and even the patterns of its use, are easy to understand. It is apparent which works have multiple volumes and which are slim, which have gilt, historical-looking bindings and which look more contemporary. Obviously, the big disadvantage for print titles is that they are not accessible remotely. To overcome their physical limitations, print reference titles will benefit from the following strategies:

- Include essential print reference titles in online interfaces and systems.
- Make it clear to patrons when print reference titles offer unique or irreplaceable information.
- Review print reference titles regularly to evaluate whether they are still the best choice for users.

Online titles, in contrast, are physically invisible. A user may have access to the library's entire online reference collection using a mobile device without any awareness of its existence. It is hard to grasp online titles' contents at a glance or to see how much information is in a given title or series.

Yet online reference sources have many advantages. Regardless of physical location, many users can access a title simultaneously. Sorting titles is simple, as is discerning how many titles cover a topic. Online resources provide the potential to jump from book to book, following cited references with the click of a mouse. Additionally, online titles can be read out loud by a machine, their font enlarged, and their text manipulated. For online library services, online reference books play a crucial role: Shachaf and Shaw (2008) found that 96 percent of reference transactions in data sets from both QuestionPoint and Indiana University used online sources to answer reference questions. Despite these advantages, online reference titles are usually excluded from public search engines by their publishers, thus removing them from the digital view of the end user.

Making online reference resources more visible requires the following:

- Good interface design by the information provider
- Communication with vendors about interface needs
- Good customization decisions by the library
- Maintenance of links and records for these frequently changing resources

For both types of resources, the challenge remains the same as it always has been: determining how to connect users with the appropriate resources to fulfill their information needs.

Often, print and electronic resources can be used in tandem to greater effect. For example, one might use the online version to search, then go to the print version to browse, read in detail, or find specific information. Searching the *Chicago Manual of Style* online is more effective than using the print index, but editors and serious researchers value the ability to browse entries in the print manual to examine related sections. After considering the nature of both physical and electronic items, library staff can ensure they are "seeing" the entire reference collection through use studies and collection portfolios.

Use Studies and Usage Statistics

Libraries have historically implemented in-house tracking systems to identify title-level use of physical reference items (Arrigona and Mathews, 1988; Biggs, 1990; Broadus, 1980; Colson, 2007; Engeldinger, 1986). Today, most vendors offer extensive usage statistics for online reference. Electronic resources or acquisitions librarians access these through administrative interfaces using the library's account information.

Many libraries face a challenge in dealing with the overwhelming amount of available statistical data. To make good use of statistics for improving digital visibility, libraries need to identify specific research questions and then track key metrics. For example, if changes are made to cataloging practices supporting digital visibility of reference titles, the library could track the sessions per month before and after this change and compare these numbers with statistics from a previous year.

Collection Portfolios

Another technique for evaluating reference collections makes use of the reports that most integrated library systems offer. Collection portfolios created for reference collections can include the existing number of titles in call number ranges, usage information by call number range, overlap analyses of print and electronic titles, and purchasing patterns. The specific data available vary by system. Portfolios provide a broad view of a collection so librarians can identify areas of imbalance. For example, a history librarian may order online reference titles in American history because the catalogs he receives specialize in that format. A portfolio view might reveal a lack of online resources in non-U.S. history, prompting examination of his current collection development practices. Once a library has utilized traditional use studies, usage statistics, and collection portfolios to understand how print and online titles complement each other in today's reference collection, staff should give some thought to describing reference materials.

What Is a Reference Title, and Why Is This Distinction Important?

Because of the emergence of new types of reference sources on the Web, it's challenging to determine what qualifies as a reference source. Such distinctions and definitions become important when trying to determine how to guide users to reference sources on the library Web site and in library buildings. While a user may not care that she is using a reference source, these sources fill specific information needs. Reference questions related to new cancer treatments are best answered by research articles, whereas overviews of the basic tenets of Islam are better addressed by an encyclopedia entry.

Each library will need to define and categorize its reference resources. These decisions should be purposeful and deliberate. Questions addressed should include the following:

- What will be considered reference?
- What overall term will be used? Reference collection? Reference resources?
- Will the library use more granular divisions of reference items, such as encyclopedia, almanac, and handbook? If so, where?
- Are there new types of reference works that require new terminology or labels?
- On the Web site and in the building, will the library label pathways to "reference" using this term or something more functionally oriented, such as *background information* or *facts and figures*? Or will they use more granular terms such as *encyclopedias* and *dictionaries*?
- How often should the library revisit the terminology used?

Through planning, a library can provide a more consistent experience for users by ensuring that the library catalog, Web site, signage, and promotional materials use the same terms. The discussion of definitions and terminology will come into play again in the next aspect of preparing for digital visibility: describing reference titles in the online catalog.

Cataloging for Digital Visibility

Because of the size of most libraries' reference collections, online and in print, the catalog will remain the authoritative place to find accurate information about reference materials. A major question for libraries is whether reference books need to be noted as such in the catalog record or whether the library will use another mechanism for isolating reference books, such as a social tagging system or a commercial product like Reference Universe. While a full discussion of cataloging reference books is beyond the scope of this chapter, specific factors supporting the collections' classification for higher digital visibility in Web interfaces are addressed, including denotation of reference titles, the importance of alternate titles, and link selection and maintenance.

Denoting Reference Titles in Online Catalogs

Searching specifically for reference titles in online catalogs is becoming increasingly challenging. Previously, a researcher could narrow a search to reference titles by limiting results to the reference location(s). This is rapidly becoming ineffective, as libraries replace print titles with online equivalents or move print reference titles to the stacks to save shelf space and enhance the reference collection's utility.

Librarians often search for reference items in online catalogs by combining words such as *dictionary* and *encyclopedia* with search terms, but this solution lacks accuracy and completeness. Adding consistent subject headings or notes fields to all reference titles, print and online, provides a more comprehensive solution. One advantage for online reference titles is that records are often added in batch loads, making it easier to tag these items for reference. For example, the authors' institution uses a 655 field with the term *e-reference* for all online titles. Combining the term *e-reference* with a user's terms limits the results to online reference titles. The size of a library's collection and its cataloging department will influence the decision of whether to note all reference materials as such in the online catalog.

Alternate Titles and Related Records

Both print and online titles will benefit from the addition of alternate titles—even those that are not official—in a notes field. For example, the *PRNews Measurement Guidebook* should be listed as the *Guide to Best Practices in PR Measurement* and as *Best Practices in PR Measurement,* since all are variant titles. The selector or the library's subject specialist may be in the best position to identify issues with the record from the user's perspective.

Reference titles may also change names when they move online. For example, the print resource *Handbook of Reagents for Organic Synthesis*'s (HROS) online equivalent is called the *Encyclopedia of Reagents for Organic Synthesis* (e-EROS). Online reference databases may also change names during marketing campaigns or repackaging efforts. Cross-referencing these titles will ensure maximum retrieval by the end user.

Libraries sometimes acquire both print and online versions of reference titles and will need to consider how to distinguish one from the other. Some libraries merge records for print and electronic titles (Giles, 2003); others add links to at least provide a pathway between records.

Link Selection and Maintenance

Link selection and maintenance are crucial activities for ensuring online reference visibility. For a given electronic reference title, there may be several options for linking. Decisions will need to be made with respect to the depth of linking within electronic publications. For annual publications, should links point to all available years or the most recent one? If it is part of a vendor's commercial interface, should the link go to the record level rather than the full-text link? Options are often limited by technology, and libraries need to verify that the chosen link types are "durable," meaning they will not expire as time passes. Figure 18.1 shows an example of the options available through Gale's Virtual Reference Library interface.

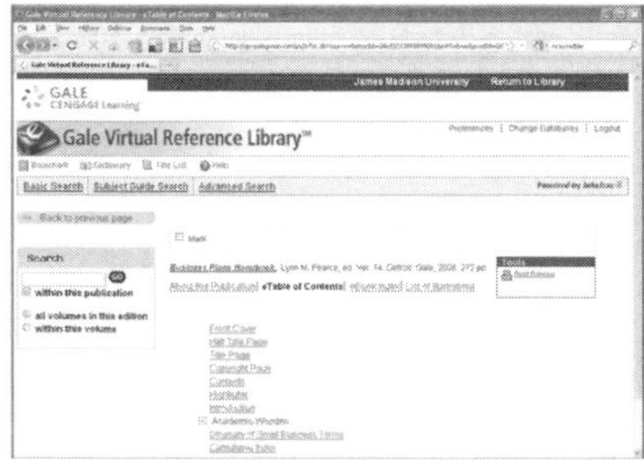

Linking to the search interface for all volumes

Linking to the full record for the most recent volume

Linking to the electronic Table of Contents for the book

Linking to the first page of the book

Figure 18.1. Various options for linking to *Business Plans Handbook:* a search interface across all volumes, full details about the book, an electronic table of contents, or the first PDF page in the book. *Screen Shot from Gale Virtual Reference Library.* ©Gale, a part of Cengage Learning, Inc. Reproduced by permission. www.cengage.com/permissions

After one selects which links to use, one of the more prosaic aspects of keeping online reference titles visible is link checking. Public reference sources, such as government Web sites, will obviously need to be checked, but even purchased reference sources change their URLs. While some online catalogs offer link-checking software, others may require a third-party link checker. The considerations discussed so far, including terminology choices and cataloging practices, will inform what metadata should be used to describe reference titles on Web pages and in Web applications.

Metadata in Web Pages and Web Applications

The library Web site and online catalog are two places a user should expect to find information about reference collections, but in today's world, library patrons may be entering the virtual library from search engines and other Web sites. Using metadata to describe the reference collection and its titles on the library Web site will improve retrieval. Reference items with accurate and complete metadata will be more likely to appear in result sets and will rank more highly in relevance algorithms. Metadata can be included in

```
<head>
<title>Smith Library Reference Collection</title>
<meta name="description" content="The reference collection provides
background information and authoritative information about facts,
both online and in print.">
<meta name="keywords" content="reference, encyclopedia, dictionary,
almanac, yearbook, handbook, facts, figures, statistics">
</head>
```

Figure 18.2. HTML metatags for a library's main reference collection Web page.

several ways: using special HTML codes, describing resources fully in Web-page text, assigning resources to categories in electronic resource portals, and tagging resources using social tagging systems.

For any Web page that includes significant information about the library's reference collections, HTML metadata should include title, description, and keyword tags (see figure 18.2). Search engines include the title and description of the text results listing, and all the codes inform relevance ranking.

Descriptive information about the collection or specific titles should be included on the text of Web pages, including database-driven systems providing electronic resource listings. The reference collection should be described with as much granularity as possible, though without duplicating the effort going into the library's catalog. For online reference collections, consider highlighting the most popular or representative titles either in the metadata or in page text. An example of a detailed description is shown in figure 18.3.

Social tagging on the library Web site or in the online catalog is another form of metadata and can facilitate user-generated title lists. While social tagging is often thought of as a casual, informal activity, librarians can take advantage of tagging capability to provide relevant lists for types of reference books (see figure 18.4).

After adding relevant metadata, be sure to test your metadata by searching a few reference titles, as well as generic search terms such as *dictionary* or *almanac,* using your library's Web site search engine. Once a library takes a new look at the reference collection, deliberates about information architecture, and establishes cataloging practices and metadata standards, it is ready to ensure the collection is displayed to maximum effect in all available interfaces.

MAXIMIZING DIGITAL VISIBILITY

When seeking to make reference collections digitally visible, libraries need to consider the multiple interfaces a user might choose: the library Web site, Google and other search engines, mobile devices, course management systems, and commercial products and sources. These interfaces offer libraries numerous ways to increase the digital visibility of their reference collections.

Figure 18.3. Electronic resource description for Sage eReference at James Madison University (http://www.lib.jmu.edu/resources/more.aspx?id=2735).

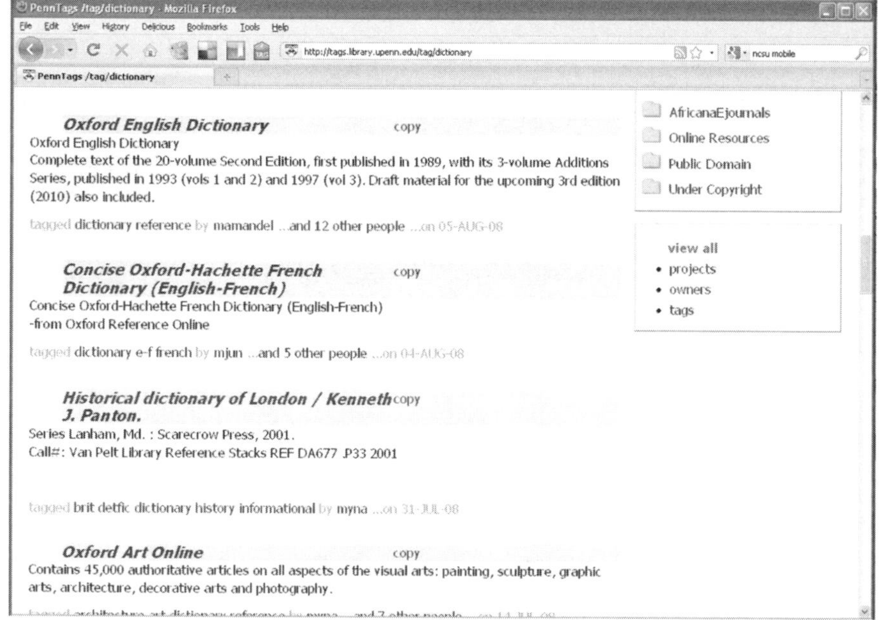

Figure 18.4. Screenshot of PennTags for *dictionary*. Used with permission.

Library Web Sites

Since libraries usually have direct control over their Web pages, it is easy to raise reference titles' visibility on the library Web site. As with the online catalog, library Web sites are an ideal promotional tool for both print and online reference collections. Specific strategies that can be employed are the following:

- Including print reference titles on the library Web site
- Creating a home page for the reference collection
- Linking to the reference collection from research guides and other library Web pages
- Searching for reference titles on the library Web site
- Providing online location maps
- Sharing items via Web 2.0 technologies

Including Print Reference Titles on the Library Web Site

Even in today's increasingly digital world, not all print sources are available online. Online versions may differ in content, and some titles lack the copyright clearance needed to publish images online. Furthermore, the online version may not have an acceptable interface. If your library has an important reference title only in print, it may be harmful to users to exclude it from the dynamically generated list of business resources merely because it is not online.

When listing physical items, include the format, location, and call number (or links to this information in the online catalog), and update this information yearly. Explain why it's worth the user's time to consult the resource in print: Are the data not available anywhere else? Does the print version contain more historical information than the online version? Is the information presented more effectively? Although the number of print titles that should be included on a library Web site is shrinking, it will be some time yet before they disappear entirely.

Creating a Home Page for the Reference Collection

Does it make sense to have a Web page dedicated to reference books? At the authors' university, the "Finding Encyclopedias, Dictionaries, and Almanacs" page, a hand-selected list of top e-reference resources, received more than 3,000 visits in one semester. This was only about 4 percent of the traffic to the main e-resource portal; however, it still represented 750 uses per month. Although the proportion of use was not high, the numbers justified the amount of time librarians spent putting the page together.

A reference collection home page might offer instructional information about understanding different types of reference information, using sources effectively, searching for them in the catalog, and evaluating free electronic reference tools such as Wikipedia. While this page can also display a selection of top sources or a menu of subjects, collections, or types of reference titles, it will likely point users to other pages for more information, such as links to the catalog, research guides, or other library Web pages.

Linking to Research Guides and Other Library Web Pages

Many Web pages on the library Web site offer additional opportunities to promote the reference collection. If links to the main reference collection page are included on pages such as "Find Books," "Getting Started," or "Research Guides," users can find them in multiple places. If the library home page offers current news or featured resources, reference titles can be included there as well. The library's deliberations about information architecture and terminology will help inform the Web site's structure and text for reference titles.

Whether database driven or static, Web pages about reference titles need to distinguish reference titles from other types of resources, illustrate what they are good for, offer a way to list them alphabetically and by subject for browsing, and include a keyword search of title and description. Good principles for pages that refer to reference titles include the following:

- Offering call numbers for each title and linking to the online catalog to provide more details
- Annotating each resource to highlight its importance and how it should be used
- Keeping the entry pages short, linking to more detailed information or bibliographies, if available
- Listing key print reference titles alongside online titles

Searching for Reference Titles on the Library Web Site

Most libraries offer some type of search input box on their Web sites. This may search the catalog, the Web site, or multiple systems. It is important to plan for how this input box will help users find reference titles. Users typing *animal encyclopedia* should find *Grzimek's Animal Life Encyclopedia,* if available. Improving the search may mean providing complete metadata about reference titles on the library Web site; it may mean enabling a Web site search to include the library catalog; it may mean offering a "how to search" page that explains different options.

Libraries may also offer a search box specifically for finding reference books, perhaps on the library reference Web page. This could search the OPAC with special limiters, a commercial product like Reference Universe, or a resource portal. Dinkelman and Stacy-Bates (2007) found most libraries in the Association of Research Libraries (ARL) had some way to search for electronic resources, including e-books, outside the OPAC. Almost all offered the ability to search for an exact electronic resource title, but only about a third offered keyword searching.

Providing Online Location Maps

As long as libraries offer print reference sources, it is important to equip users with floor maps to physical collections. Users will need directions to the reference collection, ideally to the specific section they seek. Think about where users will encounter this need: certainly in the online public access catalog (OPAC) for each reference title, near the call number and location, but also on library Web pages that describe the reference collection or reference titles.

Subscribing and Sharing Items with Web 2.0

Several Web 2.0–enabled features can also increase digital visibility. These features extend existing systems and are most effective when the underlying system has a mission of its own. For example, libraries with a "new reference titles" list could offer a Web feed subscription option so users are informed when new content is added. Most Web 2.0 technologies automatically have the ability to share and bookmark articles and entries, to generate feeds, and to publish others' feeds. Third-party applications such as AddThis (http://www.addthis.com) allow Web developers to quickly add these functions to any Web page. An example of this can be seen on Ocean City Public Library's Electronic Reference Collection home page (figure 18.5).

Even if the number of users who choose to share or subscribe to a particular source is small, the impact can be large. Shared items and feeds can be picked up by bloggers and included in other Web 2.0 systems. This also makes it possible for the library to be easily connected with other organizations and groups.

While library Web sites are perhaps the easiest interface to control, other opportunities exist with search engines, mobile devices, course management systems, and commercial products.

Google and Other Public Web Search Engines

Many library users fulfill their reference needs through Google or other search engines. Libraries need to take advantage of the opportunities offered by this trend. First, by maximizing their Web pages' metadata that describe electronic reference sources, libraries can make use of

Figure 18.5. Web 2.0 tools on the Ocean City Public Library's Electronic Reference Collection home page. Site design by SpringShare, Inc. (http://springshare.com/). Used with permission.

search engines' indexing. For example, a Google search on "jmu animal encyclopedia" finds James Madison University's biology subject guide as the first result. Second, libraries can use WorldCat.org, which is visible to the open Web. A search on the *Family Communication Sourcebook* finds this item in Google Books, and the interface offers a link to "Find in a library." This links to WorldCat.org, which shows a list of libraries with the title and their distance from the user. The existence of these new pathways presents an important opportunity for increasing digital visibility of reference resources.

Libraries also need to stay abreast of opportunities with mobile interfaces and applications. These miniature pieces of software operate without an Internet connection and have greater potential for interactivity than a mobile Web interface, which is limited by Web-available technologies.

Mobile Devices

Survey results published in 2008 by the Pew Internet and American Life Project show that 31 percent of all Americans participate in digital activities away from home or work using a cell phone. Twelve percent report they use

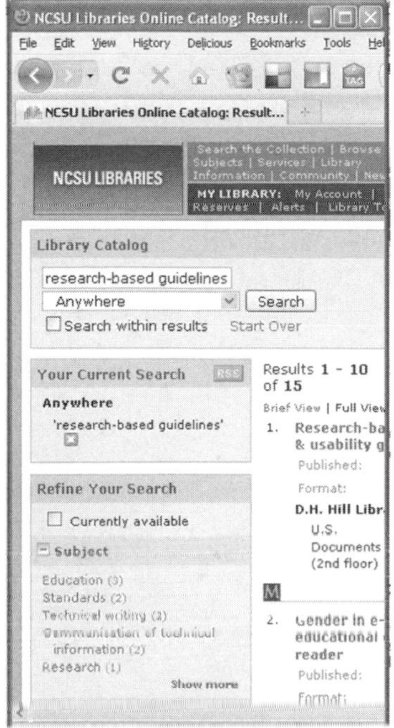

NCSU Library Catalog
results view – main interface
http://www2.lib.ncsu.edu/catalog/

NCSU Library Catalog
results view – mobile interface
http://www.lib.ncsu.edu/m/

Figure 18.6. Browsing the North Carolina State University (NCSU) library catalog with a mobile device using the native catalog interface as compared with their mobile interface. Used with permission.

mobile devices, including cell phones or personal digital assistants (PDAs), specifically to "access the Internet for news, weather, sports, or other information" (Horrigan, 2008).

The commercial sector is making mobile applications for reference tools, such as the Merriam-Webster Search for iPhone. Other companies, such as eBooks (http://www.ebooks.com/subjects/reference/) and Pocket Dictionary (http://www.pocketdirectory.com/), sell reference titles specifically formatted for mobile devices. Other sites offer free reference titles (http://manybooks.net/categories/REF). Web sites of all types are also formatting their Web pages for mobile devices.

With these market and behavioral trends in mind, libraries need to consider how their interfaces—including Web sites, search widgets, and online catalogs—appear on mobile devices. Some online catalog vendors offer a mobile interface for an additional charge. Figure 18.6 shows how different a library catalog interface can look via a mobile interface.

Course Management Systems

Reference collections at academic institutions can also become digitally visible through course management systems (CMS), such as Blackboard (http://www.blackboard.com/) or Moodle (http://moodle.org/). Library catalog vendors may offer building blocks or plug-ins that allow connections between the CMS and the library catalog. Depending on the CMS, libraries may be able to place Web 2.0 tools or locally created Web applications within an <IFRAME> within the system (Casden, Duckett, Sierra, and Ryan, 2009). At the simplest level, libraries can work with instructors to provide simple links to library subject guides or predefined search queries in the catalog for relevant reference titles.

Commercial Products and Product Features

Several commercial products can also raise reference collections' digital visibility. Reviews of specific reference titles and products are available through sources such as *Reference & User Services Quarterly* and *Choice*. This section discusses two commercial products, metasearch software and discovery tools, and interface features of online reference sources that raise their visibility.

Paratext's Reference Universe

Paratext's Reference Universe searches the indexes of more than 40,000 electronic and print reference works (Paratext, Inc., 2010). This service allows users to search even print reference books at the article and index level. Searches can be limited to a library's local holdings, to e-books only, or to print only. Titles can be browsed by publisher, title, and call number. Libraries upload local data to Paratext to permit the local-holdings view of their reference collections. There is no full text within Reference Universe, although users can link to any electronic reference item held by the library.

Credo Reference

Credo Reference is an online, full-text collection of over 500 reference titles, all with cross-references to one another (Credo Reference, 2010). While Credo Reference sells reference *content*, its extensive feature set offers libraries extra opportunities for digital visibility. Hyperlinked bibliographies connect users to the library's online catalog records via link-resolver software, and libraries can specify numerous custom navigation links that connect users with other systems.

Metasearch Products and Discovery Tools

Metasearch software, also called "federated" search software, can search many online sources simultaneously, regardless of the provider, as long as providers have made themselves available as targets. Even if a library creates a reference-specific metasearch of its online reference collections, however, evaluating the usability of such a search's results is critical. Because of the arbitrary nature of metasearch product limitations, results may be weighted toward certain disciplinary areas or source types. Although current results may be disappointing, the underlying concept of metasearch is sound, and the technology continues to develop.

Many libraries are beginning to use interfaces that provide a combined search of their online catalogs and selected electronic resources content called *discovery tools*. These interfaces may also offer metasearch capabilities, thus offering a one-stop search of catalog records for reference titles and select reference products. How reference titles appear in these discovery tools depends largely on the original cataloging and indexing, but the special features of these tools often make extra cataloging efforts worthwhile. For example, with more control over the interface and relevancy ranking, if libraries tagged all reference titles, they could choose to have reference titles appear at the top of the results list when they are included in a results set. Facets, which show the number of results in categories, could include "reference" as a category.

Features of Online Reference Sources to Enhance Digital Visibility

Online reference resources vary in their digital visibility. Therefore, libraries should evaluate reference products with some type of feature checklist for optimal digital visibility. When a desired product is missing important features, libraries can negotiate a better price and encourage the provider to add desired functionality.

Durable URLs to Electronic Reference Sources

Sadly, there are still plenty of subscription resources that do not feature durable URLs, meaning users cannot bookmark useful locations. The ideal resource will allow the user to link not just to the home page but to specific search screens, product parts, results lists, and individual titles. The more durable URLs a resource has, the better a library can integrate that resource into its Web site, catalog, and other systems and services.

Linking to Groups of Electronic Reference Titles

Libraries subscribing to a large collection of reference books from one provider may wish to link to subgroups of titles, either to titles in a disciplinary area or to a set of specific titles. Some vendors have precategorized their titles by subject; others may allow libraries to create custom subcollections, as with Gale's Virtual Reference Library. Either way, this feature is most useful when users can link to a subgroup and search within that subgroup of titles.

Hyperlinked Bibliographies and Link Resolvers

Since reference information often provides carefully selected pointers to further reading, some electronic reference resources offer hyperlinked bibliographies so users can easily follow citations to other sources or full text. A common way to do this is by enabling a library's link-resolver software so that an institution-specific button or link appears next to each citation. This offers quick access to full-text or delivery options. If the information provider is large, it may offer direct hyperlinks to subscribed full text on its platform.

Exporting Citations and Sharing Items

The ability to export machine-readable citations can also increase the digital visibility of reference titles. For example, Helen Hough (2009) has re-created her "Tests and Measures in the Social Sciences" database using RefWorks' RefShare software, which supports many types of import techniques. Users may also wish to simply share an item with their friends or colleagues. Most of today's commercial Web sites allow users to use Delicious, Digg, reddit, Facebook, and other applications to post basic information about an item to those sites.

Descriptive Information and Book Covers

By providing book covers and other descriptive information, interfaces help users understand the nature of a resource: whether it is scholarly or popular, how long the entries are, and what type of subject area it falls into. Consider figure 18.7, from Credo Reference. It is clear that the first two entries are significantly longer than the third and that the first entry is from a science-focused title while the second is focused on food. The facets along the side also help the user understand the types of resources and subject areas into which her topic falls. For librarians and experienced researchers, having the publisher information is also helpful.

Facilitating Browsing and Known-Item Searching

Browsing and known-item searching are critical functions for an online reference collection, even if this type of access is used less frequently than keyword searching. Functions should include the following:

- Title, subject, and author searches
- Hyperlinked footnotes and citations
- A "shelf list" of online reference titles, arranged by classification
- An option to "find similar" entries or titles
- An option to move quickly from the table of contents or index to pages in the book

Widgets

Major information providers such as Gale (http://access.gale.com/widgets/), EBSCO (http://supportforms.epnet.com/eit/searchbox builder/), and ProQuest (http://widgets.proquest.com) offer customizable "widgets," miniature search interfaces that librarians can paste into their own Web sites. In these three cases, users can select specific reference databases

Figure 18.7. Descriptive information in Credo Reference (http://www.credoreference.com/). Used with permission.

available through these connections. With Gale, users can select an "eBook subcollection," which can be composed of specific reference titles. Smaller information providers are also adding widgets, including FactsOnFile (http://fofweb.com/Subscription/Default.asp?BID=13), the *Oxford English Dictionary* (http://www.oed.com/services/), and *Encyclopaedia Britannica* (http://www.britannica.com/widgets), to name a few.

This section has discussed numerous opportunities for raising the digital visibility of reference sources in an array of interfaces. Once a library has prepared its collection to be digitally visible and has offered access pathways through multiple interfaces, it is ready to promote and evaluate these efforts.

PROMOTING AND EVALUATING DIGITAL VISIBILITY EFFORTS

Although this section is much shorter than the others, it is equally important. Promotion ensures that all the hard work discussed in the previous sections is fruitful. Evaluation tells a library which efforts are working.

These two activities go hand in hand. Promotion efforts can focus on specific digital visibility efforts and can then be evaluated to determine their effectiveness.

Promotional Campaigns

Many of the suggestions in this chapter are promotional in nature. Libraries can plan specific promotional campaigns to advertise new interface developments or reference products. For example, if a library creates a special library catalog search that focuses on the reference collection, a promotional campaign would advertise the existence of this tool. In the academic setting, marketing or communication classes may even be willing to take on a promotional campaign as a class project.

Specific Promotional Techniques

Libraries can use the same promotional techniques they use for other services, such as newsletters, but a few techniques deserve specific mention in this chapter because of their place in the digital information flow.

- **Feature/news items on the library Web site.** Many libraries promote the reference collection or specific reference titles through news items and features on their library Web sites, increasing the possibility the titles will be found in a library Web site search. Timely events like Black History Month can provide extra opportunities to show the relevance of reference information.
- **Promotion through virtual reference services.** If the library has recently added an important reference title, reference librarians could make a conscious effort to suggest it during virtual reference transactions.
- **Quick online polls and surveys.** Numerous freely available poll and survey tools allow libraries to gather quick feedback about specific resources' or Web pages' usefulness. Such instruments serve double duty as promotional and feedback-gathering tools.
- **Promotion of online items from physical spaces.** The library's physical reference collection is an ideal area for posters and promotional materials featuring online equivalents and additional sources. Face-to-face library instruction classes or seminars can highlight online reference sources. Veteran library users may require a physical tour of online reference resources when connecting for the first time.

Following up such activities with evaluation can track which strategies are most successful for libraries.

Evaluating Digital Visibility Efforts

Evaluating digital visibility efforts may involve traditional techniques, such as tracking use of the physical reference collection, and new metrics for online resources, such as usage statistics, Web server logs, and user studies.

Usage Statistics and User Studies

Usage statistics from electronic reference product vendors can also be used to evaluate promotional campaigns or interface changes. For example, if a library wants to increase usage of *Encyclopaedia Britannica* and conducts a month-long promotional campaign, it can compare usage for the months before, during, and after the campaign with the same numbers from the previous year. The same strategy can be used if changes are made to the library Web site regarding specific resources.

Web site use statistics show how often the reference collection home page and other areas of the library Web site are used. This type of statistic tracks usage of individual files, not clicks on hyperlinks. However, Google offers a free tool, Google Analytics (http://analytics.google.com), that shows how many users click on specific links on a specific page.

To find out if users are following links from the online catalog, some libraries have implemented lightweight logging applications that prefix the URLs used for electronic resources in the catalog with a logging application URL. For example, a link such as http://library.edu/reflog?url=www.referencetitle.com would first call the reflog application, which would simultaneously log the transaction and send the user to the resource specified.

Usability studies provide another way to determine if resources are digitally visible. Librarians can create a usability protocol consisting of several tasks that ask users to find reference information and have them begin from the interface being tested—for example, the library Web site. A human observer or software, such as Morae or Camtasia (http://www.techsmith.com/), then records the user's pathway to areas that cause confusion.

CONCLUSION

Demonstrating library collections' value through description and instruction must be coupled with making reference resources visible in the user's digital interface. As Wikipedia and other publicly available reference tools raise the visibility of reference information for the general user, libraries will need to employ several strategies for making collections digitally visible.

Libraries must first reenvision their collection and reconsider how to describe reference items in the catalog and other systems. Since numerous interfaces offer portals into the virtual library, consideration must be given not only to the library Web site but also to public search engines, course management systems, mobile devices, and commercial products. Promoting new interfaces and resources, as well as evaluating digital visibility efforts, will help libraries determine which strategies are most beneficial to their users.

WORKS CITED

Arrigona, D. R., and E. Mathews. 1988. A use study of an academic library reference collection. *RQ* 28 (Fall): 71–81.

Biggs, M. 1990. Discovering how information seekers seek: Methods of measuring reference collection use. *Reference Librarian* 29: 103–117.

Broadus, R. N. 1980. Use studies of library collections. *Library Resources & Technical Services* 24 (4): 317–324.

Casden, J., K. Duckett, T. Sierra, and J. Ryan. 2009. Course views: A scalable approach to providing course-based access to library resources. *Code4Lib Journal* 6 (March 30). Retrieved July 30, 2009, from http://journal.code4lib.org/articles/1218.

Colson, J. J. 2007. Determining use of an academic library reference collection: Report of a study. *Reference & User Services Quarterly* 47 (2): 168–175.

Credo Reference. 2010. *CredoReference-home*. Retrieved September 14, 2010, from http://corp.credoreference.com/.

Dinkelman, A., and K. Stacey-Bates. 2007. Accessing e-books through academic library web sites. *College & Research Libraries* 68 (1): 45–58.

Engeldinger, E. A. 1986. Weeding of academic library reference collections: A survey of current practice. *RQ* 25 (Spring): 366–371.

Giles, V. V. 2003. Single or multiple records for print and electronic serials titles. *Serials Librarian* 45 (1): 35–45.

Horrigan, J. 2008. *Mobile access to data and information*. Pew Internet & American Life Project. Retrieved July 31, 2009, from http://www.pewinternet.org/Reports/2008/Mobile-Access-to-Data-and-Information.aspx.

Hough, H. 2009. *Tests and measures in the social sciences: Tests available in compilation volumes*. Retrieved July 30, 2009, from http://libraries.uta.edu/Helen/test&meas/testmainframe.htm.

Paratext, Inc. 2010. *Reference universe*. Retrieved September 14, 2010, from http://refuniv.odyssi.com/.

Shachaf, P., and D. Shaw. 2008. Bibliometric analysis to identify core reference sources of virtual reference transactions. *Library & Information Science Research* 30 (4): 291–297.

19

SCHOLARLY COMMUNICATION: LIBRARY AS CONTENT PROVIDER—DIGITAL PROJECTS TO SUPPORT REFERENCE AND USER SERVICES

Linda Friend

It is difficult to imagine a functional 21st-century research library without some level of digital content, services, and access. Patrons continue to demand the flexibility and searchability of full text digital resources in various formats. Developments and opportunities in scholarly communication significantly affect the fundamental roles and future contributions of reference services, as well as the future definition of a librarian.

Changing roles and organizational developments are addressed in other chapters in this book, but nowhere do the changes seem more profound than in the ways librarians are reenvisioning services and content to manage and optimize their increasingly digital collections—and increasingly digital-expectant users. According to Byrne, regenerating the profession

> demands new organizational structures which no longer inhibit invention and exploration through hierarchy and blockages. These are structures that are tolerant and resilient, able to foster innovation and accept occasional failures. They are structures which attract, develop and retain good people in positive, team-based work environments but are also supportive of individual initiative and creativity, avoiding the tyranny of conformity to the norm. (2009, 28–29)

The volatile scholarly content environment itself is a major component of the call to rethink reference and seize this opportunity to enhance creativity in services. As libraries and librarians reinvent themselves to satisfy the escalating needs and expectations of the 21st-century scholar, student, and lifelong learner, it becomes increasingly clear that digital research will be a key feature of librarians' future viability; significant contributions to the profession will unquestionably be in the digital arena. Examples are given throughout but only begin to scratch the surface of the many creative library initiatives that are part of content provision in the digital library.

A decade ago, in her seminal essay on digital libraries and scholarly communication, Borgman (2000, 423) observed that

> digital libraries are bringing issues of space and place into conflict in some unanticipated ways. One of the promises of a global information infrastructure is for individuals to have direct access to information resources located anywhere on the network, so that they can seek and use information on their own, and can create new resources for others to use. In many respects, however, individuals are becoming more dependent on institutions for information access, rather than less dependent as predicted.

Reference librarians are one of the critical players in ensuring that such access is readily available.

In a 2006 white paper, the Association of College and Research Libraries (ACRL) confronts and explicates some of these new roles and challenges:

> The changes that are occurring—in technology, in research, teaching and learning—have created a very different context for the missions of academic and research libraries. This evolving context can afford a moment of opportunity if libraries and librarians can respond to change in proactive and visionary ways. There are diverse and unmet needs now arising within the academy—many of which closely align with the traditional self-definitions of academic and research libraries. To the extent that libraries and their leaders can reposition themselves to serve these evolving needs—which pertain in part to the centralized storage, description, and delivery of academic resources, and in part to the organization and support of scholarly communication within and across higher education institutions—libraries will emerge as even more central and vibrant resources for their institutions. (ACRL, 2006a)

Are library employees embracing and contributing to technology diffusion, and is it positively affecting productivity and efficiency in user services? In 2006, Rabina and Walczyk (2007) surveyed over 1,100 information professionals in many types of libraries to gauge their "innovativeness" as well as how early they adopt new methods—and how likely they are to be opinion leaders. One of their conclusions is that

> some of the conventional wisdoms regarding information professionals and their willingness to adopt new ICT [information and communication technology] innovations may be incorrect. Contrary to common beliefs, librarians in academic or special libraries are no more innovative than public or school librarians. Technical service librarians are not more innovative than public service librarians. Older librarians seem only a little less likely to accept innovations, and administrators appear to be no more innovative than the employees they supervise.

SCHOLARLY COMMUNICATION

The term *scholarly communication* continues to have multiple meanings. Over the last 20 years or so, various authors and organizations have defined and redefined the phrase. Currently, it is often linked to the emergence of digital scholarship and the various opportunities and issues associated with digital publishing. ACRL (2006b) defines scholarly communication as "the system through which research and other scholarly writings are created, evaluated for quality, disseminated to the scholarly community, and preserved for future use. The system includes both formal means of communication, such as publication in peer-reviewed journals, and informal channels such as electronic listservs."

Borgman (2000, 414) described it as "the study of how scholars in any field (e.g. physical, biological, social, and behavioural sciences, humanities, technology) use and disseminate information through formal and informal channels." Wikipedia appears to have borrowed its definition from one of the better existing Web definitions, although ironically that text is no longer available at the originating Web site: "Scholarly communication is '. . . the creation, transformation, dissemination and preservation of knowledge related to teaching, research and scholarly endeavors. Among the many scholarly communications issues include author rights, the economics of scholarly resources, new models of publishing including open access, institutional repositories, rights and access to federally funded research, and preservation of intellectual assets'" (Scholarly Communication, 2009).

To date, hundreds of articles, reports, and books deal with scholarly communication in its many iterations (*Library and information Science Abstracts* yields over 1,200 hits for that phrase alone). For the last two decades, Bailey has maintained an inclusive bibliography of the literature (2008), supplemented by his Weblog (2010.) A good overview of scholarly communication topics (published 15 years ago, but the issues remain relevant and fresh) can be found in *Scholarly Publishing. The Electronic Frontier* (Peek and Newby, 1996). Odlyzko from AT&T Labs defines the landscape circa 2002 by saying that "Gutenberg's invention imprisoned scholarly publishing in a straitjacket that will eventually be discarded" but observes that "the inertia of the scholarly publishing system is enormous" (2002, 17–18). Mukherjee (2009) defines scholarly communication and concentrates on journal literature, tracing scientific communication back to ancient cultures. Greco (2009) edited a compilation of relevant articles reprinted from *Journal of Scholarly Publishing* that explore many of the defining issues.

As I reviewed the literature about scholarly communication to locate examples of the significant areas where librarians had been and continue to be active participants, I found I was mentally dividing the things I was seeing into five general themes:

- Intellectual property and copyright
- The "open access" movement
- Reenvisioning of the academic library and reference librarian's roles

- The "crisis" in scholarly publishing, or "the sky is falling" doom and gloom prophesies linked to publishing economics, including the lasting effects of "The Big Deal" for journal aggregators
- Platforms and methodologies for creating coherent digital libraries and repositories

Librarians have played and will continue to play critical roles in all these areas of scholarly communication.

ROLES LIBRARIES AND LIBRARIANS CAN AND MUST PLAY—REENVISIONING THE ACADEMIC LIBRARY AND REFERENCE LIBRARIANS' ROLES

The development, care, and management of digital collections have triggered the creation of new units and the reexamination of both organizational efficiency and individual employees' functional job descriptions, particularly in large institutions. For many research libraries, digital resource development was conceived originally as a way to preserve physical objects—such as historical newspaper collections—that were fragile, unique, valuable, or some combination of these characteristics (microfilming is an early and still successful example of an archival format). Because of the specialized skills needed and the technical nature of digitization and preservation processes, many libraries developed specific departments for this activity. At the University of Pittsburgh, the Digital Research Library has a distinct physical location and a rather typical mix of "faculty librarians and production staff, who are assisted by a body of graduate students and interns. The librarians include a coordinator, metadata specialist, and technical manager" (University of Pittsburgh, 2007). New position titles have been coined to attempt to capture what librarians are now doing in scholarly communication, including interdisciplinary research librarian, scholarly communications specialist, scholarly communications and sciences librarian, and so on. Much admired and widely discussed is the University of Minnesota's systematic and active approach to identifying enhanced expectations for its reference librarians/subject liaisons, including knowledge of and active participation in scholarly communication activities and exploration of issues in collaboration with the teaching and research faculty of the university. Some of their background information appears at the Association of Research Libraries (ARL) Institute Web site (http://www.arl.org/bm~doc/scprogpdframework.pdf).

Williams (2009) further articulates Minnesota's developing plan for reconceptualizing the liaison role in *Research Library Issues.* She discusses the value of "systems thinking" in formulating dynamic position descriptions that closely align with institutional goals. In the Minnesota framework, librarians are responsible (in position-adjusted proportions) for 10 areas: campus engagement, content/collection development and management, teaching and learning, scholarly communication, e-scholarship and digital tools, reference and help services, outreach, fundraising, exhibit and event planning, and leadership. Her report takes the scholarly communication role and expands on the expectations in this particular area as an example.

The authors of the study commonly referred to as the "*Ithaka Report*" (2007, 15) noted that

> among the librarians consulted for this study, we perceived a high level of energy and excitement about the "reinvention" of librarians' mission, making them more relevant and reinvigorated with a better understanding of their purpose and potential. This new mission involves a combination of:
>
> - serving faculty research, teaching, and publishing agendas (building collections to support faculty research, providing tools, delivering everything they want to the desktop, developing technological expertise for their publishing projects, supporting the infrastructure for their courses);
> - serving student study needs (creating new physical and virtual spaces for private and group work, helping students to become more efficient researchers);
> - preservation (e.g. launching institutional repositories [IRs], as 87% of librarians in a recent Ithaka survey cited archiving and preservation of an institution's intellectual assets as a "very important" reason for having IRs);
> - making scholarship available to the wider world (open access, digitizing special collections); and
> - lowering the cost of scholarship (alternative publishing, legal experts to negotiate contracts).

Both Minnesota's efforts and the *Ithaka Report* suggest that the roles of collection development and reference librarians can be revitalized by emphasizing their strengths and the value and knowledge they bring to a scholarly communication partnership with academic departments and their institutions. My hope and expectation is that future iterations of expanded position expectations in libraries will acknowledge and reward librarians' creative abilities as content *producers*, too, and thus as active contributors in their own right to digital scholarship. Many examples already exist—Web sites that are true intellectual portals, others that act as effective guides to intellectual property options and other scholarly publishing concerns, and the publishing collaborations that are becoming the norm in higher education.

Twenty years ago, following a somewhat dismal set of findings about the understanding and appreciation of librarians by faculty at a small college (actually *mis*understanding and *lack* of appreciation), Oberg, Schleiter, and Houten concluded that "the task before librarians today is to make the invisible visible. They must settle upon their role, perform it consistently, and communicate it unambiguously. When they do, their unique services and abilities will come to be understood and valued by their communities" (1989, 226).

In his influential essay, Lewis (2007) observes that libraries have always purchased collections to support their local communities or organizations and have also always curated special collections of unique or valuable items for the world. He believes that in the future, the second role will dominate, and curation will focus mainly on digital approaches.

Web access is relatively ubiquitous now, thanks to technology's increasing availability, inevitably leading to an ever-expanding mountain of content. Navigating this complexity is a familiar, everyday task where librarians have much experience. Reference librarians are critical to digital collection building because of their connections with faculty and students, their involvement with the issues, and their in-depth knowledge of collections, both those owned by the library and those available elsewhere. As Walters notes, "To be successful information service providers, libraries need to develop services that allow content creators, content managers, and end users to manipulate the content in ways they desire" (2006, 213). There is a growing literature about the skills and knowledge required for positions in libraries with a strong digital and scholarly communication component. In one study, researchers surveyed digital library professionals working in U.S. academic libraries to identify their critical activities and skills; they confirmed the value of soft skills and project management abilities as well as in-depth comprehension of digital library infrastructure and library knowledge such as user needs, archiving, preservation, cataloging and metadata, and collection development (Choi and Rasmussen, 2006).

Graduate library and information science programs are now reflecting the profession's changes in their own curricula, with digital programs and other technology- and content-focused coursework (for example, the University of Illinois has a data-curation education program specialization, and the University of North Carolina has a course devoted to digital libraries).

I believe that at least six important and expanded scholarly communication roles currently exist for libraries and librarians to assume. These include the following:

1. Content provider (the most traditional role): subscriptions, collection development, preservation, etc.
2. Content aggregator: Web pages, repositories, research guides
3. Content enhancer: metamorphosis of content into something new
4. Issues interpreter: participation in scholarly communication and discussions
5. Instructional communicator and partner in the learning cycle
6. Content producer: original contributions to scholarship

1. Content Provider

Collection development and management within the changing world of scholarly communication continues to be a complex and unpredictable yet vital endeavor for subject specialists. Digital collections are a critical element of scholarly research in every discipline, whether it be complex astronomical data, underground energy resource maps, or digitized versions of important authors' works. E-journal subscriptions are continuously a challenge. Librarians have used the changes in scholarly content delivery to create assessment projects that track usage in sophisticated ways and collect and analyze data to assist with user services and collection decisions.

Preservation of materials continues to be an important goal in digitizing collections. Reference librarians can help with this process by engaging their communities in supporting sustainable and accessible collections. The issues are clearly outlined by Dempsey (2004), vice president and chief strategist at OCLC, who discusses the need for a critical mass of digitized resources so that stakeholder interest is sustained, the importance of platform interoperability for sharing between users and services, the significance of the capacity to identify both users and content pieces, and the potential of long-term archiving practices for sustaining the cultural record. Dempsey feels that preservation is both a "public good" and a critical complement to other user services in libraries.

2. Content Aggregator

It took librarians very little time to recognize the Internet's value for assembling useful compilations of digital resources. Anderson's Digital Librarian (http://www.digital-librarian.com/) is a good example of creating and maintaining a list of digital sites in many subject areas. Bailey's work is another example of the impact that individual librarians can have in scholarly communication. He was an early innovator in establishing and editing the *Public-Access Computer Systems Review* (1989–1996) and was an early adopter of weblog software. He established the current *DigitalKoans* in 2005, which has become a prominent source of news and discussion about scholarly communication issues including intellectual property, open access, and repositories. Crawford's "Cites & Insights" (http://citesandinsights.info/civ10i1.pdf) is a further example of a creative work associating relevant content and thus increasing its findability and usefulness.

3. Content Enhancer

In the past, library users have been expected or forced to adapt their information seeking to the library environment. With increasing access available via networks, increasing reliance on digitized collections, and increasing expectations of immediate gratification, it is no surprise that these roles have somewhat reversed themselves, and libraries are now actively crafting and adapting services to appeal to users. Reference staff, because of their deep knowledge of subject areas and user needs and behavior, are in a particularly strong position to create significant digital environments. Some examples follow:

- The Library of Congress's Web Archives, originally called MINERVA (http://lcweb2.loc.gov/diglib/lcwa/html/lcwa-home.html), where reference specialists collect and archive Web information on a particular topic, such as Darfur or 9/11. According to the Web site, "it is part of a continuing effort by the Library to evaluate, select, collect, catalog, provide access to, and preserve digital materials for future generations of researchers."
- "The Valley of the Shadow: Two Communities in the American Civil War," the University of Virginia's Virginia Center for Digital History (http://valley.lib.virginia.edu/).

In attempting to describe this trend, Choudhury (2005) notes that "collections (content) are becoming recombinant, by which I mean that the 'fixed' notion we've become familiar with is being challenged. People think of content as malleable, something that can be broken into smaller chunks, shared and repurposed or transformed."

Many libraries are seeking collaborations to develop aggregated collections. For example, Arcade (http://arcade.nyarc.org/search~), launched in January 2009, is a combined database of the collections of three major art libraries, all members of the New York Art Resources Consortium (Brooklyn Museum Libraries and Archives, the Frick Art Reference Library, and the Museum of Modern Art Library). ECAI, the Electronic Cultural Atlas Initiative, is a global consortium incorporating scholars in the humanities, social sciences, and history; archivists; librarians and curators; members of nongovernmental organizations; and information technology researchers. HathiTrust, which describes itself as a "shared digital future," is a relatively recent Committee on Institutional Cooperation (CIC)/University of California libraries initiative to establish a repository for archiving, preserving, and sharing digital monograph collections.

The University of Nevada-Reno's University Digital Conservancy (http://contentdm.library.unr.edu/) is a good example of a library developing access to both restricted and unrestricted collections and adding value for the user. The conservancy contributes to Nevada's Digital Treasures Web site, and from the University of Nevada-Reno Web site one can search all the CONTENTdm digital collections in the state, set up a personal RSS feed, save items, and use them in presentations, classes, and so on, via a PowerPoint plug-in.

Repository Initiatives: Home for Faculty Publications and Other University-Produced Content

Lynch defines a university-based repository as "a set of services that a university offers to members of its community for the management and dissemination of digital materials created by the institution and its community members. It is most essentially an organizational commitment to the stewardship of these digital materials, including long-term preservation where appropriate, as well as organization and access or distribution" (2003, 1). Furlough's insightful article (2009) provides a significant contribution to current thinking about repositories. He provides a synopsis of the repository concept as an organized method of content management and argues for considering multifunctionality from a service and user viewpoint as well as a data curation initiative (Furlough, 19). Placing repositories in a meaningful context, Furlough delivers a concise and thoughtful—as well as thought-provoking—overview of models, tools and software, and the efforts thus far to attempt to manage the proliferation of data, arguing persuasively that

> libraries are moving from a business model based on facilitating the process of scholarship, teaching and research that result in those products. No matter what technology is used, the lifecycle model for digital data curation suggests that repositories and digital data management are not distinct backroom technology operations but activities that should be functionally integrated into the mission and services of the library. (20–21)

Many academic libraries have found it effective to inaugurate their repository development by taking low-hanging fruit and digitizing theses and dissertations, the research output of their departments. When a Penn State task force surveyed ARL library Web sites in 2008, the team found that the majority already have developed or are developing programs for electronic accessibility of dissertations and theses, and most were providing open access with authorial consent. The Networked Digital Library of Theses and Dissertations (NDLTD) is an international member organization whose goal is "promoting the adoption, creation, use, dissemination, and preservation of electronic theses and dissertations (ETDs)." It boasts a Facebook site and hosts conferences where librarians and developers share information about services and user access to the intellectual output of graduate students (see http://www.ndltd.org/). Librarians have also been instrumental in contributing to policy and archiving issues for repository development, with positive results for items such as learning objects and institutional records.

Librarians are also taking advantage of repositories to highlight their own work. For example, the University of Rochester has been developing its own open source repository software product (ir+ or irplus); see http://serials.infomotions.com/code4lib/archive/2009/200912/2038.html. And librarians at the River Campus are adding their papers, presentations, and so on, to stand alongside many of the teaching departments (see https://urresearch.rochester.edu/home.action).

Walters (2007) explores the changing roles of libraries and library departments that are "reinventing themselves" as a result of the repository movement. In both of his articles referenced in this chapter, he uses the transformative nature of the act of building a repository at the Georgia Institute of Technology Library and Information Center as an example of how libraries handle change triggered by developments in scholarly communication. Various library departments contribute to a successful institutional repository, and he assigns reference and information services the significant roles of observing how faculty and students produce and use content in a repository, providing feedback for functional improvements, promoting repository services and training users and contributors in effective use of the repository, and keeping faculty informed about developments in scholarly communication, including their publication and intellectual property options.

According to the *Ithaka Report,* "libraries provide tools and infrastructure to support new forms of informal publishing, but these tend to be inward focused (toward the home institution) rather than externally focused (towards the best scholarship in a given discipline), limiting their appeal to users. As a result, institutional repositories so far tend to look like 'attics' (and often fairly empty ones), with random assortments of content of questionable importance" (2007, 16). Institutions can use the strong organizational skills of librarians, as well as their close ties to faculty, to ensure that the somewhat harsh judgment of the *Ithaka Report* is not played out in future repository developments.

Another jaundiced view of the current state of repositories is found in Salo's 2008 article, "Innkeeper at the Roach Motel." Salo argues that library-managed repositories and the open access movement have not led to increased access to scholarship, and she suggests 12 concrete steps for improvement, including active involvement of staff:

> In an ideal world, library administrators would work toward campus-wide permissions mandates like Harvard's, liaison librarians would evangelize the institutional repository to faculty as a matter of course, serials and collection-development librarians would help identify suitable content for deposit, e-reserves staff would scan analog content during slow times in the academic calendar, and technical-services librarians would help with repository metadata and authority control. (Salo, 2008, 118)

4. Issues Interpreter

Libraries are often cast in primary or supporting roles in providing information to their communities about intellectual property and copyright and, more recently, the open access movement. Decades of resource sharing have given librarians a deep grasp of copyright principles and issues. Institutions generally have developed formal statements regarding copyright (for example, Stanford University's policies, available at http://dor.stanford.edu/Resources/ip.html). Russell (2004), a librarian in the American Library Association's Washington office, covers the major points of copyright in her book through the use of descriptive scenarios.

Scholarly publishing is undergoing major changes as the transition from print to online formats continues unabated, and feasible business models and the new paradigm are still in flux. In addition, a movement toward open access has been quietly revolutionizing the traditional view of intellectual property in the United States. Licensing the full text of electronic journals is now common, and unrestricted access to this rich array of resources is a long-term subject of debate.

Initially, libraries and librarians were most closely associated with collection development, acquisitions, and budgetary issues within scholarly publishing and the open access movement. The practice of licensing e-resources, full text journals in particular, has become commonplace, and many companies joined the industry in the 1990s as content aggregators. University presses, under scrutiny, are rethinking their roles, acquisition guidelines, publication estimates, and alternatives (such as publication on demand). Publishing economics and business models have become unstable, especially in some disciplines, once open access on the Web became a technologically viable option, either provided by a journal publisher or because an individual author chooses and has the ability to make copies of original work available.

To provide open access, authors may take the route of self-archiving and making a copy available via the Web. Alternatively, a journal publisher may make content available online, either immediately or after an embargo period. The debate has heated up periodically over this decade, as various disciplines tackle the intellectual property expectations of the journals where they publish. The National Institutes of Health (NIH) Public Access Policy has encouraged more ready access in the sciences in particular and is designed to ensure retrieval by the public of the knowledge resulting from federally funded research (see http://grants.nih.gov/grants/guide/notice-files/NOT-OD-08–033.html). Libraries have been quick to provide customized information for their institutions so that researchers have local guidance about compliance. Many librarians maintain comprehensive, up-to-date scholarly communication Web sites that provide a wealth of information about open access and many other issues of interest to faculty, as well as institutional guidance and explanations about intellectual property, the NIH policy, journal subscription costs, and so on. A few examples include Harvard University (http://osc.hul.harvard.edu/osc.php), the University of Minnesota (http://www.lib.umn.edu/scholcom/), the University of Illinois at Urbana-Champaign (http://www.library.illinois.edu/scholcomm/), Johns Hopkins University (http://openaccess.jhmi.edu/), and the University of Washington (http://www.lib.washington.edu/ScholComm/Issues/oa.html).

Many knowledgeable librarians are also planning and contributing to seminars on scholarly communication topics. For example, librarians from three universities collaborated on a scholarly communication workshop in 2009 and have made their materials freely available (see http://scholarlycommunications.wustl.edu/roadshow/index.html).

ARL has been active in investigating and sharing research and serving as a resource hub for scholarly communication. In the beginning it concentrated on illuminating open access issues in collaboration with ACRL. The Tempe Principles for Emerging Systems of Scholarly Publishing became an initial rallying point calling for changes in the scholarly publishing system (see http://www.arl.org/resources/pubs/tempe/principles-2.shtml.)(Association of Research Libraries, 2000.)

The Scholarly Publishing and Academic Resources Coalition (SPARC) has also become an important source for current information (http://www.arl.org/sparc/). ACRL and ARL have partnered in developing an influential series of institutes, described as "an immersive learning experience that prepares participants as local experts within their libraries and provides a structure for developing a program plan for scholarly communication outreach that is customized for each participant's institution" [See: http://www.arl.org/sc/institute/index.shtml]. Taught by librarians from institutions with established scholarly communication programs, the institutes have benefited many librarians who have attended them. Librarians ready to establish scholarly communication initiatives at their own institutions are still finding the available background resources from the program (and the real-life example documents from institutions including the University of Minnesota and the University of California, San Francisco) extremely valuable for start-up information. The program agenda covers organizing, focusing inward, increasing staff understanding of issues, focusing outward, implementing, and evaluating. [See: http://www.ala.org/ala/mgrps/divs/acrl/issues/scholcomm/scinstitute.cfm].

"Scholarly Communication 101" is another initiative developed by librarians that has evolved into a traveling seminar; workshop content including handouts and exercises from January 2009 has been posted at the ACRL site (http://www.acrl.ala.org/scholcomm/node/32), including "The 10 Things You Should Know about... Scholarly Communication." ACRL also provides the Scholarly Communication Toolkit, especially valuable for its advocacy suggestions (http://www.acrl.ala.org/scholcomm/).

5. Instructional Communicator and Partner in the Learning Cycle

Course content is an area where reference librarians are able to make even more effective contributions with the tools available in a scholarly communication environment. Bell and Shank (2007) incorporate a chapter of definitions and examples of how librarians create—as well as locate—digital learning materials, defined as "any interactive web-based digital resource that is used for instruction" (119). Their book is a useful resource for information on librarian-initiated digital instruction projects.

Special collections reference has been a natural setting for exploring the use of digitized materials with students. In the *Chronicle of Higher Education*'s blog, a post about "Special Collections as Laboratories" highlighted a panel with participants from Yale and the University of Illinois at Urbana-Champaign at the Coalition for Networked Information's Fall Forum describing "what can happen when you turn undergraduates loose in special collections" (Howard, 2009). At Penn State University, history librarian Eric Novotny has collaborated with a teaching faculty member to explore adding student-developed content from a course project to the library's Pennsylvania History Web site (http://www.libraries.psu.edu/digital/pahistory/).

Librarians and other staff of the University of Virginia Library's Scholars' Lab assist humanities and social sciences faculty and advanced students in digital research, digital project development, text encoding, digitization of text and images, and other related services (see http://www2.lib.virginia.edu/scholarslab/consultation/index.htm).

According to their Web site, instruction librarians at the University of California, Los Angeles (UCLA), collect statistics on scholarly communication interactions, which are defined as

> communication with a student, faculty, or staff, on a range of topics associated with intellectual property and publishing, including authors' rights, copyright, use of copyrighted materials, new scholarly publishing models and open-access initiatives, and the UC eScholarship Repository. Communication may be to an individual or groups and may occur in a variety of locations or formats, for example, in person, in an office or a classroom, or via e-mail, chat, telephone or text. (UCLA Library, 2009).

6. Content Producer

Choudhury (2005) notes that "the line between research, learning and dissemination is blurring—or has always been the case and we're only returning to the original vision of higher education." With easier availability via the Web, librarians are taking on expanded roles as conceptualizers and producers of significant digital content. It has been interesting to me to see that this role for librarians—and this aspect of our profession's influence—has not as yet been framed well in the literature, although many of the examples cited here are clearly the production of original content.

Sarah Thomas, then dean of the library at Cornell University, proposed the library to be an "innovator and partner" and discussed library contributions to publishing and archiving through Project Euclid, arXiv, and DPubS (2006, 563). BePress staff offer presentations explaining the virtues of BePress software. One slide titled "Why Publish" suggests eight useful examples of ways that librarians can become publishers (Berkeley Electronic Press, 2009, slide 6). In his 2009 article on library publishing, Jingfeng Xia also recognized the library's expanding role as a producer of content (2009, 371).

The Grainger Engineering Library at the University of Illinois at Urbana-Champaign (http://search.grainger.uiuc.edu/top/staff.htm) is recognized as a location where librarians work in the forefront of digital collections and technology development. Sample projects that have been created and hosted include the following:

- Illinois Harvest, a portal to digitized collections about the state, including cemetery records, Abraham Lincoln, the James Reston papers, oral history memoirs, photojournalism, and so on: http://illinoisharvest.grainger.uiuc.edu/
- The Digital Library Federation (DLF) Collections Registry, 2002–06: http://dlf.grainger.uiuc.edu/DLFCollectionsRegistry/browse/
- The University of Illinois OAI-PMH Data Provider Registry: http://gita.grainger.uiuc.edu/registry/ (OAI-PMH is the Open Archives Initiative Protocol for Metadata Harvesting.)

To name just a few additional examples, the following are some of the many libraries that have long histories of digitizing significant materials from their collections as part of their service models:

- University of Michigan: http://www.lib.umich.edu/digital-initiatives
- University of Virginia: http://www.lib.virginia.edu/digital/
- University of Chicago: http://www1.lib.uchicago.edu/e/dl/program.php3
- Enoch Pratt: http://www.prattlibrary.org/digital/
- California Digital Library: http://www.cdlib.org/
- University of Illinois at Urbana–Champaign: http://www.library.illinois.edu/dcc/

WEB 2.0 INFLUENCES

The technological and social aspects of Web 2.0 technologies (online communities, social networks, and so on) have also been enthusiastically embraced by many librarians as another means of producing and synthesizing content. Reference librarians have become adept as content aggregators, enhancers, and producers through more than a decade of creative Web site development in support of their reference, collection-building, and instructional responsibilities.

I remember talking to a cataloging colleague about 10 years ago when we were in the market for a new integrated library system and would presumably have access to enhanced options for customization. As a former database searcher and having found free text fields and "identifiers" very useful in some databases as supplements to controlled vocabulary, I pitched to him the idea of allowing users to suggest terms they would recommend adding to cataloging records as an additional means of finding relevant items. This was certainly not a traditional approach, but not very long after, we were seeing creative Web interfaces where librarians were encouraging user input. Social tagging is now a common feature; one study relevant to librarians explores social tagging in the Code4Lib community (Tonkin et al., 2008).

While academic librarians are generally embracing social networking media as a way to connect with their students, Web 2.0 technologies such as online communities, social networks, blogs, and wikis are attracting various levels of participation in the research world. According to a survey by Robert Half Technology (2009), 54 percent of Chief Information Officers (CIOs) in a study of 1,400 randomly selected companies employing over 100 people indicated that staff are blocked from using social networking sites while at work, and another 19 percent require any use to be for business purposes only. The picture appears somewhat more encouraging in academia: Anderson (2009) cites a column in *Cell* (Bonetta, 2009) that illustrates how scientists are now using Twitter.

Harley, who has led some of the seminal work in studying faculty scholarly communication needs (using interview techniques with support from a 2007 two-year Mellon grant), observes in the interim report that while personal faculty home pages are "ubiquitous," "blogs, RSS feeds, wikis, etc., are less common ways in which scholars broadcast and receive information" (2008, 10). Scholars' adoption of social media certainly appears to follow a discipline-based path. For reference librarians, understanding the foundational communication methods of the discipline continues to be critical for them to be credible in the scholarly communication discussion. The site arXiv.org has long been the preferred place to submit and locate preprints in physics, mathematics, statistics, computer science, and quantitative biology. Some in the scientific community, such as vertebrate paleontologists, have several active communities on Facebook. A column on October 23, 2009, in *The Wired Campus* (the *Chronicle of Higher Education*'s newsfeed) reported that "a $12.2 million federal stimulus grant from the National Institutes of Health will finance a network some are calling a Facebook for scientists. Several universities, including Cornell and the University of Florida, will develop the network over the next two years in the expectation of helping scientists find other academics to work with" (Aujla, 2009). And in the scholarly communication world, practitioners look to *The Scholarly Kitchen*, a blog sponsored by the Society for Scholarly Publishing (which has a strong membership of librarians), as one way to track topics in scholarly communication (see http://scholarlykitchen.sspnet.org/). EthicShare, a collaborative virtual community, is a contemporary project using librarian expertise to develop something entirely new in collaboration with scholars and computer scientists at the University of Minnesota (see http://www2.lib.umn.edu/about/ethicshare/index.html).

Librarians have experimented with and used Second Life in promoting scholarly collections, either independently or as part of an institution-wide effort. For example, Stanford hosted a special collections open house using Second Life in July 2009 and discussed the event later via Chris Bourg's blog (see https://www.stanford.edu/group/ic/cgi-bin/drupal2/node/763). Lisa Spiro, director of the Digital Media Center at Rice University's Fondren

Library, created a blog entitled *Digital Scholarship in the Humanities* (http://digitalscholarship.wordpress.com/). A blog also exists called *The History Librarian* (http://historylibrarian.wordpress.com/category/scholarly-communication/).

SOFTWARE DEVELOPMENT

Librarians have also contributed as producers and collaborators in other ways. While libraries and individual librarians in the United States and internationally have begun to produce scholarly digital content, in some cases they have also been part of the development of the underlying platform software or infrastructure. Many of the common names in digital collections software, particularly open source, have their basis in library applications development. DLXS software for building digital collections was developed at the University of Michigan. BePress had its start at the University of California. In late 2001, James Madison University began to offer its image-archiving and multimedia software as open access. Project Euclid and DPubS were conceived at Cornell University, and DPubS was expanded to include many of the features needed for the editorial process of journal publishing during funding by a Mellon grant with Penn State University as a partner. Greenstone's suite of software was developed by the New Zealand Digital Library Project at the University of Waikato to empower users, especially libraries, to build digital libraries (see http://www.greenstone.org/). The Public Knowledge Project at Simon Fraser University provides open source software for the entire process of producing journals and conferences. Librarians have also been deeply involved in digital collection development and management projects such as harvesting data as well as in the development of various digital standards.

LIBRARY AND PRESS COLLABORATIONS

Finally, librarians have been active in partnership with university presses to produce new content in the form of monographs and other publications. As what has been referred to as "the crisis in scholarly publishing" became more evident in the first decade of the 21st century, some institutions recognized research libraries and university presses' collaborative potential. According to the *Ithaka Report*, "press directors and librarians must work together to create the intellectual products of the future which increasingly will be created and distributed in electronic media. Their efforts should be closely and intelligently connected to their campuses' academic programs and priorities in order to ensure their relevancy and institutional commitment" (2007, 16). Librarians interviewed for the report noted that besides the prestige and status that distinguish a university imprint, presses can assist them in assessing whether there is a user base for a digitized product, identifying potential markets, planning for maintenance of online versions, and building awareness via marketing.

It has become increasingly common to see presses reporting to library deans. In many cases the presses are relieved of some of the financial burdens of an obsolescent business model by becoming more of a service organization rather than an assumed revenue generator within the university structure. Penn State's University Press has reported to the dean of libraries and scholarly communications since 2006, and the merger has offered increased opportunities for reference and subject specialists to be actively involved in building digital collections; for example, responsibility for the MetalMark Books imprint is shared by the press and the libraries, and subject librarians are part of the team selecting titles for digitization.

Other examples of larger presses reporting to libraries include the University of Michigan, Massachusetts Institute of Technology, New York University, and Utah State University. Following a different model than many universities with presses have adopted, the University of Pittsburgh library is partnering with its press in the D-Scribe Digital Publishing program to create digital editions, and Ohio State University houses the press's backlist on a library server. Helping to facilitate the dialogue on campuses, SPARC published a lengthy report in January 2009 that provides a guide for presses, libraries, and information technology organizations that are exploring partnerships; international in focus, it includes a table of previous and current press and library collaborative initiatives and informative case studies from Cornell, the University of Toronto, and the University of California (Crow, 2009). In spring 2009, the University of Michigan Press announced that it would become part of the University of Michigan library system and change its focus primarily toward digital monographs. They anticipate opportunities for increasing collaborative work with the university library's existing publishing services from the Scholarly Publishing Office (Provenzano, 2009). While not in a direct reporting relationship, the California Digital Library continues its maturing eScholarship repository by partnering with the University of California Press in a new venture called UC Publishing Services (UCPubS). They expect the partnership to provide broad advantages since the library will gain new digital content and authors will benefit from the editorial, marketing, and distribution channels the press can provide (University of California Press, 2009).

Some libraries are actively embracing the role of stand-alone publisher. The University of Tennessee's Newfound Press has a mission statement that explains, "Drawing on the resources that the university has invested in digital library development, Newfound Press collaborates with authors and researchers to bring new forms of publication to an expanding scholarly universe." Librarians involved in the program are exploring and supporting the use of new media in publishing, along with retaining peer-reviewed quality. At the same time, the University of Tennessee's press is finding an external partner in the Tennessee Historical Society.

CONCLUSION

We may quibble with some of the features and implementations, but as a former "database searcher," I am thrilled by everything that users can now do by and for themselves, and by the increased ability librarians now have to participate creatively in the knowledge economy. Scholarly communication is truly verging on the "memex machine" that Vannevar Bush coveted over 60 years ago:

> Wholly new forms of encyclopedias will appear, ready made with a mesh of associative trails running through them, ready to be dropped into the memex and there amplified.... There is a new profession of trail blazers, those who find delight in the task of establishing useful trails through the enormous mass of the common record. (1945, 8)

The scholarly communication landscape has seen massive changes in the last 20 years, and any view to the future shows exponential increases. In concluding his essay, Bush uses examples of chemists, patent attorneys, historians, and doctors, who in his imagination will have access to the world of information in a linked and usable form. I like to picture librarians at the forefront of Bush's scholarly trailblazers. This chapter has given a brief overview of the changes that most affect reference librarians and how librarians are using new tools, methods, and skills to contribute to supporting and creating digital scholarship. Provided that we meet the challenges with enthusiasm and welcome the reality of living with constant change, the rewards will be considerable. Librarians will certainly continue to be key providers, interpreters, maintainers, and producers of content. I can't visualize a more exciting, innovative period to be a librarian.

WORKS CITED

Anderson, K. 2009. Scientists are using social media tools (and may be using social networks, too). *The Scholarly Kitchen* [blog]. November 2, 2009. Retrieved November 20, 2009, from http://scholarlykitchen.sspnet.org/2009/11/03/scientists-are-using-social-media-tools-and-may-be-using-social-networks-too/?utm_source=feedburner&utm_medium=feed&utm_campaign=Feed%3A+ScholarlyKitchen+%28The+Scholarly+Kitchen%29.

Association of College and Research Libraries (ACRL) and Association of Research Libraries (ARL). 2010. ACRL/ARL Institute on Scholarly Communication. Retrieved September 15, 2010, from http://www.ala.org/ala/mgrps/divs/acrl/issues/scholcomm/scinstitute.cfm.

Association of College and Research Libraries (ACRL). 2006a. Changing roles of academic and research libraries. Retrieved September 15, 2010 from http://www.ala.org/ala/mgrps/divs/acrl/issues/value/changingroles.cfm.

Association of College and Research Libraries (ACRL). 2006b. Principles and strategies for the reform of scholarly communication. Retrieved August 5, 2009, from http://www.ala.org/ala/mgrps/divs/acrl/publications/whitepapers/principlesstrategies.cfm.

Association of Research Libraries. 2000. Principles for emerging systems of scholarly publishing [the Tempe Principles]. Retrieved August 5, 2009, from http://www.arl.org/bm~doc/tempe1.pdf.

Aujla, S. 2009. Federal stimulus funds from NIH go to a "Facebook for Scientists." *Wired Campus,* October 22, 2009. Retrieved November 17, 2010, from http://chronicle.com/blogPost/Federal-Stimulus-Funds-From/8568/?sid=wc&utm_source=wc&utm_medium=en.

Bailey, C. W. 2008. *Scholarly electronic publishing bibliography.* Retrieved September 15, 2010, from http://www.digital-scholarship.org/sepb/archive/75/. (Also available in paperback and an Amazon Kindle edition.)

Bailey, C. W. 2010. *Scholarly electronic publishing weblog.* Retrieved on September 15, 2010, from http://www.digital-scholarship.com/sepb/sepw.htm.

Bell, S., and J. Shank. 2007. *Academic librarianship by design, the blended librarian's guide to the tools and techniques.* Chicago: American Library Association.

Berkeley Electronic Press. 2009. The library as publisher, ready or not. *Presentations, Paper 13.* Retrieved September 20, 2009, from http://digitalcommons.bepress.com/presentations/13.

Bonetta, L. 2009. Should you be tweeting? *Cell* 139: 452–453. Retrieved November 20, 2009, from http://www.sciencedirect.com/science?_ob=MImg&_imagekey=B6WSN-4XJWG74-4-1&_cdi=7051&_user=209810&_orig=search&_coverDate=10%2F30%2F2009&_sk=998609996&view=c&wchp=dGLzVlz-zSkzS&md5=e2a4e5166e1c05095ca9f89a51cb9713&ie=/sdarticle.pdf.

Borgman, C. 2000. Digital libraries and the continuum of scholarly communication. *Journal of Documentation* 56(4): 412–430.

Bush, V. 1945. As we may think. *The Atlantic* (July). Retrieved November 2, 2009, from http://www.theatlantic.com/doc/print/194507/bush.

Byrne, A. 2009. Owning our future: Twenty-first century librarians (the 2009 Elizabeth W. Stone Lecture). In *Strategies for regenerating the library and information profession,* ed. J. Varlejs, L. Lewis, and G. Walton, 17–31. Berlin and New York: Walter de Gruyter and K. G. Saur.

Choi, Y., and E. Rasmussen. 2006. What is needed to educate future digital librarians: A study of current practice and staffing patterns in academic and research libraries. *D-Lib Magazine* 12(9). Retrieved September 7, 2009, from http://www.dlib.org/dlib/september06/choi/09choi.html.

Choudhury, S. 2005. The cutting edge: The next generation digital library. In *The library in bits and bytes: A digital library symposium,* edited by A. Hanlon and G. Gueguen. College Park: University of Maryland. Retrieved October 20, 2009, from http://www.lib.umd.edu/dcr/events/symposium/choud hury.html.

Crow, R. 2009. *Campus based publishing partnerships: A guide to critical issues.* Retrieved November 3, 2009, from http://www.arl.org/sparc/bm~doc/pub_partnerships_v1.pdf .

Dempsey, L. 2004. Thirteen ways of looking at... digital preservation. *D-Lib Magazine* 10 (7–8). Retrieved August 10, 2009, from http://www.dlib.org/dlib/july04/lavoie/07lavoie.html.

Furlough, M. 2009. What we talk about when we talk about repositories. *Reference & User Services Quarterly* 49 (1):18–23, 32.

Greco, A. N., ed. 2009. *The state of scholarly publishing: Challenges and opportunities.* New Brunswick, NJ: Transaction.

Harley, D. 2008. *Interim report: Assessing the future landscape of scholarly communication: An in-depth study of faculty needs and ways of meeting them.* Berkeley: Center for Studies in Higher Education, University of California, Berkeley. Retrieved September 7, 2009, from http://cshe.berkeley.edu/publications/docs/SC%20Draft%20Interim%20Report%20060808.doc.pdf. (Note: Harley's interim report [2008] has been updated by a full report dated January 2010; see http://escholarship.org/uc/cshe_fsc for the announcement, with a PDF available at http://escholarship.org/uc/item/15x7385g.)

Howard, J. 2009. Special collections as laboratories. *The Wired Campus,* October 16, 2009. Retrieved October 25, 2009, from http://chronicle.com/blogPost/Special-Collections-as/8490/?sid=wc&utm_source=wc&utm_medium=en.

Ithaka report: University publishing in a digital age. 2007. Retrieved August 5, 2009, from http://www.ithaka.org/ithaka-s-r/strategy/Ithaka%20University%20Publishing%20Report.pdf.

Lewis, D. W. 2007. A strategy for academic libraries in the first quarter of the 21st century. *College & Research Libraries* 68(5): 418–434. Retrieved August 11, 2009, from https://scholarworks.iupui.edu/bitstream/handle/1805/665/A%20Model%20Academic%20Libraries%202005%20to%202025.pdf?sequence=6. (Another version is: Lewis, D.W. 2007. A model for academic libraries 2005 to 2025. *Visions of Change Conference*, University of California at Sacramento, January 26, 2007.)

Lynch, C. 2003. Institutional repositories: Essential infrastructure for scholarship in the digital age. *ARL Bimonthly Report* 226. Retrieved August 21, 2009, from http:/www.arl.org/newsletr/226/ir.html.

Mukherjee, B. 2009. Scholarly communication: A journey from print to web. *Library Philosophy and Practice 2009.* Retrieved September 5, 2009, from http://www.webpages.uidaho.edu/~mbolin/mukherjee.htm.

Networked Digital Library of Theses and Dissertations (NTLTD). Retrieved September 15, 2010, from http://www.ndltd.org/.

Oberg, L. R., M. K. Schleiter, and M. V. Houten. 1989. Faculty perceptions of librarians at Albion College: Status, role, contribution, and contacts. *College & Research Libraries* 50 (2): 215–230.

Odlyzko, A. 2002. The rapid evolution of scholarly communication. *Learned Publishing* 15: 7–19.

Peek, R. P., and G. B. Newby. 1996. *Scholarly publishing: The electronic frontier.* Cambridge, MA: MIT Press.

Provenzano, F. 2009. U-M redefining scholarly publications in the digital age. *The University Record Online.* Retrieved September 7, 2009, from http://www.ur.umich.edu/0809/Mar23_09/05.php.

Rabina, D. L., and D. J. Walczyk. 2007. Information professionals' attitude toward the adoption of innovations in everyday life. Proceedings of the Sixth International Conference on Conceptions of Library and Information Science—"Featuring the Future." *Information Research* 12 (4). Retrieved October 14, 2009, from http://informationr.net//ir/12-4/colis12.html.

Robert Half Technology. 2009. *Whistle—but don't tweet—while you work* [press release]. Retrieved October 20, 2009, from http://rht.mediaroom.com/index.php?s=131&item=790.

Russell, C. 2004. *Complete copyright: An everyday guide for librarians.* Chicago: American Library Association.

Salo, D. 2008. Innkeeper at the roach motel. *Library Trends* 57 (2): 98–121. (Also available at the University of Wisconsin repository; retrieved November 9, 2009, from http://minds.wisconsin.edu/handle/1793/22088.)

Scholarly communication. *Wikipedia.* Retrieved September 15, 2010, from http://en.wikipedia.org/wiki/Scholarly_communication. (Quoted at George Washington University's scholarly communication website [http://www.gwu.edu/gelman/scholcomm/definitions.html] and created by the Bernard Becker Medical Library, Washington University in St. Louis School of Medicine; that organization has since truncated its definition [http://becker.wustl.edu/services/scholarly/index.html].)

Thomas, S. E. 2006. Publishing solutions for contemporary scholars: The library as innovator and partner. *Publishing Research Quarterly* 22 (2): 563–573.

Tonkin, E., E.M. Corrado, H.L. Moulaison, M.E.I. Kipp, A. Resmini, H.D. Pfeiffer, et al. 2008. Collaborative and social tagging networks. *Ariadne* 54. Retrieved September 7, 2009, from http://www.ariadne.ac.uk/issue54/tonkin-et-al/.

University of California, Los Angeles (UCLA) Library. Instructional statistics frequently asked questions. Retrieved July 16, 2009, from http://www.library.ucla.edu/service/12984.cfm.

University of California Press. Publishing partnerships: UCPubS. Retrieved July 15, 2009, from http://www.ucpress.edu/partners.php?p=ucpubs.

University of Pittsburgh. 2007. Digital Research Library. Retrieved September 15, 2010, from http://www.library.pitt.edu/libraries/drl/.

University of Tennessee Libraries. Newfound Press. Retrieved September 15, 2010, from http://www.newfoundpress.utk.edu/.

Walters, T. O. 2006. Strategies and frameworks for institutional repositories and the new support infrastructure for scholarly communications. *D-Lib Magazine* 12(10): 213–225. Retrieved September 7, 2009, from http://www.dlib.org/dlib/october06/walters/10walters.html.

Walters, T. O. 2007. Reinventing the library—How repositories are causing librarians to rethink their professional roles. *portal: Libraries and the Academy* 7(2): 213–225.

Williams, K. 2009. A framework for articulating new library roles. *Research Library Issues: A bimonthly report from ARL, CNI, and SPARC* 265: 3–8. Retrieved September 9, 2009, from http://www.arl.org/resources/pubs/rli/archive/rli265.shtml.

Xia, J. 2009. Library publishing as a new model of scholarly communication. *Journal of scholarly publishing* 40(4): 370–83.

VI

STAFFING 21st-CENTURY LIBRARIES

20

WHAT SKILLS ARE NEEDED FOR THE NEXT GENERATION OF LIBRARIANS?

Sally W. Kalin

In 2007, the *New York Times* Style section featured an article on new, contemporary librarians under the title "A Hipper Crowd of Shushers" (Jeselle, 2007, 1). The article described a progressive, hip group of librarians who "combined geeky intellectualism with IT skills and social activism." The spin was colorful (one librarian had a tattoo of the Federal Depository Library Program logo on his arm) and fun ("*Today's librarians? Think high-tech party people*"). This article made me think about the kinds of people who are being attracted to librarianship today. In particular, what attributes should reference librarians bring to the dynamic library workplace of today and tomorrow?

I have been a professional librarian for several decades, moving through the ranks from reference librarian to academic library administrator. My first job was as the sole reference librarian in a small liberal arts college. The library's reference desk also served as my personal desk, so I was highly visible, able to engage easily with the students and faculty, and never off duty. I loved my job. Smugly cool and somewhat self-important, I was secure in the knowledge that I alone (well, at least in the college) possessed the keys to the kingdom of knowledge. My position was one of elegant simplicity, easily defined with unambiguous parameters. The kind of reference librarian that I was, so prevalent in the print world, no longer exists.

Steven Coffman, in his rebuttal to the argumentative question, "Are Reference Librarians Toast?" posed in *American Libraries,* writes, "There can be no doubt that reference librarians, as we know them—those of us who sit behind desks for five or six hours a day, as I did for the better part of my life, waiting for people to walk up and ask questions—those reference librarians are toast" (2002, 51). Instead, he suggests that today's reference librarians have multidimensional assignments. They are skilled in information technologies, Web development, teaching and instructional design, digital and print collection development and services, and media creation; possess subject expertise; and are branching into fields such as e-repositories and software development. They multitask, deliver professional presentations, create partnerships with other professional entities, and foster new and creative initiatives. They create gaming activities, provide media interviews, and fundraise. They do it all, and then some.

The good news is that reference librarians continue to be in demand. Radford (2008, 108) writes that "there has never been a more exciting time for reference. In fact, I've never seen any time that has even come remotely close." I concur with her. The complexity of the information world, which extends far beyond the confines of libraries and their collections, calls for information experts who can guide, consult with, and teach diverse users with a myriad of expectations. In large academic research libraries, the demand for subject specialists remains strong even as interest diminishes in maintaining subject-based, collection-centric libraries. What skills and attributes do prospective employers look for in determining which librarians can provide excellent user services and make important contributions to their libraries?

The professional literature is rife with articles and documents on core competencies for librarians. Susan Thompson (2009, 4) defines a *core competency* as "the fundamental knowledge or ability related to a specific subject area or skill set. The *core* part of the term refers to the underlying understanding from which an individual can build specific abilities related to a task or job. *Competency* implies that this understanding goes beyond a basic ability to being well qualified or proficient at the task." The *Professional Competencies for Reference and User Services Librarians* (Reference and User Services Association, 2003) defines *competencies* as "behaviors that excellent performers exhibit more consistently and effectively than average performers" (n.p.). Competencies are used to develop position descriptions and to make subsequent hiring decisions, to create training and professional development programs, to assess and evaluate services and the personnel who deliver them, and to guide organizational change.

In the past decade, a multitude of competency documents have been developed for music librarians, special-collections librarians, business librarians, information technology (IT) specialists, and others. After nearly a decade, the American Library Association (ALA) approved its *Core Competencies of Librarianship* (2009). Prominent librarians such as Roy Tennant have created their own lists for the digital age (1998). The Library Information and Technology Association of the ALA published an excellent monograph on core technology competencies for librarians (Thompson, 2009). Two important competency documents for reference librarians are the Reference and

User Services Association's *Guidelines for Behavioral Performance of Reference and Information Service Providers* (Reference and User Services Association, 2004) and *Professional Competencies for Reference and User Services Librarians* (Reference and User Services Association, 2003). The introduction to the latter states, "These competencies are focused on the abilities, skills, and knowledge that makes reference and user services librarians unique from other professionals" (n.p.).

Several years ago, Meredith Farkas, a self-described "librarian, writer, teacher, and tech geek," blogged about the "Skills for the 21st Century Librarian," or competencies she identified based on her experience as a graduate student in librarianship and as a new librarian (Farkas, 2006). It quickly became a heavily cited contribution to the growing literature on competencies. In her post, Farkas distinguishes between what she calls "basic tech competencies" and "higher level competencies." Her competencies are a combination of practical skills, such as the ability to troubleshoot new technologies, and personal characteristics, such as the ability to embrace change. Farkas's core competencies typify what many librarians and library administrators have discovered: The librarians who will thrive and excel in today's challenging information environment possess a special combination of technical *and* personal competencies.

Librarianship competencies are therefore a combination of hard and soft skills. Hard skills are also referred to as technical or professional skills; soft skills are also defined as personal or behavioral skills, and often focus on communication abilities. Hard skills are specific to a job and can be learned through experience doing the job or developed through training and education. For a reference librarian, appropriate technical skills could include an in-depth knowledge of reference resources, the ability to apply assessment methodologies, the expertise to create Web pages, or skill in using the features of chat reference software. Soft skill competencies could include the ability to create rapport with users, to engage colleagues as a mentor, and to foster teamwork.

In the mid-1990s, Daniel Goleman added the word *emotional intelligence* (EI) to the management lexicon through his best-selling books *Emotional Intelligence* (1995) and *Working with Emotional Intelligence* (1998). Emotional intelligence gives credence to soft skills; it serves as an umbrella under which to consolidate those personal traits and behaviors that lead to successful leadership, excellent services, and, for businesses, profitability. Emotional intelligence, Goleman argued, plays a greater role in employee performance than intellect (IQ) or the attainment of technical skills. He identified three emotional skills that deal with self-management—self-awareness, self-regulation, and self-motivation—and two that address how one relates to others—empathy and social skills. Good technical skills get an employee hired; soft skills allow the employee to achieve.

The iconic Jack Welch, former chief executive officer of General Electric, gave credence to the importance of soft skills in his response to a student who asked, "What should we be learning in business school?" following a lecture at Massachusetts Institute of Technology's Sloan School of Management. His response: "Just concentrate on networking. Everything else you need to know, you can learn on the job" (Fisher, 2007, 49). His hosts, surprised by his answer, soon responded to Welch and also to their employment recruiters by creating a new curriculum with an increased emphasis on the interpersonal skills that MBAs need to succeed. Libraries can take lessons from the business world's increasing focus on hiring employees with the appropriate EI to improve profitability through service quality and, ultimately, customer satisfaction. The bottom line is that both libraries and successful businesses want satisfied customers.

Is EI important for librarians? Research indicates that it is. Promis (2008, 28) writes, "There is a growing awareness of EI's importance. Soft skills, traditionally most valued in upper management, are now essential at all levels of the professional workplace." Her research discovered that despite a "clamoring for soft skills," a significant number of library job advertisements are not designed to attract candidates with EI but instead continue to emphasize hard skills. Eidson (2000) found that reference librarians with EI are better able to understand the information needs of users and that successful reference interviews are enhanced by cultivating librarians' EI. Research conducted by Williamson, Pemberton, and Lounsbury (2005) revealed that librarians who possessed personal traits such as optimism, emotional resilience, and a strong work ethic derived more job and career satisfaction from librarianship, possibly resulting in enhanced creativity and production.

Writing this essay brought to mind a favorite poem that I discovered when I was a graduate student in library science. The poem's message is more relevant today than ever.

Essay Concerning the Sufficiency of Intellect in the Attainment of Excellence in Teaching

IQ
Won't Do.

—P. J. Sokolowski

I have rarely encountered a reference librarian who was not intelligent; I have, however, encountered many more reference librarians who did not possess the interpersonal skills that would enable them to effectively engage with patrons or colleagues. Let me employ some literary license and tweak the title (with apologies to Sokolowski):

Essay Concerning the Sufficiency of Intellect in the Attainment of Excellence in Reference

IQ
Won't Do.

Consider the following case study: A librarian shares responsibility for delivering reference services with a number of fellow librarians. It soon becomes apparent that he is not well versed in all of the relevant reference tools, databases, and other resources. He sometimes struggles to craft efficient strategies to locate information, and although he always provides assistance, the quality and accuracy of his reference abilities are suspect. At the same time, he is unfailingly pleasant to the users and generates a warm and welcoming environment for them. International students especially appreciate his attention to them and seek him out. In the mornings, several students can often be found camped outside of his door waiting for his arrival. How would you judge the quality of this reference librarian, and why?

The question I pose to my readers is one that I have struggled with for years. The quality of this reference librarian's performance was judged by his colleagues almost solely on technical skills such as accuracy, timeliness, and knowledge of reference tools. With today's growing recognition of the power of soft skills to create a robust and welcoming information environment, perhaps the librarian in my scenario was a better reference librarian than his colleagues believed. Taking a lesson from the Disney company, which regards repeat attendance by "guests" as an important measurement of service quality, this librarian satisfied his patrons—including our international students—because they were willing to return to the library. Management could have improved his technical reference skills through mentoring and professional development. The message of this exercise is that libraries should strive to hire reference librarians who possess the soft skills that generate the trust and appreciation that stimulate repeat attendance, in person or online.

HARD SKILLS

I could generate a long list of technical skills that reference librarians should possess or develop. The good news is that the competency documentation referenced earlier covers these technical skills in detail, so it is not necessary to repeat them here. Technical skills for reference librarians generally fall into three areas: cognitive intelligence, academic credentials, and the practical skills or expertise necessary to perform the requirements of the position.

Cognitive intelligence relates to one's intellectual acumen, such as skills at reasoning, analyzing, and prioritizing as well as abilities in reading and writing. One could refer to this form of intelligence as "book smarts," often measured by academic honors, good grades, and scores on standardized tests. Education and experience contribute to the growth of cognitive intelligence. I have found that most reference librarians possess this form of intelligence and are distinguished by the depth and breadth of their knowledge base. Even so, as prospective employers, we continue to be attracted to candidates with vitas indicating degrees from top universities, graduation with honors, and receipt of fellowships.

The emerging controversy over the required academic credentials for librarians is becoming so intense that it merits its own chapter. Today's libraries house a mix of professional employees: They include librarians as well as professionals with expertise in human resources, IT, and public relations. The master of library science (MLS) degree and its equivalents (although the latter are partly the source of the controversy) will continue to be the standard for some time because they provide librarians with the fundamental values of the profession. I am buoyed by the high quality of candidates coming from our nationally ranked graduate schools of library and information studies, likely a result of a more rigorous and relevant curriculum and the increasing integration of internship requirements. However, I predict that academic research libraries will increasingly seek reference librarians who have second disciplinary masters and even doctorates. Having these advanced academic credentials will establish reference librarians' credibility with the teaching and research faculty at their institutions, enabling the librarians to be better liaisons and to build effective partnerships. Universities such as Ohio State and Columbia have already moved in this direction.

The technical competencies required for reference librarians will continue to evolve because our users' expectations change. For example, not long ago IT questions and support were not considered to be a reference librarian's responsibility but were delegated to another unit or to an individual with IT skills. Technology is now so integral to librarianship that we don't even discuss its separation from what reference librarians do. In his analysis of job advertisements, Gary W. White (1999) determined that "computer skills" were the primary technical skills required of subject librarians in all disciplines. At a recent ALA conference, two newly minted reference librarians, during a program uniquely titled *Thingamabobs and Doodads,* argued that tech support *is* a form of reference and that such queries should be warmly received by librarians to eliminate another barrier to access. They also advocated that everyone delivering reference service should be trained in core IT competencies such as personal computing basics, Web 2.0 fundamentals, and data management (Hibner and Kelly, 2009).

Anne Woodward (1997, 46) provides a succinct answer about the kind of IT skills that contemporary reference librarians should possess: "Basic competencies for every librarian must include knowing what the Internet is and is not; evaluating and using hardware, software, and networks; and understanding basic computer and information science concepts. We must be comfortable working with various search strategies, search engines, and emerging standards." Woodward also underscores how IT has pushed the necessity for complementary soft skills to the forefront: "True competency also entails being able to lead change within the organizations that libraries serve, as well as internally within libraries" (46). The World Wide Web was still in its infancy when Woodard wrote this, but her words are as relevant today as they were then.

SOFT SKILLS

In determining what soft skills are desired for reference librarians, or for that matter for any librarian, I found a remarkable consistency in the soft skills identified in the competency lists that are readily available in the literature. As a library administrator who hires and evaluates librarians, I have selected six skills or behavioral characteristics that I believe are critical to public services librarianship, today and tomorrow. Readers will note the strong interdependence among these attributes.

Public Service Attitude

Nothing is more elemental to reference librarianship than a positive service attitude; it is imperative that we hire reference librarians who consistently demonstrate the human element in their service delivery. We need librarians who show interest in our users and receptivity to their needs, even if the question posed is just "Where is the bathroom?" We need librarians who put the patron ahead of the conversation on their cell phone or the Web site on their computer screen. We need librarians who have positive, optimistic attitudes and pleasant demeanors. We need librarians who will bond with their colleagues to identify and deliver the new and improved services that increasingly define contemporary libraries. We need librarians who possess emotional stability, even in the face of challenging IT problems and difficult patrons. We need librarians who will go the extra mile for patrons and who are flexible enough to bend rules in the interest of good service.

Librarians still depend on users coming to them, whether the users walk in the door or make their connections through virtual means. What has changed radically is that users seeking information have many alternative avenues to pursue; the excellence of our collections and user services are often secondary to patrons, who seek convenience and ease of use first. More than 40 years ago, Mount (1966, 577) wrote about the negative reaction users have to librarians who "appear cold and disinterested." Radford (1998, 713) continued the discussion when she wrote that "talking on the phone, conversing with another person, and using the computer" were barriers "to connecting with librarians who are not to be interrupted." Libraries that do not have a strong service culture will find that they are marginalized and ignored. The reference or public service librarians must set the standard for this service excellence.

The service attitudes librarians require were honed in the reference desk environment; how relevant is a service attitude for digital and virtual reference? Very. In his "laundry list" of the personality traits needed for librarians in the new millennium, Tennant (1998, 102) includes "an abiding public service perspective." Any digital library will benefit from having staffers who understand the needs of its users and who will strive to meet those needs. Research emanating from the landmark Seeking Synchronicity study of virtual reference conducted at Rutgers indicates that reference librarians must employ specific behaviors to ensure successful virtual reference encounters. Creating relationships with distant patrons is difficult for reference librarians when body language and tone of voice, often considered the most critical elements in communications, are absent. Radford and Connaway (2007) advise librarians to build positive relationships with screenagers (young millennials born between 1988 and 1994) in order to change the image that this group has of librarians. Even though screenagers use chat frequently for social communications, they are deterred from using library chat services because they are intimidated by librarians they perceive as grumpy and unfriendly. The need for librarians who can deliver "high-tech, high-touch" user support does not diminish as libraries add more hardware and software to their suite of services. Greenwald (2009, n.p.), promoting new library services on mobile devices, shared these words of wisdom: "The human connection will make or break our institutional presence on the mobile web."

Never have service behaviors been more important to reference quality than in establishing rapport with our increasingly diverse patron base. Displaying patience, friendliness, warmth, and an interest in patrons takes on an even more critical role when encountering library users from varying cultures and backgrounds. Twenty-five years ago, I wrote the following in an article on international students in American libraries: "Hence a librarian's attitudes, behaviors, and instructional practices can do much to minimize the cultural conflicts that do occur and promote an enhanced understanding between librarian-educator and student" (Wayman, 1984, 340). According to Goleman (1998), possessing the emotional competence of *empathy* helps to leverage diversity. People with this attribute "respect and relate well to people from varied backgrounds" and "create an environment where diverse people can thrive" (184–185). The battle is still not won: Research conducted by Shachaf and Horowitz (2006) found that virtual reference service offered to African Americans and Arabs was of lower quality than that delivered to other groups.

Because libraries should be welcoming and hospitable, they can take cues from the hospitality industry. Restaurateur Danny Meyer, a strong proponent of integrating soft skills into the work environment, writes in his best-selling *Setting the Table* (2006) that successful hires are 49 percent technical skills, 51 percent soft or emotional skills. His restaurants have become world renowned for not just for the quality of their food but for the personal attention lavished on diners. For our 25th wedding anniversary, my husband and I treated ourselves to dinner at one of Meyer's restaurants, so I can provide a personal testimonial to the power of his vision. Meyer identifies five core employee skills that make his restaurants "champions of the team sport of hospitality":

- Optimistic warmth, or genuine kindness, thoughtfulness, and the sense that the glass is at least half full
- Intelligence, which includes an insatiable curiosity to learn for the sake of learning
- Work ethic
- Empathy, or an awareness of how your actions make others feel
- Self-awareness and integrity

I find Meyer's list of employee skills, rooted in the concept of EI, an excellent guide to the personal competencies that we want in our reference librarians. If we hire public service employees with these core skills, we will have libraries that are more hospitable. Meyer is demanding in his attention to core emotional skills: His new employees go through a rigorous training program that requires them to "audition" during a probationary period so that their behavioral characteristics can be determined. This might sound a bit draconian, but it reminds us that it is during the hiring process that we determine if potential librarians have the behavioral skills that we need and if they are willing to make a commitment to an organization that requires and enforces behavioral service standards. In 2009, Meyer was a featured speaker at a forum entitled *Service Excellence: Positioning Library Staffs for the Future* cosponsored by the New York Public Library and DeEtta Jones and Associates.

Collaboration

The future of libraries is in partnerships. Libraries can no longer exist as separate islands; instead, the partnerships they create make them stronger, more relevant, and better service organizations. Partnerships can be formed between libraries and external entities, including but not limited to other libraries, social service agencies, IT operations, academic departments, and school systems. One example would be an academic library collaborating with the university's computing center to develop an e-repository of faculty research. Within libraries, partnerships often exist in the form of teams, such as a project team directed to develop new services for an immigrant population. Partnerships can take many forms, but, ultimately, there is more strength in the partnership than in each of its entities acting separately. Librarians are able to use their rapport-building skills to foster collaboration among the partners or team members.

The late Ilene Rockman was a pioneer in developing partnerships between academic librarians and institutional faculty and administrators. She believed that reference librarians are ideally positioned to provide user-centered perspectives in the development, delivery, and promotion of new services. In a special issue of *Reference Services Review,* Rockman (2005, 258) wrote about the unique qualifications of reference librarians to engage in initiatives such as the development of institutional repositories (IRs):

> Reference librarians are natural partners to be involved in IRs. Their service orientation, subject experience as knowledge managers, and communication skills come easily into play as they serve as advocates for IRs, and interact with campus creators of new digital content, whether in the form of text, numeric, graphic, aural, or visual media. In addition, their knowledge and experience with interface design, policy development, and instructional techniques all contribute to the important role they play as a campus decides to develop an IR.

Tennant (1998, 102) underscored the importance of involving librarians who understand user needs in digital projects: "Many of those currently building digital libraries do not have a public service background, and it often shows in complicated and obtuse interfaces."

As collaboration becomes a core value in librarianship, the shy "lone ranger" librarian toiling privately behind closed doors becomes a relic of the past. However, becoming engaged in a new partnership or team can push a reference librarian into a larger, and sometimes unknown, context. Working outside of one's comfort zone requires behavioral characteristics such as tact and diplomacy. Such a librarian must possess a good measure of Goleman's EI, being aware of how her behaviors affect others. To be effective, she must know how far to advocate and when to compromise, when risk is acceptable, and must be able to accept a consensus when the group's decision is not to her liking. Political savvy also counts: Library directors who were surveyed in Herndon and Rossiter's study of EI ranked "ability to function in a political environment" first in the social skills needed for library leaders (2006, 267). Other important attributes are adaptability, the capacity to learn new skills, and a willingness to create bridges between team members and partners marked by diversity and generational differences.

Leadership

Leadership and supervisory qualities are not the same. Whereas it is highly desirable to have managers who are also leaders, leaders often do not have managerial responsibilities. I've observed that being unburdened by management stress and the requirement to be a "rule enforcer" allows leaders to be more creative and to openly speak their minds. We've all known reference librarians who can quiet an audience when they approach a microphone because everyone anticipates that cogent ideas and pearls of wisdom will emerge.

Because there is evidence that new librarians often move quickly into supervisory roles, we should strive to hire librarians who possess leadership potential. Goleman (1998) determined that leadership effectiveness was directly related to EI. Leaders who were considered to be top performers possessed behavioral attributes and the emotional balance that enabled them to work well with others; their technical expertise was of secondary concern. Emotionally resilient individuals "are likely to be better able to handle the stress and strain of today's information jobs than emotionally reactive individuals" (Williamson, Pemberton, and Lounsbury, 2005, 135). The old-fashioned rule-based, autocratic library manager has little place in contemporary libraries that exist in an environment of whirlwind change and galloping technology. These micromanagers can suppress creativity; they often undervalue librarians who learn new things quickly and like to experiment.

More than ever, libraries need leaders in public services with the EI to effectively shepherd teams, bring projects and initiatives to fruition, instill confidence, and motivate their colleagues. They guide and coach instead of micromanage, provide resources when needed, and encourage reference librarians to think outside the parameters of their everyday world to explore and imagine new ways of delivering information services. As contemporary libraries are buffeted by rapid change, these leaders foster transformational change, so critical to the future of our libraries: "An emotionally intelligent leader appears to have much in common with transformational leadership" (Herndon and Rossiter, 2006, 272).

Project Management

Kinkus (2007, 352) writes that "the rapid proliferation of complex library services such as virtual reference and digital repositories suggests that the role of librarians is increasingly becoming project-oriented." Within my own library, new initiatives are often developed and managed by project teams representing a variety of areas of expertise and perspectives. For example, a project team assigned to create a digital library could include a reference librarian, an archivist, a metadata specialist, a scanning specialist, and a Web developer.

Although many reference librarians have neither education nor background in project management, Kinkus found that librarians are very interested in enhancing their project management skills. What skills are important to project management? When project managers were asked what skills and characteristics were evident in the best project managers they knew, they ranked human skills first and technical skills, or the knowledge of the tools and techniques of project management, last. Project management is a natural extension of the group culture becoming so prevalent in libraries (Kinkus, 2007). Bolton (2005, 64) writes, "The emphasis of the future has to be in the leadership and interpersonal skills that ensure sound management practices. Projects fail because relationships and expectations fail."

Libraries that want to be on the cutting edge of public services should engage reference librarians who can provide vision, facilitate initiatives, and motivate others in crafting strategies that will move goals and projects to fruition. Reference librarians represent the user perspective; therefore, they should be integral to any project with a public services perspective—and that is most of them. The best librarians for this assignment are strategic thinkers who possess the attributes of both linear and creative thinking. Many are skilled at problem solving. Being cognizant of the trends and developments in librarianship and related fields enables librarians to be more forward thinking. Organizational ability is critical, since projects must adhere to timelines; contrary to conventional wisdom, organization is not an innate skill of librarians.

Communications

Communications skills have always been the heart of the reference interview, whether delivered face to face (FtF) or virtually. Effective communication skills inform how reference librarians can best deliver information for a given situation: They help to bridge the gap between reference librarians and diverse populations, between reference librarians and patrons from different generations, and between reference librarians and their distant, virtual audiences. The introduction to the *Guidelines for Behavioral Performance of Reference and Information Service Providers* states, "One constant that the shift away from in-person encounters has not lessened is the need for good communication skills. In all forms of reference services, the success of the transaction is measured not only by the information conveyed, but also by the positive or negative impact of the patron/staff interaction. The positive or negative behavior of the reference staff member (as observed by the patron) becomes a significant factor in perceived success or failure" (Reference and User Services Association, 2004, n.p.). By analyzing the transcripts of chat reference sessions, Shachaf and Horowitz (2008) discovered that more than half the librarians neglected to extend a cordial welcome or pleasant sign-off, contrary to common reference service standard guidelines. Obviously, focused attention must continue to be directed to how reference librarians communicate with their patrons.

Communications ability is the most requested soft skill in advertisements for public service librarians. In her study of library job advertisements, Starr (2004) found no advertisements in 1973 that identified communication skills as a necessary qualification. In contrast, by 1983, over 20 percent and by 2003, over 50 percent of ads called for these skills. White's (1999) analyses of job advertisements for subject librarians discovered that communications skills were the most frequently requested qualification, regardless of the discipline of the subject librarian being sought. He found similar results when he analyzed advertisements for heads of reference (White, 2000). Wu and Li (2008) had similar findings from their content analysis of medical reference position announcements.

Articulation skills underpin many new roles for librarians, including partnership development, marketing, and team building. Key among desired oral communications is the capability to present ideas clearly and persuasively and to adapt this skill to the audience. Public library reference librarians speak to community groups, persuade and inform municipal government officials, and train library users; academic reference librarians teach classes, reach out to faculty and students as liaisons, and deliver professional presentations. Today's librarians engage broadly in their communities, and the presence they establish as communicators has much to do with the perceptions of their libraries.

Libraries foster the use of their services and collections through marketing, and no marketing strategy is more valuable than positive word of mouth from a satisfied customer. A librarian's skill at communicating, whether it is evident in how she answers a reference question or through verbal or oral communications, is an opportunity to create a positive library presence and is therefore a form of marketing. When we interview prospective reference librarians, a public presentation is included in the interview. As I observe these sessions, I think about the kind of impression the librarian is making on her audience and how she would be perceived by teaching faculty, a project team, a patron, or her departmental colleagues.

Adaptability

If there is one mantra in librarianship, it is "change is the only constant." I posit that change itself is not the challenge but the rapidity of it. In an article on technostress that a colleague and I coauthored, we wrote, "For many, the feeling of being 'a hamster in a cage' increases as the number and speed of microcomputers grows. Somehow we have set our work rhythms to correspond to the steady, quick space of the computer. The faster our machines, the faster our work flows and the higher our expectations for productivity" (Kalin and Clark, 1996, 30). My mental image of change conjures up that hamster running faster and faster inside his spinning wheel.

Public service librarians should embrace change, not push it away. It's not just technology that is generating change—although it is often identified as the key culprit—but also transformations in user expectations, service patterns, budget scenarios, workloads, organizational structures, and working relationships. Reference librarians should be self-motivated to adapt to change; many learn new procedures and master new technologies on their own. Within my library, the reference librarians who are among the most innovative and adaptable to technological change are those who obtain or buy—sometimes on their own dime—the latest handheld device or software, learn it quickly, explore ways that it could be integrated into their own lifestyles, and then turn their attention to how it could be integrated into our services. Their adaptive behaviors mimic those of our users, so they are positioned to determine how the latest innovation would be adopted and perceived by our patrons. Tennant also advocates for the hiring of staff who are flexible and can enable change: "Since change is constant, organizations need staff who can guide it, using judgment and communicating well. They must be able to distinguish between whining and constructive criticism. They should sense when to advocate and when to compromise" (1998, 102).

Talented reference librarians will thrive if they are able to work for managers who support them as they adapt to change. For example, managers should provide reference librarians with the latitude to experiment and, yes, even "play" with emerging technologies. This can stimulate the creative juices, which results in innovative and enhanced services. Herndon and Rossiter (2006, 274) wrote that a transformational leader is "an agent of change, a catalyst for change, *but not a controller of change.*" Furthermore, this leader should inspire a shared vision and "move followers to transcend their own self interest for the good of the group and organization" (Herndon and Rossiter, 2006, 273). Some of the most inventive service initiatives come out of small public and academic libraries where there are fewer bureaucratic hurdles; because of their small size, they can be more agile organizations.

Traditionally, librarians are not known as strong innovators. Rabina and Walczyk (2007) found that most librarians are second-tier (early) or fourth-tier (late majority) adopters of innovation. Reference librarians can find themselves like that hamster, running faster and faster to fill in the gaps developing between the current technologies used in their libraries and users' demands for the newest and more innovative technologies. Research conducted by Williamson, Pemberton, and Lounsbury (2008) categorized librarians by personality traits. The group identified as "unadaptive" was characterized by low emotional resilience, low optimism, and low work drive. These behavioral characteristics are undesirable in public service librarians and constitute a strong argument for hiring librarians who demonstrate adaptability to change.

I don't want to give the impression that change involves only technology. Librarians deal with generational differences in our user populations and in our workforce. There can be critical differences in how reference librarians and reference managers interact with Generation X, Generation Y, and the baby boomer generations. The half-life of these generations is getting shorter, increasing librarians' need for agility to deal with each generation's members. Even so, adaptability means that librarians must be wary of overgeneralizing the anticipated behaviors of members of the various generations. Not all college students are tech-savvy, nor are all baby boomers rigid and inflexible. During a recent encounter with honors students at my institution,

I was surprised by their ignorance of basic Web 2.0 technologies. I also believe that the adaptation of the enormous cohort of baby boomer librarians to technological changes has been underestimated. Because baby boomers were not reared as digital natives, their learning curves have been especially steep and broad, yet they continue to provide leadership to the profession.

Not long ago librarians were the only professionals in libraries. Today, librarians serve alongside a cadre of other professionals with skills in areas such as IT, public relations, and human resources. How librarians adapt to and collaborate with other professional colleagues is essential to the health of the entire library. In academic libraries, forces such as interdisciplinarity and globalization are changing the curricula, research agendas, and even the makeup of the student body. Academic reference librarians' effectiveness will depend on their capacity to adapt to this emerging academic environment and to engage in new ways with faculty and students.

Reference librarians are consistently challenged to serve everyone, to treat everyone equitably, and to meet a myriad of user expectations and demands. To do this well, it is imperative that reference librarians possess the flexibility to modify their behaviors and approaches to their patrons, regardless of who they are.

CONCLUSION AND CHALLENGES

Excellent reference librarians possess a combination of strong technical expertise (hard skills) and appropriate behavioral attributes (soft skills). In recent years, employers and educators have been placing a growing emphasis on the soft skills that are critical to delivering excellent services. The good news about hard skills is that they can often be taught to librarians, as long as the aptitude and motivation to learn them exist. For reference librarians, learning new skills is a constantly evolving process.

Soft skills, in contrast, often cannot be taught because they are more innate to the individuals. Librarians without patience cannot suddenly develop it, although they can learn to manage their impatience better. The best way to ensure that reference librarians have the requisite EI is to hire for it. A 2009 advertisement in the *Chronicle of Higher Education* for a reference position at the U.S. Military Academy cleverly combined hard and soft skills: "We welcome applications from those with a record of inspired teaching, a command of academic reference tools and literature, a solid record of scholarship, and dynamic leadership characterized by the ability to embolden, teach, and empower colleagues" (n.p.).

The challenge is how to determine if candidates have these attributes. Adler and Devlin (2004) have developed an excellent list of interview questions that should help prospective employees to ferret out those candidates with the personal characteristics they seek. A hiring model that has been proposed for IT positions might also work for librarians: filtering out candidates using technical skill requirements but making the final choice based on an assessment of the candidates' soft skills as gathered through the interview and other factors (Litecky, Arnett, and Prabhakar, 2004). Herndon and Rossiter (2006) surveyed library directors to determine what EI attributes they desired in employees and then analyzed job advertisements to see if these attributes were being sought. Unfortunately, they were not, indicating that there continues to be a serious disconnect between our actual hiring practices and our desire to bring librarians with the appropriate behavioral attributes into our organizations.

Appropriate reference behaviors can be incorporated into our performance review and professional development process. Library managers should not tolerate librarians or other staff members who are disengaged, rude, or intolerant of users. When possible, training and other professional development opportunities should be used to enhance soft skills and their applications in the library environment. David Tyckoson (1992) developed an assessment tool that evaluates reference librarians on personality and behavioral factors that can impact the user's experience in a reference encounter.

Librarians should encourage graduate schools of library and information studies to recruit and enroll students who have the personal characteristics to excel in librarianship and to modify their curricula to incorporate the development of soft skills needed by future professionals. Arns and Price (2007) surveyed new library supervisors to determine what competencies they needed as managers. The respondents identified skills such as problem solving, oral communication, leading, and interpersonal skills but also indicated that their graduate programs did not adequately prepare them with these competencies. The *Standards for Accreditation of Master's Programs in Library and Information Studies,* adopted by the ALA in January 2008, states that "the design of specialized learning experiences takes into account the statements of knowledge and competencies developed by relevant professional organizations" (8). This behooves librarians to advocate for the development of competency statements that document both hard and soft skills.

At heart, I am still a reference librarian. Even though the progression of my career has seen a dramatic change in what reference librarians do, what has not changed is the formula of how they do it: with skill, courtesy, and kindness.

WORKS CITED

Adler, J. L., and S. H. Devlin. 2004. *The human resources perspective on the [academic library] job-hunt.* Retrieved July 10, 2009, from http://www.ala.org/ala/mgrps/rts/nmrt/oversightgroups/comm/resreview/hr.cfm.

American Library Association. 2008. *Standards for accreditation of master's programs in library and information studies.* Retrieved July 10, 2009, from http://www.ala.org/ala/educationcareers/education/accreditedprograms/standards/standards_2008.pdf.

American Library Association. 2009. *ALA's core competencies of librarianship.* Retrieved July 10, 2009, from http://www.ala.org/ala/educationcareers/careers/corecomp/corecompetences/finalcorecompstat09.pdf.

Arns, J. W., and C. Price. 2007. To market, to market: The supervisory skills and managerial competencies most valued by new library supervisors. *Library Administration and Management* 21 (1): 13–19.

Bolton, B. 2005. 10 tips for becoming a successful manager. *InformationWeek* 1025: 64.

Coffman, S. 2002. Be it resolved that reference librarians are not toast. *American Libraries* 33 (4): 51–54.

Eidson, M. 2000. Using "emotional intelligence" in the reference interview. *Colorado Libraries* 26 (2): 8–10.

Farkas, M. 2006. *Information wants to be free.* Retrieved July 29, 2009, from http://meredith.wolfwater.com/wordpress/2006/07/17/skills-for-the-21st-century-librarian.

Fisher, A. 2007. The trouble with MBA's. *Fortune* 155 (8): 49.

Goleman, D. 1995. *Emotional intelligence.* New York: Basic Books.

Goleman, D. 1998. *Working with emotional intelligence.* New York: Bantam.

Greenwald, T. 2009. *Catalog notices to cell phones* [Webcast]. Presentation to The Handheld Librarian 2009: An Online Conference about Mobile Library Services, July 30, 2009.

Herndon, P., and N. Rossiter. 2006. Emotional intelligence: Which traits are most prized? *College & Research Libraries* 67 (3): 670–675.

Hibner, H., and M. Kelly. *Thingamabobs and doodads: Why tech support is reference.* Paper presented at the American Library Association Annual Conference, July 6, 2009. Additional information in "Librarians Say Tech Support Can Be Reference." *Library Hotline* 38 (29): 5.

Joselle, K. 2007. A hipper crowd of shushers. *New York Times*, July 8, Style section, Eastern edition, 1.

Kalin, S., and K. Clark. 1996. Technostressed out? How to cope in the digital age. *Library Journal* 121 (13): 30–32.

Kinkus, J. 2007. Project management skills: A literature review and content analysis of librarian positions announcements. *College & Research Libraries* 68 (4): 352–363.

Litecky, C. R., K. P. Arnett, and B. Prabhakar. 2004. The paradox of soft skills versus technical skills in IS hiring. *Journal of Computer Information Systems* 45 (1): 69–76.

Meyer, D. 2006. *Setting the table: The transforming power of hospitality in business.* New York: HarperCollins.

Mount, E. 1966. Communication barriers and the reference question. *Special Libraries* 57 (8): 575–578.

Promis, P. 2008. Are employers asking for the right competencies: A case for emotional intelligence. *Library Administration and Management* 28 (1): 24–30.

Rabina, D. L., and D. J. Walczyk. 2007. Information professionals' attitude toward the adoption of innovations in everyday life. *Information Research* 12 (4). Retrieved July 10, 2009, from http://InformationR.net/ir/12-4/colis12.html.

Radford, M. L. 1998. Approach or avoidance? The role of nonverbal communication in the academic library user's decision to initiate reference encounters. *Library Trends* 46 (4): 699–717.

Radford, M. L. 2008. A personal choice: Reference service excellence. *Reference & User Services Quarterly* 48 (2): 108–115.

Radford, M. L., and L. S. Connaway. 2007. Screenagers and live chat reference: Living up to the promise. *Scan* 26 (1): 31–39. Retrieved July 10, 2009, from http://www.oclc.org/research/publications/archive/2007/connaway_scan.pdf.

Reference and User Services Association. 2003. *Professional competencies for reference and user services librarians.* Retrieved July 10, 2009, from http://www.ala.org/ala/mgrps/divs/rusa/resources/guidelines/professional.cfm.

Reference and User Services Association. 2004. *Guidelines for behavioral performance of reference and information service providers.* Retrieved July 10, 2009, from http://www.ala.org/ala/mgrps/divs/rusa/resources/guidelines/guidelines behavioral.cfm.

Rockman, I. F. 2005. Editorial: Distinct and expanded roles for reference librarians. *Reference Services Review* 33 (3): 258.

Shachaf, P., and S. M. Horowitz. 2006. Are virtual reference services color blind? *Library and Information Science Research* 28 (4): 501–520.

Shachaf, P., and S. M. Horowitz. 2008. Virtual reference service evaluation: Adherence to RUSA behavioral guidelines and IFLA digital reference guidelines. *Library and Information Science Research* 30 (2): 122–137.

Starr, J. 2004. A measure of change: Comparing library job advertisements of 1983 and 2003. *LIBRES: Library and Information Science Research Electronic Journal* 14 (2). Retrieved July 10, 2009, from http://libres.curtin.edu.au/li bres14n2/contents.htm.

Tennant, R. 1998. The most important management decision: Hiring staff for the new millennium. *Library Journal* 123 (3): 102.

Thompson, S. M. 2009. History and overview of technology competencies in libraries. In *Core technology competencies for librarians and library staff; a LITA guide,* ed. S. M. Thompson, 3–40. New York: Neal-Schuman.

Tyckoson, D. A. 1992. Wrong questions, wrong answers: Behavioral vs. factual evaluation of reference service. In *Assessment and accountability in reference work,* ed. S. G. Blandy, L. M. Martin, and M. L. Strife, 151–173. New York: Haworth.

Wayman, S. G. 1984. The international student in the academic library. *Journal of Academic Librarianship* 9 (6): 336–341.

White, G. W. 1999. Academic subject specialist positions in the United States: A content analysis of announcements from 1990 through 1998. *Journal of Academic Librarianship* 25 (5): 372–382.

White, G. W. 2000. Head of reference positions in academic libraries: A survey of job announcements from 1990 through 1999. *Reference & User Services Quarterly* 39 (3): 2665–2273.

Williamson, J. M., A. E. Pemberton, and J. W. Lounsbury. 2005. An investigation of career and job satisfaction in relation to personality traits of informational professionals. *Library Quarterly* 75 (2): 122–141.

Williamson, J. M., A. E. Pemberton, and J. W. Lounsbury. 2008. Personality traits of individuals in different specialties of librarianship. *Journal of Documentation* 64 (2): 273–286.

Woodward, A. 1997. New library competencies. *Library Journal* 122 (9): 46.

Wu, L., and P. Li. 2008. What do they want? A content analysis of Medical Library Association reference job announcements, 2000–2005. *Journal of the Medical Library Association* 96 (4): 378–381.

21

RETIREMENTS IN REFERENCE: PASSING THE TORCH TO THE NEXT GENERATION OF REFERENCE LIBRARIANS

Charlotte Ford and Lili Luo

The baby boom generation was born during the demographic birth explosion between 1946 and 1964 (U.S. Census Bureau, 2006). According to the most recent census, baby boomers constitute the largest age group in the United States (U.S. Census Bureau, 2000), and they account for a significant percentage (around 37 percent) of the labor force (Bureau of Labor Statistics, 2008). Among librarians, the concentration of baby boomers is even higher. More than two-thirds of the nation's 158,000 librarians are 45 or older (Bureau of Labor Statistics, 2007). Wilder states that "relative to comparable professions, it [the library profession] contains one third the number of individuals aged 35 and under and almost 75 percent more individuals aged 45 and over. Librarians, particularly academic librarians, are older than professionals in all but a handful of comparable occupations" (2001, n.p.).

These statistics indicate that the baby boomers' retirement will affect the library profession greatly, and issues related to the impending labor gap have been attracting attention from library professionals. Wilder points out that "the approaching wave of retirements may be the most important human resources phenomenon facing the library profession" (2002, n.p.). A number of problems that might arise along with the retirement wave have been identified in the literature, among which labor shortages are the most obvious. It is projected that 27 percent of Association of Research Libraries (ARL) librarians will retire between 2010 and 2020 (Wilder, 2001), and labor shortages will affect not just academic libraries but also public, school, and special libraries (Everhart, 2000; Lynch, 2002; McConnell, 2004). Recruitment and retention hence become ever more important and challenging given the traditional issues of low salaries and the availability of higher-paying alternative career choices for entry-level librarians (Kaufman, 2002). Acknowledging the challenges, Castiglione (2006) calls for innovative recruiting and mentoring programs to be designed to attract students to library careers, as well as effective strategies to be implemented to retain older librarians who are about to retire, reemploy retired librarians on a part-time basis, and even attract older employees from other fields into the library profession.

Another frequently discussed problem related to baby boomer librarian retirement is the loss of valuable knowledge and skills. Castiglione (2006) indicates that with the retirement of older administrators, a wealth of experience and leadership skills obtained during a lifetime of employment will be lost. There is some concern that the knowledge base may "walk out the door" with the retiring boomers (O'Connor, 2007, 67). Solutions include a variety of bridge employment options that are designed to allow more experienced librarians to mentor new librarians and to pass on important administrative and technical skills (Castiglione, 2006; Curran, 2003; Howze, 2003). The fundamental principle of bridge employment is to get retiring librarians involved in the professional development of new librarians and create a conduit to transmit their valuable knowledge and skills.

INVESTIGATING THE EFFECTS OF RETIREMENTS ON REFERENCE LIBRARIANSHIP

We were interested in exploring how the graying of the profession and looming retirements were affecting the field of reference librarianship and how libraries were responding to these changes. Along with the challenges already enumerated, reference librarianship has been under siege in recent years, facing serious questions about the relevance of reference services in an age of search engines and self-service (*Perceptions,* 2005), about the precipitous decline in reference queries at ARL libraries over the past decade (ARL and University of Virginia, 2008), and about just what, exactly, reference librarians are "transitioning" to (Hardesty, 2002). A wave of retirements could be devastating to the field, providing an opportunity for fiscally challenged libraries to drastically reduce reference staffing and services. Alternatively, mass retirements could provide an opportunity for libraries to revitalize their reference services by reconsidering the needs of library users and recruiting and training new professionals to respond energetically to these needs. Accordingly, we asked the following questions:

- To what extent are reference librarians retiring?
- Are libraries actively seeking to fill vacancies in reference?
- Are libraries offering incentives to encourage current employees to become reference librarians?
- Are they offering incentives to recruit recent master of library and information science (MLIS) graduates into reference librarianship?

- Do libraries have programs in place to mentor new reference librarians?
- What skills and abilities are libraries looking for in aspiring reference librarians?

We chose to do an online survey of academic and public libraries to get a sense of current trends in reference retirement and recruitment, and we analyzed recent job announcements to see what libraries were requiring of new reference librarians. Both strategies gave us a sense of where the profession was heading—a feel for the future. But retirements are also about the past; each individual who retires takes with him or her years of accumulated skills, along with vast stores of professional, institutional, and personal knowledge. Mindful of this fact, we also interviewed a small number of career reference librarians (all within 10 years of retirement) to get their impressions of not only where the field is heading but also what skills have become more and less important over time and what skills or talents might be lost altogether as reference librarians of their generation exit the field.

SURVEYING THE PROFESSION

To get a sense of institutional trends in retirement, recruitment, and in-house training for reference work, we invited the heads of reference or public services at 95 libraries in the United States to participate in a brief online survey on baby boomer reference librarians and retirement. The *Nation's Largest Libraries* fact sheet of the American Library Association (ALA, 2009) provided an easy way to identify a set of public and academic libraries that were likely to have large reference departments, with measurable turnover in staffing. Heads of reference or public services for the main or central library at each of these institutions were identified using the *American Library Directory* (2009), and their names and e-mail addresses were confirmed or updated through visits to each library's Web site. The Library of Congress was eliminated from the list of libraries to be surveyed (as it is an atypical library), as were four other libraries that had no readily identifiable central or main library. In the end, invitations to participate in the survey were sent to librarians at 71 academic and 24 public libraries in May 2009. A follow-up reminder/thank-you e-mail was sent out 10 days later.

Forty-one librarians responded to the survey, an overall response rate of 43 percent. The response rate was slightly higher among academic librarians, such that 80 percent (33) of the respondents worked in academic libraries and 20 percent (8) in public libraries.

REFERENCE DEPARTMENT SIZES AND TRENDS

The survey provided the Reference and User Services Association (RUSA)'s definition for reference work, which includes "reference transactions and other activities that involve the creation, management, and assessment of information or research resources, tools, and services" (RUSA, 2008). The survey then asked how many reference librarians (librarians who devoted "a significant portion of their work time to reference work") were currently employed in the respondent's library, how this number had changed in the past five years, how many reference librarians had retired from the library over the past five years, and whether the library planned to fill positions in reference as librarians retired. The number of reference librarians employed in respondents' libraries ranged from 0 to 49, with a mean of 17.4 reference librarians (the median was 15).

With regard to trends in the size of reference departments, over half of the libraries (51 percent) had seen a decrease in the number of reference librarians working in the library over the past five years. Thirty-four percent reported that the number had remained constant, and less than 15 percent had experienced growth in the number of reference positions. Public library reference departments were both larger and more vulnerable: Among the eight responding, all but one (where the number of reference librarian positions had remained constant) reported a decrease in the number of reference librarian positions. In contrast, while 42 percent of the academic libraries reported a decrease in the number of reference librarian positions, close to 40 percent of the academic libraries reported that the number had remained the same, and 18 percent actually reported an increase in the number of reference positions. Economic reasons were cited by a number of respondents as the primary reason behind the shrinking of the reference department; several mentioned that certain reference responsibilities had been taken over by library assistants.

Retirements had occurred over the past five years in almost all of the libraries: 83 percent (34 of the 41 responding libraries) had seen at least one retirement from the reference department. But it appeared that a huge wave of retirements had not yet hit: 51 percent of the libraries reported zero or one retirements, 27 percent reported between two and four retirements, and only 22 percent of the libraries had experienced five or more retirements in the past five years. However, when asked if (to the best of their knowledge) their libraries planned to fill positions in reference as librarians retired, many respondents seemed uncertain: While 51 percent said "yes," more than 36 percent said they did not know, and 12 percent responded "no." Budgetary constraints were mentioned once again as contributing to the uncertainty, and it was clear from the comments that libraries were giving careful thought to how new librarians' time might best be spent; as one respondent noted, "We are re-thinking every position when it becomes available."

MAINTAINING AND "GROWING" REFERENCE DEPARTMENTS AND LIBRARIANS

The survey also asked about strategies libraries were employing to maintain or enhance the reference departments at their institutions—by delaying retirements, hiring previously retired reference librarians on a part-time basis, mentoring new reference librarians, supporting staff with an interest in reference work in their pursuit of a professional degree, or recruiting recent master of library science (MLS) and MLIS graduates into reference librarianship. None of the libraries had programs in place to delay retirement. One librarian commented, "If anything, there is more of an incentive to retire, than delay it." Another wrote, "Quite the opposite! I'd love to be able to encourage some of the more senior faculty to move on. I need energetic, enthusiastic, technology embracing librarians, and several of my senior librarians are stuck in old patterns." However, most of the libraries seemed to value older librarians' skills: Seven of the eight public libraries reported hiring previously retired reference librarians on a part-time basis, as did eight of the responding academic libraries (nearly a quarter).

Forty-four percent (18) of the libraries reported having a mentoring program for new reference librarians in place. While all of these programs were in academic libraries, half of the public libraries said that informal mentoring of new reference librarians occurred. And the vast majority of libraries (more than 85 percent, including all of the public libraries and 82 percent of the academic libraries) offered tuition assistance, flex time, scholarships, or other incentives to assist library support staff who might be interested in a career in reference to earn an ALA-accredited MLS or MLIS degree. Both tuition benefits and flex time (or even release time) were quite common. One respondent seemed to summarize the general mood, stating that "we do everything we can to encourage library staff to consider library degrees and to consider reference librarianship." In addition, about a third of the libraries said they offered (or had offered in the past) fellowships, internships, or residency programs for newly minted librarians or MLS and MLIS candidates interested in reference.

Finally, the survey asked respondents whether all of the reference librarians currently working in their libraries held an ALA-accredited MLS or MLIS degree. Responses indicated a certain amount of flexibility in the composition of reference departments: 12 of the respondents (close to 30 percent) said that not all reference librarians at their institutions possessed an ALA-accredited master's degree. People within a few credits of finishing the MLIS degree, along with highly experienced library assistants, individuals with PhDs in other fields, and several with master's degrees in geographic information systems (GIS) were employed as reference librarians. Additionally, some of those who said their institution *did* have an ALA-accredited MLIS requirement for librarians explained that the reference desk was staffed by both professional librarians and library assistants (a common arrangement). These findings suggest that reference librarianship is a flexible field, one that apparently has room to embrace the talents of a wide range of people—from intelligent high school graduates to highly specialized PhDs.

GENERATIONAL SHIFT IN REFERENCE

More than half of the respondents (22 of the 41) chose to share additional thoughts about how the retirement of baby boomer reference librarians was affecting, or would affect, reference librarianship. Half of the comments focused on the shift away from traditional models of reference librarianship, emphasizing that fewer people were working exclusively as reference librarians and that greater attention was being given to instruction, outreach, programming, and technical work such as Web-page design and digitization projects (and less to desk duty). Several respondents cited the importance of technological skills and openness to change in the new reference environment. A typical comment was "Because reference librarianship is changing so dramatically, there will be fewer traditional reference librarians as the years pass, and more librarians who multi-task doing a bit of reference, instruction, digitizing, and other technical work."

Several of the respondents noted that while retirements had not yet hit full force at their institutions, a wave of retirements was on the horizon; others expressed concern about the economic crunch affecting their ability to fill vacancies. More than a quarter of the comments lamented the loss of knowledge (of sources and interview techniques) that accompanied, or would accompany, baby boomer retirements. "It will be very important to plan for succession, particularly in large research libraries where professionals have spent decades building knowledge that should be shared in advance of their retirement," wrote one respondent. Another commented, "Baby boomer reference librarians skills are grounded in a thorough knowledge of traditional reference sources. As they retire, there will be a gap since the reference librarian of the twenty-first century is more adept at using technology but has less familiarity with the actual source material." The general sentiment seemed to be that older and newer librarians each had something to offer. As one respondent put it, "Retiring librarians need to pass along their knowledge and skills to the next generation. But the next generation need[s] to add to that new knowledge and skills that might have evaded the retiring librarians."

Last, there was some concern about the future of service, with several comments stressing the continued importance—and challenge—of providing high-quality reference service in a time of shrinking budgets. "I've already seen a real significant change in service," wrote one respondent. "The new hires to replace the experienced are better at the behaviors of customer service, but not as knowledgeable of the resources or areas of research questioning as the more seasoned librarians. So there is still good service being provided, but it is a very different kind of service." Another considered that the "younger voices" in reference "bring great perspective to methods which we take for granted and help us to question the status quo." Even as some knowledge and skills are lost, it appears a great opportunity awaits.

RESPONSIBILITIES OF THE NEXT GENERATION OF REFERENCE PROFESSIONALS

The logical question to ask next is whether libraries are seizing this opportunity and restructuring reference librarianship in ways that meet the current needs of library users as vacancies occur due to retirements or other reasons. What responsibilities are newly hired reference librarians being asked to take on, and what skills and abilities do the hiring libraries want them to bring to the workplace?

To answer this question, we conducted a content analysis of 100 job announcements for reference and user services positions. The sample was selected from all the position announcements posted to the largest listserv for reference librarians, libref-l, using the cluster sampling method. Since we sought to investigate the most recent requirements for reference positions, we chose the time period from January 2008 to December 2008 as the cluster in sampling design to ensure currency. A total of 207 job announcements were published on libref-l during this period of time, but 107 of them were not eligible for the study because they were either recruiting nonreference positions (such as catalogers or library directors) or lacking detailed job descriptions. Among the 100 job announcements eligible for analysis, 91 were for academic reference positions and only 9 sought to recruit public librarians.

The previously mentioned RUSA definition of reference work ("reference transactions and other activities that involve the creation, management, and assessment of information or research resources, tools, and services") was clearly reflected in the job responsibilities listed in the announcements for reference and user services positions—though responsibilities also went beyond the RUSA definition to include instruction and outreach activities. Five major areas of responsibility were identified from the sample:

- *Assisting specified user groups to meet their information needs.* An essential responsibility of reference librarians is to help library users identify and locate the information they are seeking. All of the examined job posts listed this responsibility. In addition to providing information assistance to the general public, some positions required special attention to particular user groups, such as children, students and faculty in a specific academic discipline, and Spanish speakers.
- *Delivering or coordinating information literacy instruction.* Although it is excluded from the official RUSA definition of reference work, information literacy instruction is an integral part of academic reference service. Among the 91 position announcements for academic librarians, 22 percent listed job titles like "instruction librarian" or "information literacy librarian" and specified information literacy instruction as the top job responsibility; the rest simply included it in the general description of job responsibilities.

- *Managing and developing reference collections and collections in responsible subject areas.* The responsibility of collection development is twofold for many reference librarians. Not only are they expected to maintain collections of reference materials, but some academic reference librarians are also asked to assist in the development of subject-specific collections, depending on the subject areas for which they are responsible. Sixty-four percent of the examined job announcements listed collection development as a job responsibility, and most of them included both general reference collection development and subject-specific collection development.
- *Serving as liaisons to academic departments.* Liaisons are generally interpreted as academic librarians maintaining communication and collaboration with faculty and students in different disciplines on campus, in order to best serve their needs for information assistance and collection development. Among the 69 job posts that included academic liaisonship as a responsibility, 36 percent highlighted academic disciplines that the prospective librarian would be responsible for in the job title (such as "education librarian" or "science librarian") and specified the programs and departments that the librarian would be a liaison for in the job description. The remainder simply indicated that there would be liaison responsibilities, without identifying specific disciplines.
- *Developing outreach programs to promote reference and user services.* Thirty-seven percent of the studied job announcements listed outreach as a responsibility, requiring librarians to lead or participate in outreach activities to increase the user community's awareness of library reference and user services.

QUALITIES OF THE NEXT GENERATION OF REFERENCE PROFESSIONALS

The knowledge, skills, and abilities that employers were looking for in the job announcements can be grouped into 12 categories, as indicated in table 21.1. The literature abounds with efforts to identify the qualities requisite for providing reference and user services (e.g., Auster and Chan, 2003; Bauner, 1990; Griffiths and King, 1986; Kong, 1996; Massey-Burzio, 1991; Nitecki, 1984; Nofsinger, 1999; RUSA, 2003; Sherrer, 1996; Smith, Marchant, and Nielson, 1984; Stafford and Serban, 1990; Walters and Barnes, 1985). Results of these studies can be summarized into the following areas:

- Ability to conduct an effective reference interview
- Knowledge of referral methods and techniques
- Knowledge of standard print and electronic sources and the primary subject field of users served
- Communication and interpersonal skills
- Technological skills

Table 21.1.
Quality Requirements for Reference and User Service Positions

Desirable Qualities	*Percentage of Job Announcements Listing These Qualities*
Excellent oral and written communication skills and interpersonal skills	78
Ability to work both independently and as a team member	61
Interest in and knowledge of reference service, user instruction, and other assigned duties (e.g., knowledge of reference resources, information search skills, understanding of learning theories, and mastery of instructional technologies)	58
Strong knowledge of information technologies and their application in library reference work	55
Flexibility, including flexibility in work schedule (e.g., to work nights and weekends), in adapting to a rapidly changing environment, and in working with a culturally diverse user community	45
Strong commitment to user-centered service	40
Self motivation in participating in professional development activities (e.g., scholarly writing and publication, attending professional conferences, serving the professional community) and demonstrating potential for promotion	34
Organizational skills	19
Creativity and initiative	17
Ability to work under pressure, including good time-management skills and multitasking skills	11
Analytical skills	10
Enthusiasm	7

- Instructional skills
- Ability to apply library policies and procedures
- Personal traits or attributes
- Analytic and critical thinking skills
- Management and supervisory skills
- Commitment to user services

Most of the requisite qualities for reference positions identified in this analysis of job announcements overlap with the qualities identified in the literature. However, three new qualities are worth noting:

- Ability to work both independently and as a team member
- Flexibility
- Ability to work under pressure

Finally, despite the relative flexibility with regard to possession of an MLIS degree that respondents to the survey suggested, all of the job announcements required an ALA-accredited MLIS or equivalent by the time of starting the position. Thirteen percent of the positions also required or preferred a degree or experience in a subject area, and 65 percent specified required work experience.

GENERATIONAL SHIFT IN REFERENCE, PART 2: GAINS AND LOSSES

In a time of rapid technological change and economic uncertainty, libraries are working to keep their reference departments up-to-date and seeking to recruit and support librarians with skills and qualities that will allow them to face the future head-on. As the baby boomer generation of reference librarians reaches retirement age, it is worth remembering the changes they have encountered *and made possible* over the course of their careers, and asking what skills and knowledge might disappear as they leave the workforce. To gain a more holistic view of what the changing of the guard might mean, we interviewed six career reference librarians, three public librarians and three academic librarians. The average age of the librarians was 60; all but one (born in 1943) were baby boomers, all were within eight years of being eligible for retirement, and, on average, they had worked 30.8 years in reference (ranging from 24 to 35 years in the field). To put it another way, collectively, these librarians had 185 years of reference experience.

The librarians were asked what major changes they had seen in reference librarianship since they began working in the field, what newer skills they had learned on the job, what reference skills they believed had become less important over time, what new skills they thought librarians who were just coming into reference work brought to the field, and whether there were any skills or talents they suspected might be lost as baby boomer reference librarians retired. Although the librarians who were interviewed worked in diverse public and academic settings in four different states, their responses were quite similar in many ways—and echoed some of the comments from the surveys.

The number one major change listed by all of the librarians was the obvious one: the increasing use of computers and technology in the field over the past 30 years. Reference sources and reference services have moved heavily online during this time, and all of the librarians noted this. Related to this, several mentioned changes in the types of patron questions asked: an increase in the number of technology-related questions and a decrease in certain types of questions as self-service via Google has become the norm. Other changes mentioned by both academic and public librarians included a greater emphasis on instruction in reference, more teamwork, and a constantly changing array of sources and technologies to master. Newer skills that the librarians had learned on the job revolved around these changes and included, as one put it, "everything having to do with computers" (from online searching to Internet surfing to the provision of virtual reference services), new communication skills (how to communicate via e-mail, chat, Web 2.0 technologies, etc.—one person said, "How to type fast!"), instructional skills, and how to be flexible and adapt to change (in sources, technologies, and clientele). A couple of the librarians spontaneously mentioned older skills that "still mattered," including conducting the reference interview, showing respect for the user, and providing personalized service.

When asked what skills they thought newer reference librarians brought to the field, again, everyone mentioned computer and technology skills. Although all of the librarians interviewed had learned these kinds of skills on the job, they stressed that younger librarians had a much higher comfort level with technology, were capable of manipulating the digital environment, and were willing and able to set up new services. "They all have their own Facebook pages and are all Twittering," said one interviewee rather wryly, adding—more seriously—that this would undoubtedly be useful in their work. They had fresh ideas, another noted, and were willing to experiment to make them work. Additionally, several of the librarians admired younger librarians' ability to multitask.

With regard to which skills had become less important over time, all but one of the librarians mentioned familiarity with older formats—particularly print sources. Knowledge of the physical reference collection and individual tools has diminished in importance—partly because online tools have proliferated and partly because the rapid pace of change makes it difficult to "learn" individual sources. Print has "lost its value, lost its importance," said one librarian. The lone dissenting librarian said that she believed books were still valuable, even though the newer librarians might not use them as much; several of the other librarians pointed out that they still valued print resources as well but clearly saw that the print collection was in decline. An understanding of cataloging practices and the Library of Congress Subject Headings were mentioned by two of the librarians as becoming less important. An academic librarian noted that one-on-one reference now seemed less important than group instruction, and one public librarian observed that less emphasis was being placed on readers' advisory and the reference interview in her setting (with more emphasis on self-service and "give it to me, quick!").

In discussing the skills and talents that these experienced reference librarians feared might be lost with their generation's retirement, all of the librarians interviewed mentioned the library's physical collection. Knowledge of how to work with books and of the reference sources in the collection, an appreciation of the myriad formats in which information is packaged, an understanding of the value of the content of the physical library collection, and the importance of having a broad, deep, and balanced collection were all highlighted. The librarians perceived that specialized knowledge in subject fields would be lost as some of their highly educated colleagues retired—as well as a certain basic level of general knowledge (one librarian remarked that her generation seemed to have had a better education, that perhaps they had not been "so distracted"). Two of the librarians mentioned that a sense of library history would inevitably be lost—and perhaps, though hopefully not, an understanding of the historical importance of libraries and their role in protecting the freedom of information that is essential to a democracy. And one believed that certain face-to-face interpersonal skills might evaporate as more interactions took place in a virtual environment.

ENVISIONING THE FUTURE OF REFERENCE LIBRARIANSHIP

How will libraries respond to the retirement of baby boomer reference professionals? Given that roughly half the respondents to our survey reported a decline in the number of reference positions in their libraries over the past five years (and only 15 percent reported an increase); given that half the respondents stated that they either "did not know" whether retiring reference librarians would be replaced or were certain they would not be; and given that many public and educational institutions currently find themselves in difficult economic times, the future of reference librarianship may be a short one!

At the same time, reference librarians are known for their resourcefulness, wide-ranging curiosity, and capacity for learning. Talk with someone who started out in the field when all books were cataloged individually and the library had no access to online databases, and who now blogs, provides virtual reference service, and develops online tutorials as a part of her job, and this quickly becomes apparent. Reference librarianship is an adaptable profession, and in this adaptability lies its salvation.

One of the signs that the profession is adapting to fit user needs in various environments is the diversity of job titles for librarians engaging in reference. Our visits to library Web sites (as we sought to identify the current head of reference, public services, or user services at the libraries we wished to survey) yielded an impressive array of titles—obliging us to note in the introduction to the survey, "Position titles vary from library to library (e.g., reference librarian, research librarian, information services librarian, public services librarian), and reference services are often combined with related functions (such as instruction). However, for the purpose of this survey, reference librarians may be defined as those librarians who devote a significant portion of their work time to reference work, as defined above [by RUSA]." The idea that reference librarianship may vary greatly according to institutional needs was further reinforced by comments on the survey, such as the following:

- "Very few librarians [at our university] provide reference service as their primary responsibility anymore."
- "Reference librarianship is a rare bird these days. No one in our library works exclusively as a reference librarian. They all wear other hats too."
- "We have migrated from a reference/collection development model to scholarly resource librarians."
- "Our 'reference librarians' listed here for the most part are subject liaisons, and reference services is only one part of their portfolio."
- "There are fewer reference librarians who have 'reference' as their home department—some have other main jobs and report to the head of public services, not the head of reference."
- "These librarians also have collections, instruction and outreach responsibilities. They are not devoted entirely to reference."

The job announcements we studied also listed a wide range of titles and responsibilities for librarians engaged in reference work, as noted earlier. In addition to providing reference services and managing reference collections, librarians are responsible for delivering information literacy instruction, serving as liaisons to specific user communities, and developing outreach activities to promote reference services. The diversification of job responsibilities is both a result and an indicator of the constantly changing work environment. Library users' information needs evolve as changes occur in social and economic arenas, and reference responsibilities are adapting to meet those demands efficiently and effectively.

Other comments on the surveys indicated that libraries were actively restructuring and rethinking reference positions, as well as carefully considering appropriate job responsibilities in a changing environment. However, there are some clear trends. In the libref-l job postings, instruction and outreach stood out as key reference responsibilities, and these were mentioned by a number of survey respondents as well. Almost all of the baby boomer librarians we interviewed, including public librarians, also mentioned the increasingly important role of instruction in their work. We find it striking that the official RUSA definition of reference work explicitly excludes instruction and makes no mention of outreach. Perhaps this definition needs to be updated to include these essential responsibilities.

The job announcements also made it clear that today's aspiring reference professionals should have good teamwork capabilities, great flexibility, and excellent stress-management skills—all qualities that will help them survive and thrive in a complex work environment where librarians are expected to quickly familiarize themselves with ever-changing resources and use emerging technologies to guide their users through a shifting information landscape.

The baby boomer librarians we interviewed noted the accelerating pace of change in reference in recent years and the increasing importance of teamwork in libraries. They expressed admiration for their younger colleagues' comfort with technologies and their skill at multitasking—suggesting that newer reference librarians are indeed bringing these necessary qualities to the workplace. How the next generation will hold up under continued technological, social, and budgetary pressures remains to be seen; as one baby boomer librarian remarked, "New librarians don't have a clue as to what they're facing!"

However, they are not facing these challenges alone; their older colleagues are there to help. As the survey showed, numerous libraries are offering incentives to help pave the way for talented individuals to enter reference librarianship, and some are offering internships to current MLIS students and fellowships to recent graduates. A number of libraries have formal mentoring programs in place for new reference librarians, and many others have informal programs. And a respectable number of libraries—especially public libraries, it seems—hire retired librarians back on a part-time basis, hopefully helping to ensure that some of the knowledge they have acquired over the course of their careers will not be lost.

The physical library of the 20th century in which baby boomers came of age is, if not quite disappearing, diminishing somewhat in importance. Certain types of reference skills and knowledge—of printed collections and tangible tools—are waning; others—related to the use of technology, instruction, and outreach—are on the rise. This is an important moment for the reference profession to stay focused on the primary goals of assisting, advising, and instructing users of knowledge (RUSA, 2003) while maintaining a broad interpretation of what it means to do so, maximum flexibility at both the individual and institutional levels, and a willingness to experiment and to learn.

WORKS CITED

American Library Association. 2009. *The nation's largest libraries: A listing by volumes held (ALA Library fact sheet number 22)*. Retrieved July 31, 2009, from http://www.ala.org/ala/aboutala/offices/library/libraryfactsheet/ala libraryfactsheet22.cfm.

American Library Directory. 2009. Medford, NJ: Information Today. Retrieved July 31, 2009, from http://www.americanlibrarydirectory.com.

Association of Research Libraries and University of Virginia. 2008. *ARL statistics: Interactive edition*. Retrieved July 31, 2009, from http://fisher.lib.virginia.edu/arl/index.html.

Auster, E., and D. C. Chan. 2003. Factors contributing to the professional development of reference librarians. *Library and Information Science Research* 25 (3): 265–286.

Bauner, R. E. 1990. Ready reference beyond the M.L.S. *Reference Librarian* 30: 45–59.

Bureau of Labor Statistics. 2007. Librarians. *Occupational Outlook Handbook, 2008–09 ed.* Retrieved July 31, 2009, from http://www.bls.gov/oco/ocos068.htm.

Bureau of Labor Statistics. 2008. *Employment status of the civilian noninstitutional population by age, sex, and race.* Retrieved July 31, 2009, from http://www.bls.gov/cps/cpsaat3.pdf.

Castiglione, J. 2006. Managing the library labor gap: The role of bridge employment for the older library professional. *Library Management* 27 (8): 575–587.

Curran, W. M. 2003. Succession: The next ones at bat. *College & Research Libraries* 64 (2): 134–140.

Everhart, T. 2000. Looking for a few good librarians. *School Library Journal* 46 (9): 58–61.

Griffiths, J. M., and D. W. King. 1986. *New directions in library and information science education.* White Plains, NY: Knowledge Industry Publications.

Hardesty, L. 2002. Future of academic/research librarians: A period of transition—to what? *portal: Libraries and the Academy* 2 (1): 79–97.

Howze, P. 2003. Training the new head of reference: Focusing on the supervising relationship as technique. *Reference Librarian* 81: 51–58.

Kaufman, P. T. 2002. Where do the next "we" come from? Recruiting, retaining and developing our successors. *ARL Bimonthly Report* 221. Retrieved July 31, 2009, from http://www.arl.org/bm~doc/recruit-3.pdf.

Kong, L. M. 1996. Academic reference librarians: Under the microscope. *Reference Librarian* 54: 21–27.

Lynch, M. J. 2002. Reaching 65: Lots of librarians will be there soon. *American Libraries* 33 (March): 55–56.

Massey-Burzio, V. 1991. Education and experience: Or, the MLS is not enough. *Reference Services Review* 19: 72–74.

McConnell, C. 2004. Staff and leadership shortages, grow your own. *American Libraries* 35 (October): 34–36.

Nitecki, D. 1984. Competencies required of public services librarians to use new technologies. *Clinic on Library Applications of Data Processing* 21: 43–57.

Nofsinger, M. M. 1999. Training and retraining reference professionals: Core competencies for the twenty-first century. *Reference Librarian* 64: 9–19.

O'Connor, S. 2007. The heretical library manager for the future. *Library Management* 28 (1–2): 62–71.

Perceptions of libraries and information resources: A report to the OCLC membership. 2005. Dublin, OH: OCLC (Online Computer Library Center), Inc. Retrieved July 31, 2009, from http://www.oclc.org/reports/2005perceptions.htm.

Reference and User Services Association. 2003. *Professional competencies for reference and user services librarians.* Retrieved July 31, 2009, from http://www.ala.org/ala/mgrps/divs/rusa/resources/guidelines/professional.cfm.

Reference and User Services Association. 2008. *Definitions of reference.* Retrieved July 31, 2009, from http://www.ala.org/ala/mgrps/divs/rusa/resources/guidelines/definitionsreference.cfm.

Sherrer, J. 1996. Thriving in changing times: Competencies for today's reference librarians. *Reference Librarian* 54: 11–20.

Smith, N., M. P. Marchant, and L. F. Nielson. 1984. Education for public and academic librarians: A view from the top. *Journal of Education for Librarianship* 24: 233–245.

Stafford, C. D., and W. M. Serban. 1990. Core competencies: Recruiting, training, and evaluating in the automated reference environment. *Journal of Library Administration* 13 (1–2): 81–97.

U.S. Census Bureau. 2000. *Age: 2000.* Retrieved July 31, 2009, from http://www.census.gov/prod/2001pubs/c2kbr01–12.pdf.

U.S. Census Bureau. 2006. *Oldest baby boomers turn 60.* Retrieved July 31, 2009, from http://www.census.gov/Press-Release/www/releases/archives/facts_for_features_special_editions/006105.html.

Walters, R., and S. Barnes. 1985. Goals, objectives, and competencies for reference service: A training program at the UCLA biomedical library. *Bulletin of the Medical Library Association* 73: 160–167.

Wilder, S. 2001. The age demographics of academic librarians. *ARL Bimonthly Report* 185. Retrieved July 31, 2009, from http://www.arl.org/bm~doc/agedemo.pdf.

Wilder, S. 2002. New hires in research libraries: Demographic trends and hiring priorities. *ARL Bimonthly Report* 221. Retrieved July 31, 2009, from http://www.arl.org/bm~doc/newhires.pdf.

VII

THE EDUCATION AND TRAINING OF REFERENCE LIBRARIANS

22

THE EDUCATION OF REFERENCE LIBRARIANS: A DETAILED SURVEY AND ANALYSIS

Lisa G. O'Connor

> Librarians are saying that the library schools are not keeping up with the changes in practice and that they are not initiating new methods. Librarianship is rapidly shifting its attention from the mechanics of administration to the needs of the reader. What effect has this change of emphasis produced in the teaching of librarianship? The answer from competent observers is, "Very little."
>
> In all the library schools there are courses called "reference" or "reference bibliography." Usually these courses are devoted to the study of reference books—not, as one teacher wishes that they might be—to reference work. Librarians must be prepared who can answer the simple as well as the complex questions asked, in full realization of the individual differences in the inquirers and in the inquiries. (Howe, 1931)

Some sentiments seem to persist regardless of the passage of time: Taxes are too high, sports teams do not win enough, and education for reference librarians does not keep pace with the changing needs of reference work. Howe's 1931 criticism should ring familiar to anyone who has followed the debate on reference education. Complaints that reference courses are currently overly source based and unresponsive to the changing information environment are largely anecdotal, however. The reference curriculum has not been surveyed formally for nearly 15 years. This study describes the current status of reference education through the examination and analysis of course syllabi.

LITERATURE REVIEW

The literature on reference instruction is prolific. It is a mix of philosophical and pedagogical advocacy, anecdotal experience, and observation and empirical research. Much of it argues for one approach over another. This study will forgo the discussion of what should be in favor of examining the current status of reference instruction in American Library Association (ALA)–accredited library and information science (LIS) programs.

The content of reference instruction has been studied in the past, using various approaches and with diverse purposes. Bonk (1961) and Larson (1979) analyze reference curricula but largely to determine which reference types and titles compose the core. Summers (1982) surveys reference courses and found that courses were still primarily source based. He argues that reference courses should focus more on the reference process and contexts of reference services. Broadway and Smith (1989) survey reference instructors to describe the content of reference courses and the backgrounds of personnel teaching them. They conclude that although a shift in course titles might indicate services' growing importance in relation to sources, this shift was not nearly as visible in the course content. Furthermore, their data demonstrate that although instructors were adding content to the reference course curricula (CD-ROM–based information was one example cited), they were conflicted about what content might be deleted.

Richardson examines the evolution of reference textbooks from 1890 to 1990, asserting that by "identifying the common assumptions presented" in them, he can "reveal the operative paradigm of this field" (1992, 57). He found that reference instruction has moved through several schools of thought toward a paradigm he describes as a "complete, balanced perspective," which includes "(1) a presentation of the structure of reference works; (2) the process of answering reference questions by clarification and classification; and (3) a psychological understanding of the interaction between librarians and users" (Richardson, 1992, 85).

Powell and Raber (1994) survey reference instructors and examine course syllabi. They confirm Richardson's findings that curricula are moving toward a more complete and balanced treatment of source, method, professional knowledge, and user psychology and behavior. The study identifies three areas believed to need further development in reference courses: information management, particularly the relationship between needs and services; information-seeking behavior; and the application of technology to service provision. As Broadway and Smith also discover, Powell and Raber find that instructors were experiencing great difficulty deciding what to omit from their courses in exchange for what they felt need to be added.

Finally, Adkins and Erdelez (2006) focus on teaching methods for source instruction, rather than course content, used in basic, advanced, and subject-specific reference courses. Their survey of instructors in ALA-accredited library programs finds that reference source instruction remains an important component of the reference curriculum. They also conclude that instructors employ a variety of methods to teach their use despite the challenges of access due to distance education and the proliferation of numbers and types of sources.

STUDY DESIGN

This study is designed to analyze the syllabi of basic reference courses included in master of library science (MLS), master of library and information science (MLIS), or other master's degrees in LIS programs. Analysis is confined to basic courses, because the existence and offering of advanced reference courses are too highly varied across institutions. Studying only the basic course provides a more even unit of analysis. It was not always easy to determine what constituted a basic reference course. Course descriptions from course catalogs, course titles, and syllabi were all weighed in the decision about how to categorize courses. The course had to have either a title or course content that designated it as a reference course. Many courses were deemed basic reference courses despite ambiguous titles. Of course, what constitutes a reference course in terms of content is obviously debatable, but it was fairly clear operationally (such as when reference content included treatment of sources, methods, and delivery of information in information service contexts). Only one course was titled as a reference course but did not have the content of one. This course was included in the data because its title so clearly designated it as the course to fill the reference component of the curriculum.

Study Limitations

The study of syllabi cannot fully describe the range of pedagogical approaches and content in these courses. Additional research into instructional methods and the content of course lectures is necessary for the most complete picture of reference education. Also, because courses are constantly being revised and tweaked, study data merely provide a snapshot of reference instruction at this moment in time.

Data Collection

Excluding non-English-based institutions, there are 55 ALA-accredited LIS programs in the United States and Canada. Of those, I obtained syllabi from 45 institutions (82 percent). The data consist of 74 unique syllabi. Forty-eight syllabi are authored by full-time instructors or jointly by full-time and adjunct instructors, and 26 are authored exclusively by adjunct instructors. Syllabi correspond to courses taught less than two years ago.

Syllabi were initially collected directly from the Web. Those that were unavailable online were requested directly from instructors when that information could be identified. Alternatively, syllabi were requested via e-mail from the best, most likely administrative person that could be identified. For some institutions, the only e-mail was an anonymous information e-mail, and that was used barring any more appropriate contact information. In some institutions, one standard syllabus was used across all instructors. If the syllabi for individual instructors varied in any significant ways (texts, content, or assignments), they were treated as unique. These differences could have been as small as a variation in readings assigned. An attempt was made to collect syllabi from any instructor who had taught the course in the last three semesters; however, that information was more readily available at some institutions than at others. With institutions that rely on a central scheduling system that one has to log in to access, the researcher had to rely on information provided by the administration. Responses to requests for information varied from complete information to nonresponse. So it should not be assumed that this study represents the syllabi of every section of this course taught by responding institutions over the last three semesters. Certainly there are gaps.

DATA ANALYSIS

Overview of Courses

Course titles can provide some measure of major course goals. Since they have been studied in the past, they can also provide a longitudinal measure of how courses and their place in the curriculum change. Of the 55 English-language ALA-accredited basic reference courses, 11 are entitled Information Sources and Services. The next most frequently used titles are Reference and Information Services (5) and Reference Sources and Services (5). Information Resources and Services is the title of 4 courses, and Reference of 3. Two courses each are entitled Introduction to Information Sources and Services, Introduction of Information Services, and Reference and Information Resources and Services. Twenty-three courses have unique titles:

- Access to Information
- Basic Information Sources and Services
- Foundations of Information Sources and Services
- Foundations of Reference
- Information Access
- Information Access and Retrieval
- Information Access Services
- Information Seeking, Retrieval and Services
- Information Services
- Information Services and Resources
- Information Services and Users
- Information Sources and Reference Services
- Information Sources and Retrieval
- Introduction to Information Access and Retrieval
- Introduction to Information Resources and Services
- Introduction to Reference and Information Services

- Introduction to Reference Services and Resources
- Information Users and Services
- Principles of Information Services
- Print and Electronic Information Sources and Services
- Reference and Information Literacy Services
- Reference and Online Services
- Selection and Use of Information Sources

Of these 31 total unique titles, 26 (84 percent) use the term *information*, and 10 (32 percent) use *reference* (with 5 using both terms). The trend to favor the term *information* has increased since Broadway and Smith demonstrated that 76 percent used *information* and 32 percent used *reference* in 1989. Twelve course titles (35 percent) include both the *sources* and *services* concepts, which is up slightly from Broadway and Smith's reported 32 percent in 1989. But the most striking comparison to previous studies is the addition of new terms to course titles, including *information retrieval and seeking*, *users*, *online*, and *information literacy*. These terms were not frequently used in course titles heretofore.

All but five of the courses are 3 credit hours. Four of them are 4 credit hours, and one is 3.5 credit hours. Typically, a "lab" or "practice" component constitutes the additional 1–1.5 credit hours. Forty-one (75 percent) of these courses are required for the basic library-oriented master's degree, while 14 are either electives or requirements only for special tracks. These findings indicate a decline from the 91 percent reported by Broadway and Smith (1989) and 96 percent reported by Powell and Raber (1994). One should note, however, that this figure cannot be interpreted as strictly indicating such a decline in overall course offerings, because both studies report findings on survey respondents only, rather than all ALA schools. Because response rates for both studies are fairly high, one may speculate that there has been at least some downward trend in requiring basic reference courses. Researchers in this study also observed anecdotally an increasing trend to require a prerequisite information-related course for reference courses, and in many cases these prerequisites are core requirements. These courses are often titled Information Access or Information Retrieval and tend to address search strategy and construction outside any specific information service environment. (Note that some courses with similar titles were included in data for this study because their content descriptions indicated they covered these issues within information service environments and therefore act as reference services courses.)

Textbooks

Textbook selection is an important element of reference course content because required texts often provide the vast majority of the course readings and a substantial amount of overall course content. Three texts currently dominate the market for reference courses in this study. They are listed here with the number and percentage of courses requiring them.

Bopp & Smith (2001), *Reference and Information Services: An Introduction*	29 (39.1%)
Cassell & Hiremath (2009), *Reference and Information Services in the 21st Century: An Introduction*	26 (35.1%)
Katz (2001), *Introduction to Reference Work,* Vols. 1 and 2	11 (14.9%)

Katz is the most highly source focused of the three texts, with approximately 58 percent of its 682 pages of content (including both Volumes 1 and 2) devoted to materials. Cassel & Hiremath is second with 53 percent of its 346 pages devoted to sources, and Bopp & Smith is the least source focused, with 44 percent of its 594 pages devoted to materials. All three texts include introductions that focus on the purpose and use of sources and also offer lists of reference titles for each source type.

All three texts also include chapters on the reference interview, instruction, use of electronic databases and the Internet, and management and evaluation of reference services. Both Bopp & Smith and Cassell & Hiremath include chapters on selecting and evaluating materials, while Katz covers these concepts within each source-type section. Cassell & Hiremath include chapters on readers' advisory, reference for children and young adults, and the future of reference. Both Katz and Bopp & Smith cover access issues, such as full text, document delivery, and interlibrary loan. Both Bopp & Smith and Cassell & Hiremath include chapters on training reference staff for service improvement. Bopp & Smith includes chapters on history, ethics, and specific populations (including children and young adults). Full-time instructors were 20 percent more likely to require the Katz text, and part-time instructors were 23 percent more likely to require the Cassell & Hiremath text. It should be noted that only Cassell & Hiremath is satisfactorily updated, though the other textbooks offer online updates to the print copy.

Other required textbooks include the following:

Ross, Nilsen, & Radford (2009), *Conducting the Reference Interview: A How-to-Do-It Manual for Librarians*	9
Janes (2003), *Introduction of Reference Work in the Digital Age*	6
Bell (2006), *Librarian's Guide to Online Searching*	4
Jennerich & Jennerich (1997), *The Reference Interview as a Creative Art*	4
Kovacs (2007), *The Virtual Reference Handbook*	4
Walker, Janes, & Tenopir (1999), *Online Retrieval: A Dialogue of Theory and Practice*	3

Smith (2003), *Chat Reference: A Guide to Live Virtual Reference Services*	2
Ross & Dewdney (1998a), *Communicating Professionally: A How-to-Do-It Manual for Library Applications*	2
Chu (2003), *Information Representation and Retrieval in the Digital Age*	2

These optional texts clearly reveal instructors' desire to supplement required texts on issues of interviewing and communication and use of digital technologies.

Course Content

Course content is analyzed using two types of data: course objectives and course content as described in course outlines and/or schedules. While these data sources should, in theory, parallel one another (i.e., the course content should be designed to meet course objectives), analyzing them separately provides a means of triangulating findings regarding course content. In addition, these data sources provide information at two distinct levels: the desired outcomes and the plan for achieving them. The global themes of courses are apparent in the course objectives but may be lost in the detail of course outlines. At the same time, the finer detail of course outlines provides a better picture of what is actually taught.

Analysis of Course Objectives

Course objectives provide access to course aims. Analyzing them, however, presents several challenges. Objectives are written at widely varying degrees of specificity. While one syllabus might contain 4 global, multifaceted objectives, for example, another might include 12 more discrete objectives, and yet they may essentially cover the same concepts. Terminology varies incredibly as well, which makes collating objectives into unified categories difficult at times. An effort was made to summarize the common content of objectives regardless of the structure of written objectives or the nomenclature used. It should be noted that this process of reduction often required interpretation of objectives, which may yield an imperfect summary. However, an effort was made to minimize error by comparing objectives to other parts of the syllabi to ensure the most precise interpretation possible. Of the 74 syllabi studied, 68 contained course objectives suitable for analysis.

The most common course objective is related to sources. Actions include describing, evaluating, selecting, and using sources. The sources are often qualified as "basic," "core," "standard," or "important." References are also made to "genres" and "types" of tools. One syllabus requires students to describe, in detail, 150 important sources. Another asks students "to discuss problems likely to be encountered in the use of various sources." All syllabi but one includes this type of objective. This course, though it contains *reference* in its title, is an outlier and is much more like an information-retrieval course than a basic reference course.

The "reference process" is the second most common objective. Sixty-six syllabi (97 percent) address this aspect. This objective takes many forms. It is often described as constructing a search strategy (used in a holistic sense rather than in the narrower, technical sense of constructing searches for electronic sources, which will be addressed later). It is alternatively described as negotiating a reference transaction and mediating the information needs of clients. This objective often includes or is supplemented by additional objectives addressing the reference interview. Sixty-four syllabi specifically mention the reference interview, question negotiation, and/or interpersonal communication as being in service of this objective. Only 10 (15 percent) name knowledge of users' "information-seeking behavior" as an explicit outcome. Eleven (16 percent) describe knowledge of the "organization of information," "bibliographic control," or "the information environment" as a course objective. The creation of research guides or pathfinders for provision of indirect reference assistance is also addressed in 11 syllabi.

The third most common objective (in 89 percent of syllabi) relates to reference as a set of services. They require students to "understand the nature" or "describe the essential elements" of reference services. These objectives are often qualified by the context. Sometimes context is stated in terms of technology, for example, "in a digital environment" or "in an electronic era." Alternatively, context is defined by user groups. For example, 18 syllabi (26 percent) address reference services to special groups, such as "diverse" clients, patrons with "special needs," or patrons from "multiple disciplines" or in a variety of "library types." Six syllabi (9 percent) specifically refer to the management of these services, and one to the "professional and socially responsible" management of services. Another 10 (15 percent) require students to be aware of a customer service ethic in the provision of reference services, using terms such as "user centered," "sensitive to user needs," and "customer-oriented" to describe such approaches. Only 23 syllabi (34 percent) ask students to understand or be able to execute methods for assessing reference services.

Thirteen syllabi (19 percent) mandate knowledge of the history and development of reference services, and 33 (48 percent) require knowledge of current and emerging trends in information services. Knowledge of the ethics and philosophy of reference service is an explicit objective in 21 syllabi (31 percent). Six (9 percent) require the application of professional standards and competencies in the provision of reference. Assessing reference collections and information literacy instruction are two specific aspects of information services mentioned by 9 syllabi (13 percent) and 14 syllabi (21 percent) respectively.

Several objectives relate to technology and information services. Thirty-three objectives (48 percent) require "online," "Internet," or "electronic" searching skills, with a few delineating specific skills such as the use of Boolean logic and controlled vocabulary. Competence with reference services technologies is mandated in 18 syllabi (26 percent), with only one objective specifically naming use of Web 2.0 technologies. Six objectives (9 percent) address information-retrieval theories, and two mention knowledge of information systems. One syllabus describes Web-page creation as a course outcome.

Finally, a few objectives address professional issues, such as knowledge of reference literature (10 percent), reference services nomenclature (3 percent), and the reference librarian's professional characteristics (1 percent). Single mentions of problem solving, ability to work in groups, and written and oral communication also occur.

Analysis of Course Content by Course Outlines

Of the 74 unique syllabi examined, 13 contain insufficient detail about the course content to be used in data analysis. It should be understood that these syllabi vary greatly in their specificity and descriptiveness of course content. So these data should not be understood, in and of themselves, as providing a comprehensive portrait of what is currently taught in the basic reference course. Rather, it must be considered in the context of the other data from this study, particularly course objectives and readings.

The organization of class outlines and schedules provides an interesting perspective on the instructors' approaches to this course. Richardson (1992) describes reference education as composed of content on sources, users, and management of services. Traditionally, reference courses centered on sources; however, this study finds 19 percent of the syllabi are organized primarily by source-type instruction. That is, the majority of headings for the week are source types: encyclopedias, biographies, and so on. Twenty-five percent of these syllabi are authored by adjunct instructors, and three-quarters by full-time faculty. Of the total number of full-time faculty who contributed data to the study, 22 percent use this type of organization. Ten percent of adjunct faculty organize their syllabi primarily by resource type.

Forty-one percent of the syllabi are organized by a mix of source-type instruction and the other topical aspects of reference services, such as management, user education, and information seeking. Fifty-eight percent of these mixed syllabi are authored by full-time faculty, and 42 percent by adjunct faculty. Of the total number of full-time faculty who contributed data to the study, 38 percent use this type of organization. Fifty percent of adjunct faculty organize their syllabi using this mixed approach.

Forty percent of the syllabi are organized almost exclusively by non-resource-based topics. Though they might include a week or two designated to discuss resources, all other weeks are organized thematically. Sixty-five percent are authored by full-time faculty, and 35 percent by adjunct instructors. Of the total number of full-time faculty who contributed data to the study, 40 percent use this type of organization. Forty percent of adjunct faculty organize their syllabi primarily by non-resource based topics.

Course content was analyzed both for its internal content and for correlations to external factors, such as textbook selection, instructor status, and institution type. Course content seems to have a higher correlation to textbook selection than to any other factor. Syllabi varied evenly across full-time and adjunct instructors except for in few areas, noted in the following analysis. An attempt was made to compare the course content of I-School courses to the courses of all other institutions, but this analysis was compromised by a significantly lower response rate from I-Schools. No correlations were found to other institutional types (by research status or by private versus public, for example).

Three elements are common to all 61 syllabi: source genre instruction, evaluation and selection of information, and search strategy (as it is most broadly conceived as searching for information utilizing available resources), also called the reference process. The information or reference interview, occasionally also called question negotiation, was a central component of nearly all syllabi (97 percent) as well. These four areas constitute the core of the reference curriculum.

Content Related to Sources

All syllabi but one contain weeks devoted to information source genres. In 60 percent of syllabi, source types provide headings for at least half of the weeks in course outlines. Headings are typically for single source types (encyclopedias, for example) or for groups of sources (handbooks, almanacs, and manuals, for example). Obviously source-type instruction is still a central feature of reference. However, only five syllabi (7 percent) provide a list of source titles for which students should be responsible. This is in stark contrast to Broadway and Smith's findings that specific reference sources (in contrast to types of sources) are the most frequently taught topic in their 1989 study. Organization of information and bibliographic control are mentioned in 21 syllabi (35 percent).

Content Related to Technology

Content related to technology is the most common component of syllabi, after the four core areas already mentioned. Online and electronic database searching strategy is a component of 47 syllabi (77 percent). Digital reference, including e-mail and chat reference, digital reference desks, software for digital services, and the Internet Public Library (IPL), is a topic in 46 syllabi

(75 percent). Forty-one syllabi (67 percent) include use of the Internet for reference services, and 14 (23 percent) specifically mention the use of social networking or Web 2.0 technologies. Knowledge of electronic systems and online catalogs was mandated by 13 syllabi (21 percent) and 12 syllabi (29 percent) respectively. Information-retrieval theory, including such concepts as precision and recall and information retrieval models, is a component of 8 syllabi (13 percent). Gaming is mentioned by 1 syllabus.

Content Related to Users and Services

After reference interviewing, the most common content directly related to users is information seeking, behavior, and/or use. It is a component of 26 syllabi (43 percent). This is one of the areas in which there is a correlation between its occurrence and instructor type. Forty-six percent of full-time instructors include this content in their syllabi, while only 30 percent of adjunct instructors do.

Information literacy and user instruction is a component of 38 syllabi (62 percent) and is another area in which there is a correlation between its occurrence and instructor type. Seventy-five percent of adjunct faculty include it, while only 65 percent of full-time faculty do. As a caveat, one might suspect that since all three primary textbooks include chapters on information literacy and user instruction, actual coverage of this topic is higher than course outlines suggest.

Content related to other types of services is a significant component of reference courses. Services to populations in specific contexts (academic and public libraries, museums, and archives, for example) is a topic in 23 syllabi (38 percent). Thirty-one syllabi (51 percent) include services to special and diverse populations. Reference service specifically for children is included in 9 syllabi (15 percent), with only 2 of them also mentioning young adults. Inclusion of this topic is highly correlated to use of the Cassell & Hiremath text, as it contains chapters on this topic. One might surmise that since many other courses use this text, coverage of this topic is slightly higher than course outlines indicate. Specialized services to readers and genealogists are included in 16 syllabi (26 percent) and 3 syllabi (5 percent) respectively. One syllabus covers bibliotherapy. Dealing with "challenging" or "problem" patrons is mentioned in 4 syllabi (6.5 percent). Eight syllabi (13 percent) include topics related to interlibrary loan and document delivery, with 4 (6.5 percent) containing material on copyright.

Content Related to Management and Professional Issues

Management of reference services is a relatively important topic, included in 35 syllabi (57 percent). Evaluation and assessment of services, including training and improvement of services, is specifically named in 48 syllabi

(79 percent). Eight (13 percent) and 10 (16 percent) mention marketing or outreach and collection development respectively. Development of physical spaces is included in only 1 syllabus.

Of professional topics, ethics is most often included, occurring in 36 syllabi (59 percent). Twenty-three syllabi contain topics related to the history of reference. Philosophy of reference and reference policies are mentioned in eight syllabi (13 percent) and six syllabi (10 percent) respectively. Knowledge of research literature is a component of five syllabi (8 percent) and professional standards of four (6.5 percent). Thirty-four syllabi (56 percent) include knowledge of current and/or future issues and trends in information services. Workload and burnout are mentioned in two syllabi. Only one syllabus mentions interviewing and resume preparation.

Supplementary Readings

An evaluation of supplementary readings is useful, because it reveals the areas that instructors either believe are not addressed adequately by required texts or identify as issues that simply need greater emphasis or exploration. Three types of supplementary readings are assigned: professional standards and guidelines, textbook and book chapters, and journal literature.

Professional standards and guidelines are included in supplementary readings by a relatively small percentage of syllabi. Part-time instructors were 11 percent more likely to assign them. The most often assigned reading—in 26 syllabi (35 percent)—is the Reference and User Services Association's (RUSA) *Guidelines for Behavioral Performance of Reference and Information Service Providers* (2004). *Professional Competencies for Reference and User Services Librarians* (RUSA, 2008e) is assigned in 20 syllabi (27 percent). Other guidelines included in supplementary readings are the following:

ALA (RUSA) (2008c), Guidelines for Medical, Legal, and Business Responses	8 (13%)
ALA (ACRL) (2006), Information Literacy Competency Standards for Higher Education	7 (11%)
ALA (RUSA) (2008a), Guidelines for Implementing and Maintaining Virtual Reference Services	6 (10%)
ALA (2006), Library Bill of Rights	5 (8%)
ALA (2007), Code of Ethics	5 (8%)
ALA (RUSA) (2008d), Guidelines for Preparation of a Bibliography	4 (7%)
ALA (RUSA) (2006), Elements for Basic Reviews: A Guide for Writers and Readers of Reviews of Works in All Mediums and Genres	2 (3%)
ALA (RUSA) (2008b), Guidelines for Information Services	2 (3%)

Texts about professional standards not only are incorporated as supplementary course reading but also occasionally form the basis of assignments. For example, RUSA's *Guidelines for Behavioral Performance* is used in one course to provide a framework for students to describe and evaluate their reference observation and in another course to assess students' own performances in a reference interview role-playing assignment. The ALA's *Code of Ethics* and *Library Bill of Rights* are used to frame debates about proper ethical conduct in reference case studies.

Textbook chapters also constitute some supplementary readings. Instructors occasionally assign one required text but also assign chapters from one of the other three core textbooks. The *Guide to Reference Books* (Balay, 1996) is included in recommended readings. Additional assigned texts include Kuhlthau's (2000) *Seeking Meaning: A Process Approach to Library and Information Services* and Case's (2007) *Looking for Information: A Survey of Research on Information Seeking, Needs, and Behavior.*

Supplementary reading is almost overwhelming in quantity and scope. Several articles are assigned in more than 20 percent of syllabi:

- Green (1876), "Personal Relations between Librarians and Readers"
- Dervin and Dewdney (1986), "Neutral Questioning: A New Approach to the Reference Interview"
- Dewdney and Mitchell (1996), "Oranges and Peaches: Understanding Accidents in the Reference Interview"
- Ross and Dewdney (1998b), "Negative Closure"
- Taylor (1968), "Question-Negotiation and Information Seeking in Libraries"
- Tenopir (1987), "Searching by Controlled Vocabulary or Free Text?"

An attempt was made to categorize supplementary readings to ascertain the content areas they support. Not all article and book titles are self-explanatory, and only those that are have been included in this analysis. Supplementary readings tend to concentrate on several content areas. Of the 536 titles analyzed, a significant proportion deal with technologies: 76 (14 percent) cover digital reference, 63 (12 percent) the Internet, and 49 (9 percent) electronic databases, which includes online public access catalogs (OPACs) and other electronic indexes. Information literacy and instruction are also significant areas and are addressed by 51 readings (10 percent). Forty-three readings (8 percent) cover sources. Another 43 readings cover service topics, such as customer service, services to special populations, and the ethics of equal services for all patrons. The reference interview and assessment of reference are the topics of 38 articles (7 percent) and 37 articles (7 percent) respectively. Thirty-five readings (6 percent) concern information seeking. In order of frequency, other topics include information contexts (library type, for example), reference's future viability, management, locating and writing source reviews, and readers' advisory.

Assignments

Assignments are an important part of the instructional experience. They often serve the dual purposes of engaging students in learning experiences and assessing the depth and quality of learning. Course outcomes should be evident in the work students are asked to do, so assignments provide another indicator of which outcomes instructors deem most significant for students. Although an effort was made to obtain full assignment descriptions when they were not included in the syllabus, what was provided varies widely in descriptiveness and specificity. Three syllabi have no or insufficient information regarding assignments and are not included in data analysis. Seventy-one syllabi provide data for the following analysis. One should note that assignments were categorized by types of activities, not necessarily by titles, so a single assignment might be represented more than once in the data if it requires several of the activities.

Reference Problem Sets: 53 syllabi (75 percent). Problem sets ask students to solve information problems or answer questions using print, electronic, and/or Internet resources. When these problem sets clearly include use of electronic and Internet resources, they are also included in the count for those types of assignments. Eight syllabi (11 percent) require students to answer reference problems through the IPL.

Source Evaluation: 46 syllabi (65 percent). These exercises require students to compare and contrast sources or to evaluate sources. For example, some ask students to weigh selections from a specific source type, such as encyclopedias. Others require students to review a single source. Several of these incorporate RUSA's guidelines for writing reviews.

Reference Encounter/Observation: 44 syllabi (62 percent). These assignments require students to observe, either covertly or overtly, reference interactions and evaluate their experiences. Observations include both in-person and digital services. Some assignments require students to observe services in both contexts and compare their experiences.

Electronic Database Exercises: 37 syllabi (52 percent). These assignments include exercises that were part of problem sets and exercises separate and unique from problem sets. Thirteen syllabi (18.3 percent) also contain separate Internet-based exercises.

Pathfinders: 36 syllabi (51 percent). Pathfinders are alternatively called research guides, subject guides, and annotated bibliographies (where those bibliographies are structured like traditional research guides). Pathfinders are comprehensive assignments that require search strategies, searching skills, evaluation and selection of sources, and the synthesis and organization of information for clients.

Research Papers: 24 syllabi (34 percent). Writing assignments vary from research papers requiring citation of professional literature to opinion and/or reflection papers. Common topics include learning reflections, philosophy of reference, case study analysis, the role of reference in education and/or society, and the future of reference services.

Exams and Quizzes: Sixteen (23 percent) of the courses utilize exams (midterm and/or final exams) and 13 (18.3 percent) utilize quizzes for student assessment.

Underlying Skills: Fifteen (21.1 percent) of the courses require group work, and 31 (43.7 percent) require oral presentations.

A wide variety of other learning and assessment activities are described in the syllabi. Six (10 percent) require students to teach, individually or as a group. Topics include database and source instruction. One assignment asks students to teach a source electronically via a wiki. Observation of instruction is also assigned in one syllabus.

Five syllabi (8 percent) ask students to analyze a reference interview, either through a personal experience, a taped interaction, or chat transcripts. Annotated bibliographies (those that are not structured like pathfinders) are required in four syllabi (6 percent). Bibliographies are prepared in print, Web, and wiki formats. Three syllabi (5 percent) include assignments that require students to evaluate (fact-check) the information in a Wikipedia entry. One assignment, which asks students to find a similar book, addresses readers' advisory.

Other assignments include the following:

- Citation following
- Collection development policy or collection development project
- Emerging-technologies wiki
- Facilities evaluation
- Goals and mission statement creation
- Library scan or library Web site scan
- Needs assessment
- OPAC comparison

There are some notable correlations between assignment usage and instructor status. Full-time instructors are 22 percent more likely to administer exams and 16 percent more likely to assign a pathfinder. Part-time instructors are 21 percent more likely to assign a paper and 14 percent more likely to require a reference encounter or observation.

DISCUSSION

When compared to past studies, results from this study reveal several trends in reference instruction. Textbook selection is changing. Powell and Raber report that *Reference and Information Services: An Introduction* and *Introduction to Reference Work* were the primary textbooks used in reference instruction. Clearly, *Reference and Information Services in the 21st Century: An Introduction* has gained a significant market share. This change is noteworthy because, as indicated earlier, there is a high correlation between course content and textbook selection.

Table 22.1.
Content Comparison

Broadway & Smith (1989) Content	*Powell & Raber (1994) Objectives*	*O'Connor (2009) Content*
Specific reference sources (100%)	Search strategy (100%)	Search strategy (100%)
Types of print reference sources (96%)	Interview (98%)	Genres/types of reference sources (100%)
Reference query negotiation (96%)	Genres/types of reference sources (98%)	Evaluation and selection of information (100%)
Selection and evaluation of sources (95%)	Ready reference (98%)	Reference interview (97%)
Manual search strategies (91%)	Specific current reference titles (96%)	Evaluation of services (79%)
Online reference sources (86%)	Reference philosophy (90%)	Online and database search strategy (77%)
Evaluation of reference services (77%)	Bibliographic instruction (81%)	Digital reference (75%)
Information-seeking behavior (77%)	New information technologies (81%)	Internet for reference services (67%)
Reference policy and procedure (72%)	Specific retrospective reference titles (81%)	Information literacy and user instruction (62%)
Standards and guidelines (70%)	User information-seeking behavior (79%)	Ethics (59%)
Library-use instruction (70%)	Evaluation (75%)	Management of reference services (59%)
Online search strategies (67%)	Information and referral (67%)	Issues and trends (56%)
CD-ROM reference sources (65%)	CD-ROM databases (67%)	Services to special populations (51%)
Information and referral (65%)	Automated searching (65%)	Information seeking, behavior, and use (43%)
Models of the reference process (65%)	User community information needs (60%)	Services in specific contexts (39%)

In some respects, the reference curriculum remains relatively stable. Discussions of search strategy, reference source types and evaluation, and the reference interview continue to form its core across this and previous studies. Changes in course content are evident as well. Table 22.1 compares the analysis of course content across three studies and lists the top 15 topics.

Much of the change in reference instruction has occurred in the technologies and services aspects of reference practice. Digital reference is an entirely new topic to syllabi and is now covered in the majority of courses, as is use of the Internet for reference service. Management of reference services has increased in syllabi since 1994. While the "reference policy and procedure" category from Broadway and Smith's study may be analogous, this topic did not reach the top 15 in Powell and Raber's findings. The context of reference services has also become a more important concept, as services to special populations and in specific contexts are also new to the most frequently taught topics. Ethics is new to this list; however, since Powell and Raber did not include this topic at all, one might speculate that ethics was coded within another topic, such as reference philosophy. This study does demonstrate a significant increase in treatment of ethics over Broadway and Smith's findings of 44 percent. Online search technique is now covered by approximately 10 percent more courses than in past studies.

A consistent theme across recent studies of reference curricula is that although instructors feel a great need to add new content in response to the fast-changing information environment, they are less clear about what content may be given up to accommodate it. This study does reveal a few content areas that have lost ground in coverage. Making students responsible for specific reference titles has declined from 100 percent in 1989 (Broadway and Smith) to 96 percent in 2004 (Powell and Raber) to virtual nonexistence in this study. This change appears to signal a significant shift away from teaching sources to teaching source types, which remains a core component of all syllabi. Two surprising content areas appear to be diminishing within reference curricula. Information seeking, behavior, and use are named in 36 percent fewer syllabi than in 1994. User instruction, which had risen in Powell and Raber's study, is now covered in 19 percent fewer course than it was in 1994. Although readers' advisory service is not present in table 22.1, note that it declined in coverage, as well, slipping from 44 percent in 1994 (Powell and Raber) to 26 percent currently.

It is difficult to make many assumptions about changes in assignments because no data were collected in Broadway and Smith (1989) and very limited data in Powell and Raber (1994). However, there are a few observable differences (see table 22.2). Reliance on problem sets to teach the reference method has increased by 25 percent. This would tend to reinforce the conclusion that teaching reference source types is still exceedingly important in reference education. Papers are assigned slightly more often as well. The use of exams for assessment has declined significantly at 44 percent. One might

Table 22.2.
Comparison of Types of Assignments

Powell & Raber (1994)	*O'Connor (2009)*
Other* (69%)	Problem sets (75%)
Exams (67%)	Source evaluation (65%)
Reference questions (50%)	Reference encounter/observation (62%)
Papers (25%)	Electronic and online searching (52%)
	Pathfinders (51%)
	Papers (34%)
	Exams and quizzes (23%)

*Other includes class presentations, reference worksheets, journals, source evaluation, practice interviews, pathfinders, bibliographies, online searching, book reviews, literature reviews, and term-paper clinics.

speculate that they have been replaced with the many more diverse assignments described in this study.

CONCLUSION

So, is education for reference services overly source based and unresponsive to changing information environments? If, as Richardson (1992) suggests, reference education needs to be the balanced intersection of information resources, technology, and users, how well have we evolved toward this complete paradigm? This study alone is too limited to answer these questions completely. How much is "overly" source based? Clearly, teaching source types through practice query exercises and evaluation assignments is still a central component of reference education. But to assess the effectiveness of this approach will require ongoing research that measures outcomes rather than content.

At the same time, studies analyzing content have been conducted too far apart and unevenly to provide the best measures of change to curricula (data collection and analysis have not been well replicated). Regular and standardized research evaluating the content of reference education is necessary in this age of quickly changing information contexts.

This study does demonstrate, however, that reference education has not only changed over time but also is currently under great stress to accommodate continuous change. Technology and users and user contexts are now very visible components of the curriculum. What content needs to be added to reference education seems quite obvious, but, as other studies have found, what content may be sacrificed is anything but self-evident. Clearly, however, reference instructors are overwhelmed with trying to cover more aspects of theory and practice than ever. Additional and ongoing research to inform decisions about what content is essential, as well as peripheral, is critically needed by the profession at this time.

WORKS CITED

Adkins, D., and S. Erdelez. 2006. An exploratory survey of reference source instruction in LIS courses. *Reference & User Services Quarterly* 46 (2): 50–60.

American Library Association. 2006. *Library bill of rights.* Retrieved October 5, 2009, from http://www.ala.org/ala/aboutala/offices/oif/statementspols/statementsif/librarybillrights.cfm.

American Library Association. 2007. *Code of ethics.* Retrieved October 5, 2009, from http://www.ala.org/ala/aboutala/offices/oif/statementspols/codeofethics/codeethics.cfm.

American Library Association (ACRL). 2006. *Information literacy competency standards for higher education.* Retrieved October 5, 2009, from http://www.ala.org/ala/mgrps/divs/acrl/standards/informationliteracycompetency.cfm.

American Library Association (RUSA). 2004. *Guidelines for behavioral performance of reference and information service providers.* Retrieved July 28, 2009, from http://www.ala.org/ala/mgrps/divs/rusa/resources/guidelines/guidelinesbehavioral.cfm.

American Library Association (RUSA). 2006. *Elements for basic reviews: A guide for writers and readers of reviews of works in all media and genres.* Retrieved October 5, 2009, from http://www.ala.org/ala/mgrps/divs/rusa/resources/guidelines/ElementsforReviews.pdf.

American Library Association (RUSA). 2008a. *Guidelines for implementing and maintaining virtual reference services.* Retrieved October 5, 2009, from http://www.ala.org/ala/mgrps/divs/rusa/resources/guidelines/virtrefguidelines.cfm.

American Library Association (RUSA). 2008b. *Guidelines for information services.* Retrieved October 5, 2009, from http://www.ala.org/ala/mgrps/divs/rusa/resources/guidelines/guidelinesinformation.cfm.

American Library Association (RUSA). 2008c. *Guidelines for medical, legal, and business responses.* Retrieved October 5, 2009, from http://www.ala.org/ala/mgrps/divs/rusa/resources/guidelines/guidelinesmedical.cfm.

American Library Association (RUSA). 2008d. *Guidelines for the preparation of a bibliography.* Retrieved October 5, 2009, from http://www.ala.org/ala/mgrps/divs/rusa/resources/guidelines/guidelinespreparation.cfm.

American Library Association (RUSA). 2008e. *Professional competencies for reference and user services librarians.* Retrieved October 5, 2009, from http://www.ala.org/ala/mgrps/divs/rusa/resources/guidelines/professional.cfm.

Balay, R. 1996. *Guide to reference books.* Chicago: American Library Association.

Bell, S. S. 2006. *Librarian's guide to online searching.* Englewood, CO: Libraries Unlimited.

Bonk, W. J. 1961. The core curriculum and the reference bibliography courses. *Journal of Education for Librarianship* 2 (4): 28–33.

Bopp, R. E., and L. C. Smith. 2001. *Reference and information services: An introduction.* Littleton, CO: Libraries Unlimited.

Broadway, M. D., and N. M. Smith. 1989. Basic reference courses in ALA-accredited library schools. *Reference Librarian* 25–26: 431–448.

Case, D. 2007. *Looking for information: A survey of research on information seeking, needs, and behavior.* Amsterdam: Academic Press.

Cassell, K. A., and U. Hiremath. 2009. *Reference and information services in the 21st century: An introduction.* New York: Neal-Schuman.

Chu, H. 2003. *Information representation and retrieval in the digital age.* Medford: NJ: Information Today.

Dervin, B., and P. Dewdney. 1986. Neutral questioning: A new approach to the reference interview. *RQ* 25 (4): 506–513.

Dewdney, P., and G. Mitchell. 1996. Oranges and peaches: Understanding accidents in the reference interview. *RQ* 35 (4): 520–534.

Green, S. 1876. Personal relations between librarians and readers. *American Library Journal* 1: 74–81.

Howe, H. E. 1931. The library school curriculum. *Library Quarterly* 1 (1–4): 283.

Janes, J. 2003. *Introduction of reference work in the digital age.* New York: Neal-Schuman.

Jennerich, E. Z., and E. J. Jennerich. 1997. *The Reference interview as a creative art.* Englewood, CO: Libraries Unlimited.

Katz, W. 2001. *Introduction to reference work.* Vols. 1 and 2. New York: McGraw Hill.

Kovacs, D. K. 2007. *The virtual reference handbook: Interview and information delivery techniques for the chat and e-mail environments.* New York: Neal-Schuman.

Kuhlthau, C. C. 2000. *Seeking meaning: A process approach to library and information services.* Norwood, NJ: Ablex.

Larson, J. C. 1979. Information sources currently studied in general reference courses. *RQ* 18 (4): 341–348.

Powell, R. R., and D. Raber. 1994. Education for reference/information service: A quantitative and qualitative analysis of basic reference courses. *Reference Librarian* 43: 145–172.

Richardson, J. V., Jr. 1992. Teaching general reference work: The complete paradigm and competing schools of thought, 1890–1990. *Library Quarterly* 62 (1): 55–89.

Ross C. S., and P. Dewdney. 1998a. *Communicating professionally: A how-to-do-it manual for library applications.* NewYork: Neal-Schuman.

Ross, C. S., and P. Dewdney. 1998b. Negative closure. *Reference & User Services Quarterly* 38 (2): 151–163.

Ross, C. S., K. Nilsen, and M. L. Radford. 2009. *Conducting the reference interview: A how-to-do-it manual for librarians.* 2nd ed. New York: Neal-Schuman.

Smith, J. 2003. *Chat reference: A guide to live virtual reference services.* Westport, CT: Libraries Unlimited.

Summers, F. W. 1982. Education for reference services. In *The service imperative for libraries,* ed. G. A. Schlachter, 157–168. Littleton, CO: Libraries Unlimited.

Taylor, R. 1968. Question-negotiation and information seeking in libraries. *College & Research Libraries* 29: 178–194.

Tenopir, C. 1987. Searching by controlled vocabulary or free text? *Library Journal* 112 (19): 58–59.

Walker G., J. Janes, and C. Tenopir. 1999. *Online retrieval: A dialogue of theory and practice.* 2nd ed. Englewood, CO: Libraries Unlimited.

APPENDIX: INSTITUTIONS CONTRIBUTING SYLLABI

Alabama, University of
Albany, State University of New York
Alberta, University of
Arizona, University of
British Columbia, University of
Buffalo, State University of New York
California, Los Angeles, University of
Catholic University of America
Clarion University
Dalhousie University
Denver, University of
Dominican University
Emporia State University
Florida State University
Hawaii, University of
Illinois, University of
Iowa, University of
Kentucky, University of
Louisiana State University
McGill University
Maryland, University of
Michigan, University of
Missouri-Columbia, University of
North Carolina at Chapel Hill, University of
North Carolina at Greensboro, University of
North Texas, University of
Pratt Institute
Queens College, City University of New York
Rhode Island, University of
Rutgers University
San Jose State University
Simmons College
South Florida, University of
Southern Connecticut State University
Southern Mississippi, University of
Syracuse University
Tennessee, University of
Texas at Austin, University of
Texas Woman's University
Toronto, University of
Valdosta State University
Washington, University of
Wayne State University
Wisconsin–Madison, University of

23

THE *GUIDE TO REFERENCE* AND LEARNING REFERENCE LIBRARIANSHIP

Robert H. Kieft

Reference librarians of a certain age will remember their halcyon early MLS days, say, in the 1970s, and the world in which they first practiced their craft. It was a world and their's was work shaped by paper, early strategies for "library automation," needle-in-a-haystack miracles of information retrieval from that red book in the As, and endless catalog confusion in university library systems where the questioner had to go to multiple service desks in multiple buildings to consult the several record files that gave access to different collections—needless to say, with ample opportunity for becoming lost among them.

My own introduction to reference work came during those very 1970s in my first year of graduate school, when, perhaps because I had worked at the loan desk of my college library, I was hired to staff the general reference desk on Friday night from 6:00 P.M. to 11:00 P.M.[1] My training consisted of an orientation to the desk and the main library building, an introduction to the complexities of the central card catalog and the campus library system, and an orally annotated walking tour of the very large reference room. After the tour, I was pretty much left to my own devices on the assumption that Constance Winchell's 8th edition of *Guide to Reference Books* (1967) and I could make do with each other to serve the information needs of the university community, at least insofar as those needs might surface on a Friday night. I'm sure there were other lessons from librarians in addition to that guided tour of the shelves, especially in later years as I sat with the librarians at the reference desk, learning the trade by osmosis and overt instruction, absorbing or avoiding my seniors' tricks and tics, and acquainting myself with reference sources and the folkways and mores of questioners.

During those long-gone days, it was the companionable guidance of Miss Winchell (for thus, I later learned, she was styled at Columbia) that led me through those quiet Friday nights well before librarianship in the age of the Web as we know it came into being. I invoke the Ghost of Reference Past here because I am now of that "certain age" when the past becomes interesting, there being so much more of it for me now than there is of the future, and because the future is so bright with promise for the practice of reference, albeit by means or in modes that I would not have predicted back then and with resources that I could not have imagined.

REFERENCE SERVICE AND MODERN LIBRARIANSHIP

I invoke the Ghost of Reference Past also on behalf of the *Guide to Reference* (Kieft, 2008a) and its century-long role in reference service, for, as I have written elsewhere (Kieft, 2002, 2008b), the Ghosts of Reference Present and Future have very different things, at least superficially, to tell us about reference service in the world as it is now compared to the world in which the first 11 editions of the *Guide* played their distinguished part (Miller, 1992). My immediate concern in this essay is to discuss the role of the *Guide* as an educational tool (it plays many others, of course), whether in library and information science (LIS) courses or in the reference department. In deference to the ghosts, however, I want first to take a step back to the founding period of U.S. librarianship in the last quarter of the 19th century to remind readers of the three (there may be more) components of librarians' modern professional domain and cultural role.

These components are the principles (1) that various institutions in a society, and especially libraries, gather and make available collections (or "information," if you will) as public goods; (2) that these collections require a set of services, not just a set of shelves, to make them useful to readers; and (3) that the library, its collections and services, is a site of instruction and learning for everyone, not the exclusive preserve of the proven scholar or otherwise-elite reader. Whether you obey Ranganathan's five laws or subscribe to more contemporary statements of the purposes and values of libraries, reference service and to a considerable degree reference sources lie at the heart of these founding impulses of modern U.S. librarianship; indeed, reference service, together with the kinds of instructional, advisory, and educational services that proceed from it,[2] is an essential expression of modern librarianship's demotic impulse, one echoed in Google's mission: "To organize the world's information and make it universally accessible and useful" (Google). On the long road, then, from Samuel Swett Green's "Personal Relations between Librarians and Readers" (1876) to roving reference, instant messaging (IM) and Twitter librarianship, Google Scholar, the dislocation of reference collections, and beyond, librarians have developed or adopted services and guidance mechanisms to connect users of all kinds with the materials they need.

In claiming this central place for reference service, I do not undervalue the work of those who select, acquire, catalog, and maintain the resources of the library. I would argue, however, that a service that mediates the library's resources by helping people find things, negotiate the library's bibliographic and physical organization, and, more important, learn how to use what they find is the aspect of modern librarianship that most sharply distinguishes its practices from those of previous regimes. Moreover, if reference service in its several manifestations defines librarianship's central preoccupation as helping people to use collections in order to accomplish their various purposes, I would further argue that the *Guide*, together with similar publications, occupies a central place in representing or codifying that preoccupation.

THE *GUIDE TO REFERENCE* AND THE LITERATURES OF REFERENCE

Taken broadly, then, reference service exists systematically and ad hoc on multiple levels of individual and group interaction and in multiple media and locations. The *Guide*, in turn, occupies the intersection of four collateral literatures, namely, those of reference publication and bibliography, user services, library instruction, and training for library work. The earliest edition of the *Guide* by its introductory content and title, *Guide to the Study and Use of Reference Books: A Manual for Librarians, Teachers, and Students* (Kroeger, 1902), neatly maps this crucial intersection where information sources meet patrons' immediate needs through services established by reference staff, staff who have acquired knowledge, skills, and even a sense of mission for the purpose of making this very connection between sources and their potential users.[3]

These literatures have an ample and amply documented history; they are also remarkably consistent over the last 125 years. The first of the four consists of the *Guide* and similar publications that array, describe, and comment on reference sources, discussing their value, use, and place in the contexts of other reference sources and of information-finding processes. This literature is layered for varying audiences and degrees of specificity in the *Guide*, the multivolume *The New Walford: Guide to Reference Resources* (Lester, 2005–), and O'Gorman's *Reference Sources for Small and Medium-Sized Libraries* (2008). At the next level of specificity are publications that speak to broad academic divisions, such as Blazek and Aversa's *The Humanities: A Selective Guide to Information Sources* (2000) or Herron's *The Social Sciences: A Cross-Disciplinary Guide to Selected Sources* (2002). Harner's *Literary Research Guide* (2008), Green, Ernest, and Holler's *Information Sources of Political Science* (2005), Wyatt's *Information Sources in the Life Sciences* (1997), and Kibbee and Jacoby's *Cultural Anthropology: A Guide to Reference and Information Sources* (2007) address specific disciplines or subdisciplines, and all these publications model the subject guides and Web pages that individual librarians create to address specific courses or topics.

The user services literature is the largest and most varied of the four, outlining everything from the etiquette and staffing of service points to policies, procedures, standards, and best practices and on to the design of facilities, assessment, outreach, and analysis of the needs and proclivities of various user populations. Much of this literature concerns services and programs collateral to reference, which come into focus in the present context largely as the obverse of training for reference. I pass over them here, noting that this large literature at once proceeds from the public, egalitarian impulse of reference service and subsumes reference service as one of its many categories.

The third of these four is the province not only of librarians but of faculty and anyone else who advises readers about successful research. Over the years, their work has been couched as advice about the "use of books," "research methods," "writing term papers and dissertations," "how to find information," "bibliographic instruction," or "information literacy." The variety of markets and publications in which writers offer this advice ranges from first-year writing and seminar courses to academic tutoring and writing centers, term-paper workshops, stand-alone courses or class sessions on research methods (whether in the library or in seminars for undergraduate or graduate students), research sessions for senior-thesis writers, and "self-help" books for those outside academe who undertake research in their job, whether as a personal interest or in pursuit of a publishing ambition.

These texts run the gamut from such source-based guides as Hutchins's *Guide to the Use of Libraries: A Manual for College and University Students* (1935) and her latter-day successor, Gates's *Guide to the Use of Libraries and Information Sources* (1994),[4] to such process-based guides as George's recent *The Elements of Library Research: What Every Student Needs to Know* (2008), which reflects those concerns with active learning, skills transfer, and metacognition so important to current methods of teaching academic work. The library literature exemplified by the work of these and many other writers has its parallels in the multitudes of publications for students from other angles, for example, guides for writers of term papers,[5] college composition handbooks,[6] discipline-specific guides or advice for more advanced academic researchers,[7] or guides for would-be writers of books.[8] All of these, with varying emphases, couple writing and research advice with other instructions about minding the p's and q's of academic work and the several kinds of publishing.

The fourth literature, the literature proper of training and education for librarianship, extends to just yesterday from the earliest days of the profession. It begins with the exhortations and observations of such pioneers as Green in the 1870s and 1880s through the founding of reference courses in the 1890s, the publication of the first edition of the *Guide* in 1902, and on to a number of textbooks published in the 20th century. In "Learning Reference Work: The Paradigm,"[9] John V. Richardson Jr. discusses this history through a study of various editions of textbooks on reference librarianship published by Wyer and Shores beginning in the 1930s, Hutchins in the 1940s, Katz in the 1960s, Cheney and Williams in the 1970s, and Thomas, Hinckley, and Eisenbach in the 1980s. His chronological account stops short of the Bopp and Smith (2001) and Cassell and Hiremath (2006) textbooks, but it includes extensive discussion of the *Guide*'s place in the history of teaching reference, and the paradigm he develops continues to manifest itself in such documents as the Reference and User Services Association (RUSA)'s *Professional Competencies for Reference and User Services Librarians* (RUSA, 2003) and *Guidelines for Behavioral Performance of Reference and Information Service Providers* (RUSA, 2004), LIS course syllabi, library departmental training documentation, and such very recent and prospective publications as Charlotte Ford's *Crash Course in Reference* (2008) and Carolyn Mulac's forthcoming *Fundamentals of Reference.*

Thus, from Green in 1876 to the RUSA's *Competencies* and *Guidelines for Behavioral Performance* in the 21st century, from the reference courses of the late 19th century to today's brush-up or basics seminar,[10] the tools and the environment have changed but the parameters for learning the trade have not changed much. The emphasis varies from course to course and author to author, but the knowledge base for reference staff does not, and the repertory of topics codified by Kroeger in her 1902 textbook maps well onto today's syllabi, training manuals, and textbook tables of contents.

TEACHING, TRAINING, AND THE *GUIDE*

Based on these four literatures and the reformulation of the library's place in the information economy, what skills and knowledge define the work of the reference librarian?[11] A review of course syllabi, library training and reference desk manuals, and reference service teaching and conduct literature demonstrates that the paradigm developed by Richardson (1995, 19) very much holds true today, as does his conclusion about the twin poles of source teaching and process teaching that emerged, like the give-a-fish/teach-to-fish dichotomy, 100 years ago in reference education.

This paradigm for teaching reference consists of three elements: (1) reference materials' formats and their use, (2) reference methods, and (3) the mental traits of the librarian and the user.[12] Running parallel to these three is a tripartite series of tasks emerging from the reference training materials used in libraries: (1) source and search knowledge, often using sets of questions and a bibliography of basic reference works; (2) service training in everything from proper deportment and how to be welcoming or approachable to user engagement and outreach activities to the reference interview; and (3) local knowledge of the library system, policies, and locations as well as the library's user community.

The basic reference course today, as Richardson's paradigm and my own study of syllabi both show, is, again, remarkably similar in its content and methods to its predecessors.[13] A recent survey by ALA Publishing designed to gather data about the first of the three elements in each of the two trinities described in the preceding confirms this generalization.[14] The survey asked LIS professors about the following course elements:

- Percentage of course time spent on examination and use of reference sources (70 percent of the 84 respondents spend 30 to 80 percent of students' course time on this activity)
- Tasks that instructors ask students to perform: examining similar sources for purposes of comparison (78 percent), finding answers to specific questions or specific pieces of information (79 percent), determining occasions for using specific sources for specific audiences or types of questions (89 percent), judging the quality of sources (85 percent), writing annotations or reviews of sources (46 percent), and compiling subject guides using reference sources (41 percent)
- Introduction of the *Guide*
- Use of bibliographic works like the *Guide* in courses
- Concepts or practices that students find difficult to grasp about reference sources and their potential use in reference service

The responses to the last question are telling in that they not only illuminate long-standing teaching methods and goals but also the (generational?) tensions in which the *Guide* is caught—that is, in the shift from print to electronic searching and the information-seeking practices and preferences this shift entails. Themes that emerge in the answers include students' being intimidated or confused by the abundance and variety of sources, students' reluctance to use print sources or thinking they need nothing beyond Web searches, the difficulty in online courses of introducing students to a useful range of sources, searching heuristics and answering questions (which sources to use and when or for whom, or how to think about questions and the relationship of questions to sources, also known as the "reference interview"), and understanding how information is packaged to assist others in finding it.

I will say more about these concerns in the following, but I would like to note at the outset, with respect to the first item in both the LIS and library training trinities of goals, that the *Guide,* as it has been and is now published, is ideally suited to the task.[15] Through its repertory of sources, introductory material, and list-making and comment features, the *Guide* readily helps students with source choice and comparison and with knowledge of the range of sources available.[16] These same capacities, when applied in the library environment, can help both with source training and with traditional problems of collection development and management, especially now that reference departments are emphasizing online resources and services and downsizing the print collection kept near service points. The *Guide* could even go some distance toward addressing the resource deficit that online students face by offering page images of sample content, editorial matter, and tables of contents from print sources or screen captures from online sources to which their home institution does not subscribe.

Perhaps more important in the long run, though, is how the *Guide* could grow to meet other kinds of course- or training-related concerns, especially educational concerns beyond source knowledge. For example, LIS students and service point trainees come to learn in sessions on the reference interview and through observing transactions with patrons that a question is often not what it seems, that a question is often looking for something more or concealing an unrecognized need. At least in academic library settings, the question is often a request less for specific information than for broader engagement with the project at hand.[17] If that's true, then either the *Guide* needs more introductory or advisory material, or it needs to elaborate its current editor's guides and annotations to say more not only about the scope of sources for answering specific types of questions but also about how to respond to questions within disciplinary research frameworks. To this end, and given additional programming, the *Guide* could compile pathfinders on-the-fly based on markers in the record for basic works or publish pathfinders ready-made by editors or other librarians. This service would not only clarify relationships among kinds and levels of sources but could also include collateral essays on the state of scholarship in the disciplines and on disciplinary research methods and issues—in other words, the larger context that informs the work a student has been asked to do and without a sense of which "information" does not take the student very far.

Since the reference collection has always seemed to interpose another step for students between defining a project and completing it, and since so many students are impatient with the procedural and organizational aspects of doing academic work, a *Guide* that maps sources and procedures (or links to already-existing sites) for service point staff and classroom faculty could be useful (again, this goal would be served by taking advantage of the *Guide*'s ability for editors to mark basic sources and for users to offer comments about specific sources). Augmenting the *Guide* in this way and ensuring that annotations include evaluative and situational advice would also allow the *Guide* to speak to the trends toward tiering reference service and increasing the amount of time when nonlibrarian and student staff tend to the front-line service point. These staff members' needs for more on-the-job support in acquiring basic skills and improving their knowledge base[18] suggest that the *Guide* could usefully create, or partner to offer, textbook content, perhaps in the form of video or audio made by teams of LIS students and reference librarians (quick takes on the reference interview, the use of certain sources, working with certain topics or questions, and so on). The *Guide* could also create charts, tables, and graphs that would assist browsing by tabulating differences among like sources or showing a chronological succession of sources; since it is easier to browse on a printed page than it is from a list of short-entry hits, such graphical means would help staff to see source relationships and contrasts more easily. A similar addition to the *Guide* would involve the creation of materials on evaluation of reference sources and the quality of the information in them using the parameters of audience, reference context, authority, and so on common to all LIS courses and familiar in the practice of reference service. The *Guide* could also, given the creation of the requisite business relationships, link to reviews or to "best lists" from RUSA and elsewhere, recognizing that some titles listed on the latter, though not appropriate for inclusion in the *Guide* because of its primary market, might be of interest to practicing librarians in some settings.

ALA Publishing conducted its first webinar for LIS professors and librarians about use of the *Guide* on December 3, 2009, and contemplates holding more. Sessions like these could not only help to bridge the so-called practitioner/educator divide but also serve as a means for compiling tips or case studies for using specific works, the *Guide* included, in reference service, training, and LIS courses. They could also lead to a collection of reference course syllabi and other teaching documents, training program documents for new reference librarians, guidelines for reference service, librarian competency guidelines and standards for assessing reference librarian performance, and so on. Moreover, in the absence of an online textbook for reference, the *Guide* could also digitize or link to historical or primary documents about the history of reference such as those cited in Kroeger's first section, "Books and Articles on Reference Books and Reference Work," or listed on many course syllabi; it could create surveys of the history and composition of the reference literature that are deeper than those in its present editor's guides; and it could create or, again, given the establishment of the right business relationships, link to essays on trends in publishing and in reference services and collections. LIS professors have expressed an interest in hearing from reference librarians about questions their users are asking so that their students can benefit from having "real-life" examples to work on as opposed to questions reverse-engineered from sources that they want their students to learn. The *Guide* could thus become the medium through which such questions are collected, and, given the proper interactive interface, students could gain the advantages of group work on the questions.

THE NEW WINE OF THE WEB IN THE OLD BOTTLES OF REFERENCE?

Given the constancy of the goals, methods, service concerns, and knowledge base discussed in the preceding, many ask whether the world might not be changing around a profession and a set of practices that are clinging to the past.[19] They wonder about the prospects for reference librarianship in a rapidly evolving information environment where the emergence, development, and triumph of the Web as a means for communication, publication, commerce, and the distribution of entertainment have created radically different information-seeking habits and preferences from those I encountered in days of yore at a 1970s reference desk. Indeed, you don't have to read too deeply in the literature, news, or gossip of librarianship or listen too hard at a conference to hear the voices of Biblio-Jeremiahs and Chicken Littles on the one hand, of Biblio-Panglosses and Moseses on the other, and of assorted librarians, academics, public intellectuals, and bloggocrats all along the continuum from despair to optimism; all are speechmaking and publishing from every soapbox in libraryland about what these changes portend for libraries, librarians, and the culture of information provision and learning they have supported.

No one would deny that, as the Web has upended the business models of many organizations, so too are the means and institutions for accessing information morphing rapidly into something very different from what they were before the mid-1990s, a metamorphosis whose rapidity is being accelerated and complicated by the economic crisis that began in 2007. Thus, the library community adheres to its mission of providing information access and learning opportunities for all but asks in an "everything-is-miscellaneous" information universe about the value of its traditions of information organization. Libraries at once reaffirm their important cultural and social roles even as they rethink not only where and when reference librarians are needed but also, more to the point, what their role as information institutions is. Reference staffs are reshaping services around answers to such questions as "How do reference librarians contribute their advice/guidance/expertise to the work that people do online?" "How do librarians not only array possibilities for finding information but help users select the sources useful for a particular occasion?" "What is the value of the idea of a 'source' given the deliquescence of the reference collection, or even general library collection, into the 'info heap' of the Web?" "How useful is it anymore to think of packaging information into so-called sources as packages become less visible online than they are in print?" "As information packages disintegrate, how does a user gain the context or see the relationships or structures without which information is inert?" Librarians wrestle with the service challenges of the move from print to electronic text and from at-the-shelf discovery to online discovery. At the same time, they and LIS professors contend with the anxiety of losing history in the format and access disjunction of printed and digitized information.

If libraries were once the authoritative assemblages of sources presided over from the reference desk by an authoritative information hunter who was at once the search interface and algorithm, the index and repository of knowledge, and the gateway to the deep library, it is no longer true, or it is not true to the extent that librarians have believed it was. Granting the many kinds of libraries and communities that use and support them, for many populations now the Web has taken a lot of the wind out of the sails of ready reference and seems to threaten the reference service itself. Libraries are therefore asking how their role changes in an information universe where powerful and convenient search tools and searchable information are available anywhere anytime, at least to those in North American higher education settings.

The beginnings of answers to these questions may take shape around the library's traditional role as a site for learning.[20] The Web and its search engines do not (yet) serve as well as reference librarians in user situations that implicate the relationship between finding information and doing (academic) work. If students and others do their initial search on the Web, librarians become important at the level of research where contexts and strategies, the packaging and relationships that constitute knowledge, as opposed to information, are important. Google has certainly lifted the magic curtain on the librarian as the Wizard of Information Access, but the information literacy movement, in turn, exposes the true role of librarians, which is not so much to help in finding sources, although that remains important, as to help people repurpose them into their own work.[21] Google has aspects of finding information down cold but not its understanding—pieces of information are, after all, not an argument or a body of knowledge. Although the good Mr. Boole and his operators are alive and well in LIS courses on information access, the trick in reference service is to transform *and*s and *or*s from a practice of search into a logic of research, that is, into the ways of thinking about the topic. In the skills area, reference service and, by extension, the *Guide* help by arraying possibilities; in the research area, the reference interview and the *Guide*'s introductory matter and annotations offer help with the processes of ordering, choosing, and absorbing.

In this argument, I take a position that some would regard as optimistic in terms of the persistence of the "traditional" roles of reference librarians and service. Fair enough, but even from my rose-tinted vantage I am concerned about that future because I am tempted to say, without knowing the details of what takes place in LIS classrooms or library training sessions and based on the evidence of syllabi and manuals alone, that we may yet be teaching and training to a disappearing paradigm, as the hierarchically arranged *Guide* may still be speaking to a publishing paradigm that has been superseded. Even though we who work in reference now teach online, use online sources, offer online service, and devote considerable time to devising online discovery and guidance environments for our users, I am not sure that we have adequately grappled in the basic reference course with what it means for reference sources and service if we assume that (1) our users, at least in higher education, seek information first and foremost without recourse to the library and its services;[22] and (2) the "source" as a discrete package of information will be less and less useful as electronic information publication develops and the everything-is-miscellaneous world emerges more clearly.

Were we to make these assumptions, I'm not sure what the basic reference course would look like, but certainly it would shift in favor of those on the "process" model end of the continuum for learning reference, and we would not spend as much time as we now do on bringing books into the classroom or be as concerned as we now are that students think Google is the be-all, end-all. We would be working hard to persuade publishers to expose their content to indexing by search engines. The traditional concern for source-based question answering or information finding would take a back seat to Web search, discussion of user behaviors and interaction, knowledge of academic disciplines and their particular research methods and problems, and technologies for generating, using, and displaying information or incorporating it into one's own work. Moreover, LIS education would expand requirements in learning theory and would partner with rhetoric and composition and teacher training programs to train reference librarians who can work on that line between research problems and writing problems.

If the teaching of basic reference moves in this direction, I must be careful to note at the process end of the reference–teaching continuum that the process is a process toward finding and structuring information. The interactions that constitute the process(es) of reference service are not the end product but the means to ends that rely on knowledge and manipulation of the information environment, the sources, if you will, that house or are in themselves information. Even the most resolutely process-oriented courses have to refer to something or process something, and the shift I advocate here in the content of the source-oriented basic reference course is one of emphasis in which the course proceeds toward rather than starts from source training and examination. At the very least, then, the *Guide* would continue to serve as "the other" of Web search, that is, the repertory of sources that expands its capacities and helps to define search's accountability for its results. Were libraries to share their training questions and scenarios with the *Guide,* it could become the site where search meets shelf or local database. The *Guide* would become more important for general reference librarians' learning about the scholarly methods and contexts and the orders of knowledge in which students and faculty work, and for serving as a space for educators and practitioners together to leverage libraries into the digital information environment.

NOTES

1. I would like to dedicate this essay to the memory of James M. Knox, one of the world's most knowledgeable, and redoubtable, reference librarians, whose views in department meetings and advice to reference assistants were liberally salted with observations that cannot be repeated in a family-oriented essay collection like this one, and to our colleagues in that 1970s Stanford University General Reference Department, whose daily example helped to persuade me that librarianship was a fine and interesting calling.

I would also like to thank the following who have shared their classrooms, syllabi, training materials, and, in interviews, wisdom and experience with me: Barbara Bibel, Michelle Cloonan, Phil Eskew, Charlotte Ford, Nancy Huling, Kathleen Kern, Mary Niles Mack, Patrick McCarthy, Carolyn Mulac, Terry Plum, Debbie Rabina, Marie Radford, John V. Richardson, Jr., the late Allen Smith, Linda C. Smith, Jo Bell Whitlatch, Alice Witkowski, Beth Woodard, and the many other librarians and library and information science (LIS) professors who have attended discussion meetings at the American Library Association over the years as the new edition of the *Guide* took shape.

2. See "History and Varieties of Reference Services" by Richard E. Bopp, in Bopp and Smith (2001), for the range of services and activities that qualify as "reference."

3. The overlap among these four literatures and their corresponding professional practices is enshrined in the "generalist" construct of the librarian and embodied in job descriptions for positions that I and many like me have held. The mix of duties suggested by such positions as those for "reference bibliographers," "reference and instruction librarians," or "departmental liaisons" describes staff who serve at the reference desk and its electronic equivalents, appear in the classroom to discuss research methods and resources, select materials for the collection, offer specialized individual research consultation to students and faculty, and create pathfinders and bibliographies to guide library users.

4. I remember during my days as a reference and instruction librarian taking the approach of such source-oriented books as these by Hutchins and Gates. I also remember the self-critical sarcasm that prevailed among instruction librarians in the 1980s and 1990s during the move from library instruction to information literacy, when we scolded ourselves for trying (and always failing) to train students to become "little reference librarians" by subjecting them to a source-oriented pedagogy.

5. See, for example, *MLA Handbook for Writers of Research Papers,* 7th ed. (New York: Modern Language Association, 2009); J. D. Lester and J. D. Lester, Jr., *Principles of Writing Research Papers,* 2nd ed. (New York: Pearson Longman, 2007); or A. C. Winker and J. R. McCuen-Metherell, *Writing the Research Paper,* 7th ed. (Boston: Thomson Wadsworth, 2008).

6. See, for example, such recently published titles as D. Hacker, *A Writer's Reference,* 6th ed. (Boston and New York: Bedford/St. Martin's, 2009); R. Bullock, *The Norton Field Guide to Writing* (New York: W. W. Norton, 2006); or J. Ruszkiewicz et al., *SF Writer,* 4th ed. (Upper Saddle River, NJ: Pearson Prentice Hall, 2008).

7. See, for example, W. Booth, G. Colomb, and J. Williams, *The Craft of Research* (Chicago: University of Chicago Press, 1995, and later editions); A Brundage, *Going to the Sources: A Guide to Historical Research and Writing* (Arlington Heights, IL: Harlan Davidson, 1989, and later editions); or R. D. Altick and J. F. Fenstermaker, *The Art of Literary Research* (New York and London: W. W. Norton, 1963, and later editions).

8. See, for example, M. Embree, *The Author's Toolkit: A Step-by-Step Guide to Writing and Publishing Your Book* (New York: Allworth Press, 2003).

9. The endnotes for Richardson's (1995) first chapter, "Learning Reference Work: The Paradigm," are rich in citations to the historical literature of education and training for reference. His notes are augmented by Adkins and Erdelez (2006), whose article surveys course syllabi and cites previous studies on the teaching of reference in LIS programs.

10. See, for example, such online offerings as "Reference Training and the Art of the Reference Interview" (http://www.librarysupportstaff.com/reftrain.html), "Core Reference Fundamentals" (http://infopeople.org/workshop/424), or "Core Reference Skills" (http://www.amigos.org/learning/catalog/shopping/product_details.php?id=274). All of these sources were retrieved on December 16, 2009.

11. This essay concerns itself with LIS reference courses at the basic level and, as a corollary, initial training for service point staff who have not taken such a course. The very important area of ongoing professional development for reference staff does not figure here, but much of what I say in this section about the current and foreseeable content and features of the *Guide* would adapt well to that purpose. The *Guide*'s constantly updated roster of entries and its editor's guides offer immediate opportunity, of course, for independent, in-depth exploration of reference literatures outside the librarian's expertise. More systematically, however, and perhaps in the form of webinars, the *Guide* might build, around its source lists and through creation of the kinds of narrative materials discussed in the following paragraphs, short lessons in reference work and sources in the humanities, social sciences, and so on or in specific disciplines. As the new *Guide* makes its way into LIS programs and reference service point training and as the *Guide*'s editorial staff come to understand better the uses to which faculty and librarians want to put it, the "advanced" reference or professional development possibilities for it will surely begin to define themselves.

12. Given that Richardson wrote this analysis in the early 1990s, I might add a fourth, which I think is not simply an elaboration of his first element, and I would call it the *information environment*. By this phrase I mean for all practical purposes the Web, that vast world "outside the library," and the ways in which it has supplanted traditional library-based information seeking. In the context of Richardson's list, I understand this information environment not so much as a reference tool or as insight into users and their behavior but instead as a set of influences driving change in the library.

13. LIS course offerings today will often fold such classic reference service topics as information access and organization into foundation courses. Beyond basic and advanced reference courses, the concerns of reference service find their way variously into discrete courses in user services, needs, and behaviors and courses in information-access methods (searching). On the books in many LIS programs are topical courses in reference sources and service for the humanities, social sciences, business, law, health sciences, and government information; discussion of reference sources and service necessarily also finds its way into courses on special collections, rare books, and archives. In the courses beyond foundational and basic reference courses, the syllabus also will delve into disciplinary research methods and professional issues.

14. ALA Publishing conducted a survey of LIS professors in the fall of 2009 to gather data for *Guide* development and marketing purposes (personal communications by e-mail of survey results from Patrick Hogan on October 22, 2009, and Denise Beaubien Bennett on November 4, 2009).

15. Much of this discussion is adapted from my recent *Reference & User Services Quarterly (RUSQ)* article (Kieft, 2008b). Thanks to the Reference and User Services Association (RUSA) and *RUSQ* editor Diane Zabel for their kind permission to repurpose it.

16. In this regard, Adkins and Erdelez (2006) sketch desiderata for a tool with which to teach reference sources. They conclude that they would like to find ways to

present to students the sources they should know according to such successful course strategies as "students' classroom presentation of sources, hands-on assignments, and fieldwork that allows them to work with sources" (58). They describe the need for "an instruction tool to facilitate reference source instruction," one that would offer means for access to and comparison of sources, instruction in how to use specific sources (video clips, etc.), and further video clips of reference interviews for students to use as case studies.

17. This essay centers on reference service in academic libraries. From my work in the Collection Development and Evaluation Section (CODES) of RUSA and from the survey of training materials and the interviews I conducted for this piece, I know that reference service inflects differently in public libraries, where some of the concerns and *Guide* content I discuss here are less relevant.

18. I joined a session on July 11, 2009, at the ALA Annual Conference sponsored by the Hot Topics in Frontline Reference discussion group of RUSA's Reference Services Section titled "Reference Meets Reality: (Support) Staff Training in Times of Change." The session explored training practices and needs in a time when libraries staff fewer hours at service points with librarians.

19. David Tyckoson eloquently makes the argument for consistency of purpose and role in the changing information environment in his "On the Desirableness of Personal Relations between Librarians and Readers: The Past and the Future of Reference" (*Reference Services Review* 31, no. 1 [2003]: 12–16).

20. As noted earlier in this essay, the assertion of an educational role for libraries dates to the founding of the modern practice of librarianship in the United States, and concerns for teaching students how to use library resources found expression at least as early as the exhortations of the likes of Ralph Waldo Emerson to found "professorships of books" in colleges (L. Hardesty, J. Schmitt, and J. Tucker in their *User Instruction in Academic Libraries* [Metuchen, NJ: Scarecrow Press, 1986] document this history up to 1980). Today, through hiring instruction librarians, attaching instruction duties to reference and departmental liaison positions, and raising the banner of information literacy, academic libraries play their role as centers for education, a role that public libraries play in a different way.

The foundation for academic libraries' continuing in this role is laid by first-year writing and seminar programs, which have been long-standing beachheads for library instruction in the curriculum, and by the porous border between research and writing. Research is the province of both classroom faculty and librarians, each addressing the several skills and habits of mind necessary for success in the "blended" realm of scholarship, a realm where skill and method are eventually indistinguishable from product. Anyone who has ever worked in a writing center or at a reference desk knows that research and writing overlap to a high degree and are in fact phases or modes of addressing the topic at hand, that is, of thinking—distinctive modes of thought, yes, each having its own properties, but where one ends and the other begins is often difficult to ascertain. From the point of view of writing, research is a way of developing argument, and argument, reflexively, is a way of determining the sources (research) one needs to adduce as evidence. Research understood in this way looks much like rhetoric, for both research and writing are concerned with authority, audience and context, the organization of knowledge, and so on. Even in its simplest, most mechanistic instantiations, and whatever its shortcomings, the information literacy movement has finally put to rest the notion that knowledge of which sources to use is equivalent to knowing how to do research, a process fraught with the same problems and dynamics that writing is.

21. Again, given the differences in public and academic library reference service, this educational aspect of reference may have a more vigorous life in academic than in public libraries, in part because of the populations served by each and the digital divide that prevails between them. I also recognize that, were basic reference courses to shift their focus in this way, they might exacerbate the tensions that even now exist in their attempt to prepare librarians to work in these two different environments.

22. Except, of course, insofar as the library subscribes to sources that are really "in" the library and not simply "on" the Web and as the library has designed an information-seeking environment in ways that guide people to what they want.

WORKS CITED

Adkins, D., and S. Erdelez. 2006. An exploratory survey of reference source instruction in LIS courses. *Reference & User Services Quarterly* 46 (2): 50–60.

Blazek, R., and E. S. Aversa. 2000. *The humanities: A selective guide to information sources.* 5th ed. Englewood, CO: Libraries Unlimited.

Bopp, R. E., and L. C. Smith. 2001. *Reference and information services: An introduction.* 3rd ed. Englewood, CO: Libraries Unlimited (1st ed., 1993).

Cassell, K. A., and U. Hiremath. 2006. *Reference and information services in the 21st century: An introduction.* New York: Neal-Schuman (2nd ed., 2009).

Ford, C. 2008. *Crash course in reference.* Westport, CT: Libraries Unlimited.

Gates, J. K. 1994. *Guide to the use of libraries and information sources.* 7th ed. New York: McGraw-Hill.

George, M. W. 2008. *The elements of library research: What every student needs to know.* Princeton, NJ: Princeton University Press.

Google. 2009. *Why Google?* Retrieved December 19, 2009, from http://www.google.com/enterprise/whygoogle.html.

Green, S. S. 1876. Personal relations between librarians and readers. *Library Journal* 1 (October): 74–81.

Green, S. W., D. Ernest, and F. L. Holler. 2005. *Information sources of political science.* 5th ed. Santa Barbara, CA: ABC-CLIO.

Harner, J. L. 2008. *Literary research guide: An annotated listing of reference sources in English literary studies.* 5th ed. New York: Modern Language Association.

Herron, N. L. 2002. *The social sciences: A cross-disciplinary guide to selected sources.* 3rd ed. Englewood, CO: Libraries Unlimited.

Hutchins, M. 1935. *Guide to the use of libraries: A manual for college and university students.* 5th ed. rev. New York: H. W. Wilson (1st ed., 1920).

Kibbee, J. Z., and J. Jacoby. 2007. *Cultural anthropology: A guide to reference and information sources.* Westport, CT: Libraries Unlimited.

Kieft, R. H. 2002. When reference works are not books: The new edition of the *Guide to Reference Books*. *Reference & User Services Quarterly* 41 (4): 330–334.

Kieft, R. H., ed. 2008a. *Guide to reference.* Retrieved December 15, 2009, from http://www.guidetoreference.org.

Kieft, R. H. 2008b. The return of the *Guide to Reference* (Books). *Reference & User Services Quarterly* 48 (1): 4–10.

Kroeger, A. B. 1902. *Guide to the study and use of reference books: A manual for librarians, teachers, and students.* Chicago: American Library Association.

Lester, R., ed. 2005–. *The new Walford: Guide to reference resources.* 9th ed. London: Facet.

Miller, S. W. 1992. "Monument": Guide to reference books. In *Distinguished classics of reference publishing,* ed. J. Rettig, 129–137. Phoenix: Oryx Press.

Mulac, C. Forthcoming 2011. *Fundamentals of reference.* Chicago: American Library Association.

O'Gorman, J. 2008. *Reference sources for small and medium-sized libraries.* 7th ed. Chicago: American Library Association.

Reference and User Services Association. 2004. *Guidelines for behavioral performance of reference and information service providers.* Retrieved December 15, 2009, from http://ala.org/ala/mgrps/divs/rusa/resources/guidelines/guidelines behavioral.cfm.

Reference and User Services Association, Task Force on Professional Competencies. 2003. *Professional competencies for reference and user services librarians.* Retrieved December 15, 2009, from http://ala.org/ala/mgrps/divs/rusa/resources/guidelines/professional.cfm.

Richardson, J. V., Jr., 1995. *Knowledge-based systems for general reference work: Applications, problems, and progress.* San Diego: Academic Press.

Winchell, C. M. 1967. *Guide to reference books.* 8th ed. Chicago: American Library Association.

Wyatt, H. V. 1997. *Information sources in the life sciences.* 4th ed. London and New Providence, NJ: Bowker Saur.

24

PRACTITIONERS AS ADJUNCT TEACHERS

Christopher LeBeau

Who are these teaching librarians, referred to in various ways—adjuncts, part-timers, or moonlighters—these dedicated souls who flow from a full day of work into the fluorescent glare of the nighttime classroom, racing through rush-hour traffic and wolfing down burritos in order to arrive on time? While the national educational press has covered the subject of adjuncts quite fully, little has been written about the library science school adjunct in recent years. Stephanie Brown (2007) and Nancy Gershenfeld (2004) wrote separate pieces about their personal experiences as practitioners in the classroom. Gershenfeld actually moved from practitioner to lecturer. Roxanne Spencer (2003) contributed an article about her challenges and successes in the classroom as a practitioner-teacher. Barbara Moran (2001) wrote an excellent article about the rift between practitioners and library science educators, but it addresses fundamental curricular issues rather than the practitioner's experience.

This chapter looks at the situation of the library and information science school adjunct today. The following pages explore questions about motivation, satisfaction with part-time teaching, preparedness for teaching, range of responsibilities, and the pressures and pleasures of teaching. This chapter also considers ways to prepare adjuncts for teaching. Library schools depend heavily on adjuncts for support of their programs. Cultivating and retaining good adjuncts is critical for the success of library schools. Hopefully, this chapter will generate some ideas. There is, however, much more that needs to be studied.

Over the past three years I have surveyed this special group of colleagues for some answers. A survey I conducted in 2007 (LeBeau, 2008) gathered responses about librarians who transition between academic and nonacademic positions but also included a few exploratory questions about those engaged in adjunct teaching. A more recent survey conducted in the spring of 2009 sought out the adjunct audience specifically. This survey collected responses from 184 adjunct instructors who teach part-time in one of the 56 U.S. library science schools. Surveys were distributed through national professional discussion lists and through a sampling of library school adjuncts reached directly through their library schools. Personal interviews with several deans, administrators, faculty, and colleagues working as part-timers provided additional material.

For the purposes of this discussion, I should define the term *adjunct*. As an educational term it is commonly recognized as someone who teaches in a supporting or complementary role on a non–tenure track line, normally, although not necessarily, part-time. Adjunct positions are not meant to be career positions, although there are plenty of examples of teachers who have created adjunct careers. For the purposes of this chapter, I use the term *adjunct* to refer to those who teach on a part-time basis. Some schools prefer the term *part-timer* to adjunct. The term *adjunct* is used here in a neutral manner, connoting neither a higher quality nor status than the term *part-timer*. The two terms may be used interchangeably.

The numbers of students interested in library and information science (LIS) careers are not reflective of the looming questions about the future of libraries. Between fall 1998 and 2008, student enrollment in all library science programs rose 30.5 percent (Saye and Lan, 1998, 1999; Saye and Wisser, 2000, 2001, 2002, 2003, 2004b; Wallace and Naidoo, 2010a). During the same time period, the number of full-time faculty also rose 45.6 percent. A more interesting figure is the number of individual adjuncts, which rose at a higher rate of 97 percent, confirming an observation made by former Association for Library and Information Science Education (ALISE) president Connie Van Fleet in a 2008 interview. She said, "We'll probably see a sizeable number of adjunct and part-time instructors" (Zabel, 2008, 206). By head count, adjuncts make up 52.6 percent of total number of faculty; however, if counted as full-time employees, adjuncts comprise 25 percent of total faculty strength (Sineath, 1998, 1999, 2000, 2001, 2002, 2003, 2004, 2006; Wallace and Naidoo, 2010b). These numbers are striking if one considers that most LIS programs are graduate level, and the use of adjuncts is more common on the undergraduate level.

For several years there has been concern among library science faculty that the field is in serious need of more PhDs to teach in library science programs. Charles Seavey researched LIS doctoral programs, candidates, and graduates and pronounced that "finding actual librarians to fill faculty positions was edging toward the crisis state" (2005, 55). Are LIS PhDs becoming as scarce as priests in the Catholic Church? Van Fleet concurs with Seavey: "We are concerned not only about replacing ourselves in the future, but in expanding our faculties now in anticipation of the need for the next generation of librarians" (Zabel, 2008, 206). New doctorates have entered the field in numbers fluctuating between 65 and 99 (annually) during recent years, and it is not uncommon to have as many as 87 open positions each year in LIS programs (Burnett and Naidoo, 2009; Saye and Wisser, 2004a; Seavey, 2007; Sineath, 2005). The average number of LIS PhD degrees conferred has risen steadily each decade since 1930, reaching 83.5 for 2000–2007, and the decade is not even complete. But according to a study by Sugimoto, Russell, and Grant (2009), 78 percent of the last decade's new doctorates are not teaching in LIS programs. While some new PhDs head for administration, no one is quite sure where the others have found employment. There is a trend for LIS programs to hire PhDs from other fields such as computer science, business, and communications, which fills new needs for changing curricula. Many LIS faculty are concerned about this dilution and about the low numbers of LIS doctoral students. The Sugimoto, Russell, and Grant study finds that only 58 percent of LIS faculty have PhDs in the LIS field. This fact alone makes the contribution of the librarian-practitioner adjunct more critical and valuable to LIS programs.

The 2009 adjunct survey was aimed at professionals and practitioners who teach or have taught in library science programs in the last five years. Of this group, 82 percent are employed as full-time librarians. Many librarian-practitioners teaching in library science programs today have advanced degrees but not necessarily PhDs; in fact, only 8 percent of part-timers who responded have PhDs, EdDs, or equivalent degrees. Ninety-six percent of adjuncts hold a master of library science (MLS) or equivalent degree. Thirty percent shared their second master's degrees, which cover a variety of fields: musicology, instructional design, linguistics, English, public administration, journalism, Latin, accounting, business administration, and economics. There are even some with law degrees. The PhD or equivalent is not a prerequisite for teaching part-time; however, the terminal degree would advance one's eligibility. The majority of part-time instructors work as practitioners in libraries. The variety of additional degrees brings a richness, perspective, and needed specialization to the teaching experience that supports the vital role adjuncts play.

WHAT MOTIVATES THE PART-TIME INSTRUCTOR?

In the 2007 survey, part-timers revealed their motivations for taking on this extra workload (LeBeau, 2008). In that survey, librarians indicated that their highest motivating factor was "sharing knowledge with people entering the profession." It should be no surprise that people who love sharing information for a living are motivated to teach for the same reason. Another highly motivating factor for teaching was the necessity to continually learn new content and new habits of practice. Teaching compels teachers to keep current. Finally, the extra pay motivated 57.9 percent of part-timers.

Unlike some other advanced degree programs, many library science students already work in the field. Many bring to the classroom their real-world experience, often rivaling or surpassing the teachers' knowledge. Staying one chapter ahead of the students loses relevancy in this context. Thanks to students' field knowledge, however, teachers have an opportunity to learn more about field practice beyond their immediate work circles. Teachers also develop a professional network through these future librarians by virtue of interaction in the classroom. Yet there is still plenty to be learned by graduate students, and survey respondents commented frequently about "needy" students. The fact that LIS classrooms have audiences of both uninitiated students as well as more experienced students makes teaching this group all the more challenging.

The 2007 survey also found that the opportunity for adjuncts to intermingle with library science faculty did not rate highly as a motivating factor for librarians who choose to teach. The lowest-ranking motivational factor, distinct from intermingling, was the prestige factor. Only 10 percent of respondents considered the work of part-time graduate-level teaching to be prestigious. A number of practitioners already have faculty status as librarians at various universities, which may explain this attitude. Enthusiasm, passion, personal challenge, and self-fulfillment in their work help to explain motivation. Brown adds, "Many of us also agree, quietly, that working as an adjunct is a labor of love" (2007, 43). Beyond that, there is an apparent selflessness implicit in the teaching and the work overload that goes along with the job of the part-time instructor.

WHERE DO LIBRARY SCIENCE ADJUNCTS COME FROM?

Most part-timers (82 percent) come from the library field or related fields. Their backgrounds are technical services, public services, special libraries, and the administrative ranks. Five percent practice librarianship on a part-time basis. Most of the remainder are employed in related fields, such as library consultants, consortia administrators, and professionals who own information service businesses. One administrator said his best pools of part-timers are either those librarians who are roughly five years out in the field or those who are more senior in the field for more than 20 years. Librarians who are midstream in their careers tend to be heavily involved in the profession or have families that do not allow them the necessary time for teaching.

Some administrators find good teaching talent close to home. They identify recent graduates from their own programs to teach classes appropriate to their level of experience, perhaps an orientation class. At the same time, another ready source of part-time instructors is the corps of retired librarians, not ready for total retirement and with a significant contribution to make thanks to a lifetime of accumulated knowledge and practical experience.

Library school personnel may observe librarians presenting papers at conferences. A well-delivered paper topic may land a librarian a part-time teaching position. Librarians are a great source of references for their colleagues. Frequently, librarians in the field are asked to recommend people they know who might make good teachers. Alternatively, some librarians directly approach a library science program about teaching.

Once teaching begins for practitioners, they are frequently asked to teach more courses. Over 57 percent of respondents said they have been asked to teach more courses to help fill some kind of gap. Some embrace the opportunity, but most admit they prefer to protect their time and limit their teaching to one or two courses per year. Nearly half of the survey respondents reported that they teach up to 25 students per year. One-quarter of respondents teach up to 50 students per year.

WHAT KINDS OF RESPONSIBILITIES DO ADJUNCTS HAVE?

The 2009 survey reveals that adjuncts are given a large amount of responsibility. They do less teaching of required or core courses. Only 22 percent of respondents said they teach core courses, and another 4 percent teach both core and elective courses; so, frequently LIS programs decide that core courses are best taught by full-time faculty. These are the courses injected with the most theory.

Ninety-three percent of adjuncts have the authority and responsibility for designing and teaching courses. This includes developing the concept for the course, selecting the readings, writing the lectures, leading discussions, and grading. The selection of readings scored the lowest of the duties, so it appears that library schools prefer to exercise control over the readings, but even reading selection is performed by 88 percent of respondents. Several respondents made a point of saying they avoid textbooks (a comment painful to a publisher's ear) and prefer to use journal articles, which are plentiful in databases. One person went so far as to disown her own text, "I never use textbooks (not even my own!)."

Frequently, a library school will package a course so that the adjunct instructor does not have to build a course from scratch. Not only does this give a new teacher a running start, but it provides consistency in course delivery and expected outcomes. A school may require a new instructor to follow a previous syllabus the first time through a course but then give the instructor more autonomy in subsequent semesters. Many respondents indicated that their library science programs exercised oversight to make sure a course meets program goals. Of course, there are schools that allow maximum autonomy, which is embraced by some:

> Interestingly, one of the ways the department tried to appeal to me was by saying that the course I was to teach was "canned", all ready to go, as if I was just a delivery-mechanism. I don't approach teaching that way, and would've been quite unhappy had I not had the flexibility to "un-can" the course and teach it the way I wanted.

Another respondent commented, "Whenever I have taught as an adjunct I've had plenty of leeway in designing my own syllabus and lesson plans within the scope of the school's objectives and requirements."

Three-quarters of all adjuncts teach their courses solo. Online course delivery is rapidly growing. Survey respondents note that a little more than 50 percent of their teaching is now online, and another 23 percent is Web assisted. Thirty-nine percent of adjuncts are still doing some face-to-face teaching. While team teaching is not common, many adjuncts invite guest speakers to class, which is popular with the students. Guests may be other colleagues, vendors, or administrators from other libraries or systems. Students enjoy hearing from professionals working in the "real world." The ironic reality is that even the hardest-working practitioner-teacher can suddenly become the disconnected, "not-of-this-world" teacher once in front of the classroom.

Universities mostly use part-time instructors for their electives, specialty courses, or "boutique" courses. Specialty courses include topics such as cataloging, resource description and access (RDA), metadata, information architecture, vocabulary development, special libraries, technology, electronic reference or Internet reference, information literacy, library instruction, correctional library management, archival studies, multicultural literature and audiences, marketing, copyright, competitive intelligence, technical processes, library programming, storytelling, government information, public library management, media services, adult services, music librarianship, rare book librarianship, art and museum librarianship, religious archives, media for teens and youth, information technology, and legal, medical, and business resources. And "real-world" administrators love the opportunity to teach management the way it really works as opposed to its theory. Specialty courses are best taught by the adjunct with the special knowledge. LIS programs are able to leverage their curriculum, infusing it with practical, necessary, and interesting specialties, by using adjuncts.

ARE ADJUNCTS BEING CONVERTED?

One might wonder whether many adjuncts consider jumping the fence and changing careers to full-time teaching. Of course, this would necessitate obtaining a doctorate in most cases. Interestingly, in the 2009 survey, 29 percent reported they have considered full-time teaching as an alternative to their careers. In fact, according to one respondent, "There's a group of us out there that have transitioned from library work to teaching almost full time." Although only 8.5 percent are pursuing a doctoral degree, a further 17.6 percent reported that they are thinking about it. This is a fairly high number; however, based on experience, most people "thinking about" higher degrees never act on the desire. So while this is an interesting figure, we should not place a lot of stock in it.

Not only does an interest in librarianship often come later in life, but the interest in pursuing a doctorate in library science often comes even later. The time commitment necessary to pursue the degree can be overwhelming for a full-time practitioner, as can the cost. A librarian who has been used to a full-time income and benefits finds it difficult to forgo it all to return to school. Loans are more palatable to the young, but it is understandable that middle-aged professionals lack enthusiasm for piling new loans on top of their previous college loans, a mortgage, car loans, and saving for children's education. However, grants and fellowships are available, particularly through the Institute of Museum and Library Services, so one should investigate these opportunities. Doctoral programs often require residency, which also can be problematic for the professional with a family. The key to increasing the numbers of doctoral candidates is to interest potential PhD candidates at a younger age.

HOW DO WE ORIENT ADJUNCTS?

Students paying today's tuitions deserve teachers who are knowledgeable and prepared to teach. The interesting contradiction is that many librarians, who enjoy the teaching aspects of librarianship, have no formal educational training in their backgrounds. (Of course, most university faculty have no formal educational training either.) The average academic librarian learns teaching by trial and error. Anyone who has attempted to capture the imaginations of college freshmen with the wonders of the library, while these students check out the opposite sex or text the fingerprints right off their thumbs, knows the skill needed to win their attention. Library instruction classes serving juniors, seniors, or graduate students have more attentive audiences. Walking into a classroom full of enthusiastic future librarians means preaching to the choir—teaching a receptive, if not idealistic group of students, truly eager to learn and to serve. And while teaching is never easy, it does not get much better than this for the part-time library science instructor.

Still, adjuncts are well served by some kind of orientation. As Stephen Watt of the Indiana University English Department says,

> If you just line them up to teach a course and don't give them any support, it does them damage and the institution damage because you're saying, "We don't care about you as a professional. . . . All we care about is getting our lousy courses taught." (Jacobson, 2003)

One survey respondent notes she was "thrown in without much preparation about the way the institution worked. I had to pretty much figure out (with the help of the department 'godmother') how to function." An orientation is an investment by a library school in its new hires and can aid in retaining these instructors for the long run. Ideally, when library schools find good adjunct instructors, it is to their advantage to retain them. A successful relationship enables a school to focus on important things other than constantly scouting for more adjuncts. It enables better master scheduling, creates a school that runs more smoothly, and allows relationships to develop between full-time faculty and the part-time instructors.

Adjuncts who have long-standing relationships with library schools come to know more about the school's program, allowing them to be better advocates for that school. Adjuncts reflect on the school. Poorly chosen teachers do not instill confidence in a program. Adjuncts are out and about in the community, and they have many professional relationships. Through these informal channels, they wield a lot of influence. Talkative, dissatisfied adjuncts can create a negative image of the school if relationships between programs and adjuncts turn sour.

MODEL ORIENTATION PROGRAMS

Years in academia have shown that while colleges and universities are often heavily dependent on adjunct instructors, these instructors are given relatively little in the way of orientation. From 2009 survey responses it appears that library schools vary greatly in orienting new instructors, ranging from excellent to poor. Some LIS schools offer a structured annual or biannual orientation program for adjuncts. Clearly these programs, while time consuming, are very helpful. Adjuncts without the benefit of a good orientation may be told what text to use and where the classroom is but not much beyond the basics. They often have no idea how to access library resources, what programs are available for them, or even where to park. Survey comments include statements such as "Generally, I'm expected to work in a vacuum, which is not my preference," or "I don't know if they (admin) would know if I never showed up." What is not ideal is to have part-timers feel as though they were "just plugged in to fill the spot." Yet respondents from other schools said, "We have excellent infrastructure and support from tech services and others at the school."

All new instructors should benefit from some sort of orientation, whether in person or through a virtual experience. An orientation should serve a number of purposes:

- To inform about the program, its mission, and the nature of the student body
- To meet the full-time faculty (particularly ones with whom they might be working) and key administrators and to feel a part of the program
- To learn about requirements for operating in the educational environment
- To become familiar with course delivery tools and systems
- To learn some basic pedagogy and program goals
- To learn about the kinds of resources available for adjuncts and for the students

To Inform about the Program, Its Mission, and the Nature of the Student Body

People who have decided to teach in library science programs on a part-time basis may be only vaguely familiar with the program. They know their own program that graduated them, but they may not know the one they teach for now. Acquainting them with the mission and goals and the audience that the program serves is useful. Does the program target the young new professional, the seasoned professional returning for more in-depth knowledge, those with more of a technological interest, those headed for administration or for school media centers, special libraries, or archives? Many practitioners are not familiar with the division between the L-school (with its traditional library service emphasis) or the I-school (with its emphasis on information science and technology). These are debates that go on outside the practitioner's circle.

Adjuncts ought to know the characteristics of the typical student, if there is one. Do most students work full-time? Do most students have a library background, or are they coming to school with no previous library experience? What can a teacher assume? How many courses do students tend to take in a semester? All these pieces of information help to give new instructors a context for their audience.

To Meet the Full-Time Faculty (Particularly Ones with Whom They Might Be Working) and Key Administrators and to Feel a Part of the Program

It is important for new part-time instructors to meet full-time faculty and even the key administrators. This helps the newcomer feel welcome and helps all faculty to see themselves as part of a larger and complete picture. It is helpful to know the personalities and faculty perspectives. Having one time during the year that the faculty can see itself as a whole is meaningful for everyone. As a point of interest, according to the survey, 61.8 percent of part-timers are invited to participate in department meetings.

To Learn about Requirements for Operating in the Educational Environment

New part-timers will want to understand the goals of the program. Is there a special emphasis such as service learning or community-centered coursework? Does the program make heavy use of case studies? Does it stress lots of theory? Does the program like to encourage students to work with faculty on research or to turn student research papers into presentations? Does the school value face-to-face meetings even in an online environment?

New part-timers may also need a preview of some fundamentals of the higher education environment. Understanding FERPA (Family Educational

Rights and Privacy Act) regulations is essential. In addition, they need guidance in handling students with disabilities, particularly in the online environment; school policy on retaining student papers; how to handle excuses or illness; how to handle incompletes; and how to handle course materials and copyright permissions. Does anyone cover these expenses? Where are course packs made? What are general student preferences for things like e-reserves, course packs, or simple linking to database articles? Do they prefer discussion boards, real-time voice interaction, or visual communication? And what does one do about plagiarism?

To Become Familiar with Course Delivery Tools and Systems

Since the majority of part-time instructors use course delivery systems such as Blackboard and Wimba, new teachers will need orientation about these tools. Course management software is not a typical part the daily work life of most librarians, nor the lives of consultants, administrators, vendors, or whoever else decides to teach. While some library schools received very good comments about technical orientations, an equal number of comments showed much frustration with the lack of such training. Of those surveyed in 2009, 73 percent said they had some instruction in the online course delivery systems, but sometimes it is hard to achieve just the right amount of technical support:

> The school has created a plethora of tutorials to read. But so often, all you need is a human being to say "Here's what you do." It's a waste of time—and presumptuous—to believe that a tutorial can best answer instructors' concerns in all cases. That's been the biggest frustration for me. That and the habit some tech people have of instead of directly answering your question, bombarding you with URLs to tutorials, when all you need is a simple answer.

Academic librarians may have access to training on their home campuses where they have their day jobs. Some library schools can arrange a virtual training session. Other schools handle training in on-campus orientations. Or, if all else fails, new instructors have been known to call a friend who teaches with these tools and beg for some free tutoring.

To Learn Some Basic Pedagogy and Program Goals

New part-time teachers need some guidelines if their prior teaching experience has been limited to the 60-minute class they teach as part of library instruction programs. Planning and teaching a one-hour class that is mostly skill or resource based is a far cry from planning a full semester that is coherent and progressive, promotes inquiry and interaction, challenges preconceived notions, separates the A students from the B students, caters to different learning styles, and motivates students to stretch themselves and to envision themselves working in situations they never have dreamed of. Only 49 percent of those surveyed indicated that they had any guidance with teaching methods. Yet 73 percent said they were given "desired learning outcomes" for their courses.

New instructors will want to ask questions about courses. Coteaching and lurking in some of the online classes is a good way to introduce part-timers to different teaching approaches. New part-time instructors will not have developed an understanding of the curriculum, how courses tie together, what topics are covered in which courses or if they are covered at all. And new part-timers assisting with core courses will want to discuss the course content with the full-time faculty overseeing that course. "Course caucuses" are a valuable way to handle this (Jacobson, 2003). The new practitioner-teacher does not always appreciate integrating theory into coursework. For whatever reason, theory does not find a place or make its way into the daily discourse of many practitioners. Faculty need to convey more convincingly to the practitioner-teacher (and to students) the interplay of theory and practice.

Midsemester feedback can often save a course from disaster or at least from bad summary evaluations. If the library school has access to some sort of easy survey forms such as Survey Monkey or SurveyMethods, new instructors can use these to pose a few simple questions such as "What is working well for you?" and "What is not working so well?" Midterm shifts in the mechanics or delivery of the course may make the world of difference for everyone involved. Instructors should be prepared for criticism and have the humility to make necessary adjustments. Students appreciate being asked for this kind of input. Graduate students have been around classrooms for a long time. They know good teaching when they see it, and they are ready to tell teachers where a class is sagging.

Given that so much teaching involves online instruction, new instructors may be in for a small shock at the time that online teaching consumes. If lectures are used, they have to be grammatically perfect to share with the class, whereas cryptic notes suffice for a face-to-face class. Class discussion conducted in the face-to-face classroom is limited to a specific time frame. The online course discussion board can go on all week, consuming hours of both the teacher's and the students' time. New instructors need guidance in keeping an online discussion board manageable and engaging. There is an art to guiding a good discussion.

Grading often overwhelms new part-time instructors. Only 62 percent of those from the 2009 survey said they received guidance with grading. New instructors need guidance as to what constitutes an A and a B paper in the eyes of the faculty at a particular school. Some instructors find security in rubrics and need help constructing them. If instructors prefer rubrics, they need to be clear about assignment expectations, just as students need clarity with instructions and expectations. (As an instructor I am always a bit stunned when a student comments that he or she fails to see the purpose of a particular assignment that seems so brilliantly clear to me. It never hurts to spell out for students the objective of an assignment for those lacking the instructor's vision.)

To Learn about the Kinds of Resources Available for Adjuncts and for the Students

Colleges and universities are often little cities of resources and services. New instructors coming from other universities may have good knowledge of the kinds of student support for any number of issues, such as disabilities, writing assistance, financial aid, or psychological counseling. However, new instructors coming from outside academia may not be as aware of this support.

DO ADJUNCTS FEEL THAT THEY ARE OFFERING SOMETHING SPECIAL TO LIBRARY SCIENCE PROGRAMS?

This question brought 178 responses, but the most constant refrain is that their contribution is the "real-world" and "practical" experience. One respondent sums up comments from those who have been in the profession for a number of years, saying he brings "several decades of experience and history of the profession and [its] changes." Other special contributions of part-time teachers are "introductions to people in the field" and knowledge of the "inner workings of library organizations." One person noted, "I think I bring a long experience in the field and in research that complements what the full-time faculty are doing." And another said she brings the "most current reference service practices in the library, e.g. new technology, new services, etc., current change of user population and their information needs." All of this rounds out the student experience.

DO ADJUNCTS GET INVOLVED WITH THE STUDENTS?

One of the earmarks of a satisfying educational experience from a student perspective is contact with faculty. This is often a lightning rod for full-time faculty when criticizing the use of part-time faculty. On-ground programs afford graduate students an opportunity to mingle with full-time faculty, scholastically and socially; faculty serve as mentors and role models. It is an ideal collegiate experience, not exactly a Mark Hopkins experience, but maybe even better.

The reliance of distance education makes this experience increasingly difficult. Part-timers may or may not have an opportunity to mingle with students, depending on their proximity to campus. When asked if they "interact with students beyond the classroom demands," 66 percent of 2009 respondents said they did interact through either social events, field trips, mentoring, or other similar events. One instructor said she actually flies to campus for student field trips. Many part-time instructors review resumes and write letters of recommendation. Instructor–student interaction often leads to requests from students for practicums and internships.

Unfortunately, for 26 percent of the respondents, distance was a barrier to this kind of interaction. Of course, it is not always the instructor who operates at a distance. If the instructor is not in town, frequently neither are the students. So distance education takes a toll on faculty–student interaction. Lack of time for involvement was an issue for 10 percent of respondents, and only 4 percent reported they just were not interested in interacting beyond the classroom. Overall, the amount of teacher–student involvement speaks well of adjuncts in LIS programs.

HOW DO ADJUNCTS FEEL ABOUT THEIR WORK? WHAT ARE THE BIGGEST PRESSURES FOR THEM?

When asked about the biggest challenges for the part-time instructor, responses clumped around the themes of time commitment and mastering the technology. The responses speak volumes of their own. Most comments centered on the time commitment. It is difficult "balancing the demands of my full-time job and family life with the adjunct position," and "preparing for an online course is about ten times harder than face-to-face." The most problematic thing is time management: "It takes on average nine to twelve hours to prepare one three-hour class for me (and that's once I've already taught that particular class!)—that's the problem when you teach a class about technologics." Still another respondent contributed to the conversation: "Giving the lectures and leading classes is easy to plan time for, but all of the one-on-one has to be squeezed in around the rest of work and life, and that takes a toll."

Another addresses the problem of maintaining her own sense of quality while working around work: "My institution requires that my adjunct work occurs before and after regular business hours . . . so it's a time management 'opportunity' to communicate with students in a timely fashion, given my (personal) commitment to respond within twenty-four hours." Some part-timers use vacation hours to do their grading.

There were comments that highlighted the challenges of the online environment. One response stated, "The biggest challenge has been translating my light and humorous approach in a completely online format." Another explained, "Some students don't like the online environment and trying to build a sense of community in the class can be a challenge." These challenges are not unique to the part-time teaching experience. They are shared by all distance-education faculty.

Other comments took aim at administrative issues. One mentioned the abnormal way some schools dole out paychecks: "Don't expect a regular biweekly or monthly paycheck from some schools. It's not the way it works."

Paychecks may be split up before and after the drop/add period; pay may depend on the final student numbers rather than a set rate per course. Another complained of "being called to teach with little advance notice." This is not uncommon in the life of the adjunct, either.

To offset the list of pressures, there were many favorable comments. For instance,

> My biggest surprise and pleasure, which arose from my reaction from learning that students in online environment can be quite needy: I have become a popular professor because: 1) I have been diligent about timely and detailed responses to students' e-mail questions; and, 2) My written comments on assignment essays are usually quite detailed. The students really appreciate this "attention to detail."

And another offered, "I was surprised by how much freedom I was given to develop my course how I saw fit." Part-timers working for library schools that are well structured to support them said things like, "Fortunately, there is excellent support for adjunct faculty. What surprised me the most was how much I truly enjoy teaching the students." Still others talked about how much they learned from the students and how they valued the long-term relationships they enjoy with students.

FINALLY, DO ADJUNCTS FEEL VALUED?

Fifty-four percent of respondents said they felt valued by their library schools; 34 percent said "somewhat," and 11 percent gave a flat-out "no." There is room for improvement in this area if retention is a goal for schools. Feeling valued relates to the school one works for, one's level of readiness to teach, and personal expectations for the experience. The issue of pay rose to the surface frequently:

> I think they appreciate adjuncts a lot. But they don't pay adjuncts a living wage (at least when I taught) and there was this weird disconnect between the "real" faculty and the adjuncts—which is so odd because a class taught by an adjunct costs the student just as much, and makes as much impact on the student's overall education, as a class taught by the "real" faculty.

And "it takes much more time than I would have guessed, and if I work out the income/hour, based on the number of hours I work on the class and what I'm paid, my time would be better-spent in any number of ways." While salary figures for full-time faculty are relatively easy to find, pay for part-time instructors is more difficult to uncover, officially speaking. However, unofficial figures are readily shared among well-networked colleagues. As of 2008 pay appears to range between $2,200 and $6,000 per course with many variables factoring into these figures. Some schools pay a flat rate per course, while other schools maintain a complex formula that calculates hours spent on preparation, discussion boards, grading, or other teaching-related duties and numbers of enrolled students. While a high percentage of adjuncts perform all the teaching tasks that full-time faculty perform—developing the course, writing the lectures, selecting a textbook, grading, and leading discussions, their compensation is approximately 15 to 33 percent of what a full-time faculty member makes, normally minus benefits. Many adjuncts surveyed indicated that pay is inadequate commensurate to the work required. Of course, this issue is not unique to library science programs and crops up frequently in an ongoing national dialogue in academic circles. Granted, part-timers do not carry the extra professional obligations of full-time faculty, such as committee work or publication, but schools may not be compensating adequately for the number of hours actually required to teach a course. At least one library school offers part-timers extras in the way of a book budget and travel money. It is more common for schools to compensate part-timers for attending required organizational meetings.

Several respondents noted that there is a general disdain for part-timers. The tensions that run between full- and part time faculty are well documented in the national literature, especially as tenure comes under attack, but this attitude about the friction is very place specific, and not specific to LIS programs. One survey respondent added that he would feel more valued if adjuncts could "be more included in conversations about curriculum and course design." Moran has given this considerable thought and notes, "There are many educational issues that can only be addressed by practitioners and educators working together" (2001, 52). ALISE has made an effort to bridge the gap between practitioner and faculty through its Adjunct and Part-Time Faculty Special Interest Group. According to Van Fleet, "ALISE has recently undertaken a project that focuses on these valuable contributors and ways to more fully integrate them into the educational endeavor" (Zabel, 2008, 206).

Other areas where library schools could improve in making adjuncts feel more valued are improved communication and recognition. Lack of communication leads to a feeling of abandonment. Others noted that they appreciate being listed publicly as part of the faculty. One person expressed this desire: "I wish there could be a category of professor created for those practitioners who are recognized as experts in whatever kind of librarianship that they pursue." Many institutions do have category known as "clinical" faculty, which is typically a nontenured position.

What is clear is that teaching is not for everyone. While there is much library schools can do to cultivate and retain good part-time instructors, if one requires lots of back-patting and attention, then it is important to pick a library school carefully. Part-timers need to venture in with eyes wide open, ready to be creative and flexible and to live with some ambiguity. Self-starters will be the most successful. Those who cherish working autonomously will enjoy the experience, like one person who commented that he "prefers flying below the radar and not having to be too caught up in the issues of the program and the faculty. I don't particularly mind me just doing my thing." For those ready to take the ride, the fruits of the labor may result in unexpected surprises, as for one librarian who said, "I was most surprised by how much time it involved, but equally surprised by how incredibly rewarding it is—have been doing this for ten years." Roxanne Spencer sums it up: "The sense of connection, of having engaged the student's interest and enthusiasm, is what keeps many struggling teachers in the classroom" (2003, 8). Those who have been in the teaching profession for a while are familiar with the satisfaction that results from knowing you are impacting lives in a long-lasting way.

WORKS CITED

Brown, S. W. 2007. The adjunct life: The best of both worlds—working and teaching future librarians. *Library Journal* 132 (11): 42–44.

Burnett, K., and J. Naidoo. 2009. Degrees and certificates awarded by gender and ethnic origin, doctoral, 2004–2005 (Table II-3-c-5). *Library and Information Science Education Statistical Report, 2006,* ed. J. D. Saye and D. P. Wallace, 122–124. Chicago: Association for Library and Information Science Education. Retrieved May 5, 2009, from http://www.alise.org/.

Gershenfeld, N. 2004. From librarian to educator: Teaching the next generation of librarians. *Alki* 20 (1): 5–6, 8.

Jacobson, J. 2003. The challenges of managing adjuncts. *Chronicle of Higher Education* (March 23). Retrieved June 16, 2009, from http://chronicle.com/article/The-Challenges-of-Managing/45127/.

LeBeau, C. 2008. Transitions to academic libraries for business librarians and librarians' response to adjunct teaching. *Journal of Business & Finance Librarianship* 13 (3): 295–309.

Moran, B. 2001. Practitioners vs. LIS educators: Time to reconnect. *Library Journal* 126 (18): 52–55.

Saye, J. D., and W. C. Lan. 1998. Enrollment (number) by program and gender, fall 1997 (Table II-1-a-1). *Library and Information Science Education Statistical Report 1998,* ed. E. H. Daniel and J. D. Saye, 67. Chicago: Association for Library and Information Science. Retrieved May 5, 2009, from http://www.alise.org/.

Saye, J. D., and W. C. Lan. 1999. Enrollment (number) by program and gender, fall 1998. (Table II-1-a-1). *Library and Information Science Education Statistical Report 1999,* ed. E. H. Daniel and J. D. Saye, 69. Chicago: Association for Library and Information Science Education. Retrieved May 5, 2009, from http://www.alise.org/.

Saye, J. D., and K. M. Wisser. 2000. Enrollment (number) by program and gender, fall 1999 (Table II-1-a-1). *Library and Information Science Education Statistical Report 2000,* ed. E. H. Daniel and J. D. Saye, 51. Chicago: Association for Library and Information Science Education. Retrieved May 5, 2009, from http://www.alise.org/.

Saye, J. D., and K. M. Wisser. 2001. Enrollment (Number) by Program and Gender Fall 2000 (Table II-1-a-1). *Library and Information Science Education Statistical Report 2001,* ed. E. H. Daniel and J. D. Saye. n.p. Chicago: Association for Library and Information Science Education. Retrieved May 5, 2009, from http://www.alise.org/.

Saye, J. D., and K. M. Wisser. 2002. Enrollment (number) by program and gender, fall 2001 (Table II-1-a-1). *Library and Information Science Education Statistical Report 2002,* ed. E. H. Daniel and J. D. Saye, 82. Chicago: Association for Library and Information Science Education. Retrieved May 5, 2009, from http://www.alise.org/.

Saye, J. D., and K. M. Wisser. 2003. Enrollment (number) by program and gender, fall 2002 (Table II-1-a-1). *Library and Information Science Education Statistical Report 2003,* ed. E. H. Daniel and J. D. Saye, 73. Chicago: Association for Library and Information Science Education. Retrieved on May 5, 2009, from http://www.alise.org/.

Saye, J. D., and K. M. Wisser. 2004a. Degrees and certificates awarded by gender and ethnic origin, 2001–2002 (Table II-3-a). *Library and Information Science Statistical Report, 2003,* ed. E. H. Daniel and J. D. Saye, n.p. Chicago: Association for Library and Information Science Education. Retrieved May 5, 2009, from http://www.alise.org/.

Saye, J. D., and K. M. Wisser. 2004b. Enrollment (number) by program and gender, fall 2003 (Table II-1-a-1). *Library and Information Science Education Statistical Report 2004,* ed. E. H. Daniel and J. D. Saye, 73. Chicago: Association for Library and Information Science Education. Retrieved May 5, 2009, from http://www.alise.org/.

Seavey, C. A. 2005. The coming crisis in education for librarianship. *American Libraries* 36 (9): 54–56.

Seavey, C. A. 2007. LIS educators aim to prepare reflective professionals. *American Libraries* 38 (3): 23.

Sineath, T. 1998. Full-time faculty, 1996–1997 (Table I-41) and part-time faculty, 1996–1997 (Table I-43). *Library and Information Science Education Statistical Report 1998,* ed. E. H. Daniel and J. D. Saye, 32–33. Chicago: Association for Library and Information Science Education. Retrieved May 5, 2009, from http://www.alise.org/.

Sineath, T. 1999. Full-time faculty, 1997–1998 (Table I-41) and part-time faculty, 1997–1998 (Table I-43). *Library and Information Science Education Statistical Report 1999,* ed. E. H. Daniel and J. D. Saye. 32-33. Chicago: Association for Library and Information Science Education. Retrieved May 5, 2009, from http://www.alise.org/.

Sineath, T. 2000. Full-time faculty, 1998–1999 (Table I-41) and part-time faculty, 1998–1999 (Table I-43). *Library and Information Science Education Statistical Report 2000,* ed. E. H. Daniel and J. D. Saye, 29–30. Chicago: Association for Library and Information Science Education. Retrieved May 5, 2009, from http://www.alise.org/.

Sineath, T. 2001. Full-time faculty, 1999–2000 (Table I-41) and part-time faculty, 1999–2000 (Table I-43). *Library and Information Science Education Statistical Report 2001,* ed. E. H. Daniel and J. D. Saye, n.p. Chicago: Association for Library and Information Science Education. Retrieved May 5, 2009, from http://www.alise.org/.

Sineath, T. 2002. Full-time faculty, 2000–2001 (Table I-41) and part-time faculty, 2000–2001 (Table I-43). *Library and Information Science Education Statistical Report 2002,* ed. E. H. Daniel and J. D. Saye, 28–30. Chicago: Association for Library and Information Science Education. Retrieved May 5, 2009, from http://www.alise.org/.

Sineath, T. 2003. Full-time faculty, fall 2002 (Table I-41) and part-time faculty, fall 2002 (Table I-43). *Library and Information Science Education Statistical Report 2003,* ed. E. H. Daniel and J. D. Saye, 28–30. Chicago: Association for Library and Information Science Education. Retrieved May 5, 2009, from http://www.alise.org/.

Sineath, T. 2004. Full-time faculty, fall 2003 (Table I-41) and part-time faculty (Table I-43). *Library and Information Science Education Statistical Report 2004,* ed. E. H. Daniel and J. D. Saye, 28–30. Chicago: Association for Library and Information Science Education. Retrieved May 5, 2009, from http://www.alise.org/.

Sineath, T. 2005. Faculty replacement appointments, 2002–2003 (Table I-47) and unfilled, funded, full-time faculty positions, fall 2003 (Table I-47a). *Library and Information Science Education Statistical Report, 2004,* ed. E. H. Daniel and J. D. Saye, n.p. Chicago: Association for Library and Information Science Education. Retrieved October 5, 2010, from http://www.alise.org/.

Sineath, T. 2006. Full-time faculty, fall 2005 (Table I-41) and part-time faculty, fall 2005 (Table I-43). *Library and Information Science Education Statistical Report 2006,* ed. E. H. Daniel and J. D. Saye, 27–29. Chicago: Association for Library and Information Science Education.

Wallace, D. P., and J. Naidoo. 2010a. Enrollment (number) by program and gender, fall 2008 (Table II-1-a-1). *Library and Information Science Education Statistical Report 2009*, 57. Chicago: Association for Library and Information Science Education.

Wallace, D. P., and J. Naidoo. 2010b. Full-time faculty, fall 2008 (Table I-41) and part-time faculty, fall 2008 (Table I-43). *Library and Information Science Education Statistical Report 2009*, 40–42. Chicago: Association for Library and Information Science Education.

Spencer, R. 2003. New academic librarian as new adjunct faculty member: Trial by fire. *Southeastern Librarian* 50 (4): 4–9.

Sugimoto, C. R., T. G. Russell, and S. Grant. 2009. Library and information science doctoral education: The landscape from 1930–2007. *Journal of Education for Library and Information Science* 30 (3): 190–202.

Zabel, D. 2008. An interview with 2006–07 ALISE President Connie Van Fleet. *Reference & User Services Quarterly* 47 (3): 204–206.

25

OUTSIDE THE SCHOOL DOORS: LESSONS LEARNED AFTER LIBRARY SCHOOL

Amber A. Prentiss

I entered library school at the tender age of 24 for three reasons:

1. I had a BA in English.
2. I liked research, books, and computers.
3. I never wanted to work at Home Depot again.

Library school was a necessity for me. Before graduate school, my library experience consisted mostly of a history of being an enthusiastic (if often overdue) library patron and a couple of brief college stints at shelving and circulation. The terms *metadata, information literacy,* and *open access* had no resonance or meaning, and my reference knowledge could barely fill a brochure. I needed graduate school to learn MARC and Library of Congress and Dewey and Cutter, spend inordinate amounts of time finding obscure facts in reference books, and work a demanding reference graduate assistantship. When I finished my last semester, I thought I knew all that was necessary. I was wrong.

What did I learn after library school? First, the career you prepare for is not always the career you get. I trained as a generalist, taking courses in reference, collection development, cataloging, information literacy, and management. I wanted to be able to handle multiple duties in a small to medium-sized academic library. At my first position, I did reference and instruction, but I was also in charge of facilitating access to and answering questions about the college's small archive, even though I had no archival training. Four years after graduation, I now work for a giant state university. When a fellow reference librarian left, I suddenly found myself liaising with social science departments, despite a lack of depth in those disciplines (how I wish I had taken a social science reference course!). Collection development is largely handled by another department. I have not cataloged a single item since graduate school and have completely forgotten how to do so. Working in a library with a fairly flat administrative structure, I don't manage any staff or even student workers. Not quite what I expected!

In addition, the library is constantly changing. First we were instant messaging, and now we're texting. We had 500 databases, each in their own silo, and now we have federated search. E-books were out, and now they're back in. I don't believe a master of library and information science (MLIS) fully prepares anyone for day one, much less day 1,034. It's a start, a necessary but not sufficient criterion. As in any profession, the more you do, the more you learn.

Now that I've been a librarian for four years, I wanted to pass on some of my hard-won, occasionally painful lessons to you. Some of them have to do with the realities of office life and others with the peculiar organism of the library. If nothing else, I hope it will enable you to make new and different mistakes upon graduation.

THE LIBRARY IS A BUREAUCRACY WITHIN A BUREAUCRACY

The library is made up of departments, specialists, assistant to the dean of this, associates of that. It's a bureaucracy, which is not terribly surprising, considering that a large portion of our profession concerns itself with putting things in their right places. On top of that, a library is usually situated inside yet another bureaucracy: a college, university, government division, or company. For the new reference librarian, navigating the maze can be overwhelming. Will the systems department resent you for asking for server space to try out a new content management system? Will the "Web guy" be upset about your efforts to ramp up the library blog? Librarians and departments have entrenched interests, and the status quo, while sometimes dysfunctional, is at least familiar.

Before you tangle with the bureaucracy, you will want to gather some intelligence. Introduce yourself to people both inside and outside your department, read meeting minutes, keep up with the college news, and lend a (skeptical) ear to the grapevine. You will learn the office personalities: ambitious, laid-back, anxious, pleasant, contrarian, adventurous, or risk-averse. You will also map the conflicts. Sometimes reference, which is always trying to do something new on the Web site, bothers information technology (IT), which has its hands full maintaining existing systems. A new librarian may sprout innovations constantly and win public accolades, while an established one feels unappreciated for her years of quiet, steady service. Knowing your colleagues and the tenor of the office relationships makes it easier to dance around toes when necessary.

If your new project requires significant time investment by colleagues, makes a major change in the daily workflow, or requires the involvement of multiple departments, make sure not only to get approval from the higher-ups but also to try to get support for your project from the people who will carry it out. The more influential supporters (not necessarily management) you gain, the more naysayers will desist. Learn your supervisors' and colleagues' preferences and communicate accordingly. If your boss likes reports, present your idea in a formal proposal. If she wants proof of concept, show her examples of similar projects at other institutions. Some people prefer to discuss ideas informally over coffee, and others enjoy the Socratic give-and-take of the department meeting. Thank those who take the time to listen, critique, or help implement your plan. Some will persistently dislike your idea, but at least they will be aware of it (and thus can't resort to "No one told me about this!")

GET A MENTOR

Keep your eyes peeled for a good mentor or two. Mentors serve as a personal advisory panel; in other words, they are people you can trust for good advice when you're trying new things or planning a career move. Some libraries have formal mentoring programs, which may make this process easier, but others do not. Ideally, a mentor will have experienced a few years in your field and operated at different levels of responsibility. She should also be able to keep your confidences private. A mentor at your home institution can help acclimate you to the unofficial lay of the land and history of your organization, but an outside mentor can give you a more objective perspective on your organization and work life. When you are embarking on a new project, ask your mentor about her experiences starting new initiatives. If you're job searching, ask your (outside) mentor what she looks for when she sits on hiring committees.

BUILD OFFICE KARMA

Does a colleague need someone to pinch-hit a desk shift to take a child to the doctor? Volunteer. Does a favorite professor need someone to teach a freshman English information literacy section at the last minute? If you have the time, offer to do it. Being willing to help goes a long way toward impressing your colleagues and community, and you can tap that goodwill when you need it.

KEEP IN TOUCH

In addition to a mentor, it helps to have a network of library people—former colleagues and classmates, conference roommates, Facebook friends you've never met, and coworkers you see daily. You need friends familiar with the peculiar pleasures and vexations of librarianship, and, frankly, the civilians just don't get it. You also need people who can be called on to solve random reference questions (Why are termites attracted to pen ink?), explain FRBR in plain English, and demonstrate the new social networking trend of the week. Friends are also invaluable in the job hunt. Not only can they keep you apprised of job openings, but they can also tell you things a search committee can't and won't, like why the last person left, whether your potential new coworkers will drive you insane, and how closely higher-ups guard the purse strings. As I learned in Girl Scouts, "Make new friends, but keep the old. One is silver, and the other's gold."

THE LIBRARY IS THE CENTER OF CAMPUS—TO LIBRARIANS

I was the kind of kid who was always in the school library, the public library, and the academic library. Then again, I was the kind of kid who grew up to be a librarian. Unfortunately, many in the community do not feel the same way we do about libraries. They think of the library as a scary fortress patrolled by hawk-eyed crones, a relic of an analog society, a storehouse of irrelevant knowledge and thought, or a place to be avoided at all costs. I wish I had a dollar for every time a student approached the reference desk, with a perverse combination of sheepishness and pride, and told me, "I'm a senior, but I haven't used the library before." (Am I supposed to be happy for them?) The point is, marketing the library may feel superfluous for such an obvious good, but the value of the library is not readily apparent to many in our communities. We need to get out and talk with faculty, instructors, graduate students, and undergraduates and state our case. We have a singular advantage over the Googles of the world—human assistance. We can parse a question and get to the heart of a fledgling idea better than any software. We can understand not just what information is needed but what kind and format might be best for our users. We want our users to remember that certain questions are best taken to the professionals.

YOUR PATRONS ARE NOT LIBRARIANS

Occasionally, I forget that patrons do not spend 160 hours a month inside a library like I do. You can't tell a person's research experience from looking at them. A college freshman, educated in the United States, told me that he needed help finding a book since he had not used a call number since "like, the seventh grade." Often, people come to me looking for a book that's really a journal article because they don't know how to read citations. I have met graduate students, young and old, who do not understand the basics of searching, despite four or more years of undergraduate education.

I have learned the hard way not to assume prior knowledge on the part of my patrons.

In library school, I answered reference questions from worksheets and had a week to work on them. In the library, I answer questions from harried undergraduates who have 10 minutes between classes. It is a completely different experience. Frankly, sometimes the reference interview is more like a reference interrogation:

> "I need information on frozen foods."
> "What kind of information?"
> "You know, anything really."
> "So, what's your assignment?"
> "I have to design a new type of product."
> "And your product is a frozen food?"
> "Yeah. I have to describe the market and stuff."
> "So—you need market information about frozen foods?"

As frustrating as such a conversation can be, I try to remind myself that this task seems pretty impossible to a typical undergraduate. I have to back up and put myself in his position: intimidated by his first visit to the library with a strange assignment and no idea how to pursue it. Why would there be information about the frozen-foods market, and where would a person find it? How do you go about asking for it? In the reference interview, the librarian whittles down a broad, vague, tentative question to what the user wants. We don't just answer questions. Sometimes, we make questions answerable.

THIS JOB CAN BE AWESOME

I love reference. As reference librarians, we guide people in their quests to learn and create knowledge. Certainly, the life of a reference librarian involves a fair amount of printer troubleshooting and bathroom directions, but the chance to participate in true inquiry is sustaining. I love conferences with students who have questions but are overwhelmed by their options for finding answers. Those 30 minutes can turn confusion into confidence once we identify the information they seek and the places it can be found. I just feel incredibly *useful* when I finally track down an early 20th-century article in an obscure German archaeological journal or find just the right keyword to describe microorganisms living in harsh environments (*extremophile,* it turns out). This profession gives me the chance to participate in the intellectual passions of others, a chance to tantalize my brain while being of service (and getting paid). When entangled in office politics or work frustrations, remember the applause at the end of a class and the thank-you note at the end of a long week. Remember that what you do has impact and meaning. Be proud to be a librarian.

INDEX

ABOUT THE EDITOR AND CONTRIBUTORS

ANNE BEHLER is an information literacy librarian at the Penn State University Libraries, focused on instruction and outreach to first-year students. She is also the librarian for the Penn State University Park leisure reading collection and is co–project leader for the Penn State Sony Reader pilot project. Her research interests include literacy among higher-education students and outreach marketing to first-year students.

LAURA FARWELL BLAKE is head of services for academic programs in the Harvard College Library (HCL). She also serves as HCL's library liaison to the Department of English. She received her AB in English language and literature from Smith College and her MA in library science from the University of Wisconsin–Madison. From 1989 to 2008, she was a research librarian in the Widener Library. Prior to joining HCL's staff, Ms. Farwell Blake was a reference librarian and director of public libraries in Rhode Island and New York, with happy interruptions for the duties of parenthood during the mid- and late 1980s. She coauthors the section on literary reviews for *Magazines for Libraries,* was coauthor of *Teaching the New Library* (Neal-Schuman), and coordinated the Harvard conference whose proceedings were published in *Gateways to Knowledge: The Role of the Academic Library in Teaching, Learning, and Research* (MIT Press).

ELLYSA STERN CAHOY is an education and behavioral sciences librarian at Penn State University's University Park campus.. A former children's librarian and school library media specialist, Ms. Cahoy has published research and presented on information literacy, library orientation, evidence-based librarianship, and library instruction. Ms. Cahoy's article "Maximizing Local and National Assessment for Evidence-Based Librarianship," coauthored with Loanne Snavely, appeared in the Spring 2009 issue of *Reference & User Services Quarterly*. She serves on the Executive Committee of the Association of College and Research Libraries (ACRL) Instruction Section and is chair of the ACRL Information Literacy Standards Committee.

JODY CONDIT FAGAN (MLS, MA) currently serves as content interfaces coordinator and associate professor at James Madison University. She is also the editor of the *Journal of Web Librarianship*. She recently published her first book, *Web Project Management for Academic Libraries*, with colleague Jennifer A. Keach, and anticipates the publication of *Comic Book Collections for Libraries*, coauthored with Bryan D. Fagan, in January 2011.

CHARLOTTE FORD (MLS, PhD, Indiana University) is director of the library at Birmingham-Southern College. She previously served as assistant professor of library and information science at San Jose State University and at various times has held positions in reference, government documents, and cataloging at Birmingham-Southern College, Florida International University, and the Pontificia Universidad Javeriana (Colombia).

LINDA FRIEND is head of scholarly communication services at Penn State University and works with the library and the university community to develop and promote digital services. She is a past recipient of the annual University Libraries Award, which recognizes excellence in service, leadership, innovation, and achievement in librarianship at Penn State. An active member of the American Library Association, she serves on the Freedom to Read Foundation Committee, has held many committee and board assignments in the Reference and User Services Association (RUSA), and has had the privilege of being elected to chair the RUSA Machine-Assisted Reference Section (MARS) for two separate terms. She is a member of the Society for Scholarly Publishing and is currently cochair of the Web Site Editorial Committee. Her research interests include scholarly communication, assessment, the crucial role of librarians as authors and publishers, and organizational improvement.

JULIE A. GEDEON is assistant professor and coordinator of assessment at Kent State University Libraries. She is a founding member of Project SAILS (Standardized Assessment of Information Literacy Skills), a member of the TRAILS (Tool for Real-time Assessment of Information Literacy Skills) project, and a coadministrator for the Wisconsin-Ohio Reference Evaluation Program (WOREP). Dr. Gedeon received an MLS in 1998 and a PhD in educational evaluation and measurement in 2002, both from Kent State.

JIM HAHN is the orientation services librarian at the University of Illinois at Urbana-Champaign. His librarianship is centered on helping first-year and transfer students make the transition to university study. His research interests include student transition-support services and the educational aspects of mobile technology.

DANIEL HICKEY is the business and information sciences librarian at Penn State University's University Park campus. Mr. Hickey graduated from the University of Pittsburgh's School of Information Sciences in 2009, where he focused his studies on academic libraries and reference across scholarly disciplines. While studying in Pittsburgh, he helped create metadata for parts of Warhol's Time Capsules, a work of art composed of a large, uncataloged collection of Andy Warhol's personal effects. Mr. Hickey's research interests include the intersections of access, services, and collections in the digital library environment. He is an active member of the American Library Association (ALA) and the American Society for Information Science & Technology (ASIS&T).

NEIL HOLLANDS is the author of *Read On . . . Fantasy Fiction* (Libraries Unlimited, 2007) and *Fellowship in a Ring: A Guide for Science Fiction and Fantasy Book Groups* (Libraries Unlimited, 2010). He writes online for Booklist's *Book Group Buzz* and Williamsburg Regional Library's *Blogging for a Good Book*. He is a passionate advocate of books and the practice of readers' advisory, contributing articles and reviews to publications such as *Booklist*, *Library Journal*, *Reference & User Services Quarterly*, and *Public Libraries*, and presenting regularly at state and national conferences.

ALEXIA HUDSON is a reference and instruction librarian at Penn State Abington College and has worked as a reference librarian and officer of the Second Life library since 2007 as avatar Donna Upshaw. She also initiated the Penn State University Libraries' presence in Second Life and works on teaching faculty and librarians to link pedagogy and workplace information literacy with emerging technologies including virtual worlds.

SALLY W. KALIN is associate dean of University Park Libraries, Penn State University, where she is responsible for overseeing the operations of all libraries at the University Park campus. Her responsibilities include collections, public and access services, instructional programs, public relations and marketing, and university media services. Ms. Kalin collaborates with the dean and other administrators on budgeting, strategic planning, policy development, personnel, and facilities issues.

M. KATHLEEN KERN is reference librarian at the University of Illinois Library, where she comanages the virtual reference service and supervises

10 graduate students who work in the Information and Reference Desk. She is also a second-semester doctoral student at the University of Illinois Graduate School of Library and Information Science. Among her publications are *Virtual Reference Best Practices* from ALA Editions and the "Accidental Technologist" column in *Reference & User Services Quarterly*.

ROBERT H. KIEFT is college librarian at Occidental College. Prior to this appointment in 2008, he worked for 20 years at Haverford College, where he was most recently director of college information resources and librarian of the college. From 1974 to 1988, he worked at Stanford University in circulation, reference, and collection development. He earned his MLIS from the University of California, Berkeley, and a PhD from Stanford University. A member of the Collection Development and Evaluation Section of the Reference and User Services Association, he has held a number of positions in that section, including chair (2000–2001). He has published articles and reviews in *Choice, College and Research Libraries, Reference Services Review,* and *Reference & User Services Quarterly*. Dr. Kieft served as general editor of the *Guide to Reference* from 2000 to 2008 and is now consulting editor.

JAMES LARUE has been the director of the Douglas County Libraries since 1990. He is the author of *The New Inquisition: Understanding and Managing Intellectual Freedom Challenges* (Libraries Unlimited, 2007) and has written a weekly newspaper column for over 20 years. He was the Colorado Librarian of the Year in 1998 and the Castle Rock Chamber of Commerce's 2003 Business Person of the Year, and in 2007 he won the Julie J. Boucher Award for Intellectual Freedom.

CHRISTOPHER LEBEAU has been an assistant teaching professor at the School of Information Science and Learning Technologies, University of Missouri, since 2003. She holds a joint appointment with the University of Missouri-Kansas City as a business librarian. She is an active member of the American Library Association and the Business Reference and Services Section (BRASS) of the Reference and User Services Association (RUSA). Some of her publications include "How Well Do Academic Library Web Sites Address the Needs of Database Users with Visual Disabilities?" (*Reference Librarian,* 2009); "Transitions to Academic Libraries for Business Librarians, and Librarians' Response to Adjunct Teaching" (*Journal of Business & Finance Librarianship,* 2008); and a committee-authored article, "An Exploration of the Working Relationship between Systems/IT and Reference/Information Services Staff in an Academic Library Setting" (*Reference & User Services Quarterly,* 2007). Ms. LeBeau reviews for *Choice* magazine. She holds a BA from Marymount College, an MLS from Long Island University, and an MBA from Creighton University.

ELISABETH LEONARD (MSLS, University of North Carolina Chapel Hill; MBA, Wake Forest University) is the associate dean of library services at Western Carolina University and an instructor at San Jose State University, teaching information organizations and management. Ms. Leonard also teaches a professional development class for the Reference and User Services Association (RUSA): Marketing Basics for Libraries. A member of RUSA's Collection Development and Evaluation Section (CODES), RUSA's Business Reference and Services Section (BRASS), and the American Library Association's Library Leadership and Management Association (LLAMA), she has held positions on committees in these sections, including chair of the BRASS Program Planning Committee, chair of the CODES Liaison with Users Committee, and member of the BRASS Education Committee and Business Reference Sources Committee. Ms. Leonard has published articles in *Library Journal, Library Trends,* the *Journal of Business & Finance Librarianship,* and *Reference & User Services Quarterly.* She is the editor of the Economics and Business section of the current edition of the *Guide to Reference.*

LILI LUO (PhD, University of North Carolina at Chapel Hill) is assistant professor at the School of Library and Information Science at San Jose State University. Her primary research and teaching interests include information access and services in the digital age, library and information science education, research methods, and virtual librarianship.

MERIS A. MANDERNACH is the collection management librarian at James Madison University. She has an MS in library and information sciences from the University of Illinois at Urbana-Champaign. While collections have occupied her work life recently, she previously worked as a science librarian at both James Madison University and Loyola University of Chicago.

ELIZABETH MCKEIGUE is assistant university librarian for public services at Santa Clara University in California. Prior to this appointment in 2010, she was coordinator of reference services for the Lamont and Widener Libraries in the Harvard College Library. She also served as Harvard College Library's library liaison to the departments of Celtic, Germanic, and Slavic Languages and Literatures. She holds a BA in English literature and an MS in library science and completed additional graduate work in Irish studies, all at the Catholic University of America in Washington, D.C. From 1996 to 2003, she was the head of circulation and associate head of access services at Widener Library, where she was actively involved in the multimillion-dollar renovation of the building and its stacks. Ms. McKeigue also serves as an editor for *Magazines for Libraries* and is the author of the "Theatre," "International Magazines," and "Europe" chapters of that publication. Her publications also include numerous reviews of electronic library resources for *Library Journal*. She recently participated in two competitive institutes offered by the Association of College and Research Libraries: the Intentional Teacher Track of the Institute for Information Literacy Immersion Program and the Advanced Leadership Institute for Senior Academic Librarians.

LISA G. O'CONNOR earned her MLIS from the University of South Carolina and worked as a reference librarian in academic libraries for nearly a decade. After earning her PhD in the cultural foundations of education from Kent State University, she accepted a teaching post at the University of Kentucky. She teaches information sources and services, instructional services, social science information, business information sources and services, and academic libraries courses. Her research interests are in the areas of information literacy and business information seeking.

AMBER A. PRENTISS works at the University of Georgia Libraries as a reference/instruction librarian. She is a graduate of Agnes Scott College and the Graduate School of Library and Information Studies, University of Illinois at Urbana-Champaign. Ms. Prentiss was also a 2004 American Library Association Spectrum Scholar and currently serves as a director-at-large for the Reference and User Services Association.

MARIE L. RADFORD is an associate professor at the Rutgers School of Communication and Information. Prior to joining the Rutgers faculty, she was acting dean of Pratt Institute's School of Information and Library Science. She holds a PhD from Rutgers and an MSLS from Syracuse University. Her research interests are interpersonal communication aspects of reference service (both traditional and virtual), evaluation of e-resources and services, cultural studies, and media stereotypes of librarians. She has published and presented in numerous scholarly and professional venues. Her latest books are *Creating the Reference Renaissance* (Neal-Schuman, 2010) and *Conducting the Reference Interview* (2nd ed., Neal-Schuman, 2009). Dr. Radford is active in library and communication associations, including the American Library Association (ALA), the Association for Library and Information Science Education (ALISE), and the Reference and User Services Association (RUSA). Her Web site is at http://comminfo.rutgers.edu/~mradford/. She directs the online virtual reference bibliography at Rutgers (http://vrbib.rutgers.edu) and blogs at *Library Garden* (http://librarygarden.net/).

EMILY RIMLAND is an information literacy librarian in the Penn State University Libraries. She enjoys providing instruction, reference, and outreach services to undergraduate students. Her research interests include Web/library 2.0 and other instructional technologies.

JULIET RUMBLE is reference and instruction librarian and the philosophy and religion subject specialist at Auburn University Libraries. She earned a master's degree in library science from the University of North Carolina at Chapel Hill and a PhD in philosophy from Vanderbilt University.

JOSEPH A. SALEM, JR. is associate professor and head of reference and government information services at Kent State University Libraries. He has been involved in library assessment throughout his career. In addition to contributing to local assessment projects, Professor Salem serves as a member of Project SAILS (Standardized Assessment of Information Literacy Skills) as a test developer and data analyst. He received his MLS in 1999 and is currently pursuing his PhD in educational evaluation and measurement.

SUSAN SHARPLESS SMITH is the director of research, instruction, and technology services for Z. Smith Reynolds Library, Wake Forest University, in Winston-Salem, North Carolina. She received the 2008 Association of College and Research Libraries Instruction Section (ACRL IS) Innovation Award for her work as an embedded librarian in a two week sociology course that traveled by bus through the Deep South. Smith received a master's degree in library and information studies from University of North Carolina-Greensboro and a master's degree in educational technology leadership from George Washington University.

MICHAEL STEPHENS is assistant professor in the Graduate School of Library and Information Science at Dominican University in Illinois. He spent over 15 years working in public libraries while developing a passion for technology and the human connections it affords. His recent publications include two American Library Association library technology reports on Web 2.0, the monthly column "The Transparent Library" with Michael Casey in *Library Journal*, and other articles about emerging trends and technology. Dr. Stephens also maintains the popular blog *Tame the Web*. He received an Institute of Museum and Library Services (IMLS) doctoral fellowship at the University of North Texas, was named a *Library Journal* Mover and Shaker, and received the 2009 Association for Library and Information Science Education (ALISE) Pratt-Severn Faculty Innovation Award as well as a 2009 University of North Texas Rising Star Alumni Award. He spent five weeks researching and speaking in Australia as the 2009 CAVAL Visiting Scholar, examining the effect of Learning 2.0 programs in Australian libraries. Dr. Stephens speaks nationally and internationally on libraries, technology, and innovation. He is fascinated by library buildings and virtual spaces that center around users, content, digital creation, and encouraging the heart.

LYNN SUTTON is dean of the Z. Smith Reynolds Library at Wake Forest University in Winston-Salem, North Carolina. Previously, she served as associate dean at Wayne State University Libraries in Detroit, Michigan. She holds AB and AMLS degrees from the University of Michigan and a PhD in education from Wayne State University. Dr. Sutton has a wide variety of scholarly interests, speaking and publishing on such topics as intellectual freedom, gaming in academic libraries, embedded librarianship, collection development, and leadership theory. She is currently a member of the LYRASIS board of directors.

BARRY TROTT is the director of adult services at the Williamsburg (Virginia) Regional Library. He oversees the provision of reference and readers' advisory services and collection development of all adult materials and helps to manage several of the library's strategic partnerships. He is the 2010–2011 president of the Reference and User Services Association (RUSA), a division of the American Library Association. He has served as chair of RUSA's Collection Development and Evaluation Section (CODES). He edits the readers' advisory column for *Reference & User Services Quarterly* and writes for the NoveList readers' advisory database. He is also the series editor for Libraries Unlimited's Read On series and author of *Read On . . . Crime Fiction* (2008). Mr. Trott is also editor for the Selection of Materials section in the *Guide to Reference* (American Library Association, 2008).

DAVID A. TYCKOSON is the associate dean of the Henry Madden Library, California State University, Fresno. He came to Fresno as head of reference in 1997. Prior to moving to California, he held positions at the State University of New York at Albany, Iowa State University, and Miami (Ohio) University. He has an undergraduate degree in physics and a master's degree in library science, both from the University of Illinois. In the 1980s and 1990s he served at various times as an adjunct professor in the library schools at the University of Illinois and State University of New York at Albany. He has been involved with reference service for 30 years and has written extensively about reference service and the reference interview. He was elected as the 2007–2008 president of the American Library Association's Reference and User Services Association.

SCOTT VINE is the information services librarian and deputy college librarian at Franklin & Marshall College. He has also been a librarian at Carnegie Mellon University and Johns Hopkins School of Advanced International Studies. He has a BA in English and philosophy from Hiram College, an MA in philosophy from the University of Memphis, and an MLS from Kent State University. Mr. Vine coordinates the Franklin & Marshall library's reference and circulation services and acts as the library's liaison to the philosophy, psychology, math, and computer science departments and related programs. He is cochair of ACRL's 2011 Virtual Conference, serves on the editorial board of *College & Research Libraries News*, and has given talks at national and international library conferences on delivering traditional and virtual reference services.

DIANE ZABEL is the Louis and Virginia Benzak Business Librarian (an endowed position) at the Schreyer Business Library at Penn State University's University Park campus. She holds the rank of librarian. Ms. Zabel has been with the University Libraries full time since 1986. She holds a master of urban planning degree (1980) and a master of science in library and information science (1982) from the University of Illinois at Urbana-Champaign. Ms. Zabel is an active member of the American Library Association (ALA). She served as elected president of the Reference and User Services Association (RUSA), one of the divisions of ALA, for the period 2005–2006. In 2009 she was elected to the ALA Council and began a three-year term as ALA councilor-at-large. In 2006 she assumed the editorship of *Reference & User Services Quarterly*. She serves on the editorial board of the *Journal of Academic Librarianship* and the *Journal of Business & Finance Librarianship*.